Family Matters

Family Matters

Second Edition

An Introduction to Family Sociology in Canada

Barbara A. Mitchell

Canadian Scholars' Press Inc.
Toronto

Family Matters, Second Edition: An Introduction to Family Sociology in Canada
by Barbara A. Mitchell

First published in 2009 by
Canadian Scholars' Press Inc.
425 Adelaide Street West, Suite 200
Toronto, Ontario
M5V 3C1

www.cspi.org

Canadian Scholars' Press Inc. gratefully acknowledges financial support for our publishing activities from the Government of Canada through the Canada Book Fund (CBF).

Library and Archives Canada Cataloguing in Publication

Mitchell, Barbara A. (Barbara Ann), 1961–

Family matters : an introduction to family sociology in Canada / Barbara A. Mitchell.—2nd ed.

Includes bibliographical references and index.
Issued also in electronic formats.
ISBN 978-1-55130-410-6

    1. Family—Canada—Textbooks. I. Title.

HQ560.M58 2012   306.850971   C2012-905291-4

Text design by Brad Horning
Cover design by Em Dash Design
Cover image: PHOTOCREO Michal Benarek © Shutterstock

Printed and bound in Canada by Webcom

Canada

MIX
Paper from
responsible sources
FSC
www.fsc.org   FSC® C004071

Table of Contents

Part I: Understanding Continuity, Diversity, Inequality, and Social Change in Families

Part II: The Ties that Bind: Family Formation and Generational Connections

List of Boxes, Tables, and Figures

Chapter 6

Chapter 7

Chapter 8

Preface

The first family-focused course that I took was in high school, at London Central Secondary School in Ontario during my senior year. And from that time onward, I was hooked! In this class, we learned about different family structures and forms, as well as family life in foreign places and fascinating cultures. This class opened my eyes to a whole new way of seeing the world. Growing up in the 1960s and 1970s in Kitchener, then just outside of Stratford, Ontario, and subsequently London to finish secondary school, most of my friends and neighbours—in fact almost all of the people I saw in my everyday life and on television—were fairly homogeneous. They tended to be relatively middle class, living in nuclear, heterosexual, biological-parent family structures, and were from British or European backgrounds. It was rare to see deviations from this norm, since "non-traditional" family types such as stepfamilies, single-parent families, cohabiting, mixed-race, and same-sex families were uncommon at the time. Of course these family types certainly did exist, and I had experienced a single-father, adoptive, and stepfamily environment myself.

Beyond my own family and a few others, however, the most common "alternative" family structure that I observed up close was that of my rural Mennonite neighbours during my teenage years. To me, these families seemed markedly exotic and different than others, with their traditional lifestyles, distinctive dress, and highly segregated gender roles. "Older order" families still relied on horse and buggies as a principal means of transportation and lived on large farms with no electricity. Of course, once I got to know these families, in many ways, they were not that much different than my own. Similar to my own parents, these parents also wanted to raise happy, healthy, and productive children in a safe, peaceful, and loving environment.

Once I started post-secondary school at the University of Waterloo in 1981, I continued to pursue my fascination with family studies. Canadian families were also undergoing metamorphosis at the time. These changes prompted theorists and researchers (who were increasingly likely to be female) to question conventional conceptualizations and ways of studying families. Emergent trends such as women's rising labour force participation and college/university enrolment, skyrocketing divorce, and changing immigration patterns were also creating a richer and more complex tapestry of family life—patterns that sparked my interest in wanting to know more about the factors underlying processes of family social change.

Graduate school at the University of Waterloo and McMaster University allowed me to expand on many conventional themes in family sociology. This was mainly due to the

encouragement and inspiration so generously offered to me by the many terrific profes-
sors at these institutions. And although the curriculum was only beginning to incorporate
aging and generational issues, these soon became interests that I developed while working on my Master's and Ph.D. theses. In part, this was the result of the strong influence
of social demographers who had begun to document and elucidate the phenomenon of
population aging. I also developed a keen interest in life course issues and gendered
processes as I began to appreciate the value in studying families throughout the entire
lifespan, rather than at only one point in time. In addition, I realized that good health is
not experienced by all families but is integral to positive family functioning and relationships, as well as successful aging.

   Since working and teaching as a family sociologist and gerontologist at Simon Fraser
University, I have continued with this perspective on families, viewing them from a critical, gendered lens, synthesized with a dynamic life course approach. I also recognize
that aging and health/well-being issues need to receive more than just cursory attention.
Indeed, you will see throughout this book that a sociological focus on the changing roles
of women and men in families and society is fundamental for understanding a wide variety of issues relevant to our everyday lives, including our health and well-being.

   In closing, writing this introductory family textbook—which is suitable for university
courses on the family or for anyone wanting to learn more about Canadian family theory
and research—has been a way for me to share with you my own personal journey and
enthusiasm for family sociology. It has also provided me with the opportunity to contribute to a field that I believe is the most exciting and important substantive area in sociology. Therefore, my greatest wish is not only that you will enjoy reading and learning
valuable information presented in this textbook, but that you, too, will become hooked
on family sociology.

Acknowledgements

Writing a textbook like this one is an enormously time-consuming endeavour that requires
patience and dependence on others' expertise, guidance, wisdom, and support. To this end,
many people have graciously contributed their time and enthusiasm to bring this project
to fruition.

   First, I would like to extend a heartfelt appreciation to everyone at Canadian Scholars'
Press Inc. who assisted with the production of this work. In particular, I am extremely
grateful to Megan Mueller, the editorial director of the first edition, as well the editorial director of this second edition, Lily Bergh, at Canadian Scholars' Press Inc. Both
of these women provided me not only with prompt, impeccable editorial assistance
during various stages of writing, revising, and polishing the text, but also served as an
enormous source of support and encouragement. In short, they should be recognized
for their incredible professionalism, collaborative working style, and steadfast enthusiasm. This created a working relationship that was not only very productive but highly
enjoyable as well.

I would also like to express my sincere gratitude to all of the reviewers who provided me with constructive and insightful feedback on earlier drafts of the manuscript. I would especially like to thank Amber Gazso, Department of Sociology, York University; Jane Gordon, Department of Sociology and Women's Studies, Mount St. Vincent University; and Vicki Nygaard, Department of Sociology and Women's Studies, University of British Columbia. These reviewers provided me with thought-provoking and highly useful suggestions that improved the quality of this work.

Also, thanks to Dominique Falls, a graduate student in the Department of Sociology/Anthropology at Simon Fraser University, for her assistance with updating some of the material in this book, as well as to Melinda Aikin of the Department of Gerontology at Simon Fraser University for some technical assistance with table/figure formatting.

And last, but most importantly, I would like to express appreciation to my own family—from my large, extended family network to my immediate family. These people have taught me innumerable lessons about the importance and meaning of family, regardless of its changing structure or relationship history. In particular, I would like to express my gratitude to my spouse, best friend, and colleague, Andrew V. Wister and my daughter Kayzia for their never-ending support. Andrew's keen interest and expertise in family sociology has undoubtedly influenced my writings on family sociology through our endless discussions about family theory and research. Moreover, this book could not have been written without their patience, particularly given my excruciatingly long bouts of "hiding out" in the home office. In closing, the support that I have been fortunate enough to receive from these sources reinforces my fundamental belief that, indeed, "family matters."

New to this Edition

This book has undergone a significant renovation since the first edition was published in 2009. While the overarching conceptual approach, organizational and pedagogical structure, broad thematic areas, and chapter topics remain similar, several key changes were made to this second edition. These revisions involved a comprehensive updating of material in existing chapters, including coverage of theoretical and research studies and the latest in student resources (such as the further reading lists and web sites of possible interest that appear at the end of each chapter). The most up-to-date statistical information available on family trends has also been added, in addition to expanded coverage of numerous topical areas. For example, this edition provides more detailed discussion of topics ranging from the special role that aunts and uncles play in families to families dealing with disability to the consequences of the recent global economic meltdown on families in Canada and worldwide.

And finally, more examples from today's news headlines and contemporary family-related events are provided, as well as case studies and examples of situations that you may have experienced in your own lives. All of these changes and examples are geared toward showing you the vast applicability and usefulness of sociology in our everyday experiences. My greatest hope is that this will help you to better understand why, and how, families matter and have such great significance for us all.

Part I

Understanding Continuity, Diversity, Inequality, and Social Change in Families

The first part in this book (chapters 1 through 5) focuses on different ways of conceptualizing families and introduces us to broader text themes of continuity, diversity, inequality, and social change. A central theme is that definitions, meanings, interpretations, and experiences of families are not static or universal and are constantly "under construction." This idea will be critically examined in Chapter 1 and Chapter 2 when we consider various institutional and ideological practices involved in defining, theorizing, and studying families. In addition, we will learn that shifting conceptualizations of family reflect how families (in whatever shape or form) are products of particular historical, economic, and political conditions and environments, as well as our own personal lived experiences and behaviours. This temporal and contextual perspective illuminates the idea that our shared and diverse experiences in families also change over the course of our lives. Overall, these fundamental notions underlie basic tenets of the life course perspective and will be detailed in Chapter 2, along with a number of other important theoretical and methodological orientations and issues.

Moreover, in order to dig beneath the surface of the broad themes of this text, it will become apparent that we need to step outside of our own families and our own society in both time and place. Indeed, the value of situating family lives on anthropological, historical, cross-cultural, and global levels is revealed and elaborated in chapters 3 and 4. This "digging" not only facilitates a better understanding of Canadian family life, but also reveals systemic or root causes of structured sources of inequality that are historically specific or related to wider trends of inequity related to gender, social class, and ethnicity/race. Moreover, we can also contemplate how processes of globalization are influencing families worldwide for the better and for the worse, a theme that will be revisited in subsequent parts of the text. We will also see that amidst these processes of globalization, there are incredible socio-demographic, political, and technological transformations that have occurred both outside and in Canadian families. For example, in Chapter 5, we will trace evolving and gendered patterns of domestic and labour force participation—work that is fundamental to the making and reproduction of daily family life, as well as to our basic experiences of health and well-being over the life course. Yet, despite significant gains made by women and new technological advancements, many inequities persist in the division of paid and unpaid labour in most of the world's economic systems.

Chapter 1

Family Matters

An Introduction to the Sociology of Canadian Families

Learning Objectives

In this chapter you will learn that ...
- families represent a fundamental aspect of our lives and a key societal institution
- many ideological and institutional practices are involved in defining The Family
- definitions of family are socially constructed and can serve a diversity of interests and purposes
- family life—which is often viewed as a private zone or sphere—cannot easily be separated from the public sphere
- families are reciprocally linked to socio-economic, cultural, political, and technological circumstances
- the apocalyptic idea that the modern family is in decline or is falling apart is nothing new and operates largely to serve personal or political agendas

Introduction

Reflect for a moment on how your life has been and continues to be influenced by your family background as well as by certain family members such as your mother, father, sibling, or grandparent. Also try to imagine how their lives would be different if you had never been born. In addition, try to envision what life was like for your grandparents, and in what ways it was the same or different than yours. It should come as little surprise to you to realize that our unique family histories have a tremendous impact on our life courses, just as we have an enormous influence on the life courses of our own family. And since most of us live out a large portion of our lives in some sort of family setting, these experiences—both good and bad—inevitably transform and alter our lives forever.

From a life course perspective—the foundational and guiding theoretical framework of this book—we can also easily see that families cannot be ignored if we want to understand societal and institutional patterns and processes around us, as well as social change. This is because the social relationships we call family are an integral feature and institution of society. In short, families are a microsocial group that reciprocally link and reflect other macro-level institutions of society. In fact, no society has ever existed without some sort of social arrangements that are labelled kinship or familial. Thus, what people do in their families makes a significant difference not only to themselves but also to wider society. For example, if we increasingly choose to have small families, there may be repercussions not only for our own lived experiences in a family, but also for other institutions, such as the educational system and the economy.

Despite the significant impact of family life in all facets of human existence and our own intimate familiarity with some type of family, it will be shown that it is not that simple to identify or define families. It is also not that easy to situate our own personal family experiences within the context of previous family life, as well as other people's family lives. This is because our personal family stories unfold within a particular historical time and place, another major tenet underlying the life course perspective, which will be further discussed in subsequent chapters. This is why a sociological study of families is so important. Could you imagine, for instance, how misguided our theories, research, and social policies would be if we relied only on our own personal observations or "hunches" of what family is and means? Or, if we automatically assumed that family life was better in "the good old days," and that modern-day families are all falling apart? Indeed, family sociology becomes very useful (and necessary) in understanding and critically evaluating existing social patterns, as well as in gaining valuable knowledge about Canada and the world that we live in.

In this chapter we will tackle and identify some provocative issues in order to lay the groundwork for subsequent chapters. We begin by asking the question, "What are families?" with the adjacent inquiries: "What ideological and institutional practices are involved in defining family?" and "Why do these practices matter to us?" This is followed by a brief overview of selected socio-demographic, cultural, and technological trends in family life. A basic summary of these patterns also provides an introduction to fundamental concepts, terms, themes, and issues that are pivotal to defining families and a sociological study of Canadian families. Notably, social demography, or the scientific study of population, is integral to family sociology, since it addresses social trends in family life such as marriage and divorce, changes in age at marriage and child-bearing, and living arrangements. Highlighting some of these basic family patterns also allows us to consider two sides of an ongoing debate in family sociology, namely the family decline hypothesis, which purports that modern-day families, relative to family life of the past, are in trouble and in "crisis." And, as will be shown in this chapter and throughout this book, a critical analysis of this debate also helps us to critically evaluate how our reflections, definitions, and meanings of family are socially constructed and embedded within ideological and institutional practices.

"We Are Family," But What Are Families?

In the late 1970s, an American musical group called Sister Sledge (comprised of four sisters) became an international sensation with their number-one song "We Are Family." But what is family? What are families? Is a retired childless couple a family? Are same-sex couples with adopted children "families"? Is your best friend or pet considered one of your family members? Is it appropriate to talk about The Family as if it was an objective homogeneous structure with a finite number of shapes and forms?

As you can tell, defining "family" or "families" is a complicated matter. Previous scholarly definitions (particularly those formulated in the 1940s, 1950s, and 1960s) tended to emphasize that The Family was the basic institution of society and that it was a social and economic unit consisting of two adults of the opposite sex who shared economic resources, sexual intimacy, labour, accommodation, reproduction, and child-rearing (e.g., see Goode, 1963; Murdock, 1949). Similarly, cultural representations of families portrayed The Family as having two parents, one as a breadwinner husband and one as a homemaker wife, as shown in television shows such as *Father Knows Best*, *I Love Lucy*, and *Leave It to Beaver*. These family types were popularized on television in

---

Box 1.1
The Standard North American Family: SNAF as an Ideological Code

I am using the term "ideological code" as an analogy to "genetic code." Genetic codes are orderings of the chemical constituents of DNA molecules that transmit genetic information to cells, reproducing in the cells the original ordering. By analogy, an "ideological code" is a schema that replicates its organization in multiple and various sites. I want to make clear that an "ideological code" in this sense is not a determinate concept or idea, though it can be expressed as such. Nor is it a formula or a definite form of words. Rather it is a constant generator of procedures for selecting syntax, categories, and vocabulary in the writing of texts and the production of talk and for interpreting sentences, written or spoken, ordered by it. An ideological code can generate the same order in widely different settings of talk or writing— in legislative, social scientific, and administrative settings, in popular writing, television advertising, or whatever.

The Standard North American Family (hereafter SNAF) is an ideological code in this sense. It is a conception of The Family as a legally married couple sharing a household. The adult male is in paid employment; his earnings provide the economic basis of the family-household. The adult female may also earn an income, but her responsibility is to the care of husband, household, and children. The adult male and female may be parents (in whatever legal sense) of children also resident in the household. Note the language of typification—"man," "woman"— and the use of the atemporal present. This universalizing of the schema locates its function as ideological code. It is not identifiable with any particular family; it applies to any. A classic enunciation of the code can be found in George Murdock's use of files containing summaries of ethnographic data accumulated by anthropologists from different parts of the world to establish the universality of the nuclear family (Murdock, 1949). The nuclear family is a theorized version of SNAF. Characteristically, Murdock was able to generate its distinctive form even when ethnographic descriptions contradicted it. Even when the nuclear family is not the "prevailing form," it is the "basic unit from which more complex familial forms are compounded." It is "always recognizable" (Murdock, 1949: 2).

Source: Smith, D. 1999. "The Standard North American family: SNAF as an ideological code," in *Writing the Social: Critique, Theory and Investigations.* Toronto: University of Toronto Press (p. 159).

the 1950s and portrayed a family structure that was relatively common during that time, although it was certainly not the norm from a historical perspective (as will become evident later in the book). Indeed, as will be revealed in this text, these definitions and images are certainly at odds with the real lives and historical experiences of most families in Canada and throughout the world.

Most scholars today readily acknowledge that previous definitions and stereotypes of The Family were often idealized and ideologically based. In other words, they reflected a particular ideology,which refers to a body of systematic beliefs and ideas (which claim to represent the truth) and that justify or rationalize certain actions or behaviours.Yet, Dorothy Smith (1999) notes that the Standard North American Family (SNAF) continues to represent an "ideological code" since it characterizes The Family as a legally married heterosexual couple living in the same household (see Box 1.1 for further discussion). SNAF as an ideological code also continues to be foundational to many economic theories of the family and it creates a text-mediated discourse that is generated in different settings. These family-related texts are found in national and local public discussions on family life (including the mass media), social scientific research in universities and think tanks, government systems of collecting statistics, and policy making in government. These practices extend to and invade other settings (i.e., by providing the terms of policy-talk) since they generate a common ordering (i.e., "the normative family") by which other family types are compared and measured.

Put simply, these texts coordinate multiple sites of representation, are coordinated conceptually, and produce "an internally consistent picture of the world." Moreover, Smith asserts that as active agents, we all enter into and participate in such relations in ordinary and unthinking ways as these texts are reproduced in our everyday practices of thinking about families and in our own experiences in families. Yet, as we will see later in this chapter and throughout this text, these texts or representations of families are not reflective of reality and the variability that occurs within families, particularly with respect to living arrangements, economic co-operation, and sexual relations.

There are also many religious, legal, or official-based meanings of family, and these classifications may or may not be consistent with public or scholarly definitions. This is because religious organizations are particularly concerned with moral issues and obligations, and that families adhere to the teachings of their faith. Policy makers and government officials, on the other hand, while also ideological, need to establish set criteria as to what constitutes family in order to meet their specific needs. For example, they might need to produce population estimates of the number and types of poor families in a given province. And while these definitions change over time, Statistics Canada (2002), the official census and survey agency for Canada, recently defines a census family quite broadly as: "A married couple (with or without children of either or both spouses), a couple living common-law (with or without children of either or both partners) or a lone parent of any marital status, with at least one child living in the same dwelling. A couple living common-law may be of opposite sex or same sex. 'Children' in a census family includes grandchildren living with their grandparent(s) but with no parents present."

Moreover, government- or other official agency-based definitions can vary across domains (e.g., immigration policy vs. marriage laws) and these definitions determine who may receive certain formal and informal rights, entitlements, and benefits. For example, an individual may not be able to immigrate under a family reunification policy if they fall outside given certain requirements. Or, if gay and lesbian couples are not legally considered married, they may not be able to claim the same entitlements as heterosexual married couples. Therefore, far from being an obscure issue of linguistic and philosophical debate, these definitions have very real and very critical consequences. Notably, if certain individuals cannot claim to be part of a family, then they may be ineligible for benefits ranging from housing to health care and sick leave. In addition, those deemed "non-families" may be considered illegitimate, inappropriate, or immoral within the community or in other settings (Newman and Grauerholz, 2002). Thus, the term "family" is not simply a concept, but a minefield of contested values and power relationships (Silva and Smart, 1999).

Our everyday discourse or usage of the word "family" also illuminates how it can conjure up a wide array of meanings. Consider for a moment the slogans of two corporations, The Olive Garden (an Italian restaurant) and Kimpton Hotels, both popular chains in Canada and the U.S. The former uses the tag line "When you're here, you're family," while the latter uses "Because pets are family too." In fact, Kimpton Hotels is not only known for its pet-friendly policies, but also for its employee pet care benefits. All employees receive Pet Assure comprehensive pet benefits programs, such as a special I.D. program and access to veterinary service networks. And while these meanings of family may seem far-fetched to some, many individuals do consider their pets to be "one of the family" (see Box 1.2).

Moreover, many consider fictive kin or non-relatives such as friends, neighbours, or co-workers "family," despite the popular saying "Blood is thicker than water." These "kin by a fiction," in fact, may exhibit bonds that are even stronger than with blood relatives. A good example of this interpretation of domestic ties and family structure is illustrated in Carol Stack's now classic ethnography of an African-American community, *All Our Kin* (1974), which is discussed from a social constructionist approach (see Box 1.3). This approach highlights how "family" is not objectively meaningful, but instead, is constantly "under construction" and mediated by local culture (Holstein and Gubrium, 1999). We also often use the term "family" when we really mean "household," which includes all those sharing a dwelling. Household members, however, may or may not be related by blood, marriage, or adoption. Also, most people consider an aunt or uncle "family" but probably do not share a household with these relatives.

Despite the near impossibility in arriving at a single definition of families, McDaniel and Tepperman (2004) observe that there are common elements or processes fundamental to the social groups we call families. First, all close relations usually involve some relational type of attachment, emotional bonding, dependency, or interdependency. However, family relations tend to include birth to death or long-term commitments, both to each other and to the family per se. This includes a degree of familiarity—in fact the word family is derived from a Latin word meaning familiar—as well as expectations of

Box 1.2
Pets: An Integral Part of the Family

More than 50 percent of Canadian households own pets of some kind. Dogs, cats, birds, and other companion animals are living in more than five million homes. For their owners, these animals are more than pets—they are part of the family.

Each year, Canadian families spend about three billion dollars on their pets. This exceeds consumer spending on children's toys, footwear, eye care, and dental plans.

A recent survey of pet owners revealed that nearly 80 percent of respondents gave their pets holiday or birthday presents. More than 60 percent signed their pets' names on cards or letters. A slight majority (51 percent) gave their pets human names.

While virtually all pet owners talk to their pets, an astounding 94 percent spoke to their pets as though they were human. One-third of respondents spoke to their pets on the telephone or via the answering machine. More than 90 percent of pet owners believed their pets were aware of their moods and emotions.

As millions of Canadians already know, pets make wonderful, loving companions. In return for proper care and attention, pets offer unconditional love.

Pet Ownership: It's Good for Your Health
Chances are, you'll live longer and feel better if you own a pet.

Medical studies on the human-animal bond reveal that pet owners are more likely to have reduced stress levels, cholesterol levels, and blood pressure. They also experience fewer heart attacks than people without pets.

Researchers have found that the mere presence of an animal has a beneficial effect on heart function, and stroking and talking to a pet reduces blood pressure and stress.

Many hospitals and retirement homes engage in animal therapy. This may involve visits from volunteer animals or a pet that is kept at the facility. Seniors with pets are much less lonely than non–pet owners. Consequently, they do not make unnecessary visits to their doctor out of loneliness.

A study of women undergoing stress tests demonstrated that the presence of a dog had a greater effect on lowering blood pressure than the presence of friends.

Companion animals also provide psychological benefits. Pets are sympathetic, supportive, and non-judgmental listeners. Pets provide us with a distraction from our worries; they encourage social interaction and provide a soothing presence.

Source: Retrieved June 5, 2006 from The Ontario Veterinary Medical Association at http://www. ovma.org/pet_owners/ownership_benefits/index.html.

reciprocity. It also means that there can be many relational landscapes since families are not a single entity and can take many forms and structures. Aunts and uncles, for example, can play a significant role in the socialization and raising of nieces and nephews.

Box 1.3
What Is Family? Further Thoughts on a Social Constructionist Approach

Holstein and Gubrium (1999) outline their constructionist approach to family studies by considering how fictive kin represent one interpretation of family life. In the
following quote, Billy, a young African-American woman living in a midwestern
city, describes the family ties structuring her life:

> Most people kin to me are in this neighbourhood…but I got people in the South,
> in Chicago, and in Ohio too. I couldn't tell most of their names and most of
> them aren't really kinfolk to me…Take my father, he's no father to me. I ain't
> got but one daddy and that's Jason. The one who raised me. My kids' daddies,
> that's something else, all their daddy's people really take to them— they always
> doing things and making a fuss about them. We help each other out and that's
> what kinfolks are all about. (p. 4).

Here, Billy projects family structure and meaning by convincingly articulating
a familiar, recognizable vocabulary with features of her day-to-day life in order to
construct and convey what it means to be family. She uses language of care and co-
operation to establish the parameters of her "family." By actively assigning family
status in this way, Billy indicates what persons mean to one another, simultaneously
designating their interpersonal rights and obligations. She instructs her listeners in
how to interpret and understand the concrete meaning of particular social ties, publicly constituting domestic order in relation to the practical circumstances that com-
pose the life world that she confronts daily (Holstein and Gubrium, 1999: 6).

Source: Holstein, J.A. and J. Gubrium. 1999. "What is family? Further thoughts on a social
constructionist approach," in B.H. Settles, S.K. Steinmetz, G.W. Peterson and M.B. Sussman (eds.),
Concepts and Definitions of Family for the 21st Century. New York: The Haworth Press (p. 6).

Families also typically change and expand as we age. For example, as shown in Figure
1.1, we can have two (or more) families by the time we reach adulthood—the family that
we are born into (our family of orientation), and the family that we create when we marry
and have children (our family of procreation).

Second, sexual relations tend to be regulated, such that certain relations are appropriate
(e.g., between spouses) whereas others are taboo (e.g., between parent and child). Third, most
families exhibit some degree of power imbalance, such as by gender or age, which means that
ideally, more powerful family members tend to protect the less powerful family members.
Fourth, families tend to guard their members against all kinds of internal and external danger,
although in reality, we know that violence, abuse, exploitation, or neglect can occur. As will
be shown in Chapter 14, our family may be more dangerous to us than the outside world.

Figure 1.1
Mary's Two Families

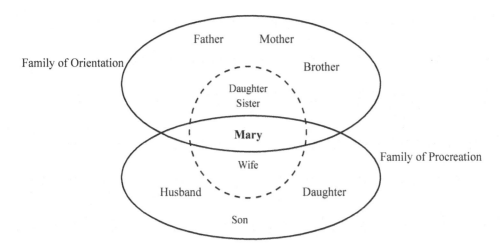

In her family of orientation, Mary is a daughter and a sister; in her family of procreation, Mary is a wife and mother. She is also a daughter-in-law in her husband's family of orientation, and perhaps a sister-in-law.

Source: Modified from E. Nett, *Canadian Families: Past and Present* (Toronto: Butterworths, 1988), p. 22.

In this textbook, the term "families" is used in a fairly broad sense to refer to a group of people who have intimate or close social relationships and a shared history together. There are also many "acceptable" family structures and relationships. And, as Eichler (1988) suggests, it is more realistic and productive to view families in broad terms (rather than as a single entity) and as interacting and varying along several key dimensions. These dimensions include procreation, socialization, sexual relations, residence, economic co-operation, and emotional ties. Within each of these dimensions, various degrees of interaction can be identified. By way of illustration, in the procreative dimension, interaction can range from a couple having children with each other and only with each other, to both having children with other partners and/or having children together, to their having no children at all.

Moreover, Eichler argues that several biases characterize the sociology of family literature, as will be further elaborated in the next chapter. For example, a monolithic bias results in the tendency to treat the family as a monolithic structure with an emphasis on uniformity of experiences and universality of structures and functions instead of on a diversity of experiences, structures, and functions. However, as will be shown in Chapter 3, there is little evidence to support the idea of "a universal family." Instead, different

Box 1.4
Relational Landscapes

Oddly enough, aunting and uncling have little clear representation in the public discourse about families. The relationship of aunts and uncles with nieces and nephews are rarely discussed or examined in any comprehensive way. Yet relationships among siblings are among the more resilient, long lasting, and intimate of family ties, and with the introduction of children, the roles of aunt and uncle are added to the bonds linking siblings and their parents or spouses.

Even the terms "aunting" and "uncling" are relatively new; they appeared only recently in the popular and academic literature on families, and then amid some controversy. Among the early appearances of the terms was an article I wrote and submitted for review to a leading academic journal. The article was published in due time, but not without some spirited exchanges. One of the reviewers questioned the terms "aunting" and "uncling" and lamented over their inclusion in the family lexicon, perhaps thinking they were unnecessary, unusual, or simply dreadful. The story illustrates the invisibility of the family work of aunts and uncles because specific terms to describe what they do are not in common usage. We have heretofore no common terms by which to describe our expectations of aunts and uncles or their typical activities and to differentiate them from the expectations and activities of other family members such as parents or grandparents. Terms such as "aunting" and "uncling" have a clear linguistic parallel with the term "parenting", a word in common usage, but the former still sound foreign to some ears, as they did to the journal reviewer. The gap in our common language is suggestive of how the family positions of aunts and uncles are rarely discussed in any formal way. The family work of aunts and uncles, nieces and nephews is neatly hidden from public view and acknowledgement, although as we shall see, aunts and uncles routinely discuss among themselves and their intimates their relationships with nieces, nephews, and other family members, and their contributions to family work are varied, consequential, and apparently commonplace.

The invisibility of aunts, uncles, nieces, and nephews, as well as relationships among adult siblings more generally, in the field of family studies contrasts sharply with the lived experience of actors who know quite clearly the importance of each to the other. Family members commonly talk among themselves, visit, phone, e-mail, circulate family photos in person or via web sites, and celebrate holidays, birthdays, and anniversaries. In their contacts, they share news and gossip, and all of this occurs across households of grandparents, parents, adult siblings (some of whom are single), and close friends, including coworkers. To be sure, not all families are in frequent communication, but then not all exist in isolated households. One need only recall travel patterns on major North American holidays to confirm this.

Source: Milardo, R.M. 2009. "Relational landscapes," in *The Forgotten Kin: Aunts and Uncles*. New York: Cambridge University Press (pp. 1–2).

family forms—from monogamous to polygamous—are found historically and world-wide. These family forms are reciprocally linked to the economic and political conditions in which families live their daily lives. For example, polygamy, which is a common family form in many parts of the world, can be traced to structural arrangements of economic control and power. A conservative bias, on the other hand, results in the tendency to ignore changes in family life. Instead, Eichler argues that the boundaries of contemporary families need to be recognized as fluid and ever-changing. Notably, in a period of rapid social, technological, and economic change, family lives change and transform such that definitions of family continually need to be re-evaluated.

In summary, many of the issues raised so far beckon us to rethink The Family as an objective condition apart from acts of interpretation, as well as a private zone or entity and as separate from public life. Instead, Gubrium and Holstein (1987) assert that The Family can fruitfully be considered "a way of interpreting, representing, and ordering social relations." The Family's social organization is "not to be discerned through carefully focused attention to its component parts," but instead "is gleaned from the diverse categories and varied contexts in which considerations of family order are raised." Similarly, Fahey (1995: 687) observes that a focus on a simple public/private dichotomy (which is common in sociological practice) points to the "multiple, cross-cutting, context-specific zones of privacy found in social life." Thus, it is recognized that meanings of related family experiences cannot be separated from the interpretations of those studying families (Gubrium and Holstein, 1987). It is therefore useful to adopt descriptive practices that allow for both deviance and normality as categories of domestic definition, regardless of household location or setting. Yet, as will be further shown in the next section, there remains a tendency to produce normative or ideological visions of family life as if The Family were one distinct and immutable structure or form.

"The Sky Is Falling": The Family Decline Hypothesis

It is common to hear people idealize the past, when family life was supposedly stable and harmonious, free of conflict, and devoid of serious social problems. As a result, past family life is romanticized through a lens of "rose-coloured glasses" and was assumed to be simpler, happier, and less stressful. And indeed, we do hear startling statistics on the news and from religious and political leaders about family demise in modern life. This includes aspects such as declining marriage and fertility rates, skyrocketing divorce rates, latchkey children, drugs and gangs, and how the elderly are being abandoned by their children, and we worry that our society is now rejecting marriage and commitment to family relationships. Similarly, in the academic literature, scholars point to these and similar trends that contribute to an acrimonious debate about family life and the future viability of the family.

Dave Popenoe (1996, 1993, 1988), an American family sociologist, has been at the forefront of this debate with the view that the family is deteriorating and is in crisis. His main argument is that the family as an institution is in unprecedented decline since individuals are in the process of rejecting the bedrock of family functioning: the nuclear family. The rise of alternative family forms (e.g., single-mother families, cohabitation), the absence of fathers in many families (particularly in the United States), and other similar changes are purported to be the main causes of family decline. In his book, *Life without Father* (1996: 1, 3), for example, he writes:

> And according to a growing body of evidence, this massive erosion of fatherhood contributes mightily to many of the major social problems of our time ... [among them] crime and delinquency; premature sexuality and out-of-wedlock teen births; deteriorating educational achievement; depression, substance abuse; and alienation among teenagers; and the growing number of women and children in poverty.

As a result, he argues that the family is becoming ill suited to serve its two most basic functions: rearing children and providing sustained emotional sustenance to its members. On the other side of this hotly contested debate are those who maintain that "families are no worse than ever before"; these are the "family change perspective" theorists. These proponents argue that what is in decline is our normative idea of what a family is, or rather a particular historical ideological vision of the family. This depiction is usually represented by the prototypical 1950s family previously discussed—a family type in which parents marry for life, children are born inside the marriage, and the mother works inside the home while the father works outside the home to provide for the family

Figure 1.2
Life Expectancy by Sex, Canada, 1921–2004

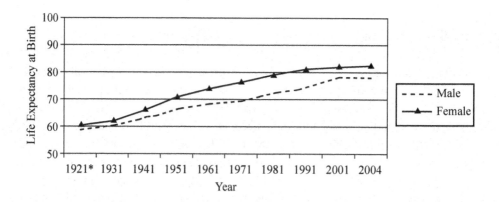

*1921 life table excludes Quebec

Sources: Adapted from M. Novak and L. Campbell, *Aging and Society: A Canadian Perspective*, 4th ed. (Toronto: Nelson Thomson Learning, 2001), p. 55; Statistics Canada, "Deaths," *The Daily* (December 20, 2006).

(Casper and Bianchi, 2002). Feminist scholars such as Judith Stacey (1996) argue that the family is not in decline but is undergoing metamorphosis as many come to realize that this vision of the traditional family is no longer viable or even desirable.

Moreover, some theorists (e.g., Coontz, 1992; Gee, 2000) argue that family life, even during the 1950s, was never "golden" or stable. Social problems such as poverty, alcoholism, drug addiction, family violence, and incest were prevalent, although often hidden behind closed doors. Also, previous to this time, sickness, disease, and war created very low life expectancy, as shown in Figure 1.2. These conditions robbed family members of infants, husbands, wives, and parents at young ages. As a result, the family change perspective highlights change as well as patterns of continuity such that the social and personal problems we think of as recent also existed long ago, albeit with different underlying circumstances. For example, we often hear alarming figures on the number of children raised in lone-parent households, yet rates of single parenthood were almost as high in the 1930s (see Table 1.1). However, single-parent families at this time were typically formed when one parent died at a young age or when a father deserted the family because of economic hardship. Today, they are more likely to be created by divorce or by individual choice. Thus, family life has almost always been diverse, as noted by the late Ellen Gee, a prominent Canadian family sociologist, who is well known for her historical, life course research on family change (see Box 1.5).

These observations highlight the necessity of identifying historical benchmarks as well as personal or institutional motives with respect to assessing family change. For example, when we assert that family life was somehow better in the past, how are we defining family

---

Box 1.5
Family Diversity

Family diversity is the norm in Canadian society, past and present. Only for a short period of history— the post–World War II "baby boom" years (circa 1946–62)— did Canada (and U.S.) families approach uniformity, centred around near-universal marriage and parenthood, family "intactness," and highly differentiated gender roles. This period was anomalous in terms of family life; a time when the gap between "actual" and "ideal" narrowed to an unprecedented degree. This was due, in part, to improved mortality levels (death contributed less to family breakup) and also to substantial economic growth (men's wages alone could support a family). It is also no coincidence that the then pre-eminent U.S. sociologist Talcott Parson's conceptualization of the homogenous modern family model was developed at this time in history…It is very important not to examine today's families in the light of that period; to do so is to overestimate familial change and trends related to diversity.

Source: Gee, E.M. 2000. "Contemporary diversities," in N. Mandell and A. Duffy (eds.), *Canadian Families, Diversity, Conflict and Change*, 2nd ed. Toronto: Harcourt Canada (pp. 78–111).

Table 1.1
Percentage of Lone-Parent Families in Canada, 1931–2006

Year	Percentage
1931	13.4
1941	10.5
1951	9.9
1961	8.4
1971	6.8
1981	6.0
1991	13.0
2001	16.0
2006	15.9

Source: E.M. Gee, "Contemporary Diversities," in N. Mandell and A. Duffy (eds.), *Canadian Families, Diversity, Conflict, and Change,* 2nd ed. (Toronto: Harcourt Canada, 2000), pp. 78–111; Statistics Canada, "Update on Families," *Canadian Social Trends,* Catalogue no. 11-008 (Summer), pp. 11–13; Statistics Canada, "2006 Census: Families, Marital Status, Households and Dwelling Characteristics," *The Daily* (September 12, 2007).

and which past are we referring to? Whose interest is being served in holding onto a certain definition or vision of family life? With these questions in mind and in consideration of the family decline hypothesis and the family change perspective, we will review some key socio-demographic, cultural, and technological changes in the family in order to critique this debate in greater detail. And while this discussion is only intended to briefly highlight some key patterns and issues, these and other fundamental patterns and processes integral to understanding Canadian family life will be explored in more depth in subsequent chapters.

Evaluating the Family Decline Hypothesis: A Brief Overview of Key Socio-demographic, Cultural, and Technological Trends in Family Life

Contemporary family life is often deemed in collapse or in crisis based on a number of social behaviours and assumptions. One of these is based on the tendency for young adults to take longer to establish themselves in adult roles and statuses since they are marrying and having children later than ever before (if at all). Therefore, it is assumed that young people are rejecting the institution of marriage and family. Moreover, it is observed that today's individuals are engaging in a wider array of less permanent living arrangements, such as non-marital cohabitation and returning to live with parents as "boomerang kids." It is also argued that we live in a hedonistic divorce culture by marrying more than once. Further, many point to the emergence of non-traditional family forms and behaviours due to technological advances, such as in the areas of work, medical, digital, and reproductive technologies. And while these technologies make our lives easier and lengthen our life expectancy, some purport that we are living with more chronic illness and stress, with little time left for our families. These technologies are also blamed for undermining certain family communication and interaction patterns, as witnessed by the privatizing effects of some electronic technologies (i.e., television, computers, cellphones, iPods). They also further contribute to our ability to reject or delay "natural" family-related transitions, for example, through the usage of in-vitro fertilization and surrogate motherhood.

For example, few trends in the family have been as significant as the increase in the prevalence of unmarried cohabitation in Canada, a topic to be further explored in Chapter 6. From 1981 to 2006, the proportion of common-law families increased from 5.6 percent to 15.5 percent of all census families. Between 2001 and 2006 there was a particularly high growth rate (increasing by 19.8 percent), making this the fastest growing family structure in Canada (Statistics Canada, 2007). Moreover, there has been a dramatic increase in cohabitor households with children. These trends have created concern about the impact of

---

Figure 1.3
Profile of the Canadian Family, 2006 Census

Total Number of Families = 8,896,840

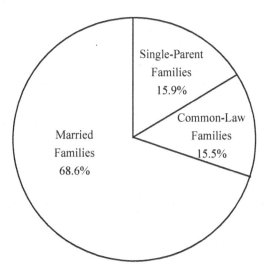

Source: Statistics Canada, "2006 Census: Families, Marital Status, Households and Dwelling Characteristics," *The Daily* (September 12, 2007).

cohabitation on marriage and family life, since these unions are viewed as less committed, and are found to be more fragile than legal, marital partnerships (Riedmann et al., 2003).

However, many assert that living together before or as an alternative to marriage is not something new. In fact, cohabitation has existed long enough to predate marriage. Until the mid-18th century, the difference between the two statuses was fluid in many countries, such as England (Wu and Schimmele, 2003). It is further argued that the growing popularity of cohabitation does not mean a rejection of marriage or family since the vast majority of Canadian families are comprised of married parents, as shown in Figure 1.3. Moreover, for those who choose to cohabit rather than be married, it is asserted that these couples are still entering into intimate partnerships that often serve the same functions as marriage, albeit without a marriage certificate. For example, people who choose to live together report that it allows them to pool resources with a loved one, as well as an opportunity to "test the waters" in order to avoid divorce later on.

Other cohabiting individuals maintain that it is their personal choice and that the state or religious institutions have no business in defining or regulating their private life. In short, they claim that a piece of paper does not guarantee commitment or a lifetime of happiness. Yet others point to some parts of the world like Africa, Latin America, and Sweden, and maintain that not only does cohabitation have a long history in these societies, but that it is widely practised and highly accepted. Thus, it is also argued that as the legal and social distinction between legal marriage and cohabitation increasingly blur, cohabitation should not be a sign of family demise.

Similarly, the popular media and other commentators have played a large role in the public perception that there has been a large increase in unmarried people, suggesting that society is rejecting the institution of marriage. And statistics do reveal shrinking marriage rates, rising ages of first marriage, and the growth of non-traditional living arrangements (such as cohabitation). Notably, the latest ages of first marriage are now evidenced: the average age of first marriage for women is 29.1 and 31.1 for men in 2008 (Statistics Canada, 2008). If we compare these average ages to the timing of first marriage in previous decades, these age differences are startling indeed! Figure 1.4 shows that in 1960, for instance, the average age of first marriage for women was 23, while it was about 26 for men (Dominion Bureau of Statistics, 1962).

If we take a longer historical view, we can see that average ages of marriage (as well as parenthood) have fluctuated widely. Figure 1.4 also reveals that the average ages of first marriage (for men) were relatively similar in the 1930s compared to recent trends, with only about a two and a half year increase in average age. Moreover, when calculating marital rates, it is important to realize that delayed marriage (since most people eventually marry) is an important contributing factor to lower marital rates. Thus, many argue that the fact that young people are delaying marriage is not a sign of a dwindling commitment to marriage, but rather evidence of a general extension of young adulthood and more carefully planned life course choices.

Furthermore, young people are taking longer to establish themselves in adult roles due to changing economic policies, education, and labour market demands. It is also argued that other socio-demographic changes (i.e., increased life expectancy) and alternative

Figure 1.4
Average Age at First Marriage, by Sex, Canada, 1921–2008

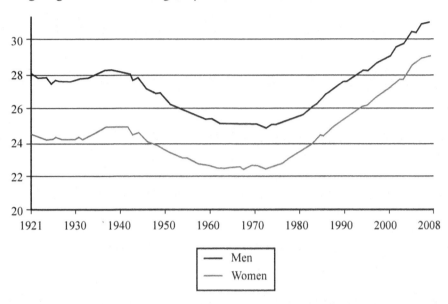

Note: Since 2003, the definition of marriage has been changed in some provinces and territories to include the legal union of two persons of the same sex. Age at first marriage for same-sex couples tends be higher than for opposite-sex couples.

Sources: For 1921 to 1987: Statistics Canada. *Marriage and Conjugal Life in Canada.* Ottawa: Statistics Canada, 1992. (Cat. No. 91-534E); for 1988 to 1999: Statistics Canada, Demography Division; for 2000 to 2004: Statistics Canada. *Mean Age and Median Age of Males and Females, by Type of Marriage and Marital Status, Canada, Provinces and Territories, Annual* (CANSIM Table 101-1002). Ottawa: Statistics Canada, 2008; and for 2005 to 2008: Statistics Canada. Canadian Vital Statistics, Marriage Database and Demography Division (population estimates). Ottawa: Statistics Canada, 2011.

Retrieved January 18, 2011 from Human Resources and Skills Development Canada (2011), Family Life and Marriage, http://www4.hrsdc.gc.ca/.3ndic.1t.4r@-eng.jsp?preview=1&iid=78

family forms provide the opportunity to experience a wider variety of living arrange-ments and relationship partners, many of which are familistic or family-oriented in nature (Mitchell, 2006). Furthermore, historical data again reveal that many people chose not to marry in earlier times. The percentage of Canadian women who had never married by the age of 45–49, for instance, was exactly the same in 1891 as it was in 2001, at 10 percent of the population (Mitchell, 2006: 38).

Moreover, we could examine many other socio-demographic trends, and provide counter-evidence to every purported claim offered by those in the family decline camp. For example, in the past, there were no problems with the aged because most people never aged. In other words, with low life expectancy, people died relatively young. Thus, we could counter the argument that "life was better for the elderly in the past" with the compelling fact that, unlike previous times, grandparents now have the opportunity to live long enough to watch their children (and grandchildren) grow up. From this vantage point, this increased generational overlap of lives could easily be interpreted as creating both new opportunities and challenges for aging families. In addition, many assert that Canadian family life is increasingly diversifying, making family decline arguments untenable. Indeed, current trends paint a portrait of rising cultural and structural variation in family life rather than a linear trend toward one monolithic "troubled" type of family.

Family Doom and Gloom Is Nothing New
It is also fascinating to note that throughout history, social scientists and the general public have always expressed concern over the demise of the family. In the 18th century, for instance, industrialization arose and farming began to decline. This led commentators to report that these changes brought with them "the break in the web of connections between the family and the community; the dispersion of the household group, with the young increasingly inclined to seek their fortune in a new setting; the improvement in the status of women; the erosion of parental authority; and a growing permissiveness in the area of sex," all of which were interpreted as signs of impending family demise (Demos, 1975: 66). In a similar vein, a well-known author writing in the 1920s (Groves, 1928) asserted that marriages were in "extreme collapse," in addition to citing numerous other problems purported to plague families at that time, such as high divorce, hedonism, sexual promiscuity, independence, and financial strain.

And by the late 1950s, many religious writers, politicians, educators, and parents were also worried about family decline, given social problems like juvenile delinquency and the emergence of popular culture, which targeted youth. Magazines like *Time*, for instance, ran stories about rampant delinquents in the streets (Liazos, 2004). Many were also concerned that families were being torn apart by the new music of rock 'n roll because it was ruining the moral fabric of communities. When Elvis Presley (known as "the King of Rock and Roll") sang "Hound Dog" on *The Milton Berle Show* on June 5, 1956, the official response was that television networks ban the filming of Presley from the waist down. The intensity of his pelvis-shaking made his teenaged fans scream, and his "vulgarity" and "animalism" were perceived to contribute to promiscuity and already weakening family values. And since that time, every decade has produced a multitude of alarmist concerns about family breakdown. For example, in the 1970s, there was a great deal of concern that family life was eroding as women began to enter the paid labour force in record numbers and divorce rates began to climb.

Summary

Despite the enormous difficulty inherent in defining families, our personal experiences of family constitute a significant influence on our lives and the family remains a fundamental institution in society. In this chapter, we explored changing and varied meanings of family. In particular, it is recognized that there are many ideological and institutional practices involved in defining families. Against an objective and private image of family life that many of us take for granted, "domestic order can be conceptualized as a working, experiential issue in collective representation, or a socially symbolic reality" (Gubrium and Holstein, 1987: 783). Therefore, the tendency to objectify families and dichotomize the public/private into two separate spheres should be understood as "a flexible cultural image which is put to use in a wide variety of situations which serve a great diversity of purposes and interests" (Fahey, 1995: 687).

Furthermore, a "normative" domestic order generates ideological codes that operate largely outside of our consciousness. As a result, these codes generate texts that are all around us and give substance to a version of The Family that masks the actualities of people's live. The consequences of these everyday practices are obviously enormous since they penetrate into a wide variety of settings in largely unthinking ways. As stated by Smith (1999: 171), "ideological codes may have a peculiar and important political force, carrying forward modes of representing the world even among those who overtly resist the representations they generate."

In this chapter we also critically evaluate the family decline hypothesis. This hypothesis purports that modern-day families are troubled and in demise relative to earlier family life, yet this hypothesis is based largely on pessimistic speculation and suggests ideological or personal agendas tied to meanings of family. From a life course framework, this chapter underscores the importance of situating family life and social change in its relative historical time frame and socio-political location. In particular, it can be socially and politically dangerous and inaccurate to rely on the prototypical 1950s "Leave It to Beaver" family as the benchmark for "traditional" family life. From a longer-range life course perspective, this nuclear family structure was actually a historical fluke. It is also not a universal norm from an anthropological or cross-cultural lens, a theme to be explored in more detail in Chapter 3. Indeed, a critical analysis of the family decline hypothesis using socio-demographic data and other evaluation methods is necessary in order to anchor speculation, hypotheses, and theorizing about families and family change (Casper and Bianchi, 2002).

A closer inspection of the family decline hypothesis also suggests that families—in whatever shape or form—have always struggled with external circumstances and inner conflicts. And, in many ways, families may be better off now than in previous times due to improved life expectancy, economic and technological conditions, and a wider range of choice in family-related behaviour. This is not to say that contemporary families are without their share of problems and complexities, but are as alive, vibrant, diverse, and socially significant as ever before.

Questions for Critical Reflection and Debate

1. Ask several people outside of your class to define family. In what ways do these definitions reflect themes and issues covered in this chapter?

2. Some individuals argue that the "normative" institution of the family is oppressive because it is a private domain characterized by hierarchical relationships and inequality (e.g., such as age and gender-based segregation). Do you agree with this viewpoint?
3. Debate the following: Family decline today is cause for alarm.
4. Provide some specific examples of how ideological codes and practices might operate outside your conscious intention as a student, as well as for a social scientist, or a political or religious leader.
5. To what extent has personal "choice" replaced institutional constraint on young people's family-related decisions, such as when and whom to marry? How might this vary by gender, ethnicity, and social class in Canadian society?
6. Try to predict what Canadian family life will look like in 50 years. For example, do you think that the institution of marriage will become replaced with new forms of family living? How might new technological advancements (e.g., medical, reproductive, electronic) shape future family life courses?

Glossary

Families are a basic social institution and, in the broadest sense, are a group of people who have intimate social relationships and a shared history together.

Family change perspective assumes that families have always been changing (despite much continuity) and that in some ways, modern-day families may be better than ever.

Family decline hypothesis refers to the idea that families today are in demise or are falling apart and have serious problems.

Fictive kin are non-relatives whose bonds are strong and intimate, such as those between very close friends.

Ideology is a system of beliefs and ideas that justifies or rationalizes action.

SNAF as an ideological code is a conception of The Family as a legally married couple sharing a household. It is a constant generator of procedure for selecting text-mediated discourse (e.g., vocabulary) and can generate the same order in widely different settings. It stands for Standard North American Family.

Social demography emphasizes the scientific study of population from a sociological perspective.

Further Reading

Cheal, D. (Ed.). 2010. *Canadian Families Today: New Perspectives,* 2nd ed. Don Mills: Oxford University Press. Presents a compilation of original essays on issues and trends affecting Canadian life with an emphasis on multiple perspectives, inequality, and diversity.

Coontz, S. 1992. *The Way We Never Were: American Families and the Nostalgia Trap.* New York: Basic Books. Examines two centuries of family life and shatters a series of myths and half-truths that burden contemporary families.

Fischer, C.S. 2011. *Still Connected: Family and Friends in America Since 1970.* New York: Russell Sage Foundation. Noted sociologist Claude Fischer examines long-term trends in family ties and friendships and paints an insightful and ultimately reassuring portrait of Americans' personal relationships.

Mandell, N., and A. Duffy. (Eds.). 2010. *Canadian Families: Diversity, Conflict, and Change*, 4th ed. Toronto: Thomson Nelson. Contains 12 articles that critically explore a wide array of issues relevant to Canadian families with an emphasis on the effects of gender, race, class, age, economics, sexual orientation, and violence.

McDaniel, S.A., and L. Tepperman. 2011. *Close Relations: An Introduction to the Sociology of Families,* 4th ed. Toronto: Pearson/Prentice-Hall. Provides a comprehensive overview of the history, structure, and the future of family life in Canada, in addition to making international comparisons.

Skolnick, A.S., and J.H. Skolnick. 2010. *Family in Transition*, 16th ed. New York: Pearson and Allen/Bacon. Is a very popular reader on American families and intimate relationships, and explores myths about family life from a socio-historical and economic perspective.

Related Web Sites

B.C. Council for Families, established in 1977, is a non-profit society devoted to strengthening, encouraging, and supporting families through information, education, research, and advocacy. It is the relationship affiliate of the Canadian Health Network, and its web site has useful publications and resources for all Canadians, www.bccf.bc.ca.

National Council on Family Relations is a national political and professional organization committed to educating the public about family issues and offers a multitude of resources and links to other family-related sites, www.ncfr.org. Facebook: NCFR

Real Women of Canada provides a good example of a national, conservative organization that views contemporary family life as fragmented. Its mission is to promote equality for homemakers and emphasizes values congruent with "traditional" family life, www.realwomen.ca. Facebook: REAL women of Canada

Sociological Images encourages students to exercise and develop their sociological imaginations with discussions of compelling visuals that span the breadth of sociological inquiry. For family-related images, search for postings under the tag "marriage and family," which has over 350 images in its archives, www.thesocietypages.org.socimages. Also see Facebook: Socimages, Twitter: SocImages, YouTube: www.youtube.com/socimages

Statistics Canada is our official federal government agency that provides statistics and information on many family-related areas such as marriage and marital status, living arrangements, economy, society, and culture, www.statcan.gc.ca.

References

Casper, L.M., and S.M. Bianchi. 2002. *Continuity and Change in the American Family*. Thousand Oaks: Sage.

Coontz, S. 1992. *The Way We Never Were: American Families and the Nostalgia Trap*. New York: Basic Books.

Demos, J. 1975. "The American Family in Past Time." In A. Skolnick and J. Skolnick (eds.), *Family in Transition*, 2nd ed. Boston: Little, Brown.

Dominion Bureau of Statistics. 1962. *Canada Year Book*. Ottawa: Queen's Printer and Controller of Stationery.

Eichler, M. 1988. *Families in Canada Today: Recent Changes and Their Policy Consequences*, 2nd ed. Toronto: Gage.

Fahey, T. 1995. "Privacy and the Family: Conceptual and Empirical Reflections." *Sociology* 29: 687–702.

Gee, E.M. 2000. "Contemporary Diversities." In N. Mandell and A. Duffy (eds.), *Canadian Families, Diversity, Conflict, and Change*, 2nd ed. (pp. 78–111). Toronto: Harcourt Canada.

Goode, W.J. 1963. *World Revolution and Family Patterns*. Glencoe: The Free Press.

Groves, E.R. 1928. *The Marriage Crisis*. New York: Longmans, Green.

Gubrium, J.F., and J.A. Holstein. 1987. "The Private Image: Experiential Location and Method in Family Studies." *Journal of Marriage and the Family* 49: 773–786.

Holstein, J.A., and J.F. Gubrium. 1999. "What Is Family? Further Thoughts on a Social Constructionist Approach."*Marriage and Family Review* 28: 3–20.

Liazos, A. 2004. *Families: Joys, Conflicts, and Change*. Boulder: Paradigm.

McDaniel, S.A., and L. Tepperman. 2004. *Close Relations: An Introduction to the Sociology of Families,* 2nd ed. Toronto: Pearson/Prentice-Hall.

Mitchell, B.A. 2006. *The Boomerang Age: Transitions to Adulthood in Families*. New Brunswick: Aldine-Transaction.

Murdock, G.P. 1949. *Social Structure*. New York: Macmillan.

Newman, D.M., and L. Grauerholz. 2002. *Sociology of Families*, 2nd ed. Thousand Oaks: Sage.

Popenoe, D. 1988. *Disturbing the Nest: Family Change and Decline in Modern Societies*. New York: Aldine de Gruyter.

Popenoe, D. 1993. "American Family Decline, 1960–1990: A Review and Appraisal." *Journal of Marriage and the Family* 55: 527–555.

Popenoe, D. 1996. *Life without Father*. New York: Free Press.

Riedmann, A., M. Lamanna, and A. Nelson. 2003. *Marriages and Families*. Scarborough: Thomson Nelson.

Silva, E.B., and C. Smart. 1999. "The 'New' Practices and Politics of Family Life." In E.B. Silva and C. Smart (eds.), *The New Family?* (pp. 1–12). London: Sage Publications.

Smith, D. 1999. *Writing the Social: Critique, Theory, and Investigations*. Toronto: University of Toronto Press.

Stacey, J. 1996. *In the Name of the Family: Rethinking Family Values in the Postmodern Age*. Boston: Beacon.

Stack, C. 1974. *All Our Kin*. New York: Harper and Row.

Statistics Canada. 2002. *Census of Canada: Profile of Canadian Families and Households: Diversification Continues*, Catalogue no. 96F0030XIE2001003. Ottawa: Statistics Canada, Ministry of Industry.

Statistics Canada. 2003a. "Marriages." The Daily, June 2.

Statistics Canada. 2003b. "Update on Families." *Canadian Social Trends*, Catalogue no. 11-008, Summer: 11–13.

Statistics Canada. 2007. *Family Portrait: Continuity and Change in Canadian Households in 2006, 2006 Census*. Ottawa: Statistics Canada, Demography Division.

Statistics Canada. 2008. "Crude Marriage Rates, All Marriages, Canada," CANSIM Table 101-1004.

Vanier Institute of the Family. 2002. *Profiling Canada's Families II*. Ottawa: The Vanier Institute of the Family.

Wu, Z., and C.M. Schimmele. 2003. "Cohabitation." In J.J. Ponzetti (ed.), *The International Encyclopedia of Marriage and Family Relationships,* 2nd ed. (pp. 315–323). New York: MacMillan Reference.

Chapter 2

Family Theory and Methods

Windows on Families and Family Research

Learning Objectives

In this chapter you will learn that ...
* sociologists use a variety of theories to explain the structure and dynamic of families
* family research is invaluable to human knowledge and understanding
* theory and research depend closely on each other
* there are two equally scientific and complementary methodological approaches to studying families—quantitative and qualitative
* a researcher's choice of theory and methods, as well as his or her own values, biases, and behaviours, can influence the entire research process
* it is important to critically evaluate research in order to make meaningful interpretations

The fascination of sociology lies in the fact that its perspective makes us see in a new light the very world in which we have lived our lives. This also constitutes a transformation of consciousness.

—P.L. Berger, *Invitation to Sociology: A Humanistic Perspective*

Introduction

What makes some families more prone to poverty and homelessness than others? Why are women more likely to do more housework and child care than men, even when they work full-time outside the home? What makes some children vulnerable to sexual or physical abuse and neglect? To make advancements on these kinds of intellectual and practical questions, researchers operate in two distinct but highly related worlds—the abstract (the world of concepts/ideas) and the concrete (the observable/empirical world). Indeed, scientific theories link these two separate domains, and in doing so provide descriptions, summaries, integration, and explanations about what is known from research. Theories also guide subsequent research and practices that will increase our knowledge and further understanding, as well as new sets of solutions (Chibucos and Leite, with Weiss, 2005). For example, if we theorize that children are more likely to be abused when parents lack institutional support and good parenting skills, we can test these ideas in order to improve our social programs targeted at this social problem.

Although a wide variety of terms (e.g., paradigm, conceptual framework, model) indicate the same general ideas as the term "theory," theorizing can be defined as "the process of systematically developing and organizing ideas to explain phenomena and a theory is the total set of empirically testable, interconnected ideas formulated to explain those phenomenon" (Chibucos and Leite, with Weiss, 2005: 1).Thus, research is integral to this process, since if one addresses questions only on a conceptual level—or vice versa—if one deals only with observable information without trying to systematically explain it, then scientific theory development or answers to our social problems will not be found. In this chapter, an overview of main "classical" and emergent sociological theories and conceptual frameworks relevant to families will be outlined. And since research is integral to knowledge building, a brief introduction to family research methods will also be provided.

Structural Functionalism: Families as Stable and Harmonious and *Leave It to Beaver*

This perspective can be traced to early attempts by August Comte (1798–1857) and Emile Durkheim (1858–1917), who sought to establish the study of society as a science. It views the family as a social institution that performs essential functions for society to ensure its stability. Society is envisioned as a biological organism, made up of interdependent parts or institutions, such as family, education, religion, and workplace that enable the larger whole (or society) to function. The best-known and leading proponent of the structural-functionalist perspective was Talcott Parsons (1902–1979), whose ideas were enormously influential during the 1950s and 1960s. He began his career as a biologist, and later taught sociology at Harvard University from 1931 until just before his death. His work was influenced by the earliest functionalistic theorists to focus on the family, particularly British anthropologist Malinowski.

In 1913, Malinowski published a classic work *The Family among the Australian Aboriginees*, which drew on 19th-century debates about families and which became the basis for most sociological theories in the first half of the 20th century. His basic argument was that The Family consisted of a man, woman, and their children, and that this family was universal. He asserted that this family form could be found in all societies, including diverse European societies and among the Aboriginal groups of Australia. Moreover, he assumed that this universal family was rooted in biological sex differences, which supports the need for a strict gendered division of labour. In addition, he assumed that a major function of the family was to provide a home, to organize sexual reproduction, and to provide nurturance and love to its members.

At Harvard, Parsons and colleague Bales (1955) applied this theory when they co-wrote *Family, Socialization, and the Interaction Process.* Similar to Malinowksi, they maintained that families function best when husbands and fathers carried out and specialized in instrumental roles and mothers carried out expressive roles. This idealization is similar to the nuclear family depicted on the *Leave It to Beaver* television situation comedy, which was produced between 1957 and 1963 (with reruns still shown). In his instrumental role as breadwinner, Mr. Cleaver ("the Beav's" dad) was hard-working and confident, while Mrs. Cleaver ("the Beav's" mom) was nurturing and caring in her expressive role as full-time homemaker. Indeed, this ideological view of a woman's role in society was widespread at this time, as illustrated in the depiction of a housewife in a Canadian encyclopedia in 1958.

Families have three primary functions, all of which lend order, stability, or homeostasis to the larger society. First, families must ensure that society has an ongoing supply of new members and to be a source of socialization. Thus, the family must control and regulate reproduction, as well as socialize offspring to learn attitudes, beliefs, and values appropriate to their society and culture so that they can function effectively in society. Second, families need to provide economic support for family members, such as providing food, clothing, and housing. Third, families need to provide emotional support for family members by providing intimacy, warmth, safety, and protection. This is deemed to be an antidote to the dehumanizing and alienating forces of modern society. In short, this family function provides a useful service to society by offering a "haven in a heartless world" (Lasch, 1977).

Social Conflict, Political Economy, and Gender Theorizing: Inequality, Class, and Power Relations as Fundamental Features of Family Life

Figure 2.1
The Role of the 1950s Housewife

The housewife accepts her never-ending work, not for its own sake but to keep one corner of a hurried world secure and bright and warm. She encourages the first steps, the first wondering contact with the world. She offers love where there is hurt or pain, and share the delights that tumble in and fill the house with laughter.

Source: This photo and caption appeared inside the front cover of the 1958 *Encyclopedia Canadiana, The Encyclopedia of Canada*, Vol. 10 (Ottawa: The Grolier Society of Canada Ltd.) (copyright ©1958).

Functionalist ideas pervaded all aspects of sociological thinking from the 1930s until they were challenged by conflict theorizing in the late 1960s. Rather than stressing order, equilibrium, and consensus, the focus of conflict theory is on power relations and inequality and how political and economic processes affect family life. At a macro level, inequality may be between the family system and the work/employment/economic system, between males and females, between social classes, or between age groups. At the micro level, inequality may occur between certain family members, such as between parent and child, or between a daughter-in-law and mother-in-law, or between siblings. Furthermore, conflict is not necessarily viewed as bad or disruptive of social systems and human interactions since it is seen as an assumed and expected feature of society and human behaviour (Eshleman and Wilson, 2001).

Social conflict theory (including political economy theory to be discussed later) has its roots in the work of Karl Marx (1818–1883), who studied the transition from feudalism to capitalism as two major classes developed—the bourgeoisie and the proletariat. These two classes were primarily in opposition to each other and interdependent since the proletariat class was vulnerable to exploitation and alienation under the dominant, ruling bourgeoisie class. Although Marxist analysts have generally given little attention to the study of the family per se, Marx's colleague, Frederick Engels, wrote the first conflict framework of the family. In his book, *The Origins of the Family, Private Property, and the State* (1894), Engels traces the relationship between the mode of production and the type of family that exists in society. For example, he argued that the communal family systems of technologically simple societies seemed to be more egalitarian than patriarchal, monogamous families, which were based on private property (Porter, 1987).

Since Marx and Engels were primarily concerned with economic relations, families were primarily viewed as sites for the reproduction of labour power that ultimately benefits the capitalists. Also, domestic labour, which is primarily done in the household, did not fit into standard Marxian concepts such as surplus (or unpaid labour) value. Domestic labour was also seen as a "natural" role for women (Sydie, 1987), though they did regard it as the major source of women's oppression. In Marx and Engels's view, only as women became members of the paid labour force could they achieve political and social influence. This would remove gender inequalities in society and produce truly egalitarian marital relationships.

A Political Economy View on Family Life: The Family as a Unit of Consumption

Although not a unified discipline, a political economy view on the family is useful for further understanding contemporary family life since it elaborates on the role of economic processes in shaping society and history. This approach makes extensive use of class analysis in making sense of society and history, particularly in the context of political, cultural, and socio-economic processes. Political economists assume that the dominant class in any society is advantageously placed to exact obedience or compliance from the subordinate classes. This implies a relationship not only between class and ideology, but also between power and ideology—the organized and structured power of a given class. Therefore, there is an element of social control since dominant groups are able to manufacture consent, a term used to denote how the mass media filters information so that the interests of elite groups go unchallenged. Thus, while many of us assume that we willingly engage in certain behaviours as free agents, in reality, this may be only illusory (Côté and Allahar, 1994).

In order to apply some of these ideas to specific aspects of family life, we need to consider how our industrial economy and capitalist mode of production (based on liberal democracy) shape our choices, lifestyles, and behaviours. Family forms are viewed as historically embedded outcomes of global capitalist practices and changes in work patterns and technology (Luxton, 2005), as discussed in Box 2.1. This reduces families to units of consumption that foster cultural values of individualism and hedonism rather than collectivist goals. Since capitalists rely on the consumption of commodities (or goods) in order to survive, families must be "encouraged" to consume goods and services, which can extend to education and parenting. For instance, Barkley (2003) argues that we live in a culture that has commodified parenting through a constant barrage of parenting magazines, books, television channels, and programs, yet parents have not voluntarily participated in the process. Indeed, according to Barkley:

> In our post-industrial society, social activity has become commodified; our needs have been absorbed into the marketplace and sold back to us. Most activities related to our children now require the intervention of the marketplace. Sales people and "experts" help us to decide on the right clothes, pets, the timing of talks about sex, the correct bedtime, normal versus abnormal adolescent behaviour, how to monitor television, how to discipline, how to deal with homework, anger, activities, entertainment, computers, sports—the list is endless, and exhausting. (Barkley, 2003: 278)

Moreover, from this perspective, the advertising industry aggressively targets certain social groups of people (e.g., young people) to buy their goods and may, in fact, even appear to embrace the values of oppressed or marginalized groups (e.g., the "gangster" subculture with its identifiable music and clothing). Consequently, capitalist enterprises are able to sell more hip-hop and designer clothing, jewellery, running shoes, alcohol, and tobacco (Côté and Allahar, 1994). Similarly, the fast-food industry bombards us with ads that target children and families since they are able to provide quick and inexpensive meals (albeit with little nutritive value). Added "bonuses" such as free plastic toys also "bully" parents into buying these meals for their children. Overall, a conflict/political economy perspective situates family life and their decision making in the context of political, socio-economic, cultural, and environmental processes.

Feminist and Masculinity Perspectives: Gender and the Family

Similar to the conflict/political economy perspective, there is not "one" unified feminist theory and feminist theoretical perspective. Socialist feminists, for example, tend to analyze the relationship between the processes of capital accumulation and "the reproduction

Box 2.1
The Effect of the Industrial Economy on Families:
A Political Economy Approach

In the modern industrial economy, the responsibility of the family for the material welfare of its members declined with the professionalization of health care and the slow emergence of state care for those in need. The traditional pattern of home births, home remedies, and informal kinship support systems was increasingly replaced by hospitals, clinics, and publicly funded welfare offices. In this sense, the general direction of the 20th century has been toward the building of public institutions to support individual existence (Strong-Booag, 1979; Struthers, 1983). Nonetheless, these institutions do not fully respond to individual needs, and families have maintained an important support role for family members as well as for kin. The processes of social and economic change may have encouraged some sense of individualism, but family and kin still provide an important framework for personal welfare in the late 20th century much as they have since the 17th century.

The instability of the family during the urban growth and industrial development of the mid-19th century caused considerable concern among politicians and other public leaders, who feared that widespread social disorder would result from the rapid pace of social change. These leaders believed that the family was in peril as a social institution, and so they promoted new ideals for family members, especially for women and children, who were most affected by the new modes of production. The major development for children was the establishment of schooling as a dominant experience growing up. For women, the result was a definition of their responsibility that limited them to the home and to the roles of wives and mothers.

Source: Gaffield, C. 1990. "The social and economic origins of contemporary families," in M. Baker (ed.), *Families: Changing Trends in Canada.* Scarborough: McGraw-Hill Ryerson Ltd. (p. 33).

of labour power." Capitalism relies on the existence of workers to supply labour power in addition to unpaid domestic labour (which is mainly performed by women) in order to survive. Radical feminists, on the other hand, tend to emphasize differences between men and women and the ways in which men's power oppresses and controls women and creates unsafe places for women and children (e.g., see Luxton, 2005 for further discussion). Despite considerable variation in theories, five basic themes that appear in feminist approaches can be identified (Osmond and Thorne, 1993; Seccombe and Warner, 2004):

1. Emphasis is placed on the female experience, since social life has traditionally been studied through the gaze of men.

2. Gender is an organizing concept of social theory and is seen as a set of relations imbued with power and inequality.
3. Gender and family relations need to be contextualized in their respective socio-cultural and historical situations and vary by social class, ethnicity, and geographic location.
4. There is not one single unitary definition for The Family.
5. Instead of taking a "value-neutral" orientation, feminists purport that inequality exists and should be eliminated.

Generally, feminist theorists have been very critical of traditional sociological approaches, especially ones that ignore power and inequality and how this is structured by gender, in addition to other root sources of disadvantage, such as by race, ethnicity, social class, sexual orientation, and age. Thus, a feminist perspective recognizes how social interaction, including discourse (i.e., the usage of language and symbols) is socially constructed and mirrors privilege and inequities as depicted in Figure 2.2. Feminists also tend to assume that if reality is socially constructed, it can therefore be reconstructed. As a result, feminist theories are designed to uncover the mechanisms by which inequality is maintained so that new mechanisms can be constructed to dismantle it (Seccombe and Warner, 2004). Moreover, it is assumed that around the world, women in developing nations face very different challenges than do women in advanced industrialized nations. Therefore, poverty, environmental degradation, and starvation can also be key concerns for many feminists.

Since feminism grew into an important social movement during the 1960s, scholars have been researching women in greater depth. However, the theoretical study of men and their various masculine identities is a relatively new field (e.g., see Carrigan, Connell, and Lee, 2002). From this lens, theorists are interested in historical conceptualizations of masculinity and masculine identity and its social construction. Family-related topics of interest might include: men's socialization; men, relationships, and sexuality; men and power/violence; and men and fatherhood. And while masculinity studies can be found in other disciplines (e.g., cultural studies), a sociological perspective typically centres on common Marxist-feminist themes such as power and oppression; the public and the private domain; and social, cultural, and political change (e.g., see Whitehead and Barrett, 2001).

Social Constructionism and the Symbolic Interaction Perspective: Families Creating Their Own Realities

Social constructionism is a sociological theory of knowledge that became prominent in the U.S. with the publication of Berger and Luckman's 1966 book entitled, *The Social Construction of Reality*. This sociological theory of knowledge focuses on the idea that social phenomena are created or constructed in particular social and cultural contexts. In other words, what may appear as a "natural" or a singular reality is actually an "inven-

Figure 2.2
Social Interaction from a Feminist Perspective

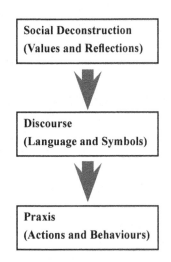

Social Deconstruction (Values and Reflections)	**Recognition that reality is socially constructed** Consideration of privilege of sex, class, race, nationality, sexuality, ethnicity, and ability
Discourse (Language and Symbols)	**Heightened awareness that our language and symbols mirror the privilege and inequities** Reordering the categorizations and thereby the stratifications valued in society in the ways we interact
Praxis (Actions and Behaviours)	**Acting on beliefs** Realize social change by working to modify existing gender and societal relations

Source: B.B. Ingoldsby, S.R. Smith, and J.E. Miller, *Exploring Family Theories* (Los Angeles: Roxbury Publishing, 2004), fig. 8.1, p. 194.

tion" or construction reflective of a particular group, culture, or society. Thus, a major consideration is given to uncovering the manner in which individuals, families, or other social groups participate in the creation of their perceived reality, such as in the creation of family rituals and stories, childhood memories, and romantic "ideals" (e.g., see Bulcroft, Smeins, and Bulcroft, 2005).

In contemporary times, social constructionism is viewed as a source of the "postmodern movement" (e.g., the "deconstructing" of asserted knowledge), and has been influential in the field of cultural studies. Its roots can also be traced to other popular sociological theories of the family such as symbolic interactionism. Symbolic interactionism emerged in the United States in the 1920s at the University of Chicago. Based on the work of Charles Horton Cooley (1909) and George Herbert Mead (1934), as well as other influential sociologists during the 1920s and 1930s, the term "symbolic interactionism" was later adopted by Herbert Blumer (1969) to describe the process of interpersonal interaction. Applied to family studies, this perspective emphasizes micro or internal family interactions, and the ongoing action and response of family members to one another. Family interactions are the result of reciprocal acts whereby individuals are acting, negotiating, and responding to one another as minded beings. Interactions occur via symbols, or gestures or words that have shared meaning.

Interpretations and meanings are anchored in actual situations of social interactions, and through interactions, a person develops a sense of self. For example, through primary relationships with "significant others," such as parents or peers, a child acquires a sense of competencies and a feeling of self-worth. A person's self is composed of a socialized component called the "me," plus an "I," which refers to the more spontaneous behaviour that arises out of biological needs and immediate sensations (Mead, 1934).

Therefore, unlike the structural functionalists who consider the family as a standard structure, these theorists view the family as the creation of its members as they spontaneously interact with one another in joint action. Thus, a family takes on a reality of its own based on subjective meanings and interpretations, role playing, and the interchanges of its members. This reflects the famous Thomas theorem introduced by Thomas and Thomas (1928: 572), which states that, "If people define situations as real, they are real in their consequences." For example, if you interpret the glances and words that your date is exchanging with others at a party as flirtatious, your interpretation of reality could result in a certain outcome, such as jealousy, accusations, and the ultimate breakup of the relationship.

Social Exchange Theory: Family Life as "Fair Trade"

Similar to symbolic interactionism, social exchange theory is a micro-level theory that focuses on the interaction between individual actors. However, social exchange theory views family life and decision making in terms of costs and benefits. Early proponents include George Homans (1910–1989), who drew from the work of developmental psychology, and Peter Blau (1918–2002), who was heavily influenced by the field of economics. Exchange theorists assume that humans are primarily motivated by self-interest and seek to maximize rewards or profits in relationships while minimizing costs or possible punishments. Humans are also seen as rational beings, who consciously calculate relative costs and rewards, although rules and/or the importance of any exchange are variable across people and cultures. Moreover, exchanges are regulated by norms of reciprocity and are characterized by interdependence (Gouldner, 1960).

Although this approach is criticized for its "market relations" type of analysis and failure to address why people hold varying amounts of resources in the first place, it has been used to study topics such as dating, marital satisfaction, divorce, and other relationship patterns. Applied to the area of mate selection, most of us have an idea of how much we are "worth" in terms of our looks, personality, ability, and even possessions. As a result, we expect to get the "best return" for what we provide in relationships at the least cost to ourselves. For example, if we perceive ourselves to be fairly attractive and intelligent, we expect to find a mate who is also smart, good looking, or has some other benefit such as an exceptionally pleasant personality (Ward, 2002). Further, norms of reciprocity suggest that both partners should perceive some gain or reward from the exchange or interaction. In other words, there should be a sense of balance such that if the exchange results in a net loss for one partner, then the relationship could be in trouble (Seccombe and Warner, 2004).

The Family Development Perspective: A Hybrid Theory

Originating in home economics and elaborated by sociologists during the 1930s, the family development approach tries to synthesize the ideas of several approaches into one unified theme (Eshleman and Wilson, 2001). For example, from rural sociologists these sociologists borrowed the concept of stages of the family life cycle, and from child psychologists they used the concepts of developmental needs and tasks. From the structural-functionalist and symbolic interactionist approaches they borrowed the concepts of family functions and sex roles and the idea of the family as a system of interacting actors (Hill and Hansen, 1960).

This perspective proposes that family members accomplish developmental tasks as they move through stages in the family life cycle. Although there are many variations on family life cycle, the best known is that of Evelyn Duvall, who developed an eight-stage model of the family in the 1950s. These stages entail: married couple, no children; the child-bearing family; the family with preschoolers; the family with school-aged children; the family with adolescents; the family as "launching pad" (e.g., children leaving home); the middle-aged "empty nest" family; and the aging family from retirement to death. Throughout the life span, members' roles, expectations, and relationships change, largely depending upon how they adapt to the presence or absence of child-rearing responsibilities (Duvall, 1957).

Since the 1960s, there has been a great deal of attention on the analysis of marital satisfaction over the life cycle from this perspective. However, you can probably see many aspects of family life that do not fit neatly into the life cycle approach, such as the refilled "empty nest," which is covered in Chapter 10. This approach has also been based on White, middle-class families and has generally ignored diversity such as same-sex households and social change, although it is constantly undergoing reformulation (e.g., see White and Klein, 2002).

Emergent Family Theory: The Life Course Perspective

Although not considered a formal theory by some, a notable emergent framework in the field of family sociology is the life course perspective (e.g., see Giele and Elder, 1998). This approach draws upon a variety of disciplines in addition to sociology (e.g., social demography, history, economics, and developmental psychology). It is particularly relevant to contemporary trends in family life, given its relevance to population aging and health-related issues. Indeed, it is generally considered the dominant perspective in the field of social gerontology at the present time. The family is perceived as a micro social group within a macro social context—a "collection of individuals with shared history who interact within ever-changing social contexts" (Bengston and Allen, 1993: 470).

This perspective has its roots in age stratification theory and draws heavily on prominent American sociologist C. Wright Mills's (1959) call for a theoretical orientation that bridges individual biography and history and the intersections of these domains within the social structure. Therefore, this perspective can link macro (history, social structure) elements and the micro (or individual/interpersonal) level (Chappell, Gee, McDonald, and Stones, 2003). The life course of individuals and their families is embedded and shaped by their relative historical, cultural, and geographic location, as well as by factors such as age, gender, family history, socioeconomic status, and ethnicity/race.

This perspective is concerned with lifelong developmental processes in the family. The life course can be defined as "trajectories that extend across the life span, such as family or work; and by short-term changes or transitions, such as entering or leaving school, acquiring a full-time job, and the first marriage" (Elder, 2000: 1615). Transitions are also subject to reversal, such as being divorced or returning to the parental home. Age and social time are connected by the concept of normative timing. In other words, societies have expectations or social clocks about the "appropriate" age for people to take on (or exit) from social roles. Some of these expectations are formal (e.g., retirement at age 65) or they may be embedded in wider social and cultural norms (e.g., at what age one should marry).

Another key principle is that individuals and families have differential access to resources (e.g., economic and social) and this can shape the timing and nature of transitional behaviours and other family-related decisions. For example, young adults with fewer resources and supports have less opportunity to delay adult roles and responsibilities. Moreover, family lives are "linked" or lived interdependently, such that the actions of one family member can affect the actions or circumstances of another. Becoming a parent, for instance, creates the counter-transition of grandparenthood with its new sets of generational roles and responsibilities.

Finally, the timing and nature of transitions and events can result in impacts that are felt as one ages, and can be envisioned as "ripple effects." For example, if a young person drops out of high school, leaves home at a young age, and becomes homeless, this situation can have far-reaching consequences for the rest of his or her life (i.e., poverty and poor health in old age). Thus, this approach emphasizes how cumulative disadvantage (or advantage) can set up a chain reaction of experiences that reverberates across the life course—a social inequality perspective that has valuable utility for creating effective social policy and programs (e.g., see O'Rand, 1996; also see Chapter 15).

Other Windows on Families

It should be recognized that these theories are not the only frames of reference used in family sociology. For example, some sociologists draw upon social ecological theory, a multidisciplinary perspective that integrates a life course perspective and calls for simultaneously considering family-level variables and contextual variables. It has received considerable attention from theorists and researchers as both a developmental and a historical framework for the study of intergenerational relations, and is often used to study substantive areas such as family violence and elder abuse (see Chapter 14 for overview and application). Another popular theory is family systems theory, which bridges family sociology and family therapy. From a family systems perspective, a family is viewed like a machine, with parts or family members that interact in a meaningful way (Chibucos and Leite, with Weiss, 2005). Therefore, problems in families cannot be understood and solved without taking into account the entire family system.

Thus, family sociologists can synthesize theoretical ideas from several sources. For example, they could integrate elements of feminism with queer theory, a theory that questions the use of socially constructed categories of sex/gender. Sociologists can also be influenced by other disciplines, such as biology and psychology, resulting in cross-disciplinary hybrid "windows" on the family (e.g., see Chapter 7 for theories on child socialization). Bio-social theory, for example, suggests that biology always interacts with culture in creating certain family forms (Walsh and Gordon, 1995). Alternatively, they may use models or other types of less formal theory, such as the Double ABCX model used in family stress/abuse research, which is covered in more detail in Chapter 14. Moreover, by rigorous scientific standards, some of these "theories" would be considered "conceptual frameworks," since they are based on loosely interrelated concepts or are only partially applied to substantive topics (Porter, 1987).

Which Theory Is Right? Critically Evaluating Family Theories

Students often wonder which theory is the most accurate, given varying (and often conflicting) foci and assumptions about the nature of reality and social life. Indeed, each theory or conceptual framework contains its own set of concepts defined to explain family life efficiently within *its* world view (see Table 2.1 for summary of key concepts), and this influences how researchers ask (and answer) questions about the family. Yet, on a broad level, all theory is a kind of discourse that seeks generalization, as elaborated by Canadian family theorist David Cheal in Box 2.2.

It should also be remembered that theoretical frameworks have evolved from the efforts of social scientists to understand large-scale social changes taking place in industrializing Europe and North America during the 19th century, yet these theories changed throughout the century in response to differing conceptions and conditions of family life. Thus, the effort of family sociologists to develop tenable explanatory frameworks is constantly being challenged by social and technological change. This is illustrated in the structural-functionalist theorizing that held sway during the 1950s and 1960s, a time in which the heterosexual nuclear family structure with rigid gender roles was more prevalent than today. In this way, each perspective represents an "intellectual heritage" that reflects a distinct socio-historical location and has been modified and expanded through the years by many contributors (Porter, 1987). As a result, some theories are now viewed as "outdated" and not reflective of contemporary family life, although some fundamental concepts or tenets may reappear in newer theories. In addition, each perspective has its own relative strengths and limitations based on its primary emphasis or conception of the phenomenon under study (also see Table 2.1).

Box 2.2
What Is Theory?

Theory is a kind of discourse. It is a set of topics and a way of talking about those topics. Not all discourse is theoretical discourse, however. Theory is the kind of discourse that seeks generalizations. It moves from the particular to the general, and makes statements that apply to a large number of cases under a variety of conditions. The purpose of theory may be to explain, or to construct a narrative, or to summarize knowledge, but the form of argument is always one of generalization. Theory is that discourse which takes particular cases and places them in a context where they can be compared with other cases having similar or different properties.

The principal means by which generalizations are made in theoretical discourse is through the use of concepts that identify types of objects. Concepts are the heart of any theory, and definitions of concepts therefore rightly receive a great deal of attention in the process of theorizing. A renewal of family theory must include renewed attention to problems of definitions in family studies, including the problem of defining family itself.

If the goal of theory is generalization, we need to pay attention to the different levels of theory. This involves including in our repertoire of theories those theories which are general in the sense of applying to aspects of society beyond family relations. Concepts such as industrial society and post-industrial society are relevant here, and seem likely to become more important as we try to take account of changes in family life.

Source: Cheal, D. 2005. "Theorizing family: From the particular to the general," in V.L. Bengtson et al., *Sourcebook of Family Theory and Research.* Thousand Oaks, Calif.: Sage (pp. 29–30).

Family Research Methods: A Brief Introduction

As previously stated, research and theory are interdependent—research without any underlying theoretical reasoning is simply a string of meaningless bits of information, whereas theory without research is abstract and speculative (Mills, 1959). Fundamentally, there are three basic ways of knowing (see Table 2.2) and two basic "ideal types" of conducting research (see Figure 2.3). One way of conducting research is by adopting the "traditional" scientific method or deductive approach, whereby the researcher begins with a theory and develops hypotheses about what he or she expects to observe. For example, social exchange theory purports that those with more resources in a relationship hold the balance of power. Therefore, we might hypothesize that in a dual-career couple, the partner who earns the higher salary will do less housework, on average. We would then collect data from couples (e.g., on their income, distribution of domestic work) and try to determine if there is support for our hypothesis. Surveys, interviews, and experimental designs would be popular methods of collecting data from this approach and these data are usually amendable to quantitative analysis (e.g., by statistically analyzing these data using numeric and coded forms).

Alternatively, we might adopt an inductive approach, which begins with systematic observations and is often used in qualitative research. Typically, these observations help us to move toward more abstract concepts and ideas that contribute to the further development of theory. This approach is favoured by those who do not want to begin their research with predetermined ideas or when a theory on that topic is not explicit or well developed enough to predict certain outcomes. Inductive styles of research are also popular among those who want to collect "quality" data rather than engage in "number crunching."

For instance, a social constructionist interested in the study of family rituals might want to explore how ritualized aspects of religious behaviour coincide with family life and events. While data could be collected in a variety of ways, one possible approach is narrative analysis. Narrative analysis is concerned with the knowledge base and stories that people and groups use to give meaning to their experiences. Researchers can examine family narratives or family stories to understand how family members "reauthor" their own lives in line with alternative and preferred stories of identity and ways of life. This is done in order to reveal how families use religious meanings and symbols to construct experiences and to develop their sense of self as a family over time (Chatters and Taylor, 2005). Generally, attention in qualitative research is paid to uncovering and understanding subjective meanings rather than assuming singular or "objective" realities, process rather than cause-effect, as well as the daily lived experiences of family members. Common types of data collection would include in-depth interviews, direct observations or ethnographies, document analysis, or case studies.

And while the descriptions of these approaches illustrate two very different styles of reasoning or doing research, in reality, researchers adopting one approach do not always follow these steps in perfect sequence. One might begin with a theory and a set of rigid hypotheses, but then modify this work as the research progresses. Indeed, science depends upon continuous movement between theory and observation (Seccombe and Warner, 2004). Also, qualitative researchers may be interested in quantifying some data, while quantitative researchers may also collect data via open-ended questions, which can contain subjective data. Furthermore, there are different styles of doing research under the rubric of either quantitative or qualitative methods, and these methods may be shared with other disciplinary foundations (see Figure 2.4 for examples of three types of qualitative methodologies).

Moreover, mixed methodological approaches are becoming highly popular since no single methodological orientation can answer all our questions about families. Mixed methods can be used in a single study, which could entail the collection of both quantitative and qualitative data. These studies could be sequential, starting with quantitative methods (e.g., statistical analysis of census data) and then use qualitative methods (e.g., case studies) to further probe meanings of emergent themes uncovered in the initial analyses. Alternatively, the study could begin with a qualitative study, or it might combine

Table 2.1
How Sociological Theories View Families

Theoretical Perspective	Key Concepts
Structural Functionalism	Order, stability, equilibrium, consensus, harmony, socialization, instrumental/expressive roles
Example: What are some long-term consequences of parental divorce for children?	
Feminist Perspective	Gender inequality, women's subordination, patriarchy, social change
Example: How does women's disproportionate participation in unpaid work affect their economic standing and well-being later in life?	
Symbolic Interactionism	Day-to-day interactions, communication, symbols, subjective meanings, perceptions, definition of the situation, role playing, joint action
Example: How does religion help families understand and cope with normative and non-normative events?	
Social Exchange Theory	Rewards, costs, profit, reciprocity, expectations, self-interest, humans as rational
Example: Why do abused women stay with their partners?	
Family Development	Expectations, norms, family career, life stages, developmental tasks
Example: How does marital satisfaction change over the life cycle?	
Life Course Approach	Age-related transitions, counter-transitions, social timetables, diversity, linked lives, cumulative advantage and disadvantage
Example: How does the timing of life course transitions during young adulthood affect intergenerational relationships?	
Conflict/Political Economy	Capitalist economy, inequality, class struggle, ideology and illusion, manufacturing consent, social control, production, consumption
Example: How does capitalism influence family patterns of consumption?	

Table 2.2
Three Ways of Knowing Applied to Family Studies

1. Scientific approach to knowing
    View of knowledge: There are objective truths, processes, or realities to be discovered about families.
    Criteria for evaluating family theories: Good theories should be relationally constructed (e.g., internally consistent, simple, coherent) and empirically relevant (testable, fit well with data).
    Goals: Explanation and prediction.
    Scholarly style: Analytic, causal, deductive or inductive, deterministic or probabilistic, factual, logical, materialistic, structural, observant, quantitative.

2. Interpretive approach to knowing
    View of knowledge: Truth is subjective, and all knowledge about families is created by interpreting actors engaged in conversations with one another.
    Values: Family science is values-relevant, and family scientists should become aware of and open about their own values.
    Criteria for evaluating family theories: Good theories should have literary qualities (e.g., elegance, imagination, narrative power). They should be based on data grounded in the experiences of family members.
    Goals: Understanding.
    Scholarly style: Artistic, intuitive, phenomenological, postmodern, processual, self-reflective, speculative, symbolic.

3. Critical approach to knowing
    View of knowledge: Truth is defined by those in power, who impose their definition of the situation on others.
    Values: Family theories are value-laden. Opportunities for change are created only when the values underlying theories are exposed and challenged.
    Criteria for evaluating family theories: Good theories contextualize phenomena and allow for pluralism. They are emancipatory, prescribe changes, display the theorists' ethical stances, and fit well with the theorists' personal experiences.
    Goal: Emancipation or empowerment of oppressive peoples and social groups.
    Scholarly style: Constructivist, dialectical, feminist, liberal or radical, postmodern, pluralistic.

Source: Adapted from D.M. Klein and J.M. White, *Family Theories* (Thousand Oaks: Sage, 1996), p. 48.

both methods simultaneously, but at different levels of aggregation (Greenstein, 2006). For example, a researcher could do a statistical analysis of the factors that increase the

Figure 2.3
The Wheel of Science

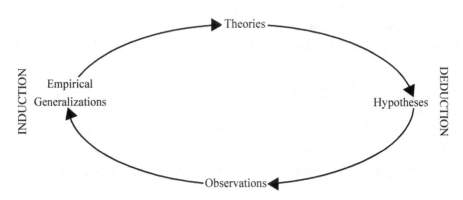

Source: Adapted from Walter Wallace, *The Logic of Science* (New York: Aldine deGruyter, 1971). Copyright © 1971 by Walter L. Wallace.

likelihood of getting divorced, while at the same time conducting in-depth interviews of recently divorced couples.

Furthermore, no discussion of research methods would be complete without mentioning the role of researcher values and biases (also see boxes 2.3 and 2.4) and the topic of research ethics. This is because researchers invariably hold values orientations that are shaped by such factors as their gender, age, ethnic and religious identification, and family history. These values can influence the entire research process, from the choice of theory, the framing of the research question, a preferred style of data collection, and the interpretation and application of findings. For example, if one values the traditional nuclear family as "ideal" for raising children, then one might speculate that deviation from this structure would result in negative outcomes. This is illustrated by the past tendency of functionalist researchers to assume a "deficit" model of the family, whereby single-parent, step-, and same-sex families were automatically expected to produce negative outcomes for children (e.g., low education, poor socio-emotional adjustment). Yet, after decades of research, many problems found in "non-intact" families (as they were commonly conceptualized) are found to be due to a lack of economic or community resources rather than family structure per se.

Therefore, it is crucial for family sociologists to be self-reflective in order to contemplate how their own values influence their work. They also need to consider whether or not they are explicit in their theorizing. Some argue that researchers should strive for transparency so that any implicit theorizing, research design, and reporting of results can be examined in a full and open scholarly debate (Bengtson et al., 2005). In this regard, feminist theorists have been particularly upfront in showing that they are value-committed. That is, they are often lauded for their general tendency to acknowledge that

Figure 2.4
Examples of Qualitative Methods

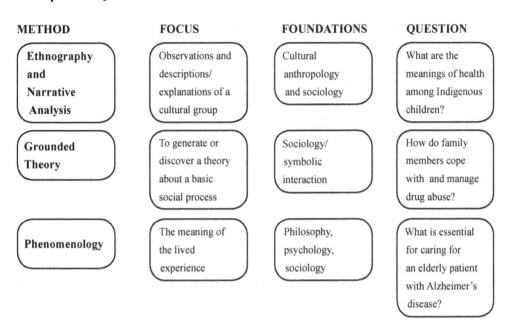

METHOD	FOCUS	FOUNDATIONS	QUESTION
Ethnography and Narrative Analysis	Observations and descriptions/ explanations of a cultural group	Cultural anthropology and sociology	What are the meanings of health among Indigenous children?
Grounded Theory	To generate or discover a theory about a basic social process	Sociology/ symbolic interaction	How do family members cope with and manage drug abuse?
Phenomenology	The meaning of the lived experience	Philosophy, psychology, sociology	What is essential for caring for an elderly patient with Alzheimer's disease?

Source: Adapted and modified from W. Jackson, *Methods: Doing Social Research*, 3rd ed. (Toronto: Prentice-Hall, 2003), p. 143.

they are aware of their values (i.e., gender equality), a reflection of a particular ideological position, and of a belief that research cannot be truly value-free (Chibucos and Leite, with Weiss, 2005). Thus, it is important to critically evaluate the sources and positions (explicit and implicit) of research in order to make meaningful interpretations.

Finally, in order to answer questions about family life, researchers can encounter a number of ethical issues and challenges. How do families feel about being observed? If they know that they are being studied or watched, will they change their behaviour? Would it be morally right to observe their behaviour without telling them? Should participants be forced to answer questions that are highly sensitive in nature and could cause psychological harm? What do we do if we suspect that a family member is being cheated on or abused? Fortunately, these and other concerns over the use of human subjects are now widely discussed and it is now a routine procedure for researchers to have their research approved by ethical review boards by granting councils and universities.

However, attention to ethical issues is a relatively recent development. It was not until the middle of the 20th century that the government and other agencies became involved in the regulation of research using humans (Seccombe and Warner, 2004). In

Box 2.3
Seven Biases in Family Literature

Canadian family sociologist Margrit Eichler identifies seven biases evident in studies of families. These biases can influence every stage of the research process and the process of understanding changes in structures and processes in family life:

1. Monolithic bias— a tendency to treat the family as a monolithic structure by emphasizing uniformity of experience and universality of structure and function over diversity of experiences, structures, and functions.
2. Conservative bias— an over-romanticized view of the nuclear family in the past which overlooks problematic aspects of family life throughout history.
3. Sexist bias— an assumption of a natural division of labour between the sexes.
4. Ageist bias— familial interactions that are considered mainly from the perspective of the middle-aged adults without considering the perspectives of the children or the elderly.
5. Microstructural bias— a tendency to treat families as encapsulated units rather than taking external factors into account.
6. Racist bias— a bias which devalues families of culturally or ethnically non-dominant groups.
7. Heterosexist bias— a bias that assumes that a heterosexual family is the only natural unit.

Source: Eichler, M. 1997. *Family Shifts: Families, Policies and Gender Equality.* Toronto: Oxford University Press.

Canada a tri-council policy statement (involving medical, social science and humanities, and natural science/engineering councils) for the ethical conduct for research involving humans was only established in 1998. The guiding ethical principles of this policy include respect for human dignity, free and informed consent, vulnerable people, privacy and confidentiality, justice and inclusiveness, balancing harm and benefits, minimizing harm, and maximizing benefit.

Prior to the establishment of regulations, there were many studies that generated a great deal of controversy with respect to their violation of these principles. One such example is Laud Humphries's (1975) infamous "Tearoom Trade Study," which took place in the mid-1960s. Humphries, a doctoral student in sociology at Washington University, was interested in learning what motivates men who have anonymous sex in public washrooms. He was interested in their personal characteristics and the nature of their sexual activity. In the first part of his study, he befriended men in public washrooms by acting as a "lookout." He also wrote down the licence plate numbers of these men, and then obtained identifying information via a policeman. In the second part of

Box 2.4
Personal Values and Family Sociology: A Male Perspective

Perhaps in other areas of sociology such a caveat about the role of personal values is less important. But there are few areas in the social sciences so fraught with ideology and subjectivity as family sociology. The personal values of sociologists concerning the family range from open antipathy toward almost everything the family stands for to the option that the traditional family can hardly be improved upon. And the family itself is viewed "objectively" within sociology as an institution that ranges from being highly oppressive, concealing dangerous anti-democratic and anti-egalitarian attitudes, to one that is immensely liberating, inculcating the supreme values of human civilization.

It defies logic and human nature to think that the personal values of social scientists do not in any way shape their sociological views. In my experience, there are few other areas of sociology in which a scholar's personal life history so clearly comes out in his or her work. Historically, most analyses and interpretations of the family have been suffused with the special interests and biases of men. This is true, for example, in much of the writing that bemoans the loss of the traditional family. For men, the traditional family seems to have been a largely unconditional benefit (especially in conjunction with the double standard of sexual behaviour), and it would seem that many men are not willing to give it up without a fight. In recent years more family analysts have been female; they too have often written from the point of view of their own gender. To many women the traditional family appears not so much a benefit as a cost, and it is not surprising that "the decline of the traditional family" has come to be viewed in a less negative, and indeed sometimes a totally positive light.

What is often omitted from both of these gender-driven positions, however, is a consideration of the family from the perspective of the interests of children. As family scholars are no longer children, this is understandable, but it is nonetheless regrettable, for children could be said to be, after all, the main reason for the institution of the family in the first place. When I analyze the family, I am realistic to know that I can never completely overcome my bias as a male. Yet to me the family is primarily a social instrument for child rearing, and I value "strong families" for that reason. I hold to the old idea of parents living together and sharing responsibility for their children and to each other.

Source: Excerpt from preface, Popenoe, D. 1988. *Disturbing the Nest: Family Change and Decline in Modern Societies.* New York: Aldine de Gruyter (pp. vi–viii).

the study, he used this information to contact and interview these men in their homes. However, he disguised himself and purported to be doing a study on health issues.

Clearly, he used very deceptive methods, although he justified this work by claiming that it was for the benefit of social knowledge. Many at the university did not support his argument, and wanted his Ph.D. to be rescinded.

Summary

In this chapter, an overview of key theoretical perspectives used to study families is outlined. These theories are empirically testable interconnected ideas that explain some phenomenon and increase our understanding of family and social life. In other words, theory is an attempt to move beyond the "what" of our observations to the questions of the "why"and "how" of what we have observed (Bengtson et al., 2005). It is also noted that theories do not develop in a vacuum but within a particular social, historical, and political context. There are also many practical impacts from ongoing theoretical explanation. For example, if our empirical results consistently provide support for our theory, then there are many implications for prevention, intervention, or treatment of persistent family problems. Thus, theory should not be viewed as "dry" or "boring." Rather, it should be seen as an exciting opportunity to improve our understanding of a particular aspect of family life by developing conceptual and empirical linkages about what people actually do (and need) in their everyday life (Chibucos and Leite, with Weiss, 2005).

   The relationship between theory and research is noted by identifying three ways of knowing and two general orientations to conducting research—deductive and inductive—as well as quantitative and qualitative research methodologies. These methodologies are equally scientific and complementary, and it is important for sociologists to choose a research approach that can best describe the human reality they wish to study (Ambert, 2006). Finally, a discussion on methods is incomplete without acknowledgement of the *ethics of research*. In short, ethical issues require ongoing sensitive reflection so that we become good researchers, as well as critical consumers, of family research.

Questions for Critical Reflection and Debate

1. Critically reflect on how your own definition of "family" could affect the way that you theorize and research family life.
2. Debate the following: Theory and research should remain value-free.
3. Consider how social context (i.e., one's historical and political location) shapes theory creation and development. Also consider how a theorist's gender, family, and ethnic background might influence the process of theorizing about some aspect of family life.
4. Collect some articles from newspapers or magazines that deal with some aspects of families. To what extent are "the facts" presented? What seems to be missing from these stories that would have allowed you to more accurately assess their accuracy?
5. Imagine that you are a family researcher hired to study a sensitive area of family life

(e.g., child abuse, sexual relations). What kinds of strategies might you use to study what goes on behind closed doors? What ethical issues might arise?

6. Critically evaluate the advantages and disadvantages of using the Internet to research family life.

Glossary

Deductive approach involves the process whereby the researcher begins with a theory, develops hypotheses, and then collects data in order to test the hypotheses.

Ethics of research extends beyond regulations (i.e., informed consent) to include underlying ethical assumptions and implications related to the entire research process, from initial topic selection to application of findings.

Inductive approach entails beginning with data collection or observations, finding patterns, and developing theoretical understandings based on these patterns.

Manufacture of consent refers to how elite groups and dominant institutions (e.g., mass media) shape social behaviour in insidious ways rather than through physical coercion.

Narrative analysis is concerned with the knowledge base and stories that people and groups use to give meaning to their experiences.

Qualitative research focuses on verbal or subjective descriptions of behaviour, and typically includes in-depth interviews, direct observation, document analysis, or case studies.

Quantitative research usually gathers data that can be presented in the form of numbers (e.g., surveys) and is analyzed using statistical techniques.

Theories are perspectives that explain why and how processes and events occur and contain concepts and empirically testable interconnected ideas.

Further Reading

Anandalakshmy, S., N. Chaudhary, and N. Sharma. 2008. *Researching Families and Children: Culturally Appropriate Methods*. Thousand Oaks, Calif.: Sage Publications. A collection of essays that highlight indigenous issues that arise while conducting research in the Indian context. Emphasizes the importance of the perspective of the participant respondent in research, a theme that can be applied to other cultural groups.

Greenstein, T.N. 2006. *Methods of Family Research*. Thousand Oaks: Sage. Teaches students basic concepts, quantitative, qualitative, and mixed methods using real-life examples, as well as how to critically "consume" research.

Lloyd, S., A. Few, and K. Allen (Eds.). 2009. *Handbook of Feminist Family Studies*. Thousand Oaks, Calif.: Sage Publications. Outlines feminist theory, methods, and praxis for the field of family studies and includes a variety of perspectives including: racial-ethnic feminisms; postmodern, constructionist, and bio-social views; as well as frameworks for theorizing motherhood.

Seymour, J., and E. Dermot (Eds.). 2011. *Displaying Families: A New Concept for the Sociology of Family Life*. Basingstoke: Palgrave Macmillan. This edited collection of studies uses the concept of "displaying families" as a novel way to understand contemporary family and intimate ties. It addresses how, in a world of fluid relationships, family life must not only be "done" but how it can also be "seen to be done."

Smith, S.R., R. Hamon, B. Ingoldsby, and J. Miller. (Eds.). 2009. *Exploring Family Theories*, 2nd ed. Toronto: Oxford University Press. A combined text/reader that integrates theory with research and applications. Presenting a diverse variety of perspectives, it offers students a unique and highly readable introduction to family theories.

White, J.M., and D.M. Klein. 2008. *Family Theories*, 3rd ed. Thousand Oaks: Sage. This book provides an overview of six popular theoretical perspectives used in family studies research—exchange, symbolic interactionism, family development, systems theory, the ecological perspective, and postmodernism.

Related Web Sites

Critical Thinking and Evaluation of Sources is a scholarly article that can be downloaded at www.ccc.commnet.edu/library/workbook/critical.htm.

Social Science Space is on online social network forum which brings together various social scientists, writers, and bloggers to discuss current issues in social science fields, http://www.socialsciencespace.com/. Facebook: Socialsciencespace, Twitter: socscispace

Theory.org focuses on social theory and popular culture and provides commentary on various theorists and articles on topics such as the media, sexuality, identity, and gender roles, www.theory.org.uk. Facebook: Theory.org.uk and Friends, Twitter: davidgauntlett

The Panel on Research Ethics is an advisory panel consisting of Canada's three federal research agencies, CIHR, NSERC and SSHRC. This web site focuses on issues relating to the second edition of the *Tri-Council Policy Statement: Ethical Conduct for Research Involving Humans,* www.pre.ethics.gc.ca/eng/index.

References

Ambert, A.M. 2006. *Changing Families: Relationships in Context*. Toronto: Pearson Education.

Barkley, J. 2003. "The Politics of Parenting and the Youth Crisis." In L. Samuelson and W. Antony (eds.), *Power and Resistance: Critical Thinking about Canadian Social Issues*, 3rd ed. (pp. 275–292). Nova Scotia: Fernwood Publishing.

Bengtson, V.L., A.C. Acock, K.R. Allen, P. Dilworth-Anderson, and D.M. Klein. 2005. "Theory and Theorizing in Family Research: Puzzle Building and Puzzle Solving." In V.L. Bengtson et al. (eds.), *Sourcebook of Family Theory and Research* (pp. 3–29). Thousand Oaks: Sage.

Bengtson, V.L., and K.R. Allen. 1993. "The Life Course Perspective Applied to Families over Time." In W. Boss, R. Doherty, W. LaRossa, W. Schumm, and S. Steinmetz (eds.), *Sourcebook of Family Theories and Methods: A Contextual Approach* (pp. 469–499). New York: Plenum Press.

Berger, P.I. 1973. *Invitation to Sociology: A Humanistic Perspective*. Woodstock: Overlook.

Blumer, H.G. 1969. *Symbolic Interactionism: Perspectives and Method*. Englewood Cliffs: Prentice-Hall.

Bulcroft, R., L. Smeins, and K. Bulcroft. 2005. "Cultural Narratives and Individual Experiences in Relationships." In V.L. Bengtson et al., (eds.), *Sourcebook of Family Theory and Research* (pp. 278–280). Thousand Oaks: Sage.

Carrigan, T., B. Connell, and J. Lee. 2002. "Toward a New Sociology of Masculinity." In R. Adams and D. Savran (eds.), *The Masculinity Studies Reader* (pp. 99–118). Oxford: Blackwell Publishers.

Chappell, N., E. Gee, L. McDonald, and M. Stones. 2003. *Aging in Contemporary Canada*. Toronto: Prentice-Hall.

Chatters, L.M., and R.J. Taylor. 2005. "Religion and Families." In V.L. Bengtson et al. (eds.), *Sourcebook of Family Theory and Research* (pp. 517–530). Thousand Oaks: Sage.

Cheal, D. 2005. "Theorizing Family: From the Particular to the General."In V.L. Bengtson et al. (eds.), *Sourcebook of Family Theory and Research* (pp. 29–31). Thousand Oaks: Sage.

Chibucos, T.R., and R.W. Leite, with D.L. Weiss. 2005. *Readings in Family Theory*. Thousand Oaks: Sage.

Cooley, C.H. 1909. *Social Organization*. New York: Scribner's.

Côté, J.E., and A.L. Allahar. 1994. *Generation on Hold: Coming of Age in the Late Twentieth Century*. Toronto: Stoddart.

Duvall, E. 1957. *Family Development*. Philadelphia: Lippincott.

Elder, G.H., Jr. 2000. "The Life Course." In E.F. Borgatta and R.J.V. Montgomery (eds.), *The Encyclopedia of Sociology*, vol. 3 (pp. 1614–1622). New York: Wiley.

Eshleman, J.R., and S.J. Wilson. 2001. *The Family*, 3rd Canadian ed. Toronto: Pearson.

Giele, J.Z., and G.H. Elder, Jr. 1998. *Methods of Life Course Research: Qualitative and Quantitative Approaches*. Thousand Oaks: Sage Publications.

Gouldner, A.W. 1960. "The Norm of Reciprocity: A Preliminary Statement." *American Sociological Review* 25: 161–178.

Greenstein, T.N. 2006. *Methods of Family Research*, 2nd ed. Thousand Oaks: Sage.

Hill, R., and D.A. Hansen. 1960. "The Identification of Conceptual Frameworks Utilized in Family Study." *Marriage and Family Living* 22: 299–311.

Humphries, L. 1975. *Tearoom Trade: Impersonal Sex in Public Places*. New York: Aldine de Gruyter.

Jackson, W. 2003. *Methods: Doing Social Research*, 3rd ed. Toronto: Prentice-Hall.

Klein, D.M., and J.M. White. 1996. *Family Theories*. Thousand Oaks: Sage.

Lasch, C. 1977. *Haven in a Heartless World: The Family Besieged*. New York: Norton.

Luxton, M. 2005. "Conceptualizing 'Families': Theoretical Frameworks and Family Research." In M. Baker (ed.), *Families: Changing Trends in Canada*, 5th ed. (pp. 29–51). Toronto: McGraw-Hill Ryerson.

Mead, G.H. 1934. *Mind, Self, and Society*. Chicago: University of Chicago Press.

Mills, C.W. 1959. *The Sociological Imagination*. New York: Oxford University Press.

O'Rand, A.M. 1996. "Precious and the Precocious: Understanding Cumulative Disadvantage and Cumulative Advantage over the Life Course." *The Gerontologist* 36: 230–238.

Osmond, M.W., and B. Thorne. 1993. "Feminist Theories: The Social Construction of Gender in Families and Society." In P.G. Boss, W.J. Doherty, R. LaRossa, W.R. Schumm, and S.K. Steinmetz (eds.), *Sourcebook of Family Theories and Methods: A Contextual Approach* (pp. 591–623). New York: Plenum.

Parsons, T., and R.F. Bales. 1955. *Family, Socialization, and the Interaction Process*. Glencoe: Free Press.

Porter, E. 1987. "Conceptual Frameworks for Studying Families." In K. Anderson et al. (eds.), *Family Matters: Sociology and Contemporary Canadian Families* (pp. 41–61). Toronto: Methuen.

Seccombe, K., and R.L. Warner. 2004. *Marriages and Families: Relationships in Social Context*. Toronto: Thomson Wadsworth.

Sydie, R. 1987. *Natural Women, Cultured Men: A Feminist Perspective*. Toronto: Methuen.

Thomas, W.I., and D.S. Thomas. 1928. *The Child in America: Behavior Problems and Programs*. New York: Knopf.

Walsh, A., and R.A. Gordon. 1995. *Biosociology: An Emerging Paradigm*. Westport: Praeger.

Ward, M. 2002. *The Family Dynamic: A Canadian Perspective*, 3rd ed. Toronto: Nelson Thomson.

White, J.M., and D.M. Klein. 2002. *Family Theories*, 2nd ed. Thousand Oaks: Sage.

Whitehead, S.M., and F.J. Barrett (Eds.). 2001. *The Masculinities Reader*. Cambridge: Polity Press.

Chapter 3

Canadian Families in Anthropological, Cross-cultural, and Global Perspective

Learning Objectives

In this chapter you will learn ...
- that in order to understand contemporary Canadian family life, we need to look backwards in time (or historically), as well as outwards into other societies
- that cross-cultural studies do not support the idea of the "universal family," despite some commonalities
- how everyday family life, family structure, and gender roles are profoundly shaped by cultural, economic, religious, and political systems in all societies
- how worldwide globalization processes, such as the growth of mass commercialization, information technologies, rising power differentials, and population processes, influence families
- that a global perspective prompts an understanding of how families from around the world are connected, despite differing family lifestyles

Introduction

Since the beginning of humankind, families have always existed in some form or another. However, this form, in terms of what it looks like, what it does, and how it operates depends on many complex factors. In other words, families do not operate in a vacuum, and it is imperative that we try to understand families within the context of their environments. Moreover, families are not just passive recipients of social structure, or the social, economic, and political forces around them (Leeder, 2004). In a dynamic or reciprocal dance, the family acts and reacts to these social arrangements, and adapts in an ongoing manner that makes it highly flexible and changeable. Consider, for instance, how Canadian pioneer families negotiated their lives in the context of their harsh environment compared to contemporary farm families living in Canada, with access to electricity, running water, and the latest in farm machinery. And how might rural Canadian life be different from rural life in an underdeveloped region in the world, such as Africa? Chances are that family life in an underdeveloped area would be at least as challenging as for our pioneer families, although it is highly probable that the arms of "modernity" and global capitalism have reached into these populations, as illustrated in figures 3.1 and 3.2.

In order for us to truly comprehend Canadian families, it is necessary to look backwards in time (or historically) as well as outwards—by examining family forms and structures in our past, as well as in societies outside of our own. In the first chapter, one conclusion was that there is much mythology surrounding previous family life, such as the belief that we have somehow lost the "traditional" family, and the related assumption about life in the "good old days." In this chapter, we further develop this theme

Figure 3.1
Coca-Cola Is One of the Largest
Corporations in the United States and
Sells Its Products in More Than 200
Countries, Such as Zimbabwe

Figure 3.2
A South African Mother
Buying Coca-Cola for Her
Family

Source: USAID from the American People, www.usaid.
gov/privacy.html

Source: ig.biz/beverages, www.sigcorpor
oplast.com/customermagazine/content/
view

by considering additional material focused on family lives in the context of place and time, major tenets underlying our guiding life course theoretical framework. This will be facilitated by integrating some cross-cultural work conducted in the field of anthropology, a perspective that is complementary to sociology. Both specialize in the study of human behaviour, although anthropologists (particularly cultural anthropologists) have a particularly strong interest in families in other cultural contexts. Finally, we will also consider how processes of globalization, capitalization, economic, and population change are affecting families worldwide.

A Short Anthropological History of Canadian Families

Hunting and Gathering Families

It is estimated that 99 percent of human history involved hunting and gathering as the principal means of subsistence. For thousands of years, Canadian hunters and gatherers moved with the seasons following available food supplies (Mandell and Momirov, 2005). Groups comprised of between one and five families hunted and trapped wild game such as caribou, moose, beaver, and bear and also fished, hunted small animals, and gathered wild berries and vegetation (Leacock, 1991). These families travelled light, lived frugally, and seldom recorded any aspects of their lives. Their life expectancy was very short, and they developed shared economies and leadership based on residence, gender, age, and ability (Druke, 1986).

These families exhibited diverse but distinct structures and organizations. For Aboriginal families (the first inhabitants), the family was the basic unit of the community, and their socio-economic and political systems were based on kinship networks, which were large and extensive. Many families were matrilineal, whereby mothers, daughters, and sisters worked together. Hierarchies existed, but Native men considered the work of women to be as important as and equal to that of males. Women and children did most of the harvesting and gathering of fruits, vegetables, and firewood, while men's hunting and fishing often took them far away from home for long periods of time (Mandell and Momirov, 2005). Moreover, both genders had freedom to perform non-traditional work if they displayed a particular talent (Anderson, 2000).

These cultures persisted in Canada well into the 1800s, and were described by colonizing Europeans as among the most highly developed in the world. In the mid-1800s, when the first major wave of White immigrants settled into the Canadian West, they discovered about 30 bands in Quebec and Labrador, and a Native population of 150,000 peoples harvesting herds of millions of buffalo in the West. Europeans brought the use of plows, irrigation, animal culture, and horsepower. Thus, agriculture is a relatively recent phase in Canadian history, and this allowed for greater productivity, greater population density, and political centralization (Mandell and Momirov, 2005; Nett, 1988).

The European Conquest

In the late 1500s and early 1600s Jacques Cartier arrived from France, which marked the beginning of settlements in Canada. Over time, French settlers (also known as Acadians) were joined by settlers from the British Isles and Germany. This led to the establishment of trading posts and trade with First Nations families. Over time, Aboriginal peoples became dependent on the Europeans who introduced alcohol to them, as well as other goods such as guns, knives, and axes. Unfortunately, Europeans also brought disease, destruction, and defeat, which dramatically reduced the Aboriginal population. Also, diets and lifestyles were dramatically affected, and their life expectancy dropped. Moreover, most Aboriginal peoples never accepted some European ideals of unequal spousal relationships, premarital chastity, marital fidelity, male courtship, and male dominance (Mandell and Momirov, 2005). Once the Canadian Confederacy (1867) was established, the Canadian state implemented a policy of "civilizing Indians," an ideology fraught with racist assumptions and marriage regulations, which will be further explored in the next chapter.

Pre-industrial Economies and the Shift to Industrialization

The pre-industrial economy, which predominated in various parts of Canada up until the 19th century, was organized on the basis of a family-based economy. Family members relied heavily on each other to keep the household running, and homes were both places of residence and places of work as settlers produced most of their goods and services in their own homes (Nett, 1988). In 1617, the first French family arrived in Quebec, and harsh conditions meant that many families struggled to eke out a living. In New France, rules governing inheritance and marriage protected women's rights and property. Conversely, in English Canada, common law dictated that men held all power and property in families so that once women married, they lost all legal status and could not control property. Slavery also existed in Canada. Notably, from the late 1600s until the early 1800s, Black slaves were held in Quebec, Nova Scotia, New Brunswick, and Ontario (Mandell and Momirov, 2005).

By the turn of the 18th century, most Canadian families lived in rural settings in Quebec, Ontario, and the Maritimes. With these agricultural settlements, populations stabilized and women's family positions became more traditional. Most of the well-paying jobs were not available to women or girls, who often lacked specialized training and education (Bradbury, 2005). Apprenticeships were also common among children at an early age to learn trades and skills. For instance, working-class boys of age nine or 10 apprenticed in jobs as carpenters, blacksmiths, accountants, lawyers, or doctors, whereas working-class girls often filled domestic contracts around the age of 10, which lasted until they were married (Mandell and Momirov, 2005). And by the end of the 18th century, many families began to move west in search of a better life, although life was often very severe for these pioneering families, as illustrated in the book *Pioneer Girl*.

Pioneer Girl contains a collection of letters, written in 1887 by 14-year-old Maryanne Caswell. These letters, published first in a newspaper in 1952 and then as a book in 1964, are an account of the trials her family faced when they moved from Ontario to the Prairies to find a better life. In one letter to her grandma, she describes some of the harsh realities of her daily life:

> The mosquitoes were terribly vicious as we neared home. Berry became unmanageable, broke from me, upsetting and scattering the pots, pails, laundry and water barrel. So ended our first of July, 1887. During the night the rain came in torrents. The knot-holes of the roof-boards leaked and rivers flowed inside and out. Mother, as she frequently had to do, put pots and pans on the beds to catch the drips. We dared not move the least bit or water is spilt. The quilts take such a long time to dry

thoroughly hanging on poles of the garden fence and this hot, golden sun burns and fades them very much.

Small-scale farming was gradually replaced with large-scale commercial agriculture. Employment opportunities also expanded in shops and factories. Factories increased from 2.4 million in 1851 to 5.4 million in 1901 in cities like Montreal, Quebec, and Hamilton. With the shift to industrialization and urbanization, work and family life increasingly became separate spheres, although different family forms occasionally emerged when women, rather than men, took on paid work or earned high-income-generating jobs (e.g., see Box 3.1 for an example of this in Paris, Ontario, between 1880 and 1950). Femininity became associated with women's domestic and child-rearing work in the home, while masculinity was associated with the world of paid work. Generally, it was considered demeaning for married women to labour for wages since it was thought to compromise the husband's authority as household head and could be potentially damaging for children's moral and cognitive development (Wilson, 1991).

During the 20th century women gradually gained more political rights, but only after many years of speeches, protests, and legal battles. In Britain, the Married Women's Property Act of 1870 was viewed as a significant milestone for women's rights because it allowed them to control their earnings, their bank accounts, and their property. Similar laws were introduced in most Canadian provinces within the next few years. And although marriage was traditionally a religious contract, it gradually became a legal one that could be broken through divorce proceedings. In 1925, the grounds for divorce became identical for women and men (see Table 3.1 for a brief history of key changes governing marriage and divorce in Canada). Yet marital property had to be divided according to certain rules, and one parent was usually granted custody of the children (Baker and Dryden, 1993).

During early industrialization, children under the age of 15 from poor or working-class families often were employed in paid wage labour in order to contribute to the family economy. Often their father had died, was sick, drank, or earned insufficient wages (Bradbury, 1993). Unfortunately, these children were sometimes exposed to dangerous working conditions (see Box 3.2). Over time, the changing role of children involved them less and less in work at home and eventually school attendance was required for all. By the end of World War One, with corporate capitalism or full industrialization, the only individual considered to be working was the husband-father. Between the two world wars (1920–1940), a consumer society was born, and families were exposed to a new advertising industry, which created a new awareness and demand for consumer goods. Therefore, the sole wage–earner family came to be seen more in terms of its economic role as a consumer rather than a producer (Nett, 1988).

At the beginning of World War Two, many women began to work in the paid labour market when men left for military service. When they returned, women left their employment due to the widespread belief that it was harmful to children for their mothers to be in the labour force. However, since the 1970s, more and more families

> **Box 3.1**
> **The Gender of Breadwinners: Women, Men, and Change in Two**
> **Industrial Towns, 1880–1950**
>
> In Paris [Ontario], men took on the characteristics of dispensability and irregularity in employment that dual labour market theorists have commonly associated with the secondary sector and with women. Those who stayed on irregular work, who commuted to jobs elsewhere, or who were among the male minority with secure local employment, were members of households where the family income was collectively amassed, not won by a male breadwinner. Similarly, in these households, domestic labour was derived from several sources rather than delegated to a single homemaker. These circumstances evoked some changes in thinking about women's and men's roles and in the practice of domestic gender divisions, but the influence of patriarchal ideology continued to cast women as the primary custodians of kin. In Paris, mill families coped by generally accepting mainstream prescriptions about what was manly and womanly work within the home. To accommodate lifelong female wage work they rather remade the boundary between the household and the market by purchasing goods and services conventionally created within the home. They also reconstrued the borders of the household itself, clubbing together as female kin, sharing houseroom, trading domestic labour, and determining by their own logic of mutual advantage who ought to go to the mill and who might better stay home.
>
> *Source:* Parr, J. 1990. *The Gender of Breadwinners: Women, Men, and Change in Two Industrial Towns 1880–1950.* Toronto: University of Toronto Press (pp. 235–236).

with only one income earner have found it difficult to meet the new "needs" that the economy created for families. The feminist movement was also instrumental in creating more equal opportunities for women in education and labour. When compared to the 1950s family, the percentage of two-income workers has skyrocketed. In 2003, 80 percent of married women were in the paid labour force, whereas it was only 11 percent in 1951 (Statistics Canada, 2003a).

Moreover, family life has increasingly become culturally diversified as immigration patterns changed, a theme that will be further explored in the next chapter. Notably, the proportion of Aboriginal families has declined substantially over time, such that modern Canada is dominated by British ethnicity, with 49 percent of the population claiming this ancestry (Statistics Canada, 2003b). Conversely, less than 5 percent of the Canadian population claim Aboriginal ancestry, which includes First Nations or Native Indians, the Métis, and the Inuit. There are currently 621 bands in Canada, with about 500 members in each (Frideres, 2000).

Table 3.1

A Brief Chronology of Changes in Laws Governing Marriage and Divorce in Canada

Prior to 1758	No divorce law existed since the Church of England in Upper Canada and the Roman Catholic Church in Lower Canada did not recognize divorce.
1758	New Brunswick allows divorce on the grounds of adultery and desertion.
1787	Nova Scotia allows divorce on the grounds of adultery.
1800–1837	Marriage contract introduced in Western provinces in which a husband agreed to support his family *à la façon du pays* (i.e., according to the custom of the Aboriginal peoples) and to marry as soon as a clergyman was available.
1867	With Confederation, federal Parliament gained exclusive authority in divorce, yet it did allow existing provincial laws in Nova Scotia, New Brunswick, and British Columbia to stand.
1925	Women could now sue for divorce on the same grounds as men (previously, men had to prove adultery, whereas women had to prove adultery and either desertion for two or more years or extreme physical or mental cruelty—now they both had to prove only adultery).
1968	All provinces except Quebec and Newfoundland had divorce laws with adultery basically the sole grounds for divorce.
1985	Law amended to show "no fault" of either partner; waiting period for divorce on grounds of marriage breakdown reduced to one year.

Source: M. Ward, *The Family Dynamic: A Canadian Perspective*, 3rd ed. (Toronto: Nelson Thomson Learning, 2002), pp. 227–228.

Canadian Families in Cross-cultural Context: The Myth of the Universal Family

The preceding discussion highlights the fact that Canadian families have taken on many forms and cannot be characterized by one monolithic structure. Similarly, there is no single type of marriage or family pattern that is found exclusively throughout the world. As will be shown in this section, there is widespread diversity in what is socially accepted, tolerated, or even expected. With this in mind, variations in family structure throughout the world will be highlighted, with a focus on marriage structures, patterns of authority, rules of descent, and patterns of residence.

Box 3.2
Working Families: Age, Gender, and Daily Survival in Industrializing Montreal

Most young children's jobs involved long and tedious hours, either repeating monotonous tasks or, as in the case of message boys, continually coming and going or sitting around waiting for errands to run. Hours were the same for children and adults—ten hours or more, six days a week. Lucks and Blackeby were shocked to see young children whose appearance and condition by the afternoon of a hot summer's day was "anything but inviting or desirable"...They had to be at the mills or factories at 6:30 a.m. necessitating their being up from 5:30 to 6 o'clock for their morning meal, some having to walk a distance of half a mile or more to their work. The tobacco of the cigar manufactories and the lead in printing shops exposed them to substances that were health hazards. The commissioners hearing evidence in 1888 were pained to see that working with tobacco had already stunted children's growth and "poisoned" the blood of some of the young witnesses. They appeared "undersized, sallow and listless."

The relationship of these young workers, their parents, and the employer was complex. Parents appear to have endowed the employer with the patriarchal and disciplinary powers usually attributed to a father. Indeed, some employers claimed such powers for themselves. M. Fortier justified beatings in his factory by arguing that children had not been beaten "other than what they have deserved for wrongs they have committed, the same as a parent would punish a child." He and his manager claimed that parents asked them to discipline their children, especially in situations where parental control failed. One boy's mother told him to "use any means in my power to chastise the body as she could not get any good at all out of him." When "apprentices" in his factory failed to turn up on time, he first notified the parents, then "had the child arrested." Employers were apparently using the [Quebec Manufacturing] Act with respect to masters and apprentices against any workers who absented without permission.

Source: Bradbury, B. 1993. *Working Families: Age, Gender, and Daily Survival in Industrializing Montreal.* Toronto: University of Toronto Press (p. 130).

Marriage Patterns

There are four types of marriage: monogamy, polyandry, polygyny, and group marriage. In Western cultures and countries such as China, monogamy is the preferred form of marriage, in which there are only two spouses. In the 21st century, bigamy and sexual relations outside marriage are generally socially or legally frowned upon. However, since divorce and remarriage have become increasingly common, the practice of serial monogamy—or having more than one sexual partner in sequence—has become more prevalent.

Polygamy or plural marriage is the practice of having more than one husband or wife. There are three forms of polygamy: polygyny, polyandry, and group marriage. Many societies permit polygyny, in which a man can have multiple wives, and it is generally a sign of wealth and power. This practice is found in many cultures, such as in the Middle East, Asia, and Africa, and in some fundamentalist Mormon groups in the United States (e.g., in rural areas among Utah's borders with Arizona and Colorado) and Canada (e.g., Bountiful, British Columbia), and is commonly sanctioned by religion. Polyandry is the practice of having two or more husbands. It is very uncommon although considered to be the ideal marriage form in societies such as the Toda of India, the Marquesians of the Polynesian Islands, and among some Tibetans. Group marriage is relatively rare and involves the marriage of two or more men to two or more women.

In the West, the choice of a marriage partner is largely voluntary and depends upon the attachment between the partners. In most Western, industrialized societies, the most common reason for marrying is for love, based upon a mutual emotional and/or physical attraction and the desire to form a lifelong commitment. In other parts of the world, such as many parts of Africa, Asia, and the Middle East, as well as within some cultural groups in Western societies, the choice of mates is deemed too important to be left to the individual and is often arranged, a topic that will be revisited later in the text.

Practices and behaviours with respect to the timing of marriage also vary widely throughout the world, particularly between less developed and more economically developed countries. Some of this variability is shown in Table 3.2, which presents the rank-ordered top 20 countries in the world that have the highest percentage of girls married by age 18. This type of marriage is referred to as child marriage, and if present trends continue, 100 million girls are estimated to marry over the next decade, according to the International Centre for Research on Women (2010). This group argues that traditional practices of child marriage are harmful since they undermine global development efforts focused on creating more educated, healthier, and economically stable populations. Girls living in poor households are more than twice as likely to marry before 18 as girls in higher-income households. Those younger than 15 are also five times more likely to die in childbirth than women in their 20s. Child brides also face a higher risk of contracting HIV because they tend to marry much older men who have had more sexual partners. These girls are also more likely to experience domestic violence and signs of sexual abuse and post-traumatic stress such as feelings of hopelessness and severe depression.

Patterns of Authority and Descent

Cross-cultural research establishes that women and men are often treated very differently in many parts of the world. The term "patriarchy," which translates to "rule of the father," refers to a form of social organization in which the norm or the expectation is that men have a natural right to have authority over women. This pattern of authority is manifested and upheld in a wide variety of social institutions, including educational, religious, legal, and economic institutions. For example, the educational system may enforce unequal or

Table 3.2
Child Marriage Around the World

Rank	Country	% Girls Married Before 18
1	Niger	74.5
2	Chad	71.5
3	Mali	70.6
4	Bangladesh	66.2
5	Guinea	63.1
6	Central African Republic	57.0
7	Mozambique	55.9
8	Burkina Faso	51.9
9	Nepal	51.4
10	Ethiopia	49.2
11	Malawi	48.9
12	Madagascar	48.2
13	Sierra Leone	47.9
14	Cameroon	47.2
15	Eritrea	47.0
16	Uganda	46.3
17	India	44.5
18	Nicaragua	43.3
19	Zambia	41.6
20	Tanzania	41.1

Source: International Centre for Research on Women (2010). Analysis of Demographic and Health Survey. Rankings are based on data in which women ages 20–24 reported being married by age 18, retrieved from www.icrw.org/child-marriage-facts-and-figures.

no formal education for girls, and religious institutions may attribute male dominance to "God's will." Conversely, a less dominant form of authority is matriarchy, in which the norm is that the power and authority in society should be vested in women. In between these two extremes are egalitarian patterns, in which power and authority are equally present in both men and women. Countries such as Canada, the United States, and some Scandinavian countries are close to, or headed in this direction, although many vestiges of patriarchy remain (Seccombe and Warner, 2004).

Turning to patterns of descent, contemplate where your last name came from and how property is passed down in your family. There are many ways in which a family's descent or heritage can be traced. Industrial nations usually use a bilateral pattern of descent, whereby descent can be traced through both female and male sides of the family. In Canada, for instance, both of our parents' parents are seen as related to us, as two sets of grandparents. Yet, in many parts of the world we see a patrilineal pattern, in which lineage is usually traced through the man's family line. As a result, minimal connections would be established with your mother's side of the family. We also see traces of this practice in Canada, as reflected in the tendency for our last names to reflect the father's lineage. Moreover, a few societies can be characterized as having matrilineal descent patterns. However, it is not the mirror opposite of the patrilineal pattern, since women often pass on their lineage through male members of the family. In other words, lineage is not the same as power (Seccombe and Warner, 2004).

Patterns of Residence

Another aspect of diversity of family patterns found worldwide is the residential patterns of family members. In industrial societies, the norm is for newly married couples to live separately from either set of parents, known as neolocal residence, which means "new place" in Greek. However, in many parts of the world, patrilocal residence is practised, with the expectation that the son and his wife will live with the husband's father. Matrilocal patterns, which are less common, dictate that the newly married daughter and her husband live with the wife's family.

Extended or joint family living, rather than the nuclear family, is normative throughout many parts of the world. And, with increasing immigration and cultural diversity in Canada, a rising number of families live in multigenerational households, defined as three or more generations living under one roof. This practice remains common in families from countries with a history of extended family living (i.e., India) and is still practised for cultural, economic, or practical reasons. Finally, there has also been a tendency for young adults (sometimes with partners and/or children) to stay at home longer, or return to the parental home after an initial "launch," in many industrialized countries, a topic explored later in Chapter 10. This living arrangement occurs for economic, cultural, or health-related reasons and has become more socially acceptable due to changing times. These family-centred trends run counter to the overall rise in the number of one-person households, especially among young unmarried and widowed females in addition to female-headed households.

Overall, these findings reveal that family forms and structures are highly diverse worldwide. Patterns of marriage, authority, descent, and living arrangements also have very real consequences for the way that we live our family lives. They also reflect whom we should marry, who should have power in the family, the status of family members, and the distribution of resources in families. In addition, they mirror divergent expectations with respect to where and with whom we live.

Myths and Half-Truths: Families Worldwide Are Also Similar

Although families around the world have looked and continue to look different based on these diverse patterns, or based on dress, food, or rituals, basically they share much in common. One of the unifying themes among all families is that they are a source of procreation.

In other words, it is within families that children are born and reared, a universal function on which sociologists and anthropologists can agree. However, procreation is more than birthing, and there are dissimilarities when it comes to the context of how births occur and the life chances of those babies and mothers. For example, birthing huts in rural Africa differ from birthing rooms in modern hospitals, and the probability that the mother or baby survive depends on economic conditions of the society and where the family fits into the social stratification system.

Another condition unifying families is that they are primary agents of socialization, a topic to be discussed in greater detail in Chapter 7. Moreover, as discussed in Chapter 1, families also tend to regulate and legitimate sexual behaviour, and families are also responsible for the care (emotional and economic) provision of their members. And finally, another consistent theme that emerges is that families provide status to their members. Indeed, the family is the place in society where race/ethnicity, class, and gender converge since it is the locus of intersection of these forces (Leeder, 2004).

Worldwide Trends: Globalization, Capitalization, Information Technologies, and Families

In light of important historical and cross-cultural patterns in family life, let us consider Canadian families within the context of globalization, as well as several salient issues facing families. Globalization refers to the world scale of economic and other market activity facilitated by the expansion of telecommunication technology and the growth of multinational corporations operating throughout the world. Hence, our postindustrial economy is characterized by information technology, paper speculation (the stock market), and the predominance of the service sector. Consequently, national economies are vulnerable to worldwide financial fluctuations more than ever before. This was quite evident in the recent 2008–2009 recession largely generated by a lack of controls over the paper economy and risky borrowing that originated in the U.S. (Ambert, 2012).

Globalization is also a vast social field, in which dominant or hegemonic social groups, states, interests, and ideologies, collide with counter-hegemonic or subordinate social groups. In the past three decades, transnational interactions have intensified significantly, from production systems and financial transfers to the worldwide dissemination of information and images through the media, or the mass movements of peoples, whether as tourists or migrant workers or refugees (de Sousa Santos, 2006).

Overall, the processes of globalization are multifaceted, with economic, social, political, cultural, religious, and legal dimensions. Globalization also seems to be related to a vast array of transformations across the globe, such as the rise in feminine employment, delayed family transitions, and rising inequality between rich and poor countries as well as between the rich and poor in each country. Moreover, globalization is often linked to environmental disasters, ethnic conflicts, international mass migration, the proliferation of civil wars, globally organized crime, formal democracy as a political condition for international aid, terrorism, and so on (de Sousa Santos, 2006).

Figure 3.3
A Cartoonist's Depiction of Globalization

BILL PROUD

"Globalization never did me any harm."

Source: CartoonStock.com

And while there are many debates with respect to the origin, nature, and meaning of globalization, it appears that the idea of globalization as a linear, homogenizing, and irreversible phenomenon oversimplifies certain patterns and processes (de Sousa Santos, 2006). Nonetheless, processes of globalization are deemed to affect families worldwide. This is because they impel structural and processual changes in families, from their economic opportunities and activities, to the increased need for schooling and education, and changing gender roles. For example, a general rise in education and increased consumerism means that children lose their utilitarian value to families, especially in industrialized countries, a value that had been very obvious in former centuries.

Women also begin to gain more social and political power as their roles become less tied to motherhood. As a result, families begin to shrivel in size, extended families become the exception, more women work outside the home, and young people defer marriage and parenthood. And in many parts of the world, these processes also present challenges to families in holding on to their long established cultural traditions and practices (Roopnarine and Gielen, 2005). Exposure to the media, for example, via satellite television and the Internet, exposes families to alternative lifestyles and Western values that often emphasize consumerism and individualism.

Pressing Issues for the World's Families
In addition to meeting the challenges of changing family structures and gender roles, families around the world are also experiencing pressures in their ability to raise their children, care for their elderly, and maintain healthy, close relationships. Issues that are particularly salient at this time include war, terrorism, and armed conflict; poverty and economic instability; migration; and world population growth (Leeder, 2004). With respect to the first pressing concern, as you read this book, all kinds of war, conflict, and terrorist acts are being experienced in many parts of the world. Indeed, the history of humankind is also one of conflict and war, and this horrible reality has dire consequences for societies and families. Although there are innumerable examples, this is illustrated in the Pol Pot regime (see Box 3.3). These events also influence Canadian society; for instance, as refugees flee countries, our young people join the military to fight wars, or individuals experience the psychological trauma of terrorist threats.

Another pressing challenge facing families worldwide is poverty and economic hardship, a state that negatively experiences every aspect of family daily life and functioning. In Canada, these issues remain a significant social problem (and will be further explored in Chapter 13), particularly when we compare poverty rates to other industrialized societies such as the Scandinavian countries, which tend to have strong social safety nets.

The World Bank has estimated that that there are an estimated 1.4 million poor people who live on $1.25 a day or less. And while the International Labour Organization revealed stability and improvement in poverty reduction in most countries from the late 1990s through the late 2000s, spikes in unemployment and vulnerable employment occurred following the 2008 global financial crisis. This crisis was precipitated by the bursting of the housing price bubble and banking collapse in the United States. It rapidly spread to most of the world and is considered the worst financial crisis since the Great Depression, at least in developed countries. Notably, 34 million people lost their jobs and 64 million more people fell under the $1.25 a day poverty threshold. Millions of workers have also been coping with job losses, prolonged unemployment, reduced working hours, lost or reduced income, and aggravated poverty. To date, the labour markets in many developing countries still remain in crisis, although there are some signs of slow recovery (Otobe, 2011).

Box 3.3
Genocide and Family Life: The Pol Pot Regime and the Killing Fields

In 1975 the government of Cambodia came under the control of the Khmer Rouge, an authoritarian rule led by Pol Pot. His attempt to rid Cambodia of all Western influences resulted in genocide. Under Pol Pot and the Khmer Rouge, an estimated two million people were killed. In what has been called "the killing fields," whole families were slaughtered, tortured, disemboweled, and maimed. Children were separated from their families and placed in camps, forced to inform on their own parents. The horror that occurred has led to a form of hysterical blindness among many mothers and women, who were forced to watch the brutalities acted on their families. In 1978, the Vietnamese Army invaded Cambodia, and millions of refugees fled the country seeking safety as they ran across Thailand through mine fields. This caused further maiming and death. Finally, when those who survived reached safety, they lingered in refugee camps...[these refugees arrived in the United States and Canada] with trauma deep in their psyches. The experience has had severe consequences in terms of family lives, and many of them arrived poor and in need of extensive assistance. But Cambodians are a very proud people, seeking harmony and maintaining politeness. Family life, although disrupted, is still most important for the maintenance of culture and their very survival.

Source: Leeder, E.J. 2004. *The Family in Global Perspective: A Gendered Journey.* Thousand Oaks, Calif.: Sage Publications (pp. 92–93).

Women and men are affected differently by economic recessions and this can depend upon which economic sectors are being affected. For example, since men tend to be concentrated in heavier manufacturing, construction, and mining, the level of job losses would depend on which sectors are most affected in the global economic crisis in a given country. However, given persistent ascribed gender roles that affect patterns of paid and unpaid work (e.g., women earn only about three-quarters of men's wages in the non-agricultural sector of 56 countries, as cited in Smith, 2006), women are particularly vulnerable to long-lasting negative socio-economic effects. Indeed, there is fear that in the wake of the global economic crisis the progress made in the past decades in advancing women's position in the world of work is being wiped out (Otobe, 2011).

Although women who were already in disadvantaged positions in the labour market prior to the crisis have generally suffered less in terms of the number of job losses, the overall reduction of employment and income for poor families has serious implications for the reproduction of gender inequities. When the resources and incomes available to poor households are being diminished, women and children are likely to be the worst affected. For example, children drop out of school because parents cannot afford to have them attend, and this has an intergenerational impact on poverty. There is also a gender bias against females in the household in many poor developing countries, in that they have less access to education, food, and health provisions relative to males (International Labour Office, 2011).

And with rising poverty, another related trend is the growth of substandard housing (e.g., slums, shantytowns), as well as many related health and well-being issues. Economic hardship and crisis increase infant mortality and malnutrition, with severe long-term costs from stunting (the failure to thrive). Damaging effects can also be found in increases in the numbers of street children, in suicide and crime rates, in abuse and domestic violence, and in ethnic tensions (Human Development Report, 2010).

Another example of a global health concern is the HIV/AIDS epidemic, as illustrated in Figure 3.4, with an estimated 33 million people worldwide currently living with HIV, and 1.8 million deaths due to AIDS in 2009 (UNAIDS, 2010). And while deaths due to AIDS have fallen (mainly due to access to life-saving drugs and the anti-retroviral programme), there are still a staggering number of new cases each year (e.g., 2.6 million cases were reported in 2009). The worst affected areas are sub-Saharan Africa, South Asia (particularly India), and China. In South Africa, for instance, AIDS deaths have fallen by nearly 25 percent, however, it is estimated that an alarming 10.9 percent of the population (5.5. million people) were HIV positive in 2010.

The implications for poverty from these staggering numbers are many, ranging from their effect on slowing economies to affecting agricultural productivity and thereby contributing to persistent food shortages (Rank and Yadama, 2006). Family structure and relationships are also affected, for example, when grandparents are left to raise grandchildren who are infected with the disease after parents have died. Fortunately, many grass-roots organizations have formed to assist these families. One noteworthy initiative is the Grandmothers to Grandmothers Campaign (see Box 3.4), which was recently established in Canada to assist African grandmothers.

Figure 3.4
Global HIV/AIDS Estimates for Adults and Children, 2009

People living with HIV........33 million (31.4–35.3 million)
New HIV infections 2009......2.6 million (2.3–2.8 million)
Deaths due to AIDS in 2009....1.8 million (1.6–2.1 million)

Source: UNAID Global Reports (2010 Edition): UNAIDS Report on the Global Aids Epidemic, retrieved from http://www.unaids.org/globalreport/Global_report.htm.

Box 3.4
The Grandmothers to Grandmothers Campaign

"It's quite extraordinary to see the bond that has developed between grand-mothers on both sides of the ocean. In a dramatic way, it helps to redefine the chasm between the developed and developing nations. It goes without saying that the chasm exists in the realms of poverty, conflict and disease, but in the realms of sophistication, intelligence and fundamental human decency, nothing separates the African grandmothers from the Canadian grandmothers. They are as one."—Stephen Lewis.

The Stephen Lewis Foundation launched the Grandmothers to Grandmothers Campaign in March 2006, in response to the emerging crisis faced by African grand-mothers as they struggled to care for millions of children orphaned by AIDS. The Campaign aims to raise awareness, build solidarity, and mobilize support in Canada for Africa's grandmothers.

The campaign has since evolved into a dynamic and responsive national move-ment and currently boasts more than 240 grandmother groups across the country. Many of the groups have organized into regional and national networks in order to support each other's development and fundraising.

Funds from the Grandmothers Campaign go to African grassroots oragnizations working with grandmothers and the children in their care in partnership with the Ste-phen Lewis Foundation. The SLF collaborates with grassroots groups who support grandmothers' immediate needs such as nutritious food, health care, transportation, home visits, adequate housing and bedding, school fees, uniforms, and supplies for orphans, as well as longer-term needs such as parenting and business skills, micro-credit grants, bereavement counselling, HIV awareness training, counselling, and testing, and grandmother support groups.

Canadian grandmother groups are tremendously active in their communities. They put on concerts, organize card tournaments, and sell jewellery. They visit count-less schools and community organizations. They bake, cook, sew, knit, paint, write, organize cycle tours, walks, and even ride motorcycles. All proceeds go to partners of the Stephen Lewis Foundation—grassroots organizations in sub-Saharan Africa that support African grandmothers and the children in their care.

Source: The Stephen Lewis Foundation, About the Campaign, retrieved June 17, 2011 from http://www.stephenlewisfoundation.org/get-involved/grandmothers-campaign/about-the-campaign.

Another issue for families worldwide is migration, since it is one means for women and men to try and escape poverty and build a better life. However, many poor migrant workers become deeply indebted to labour recruiters and are trapped in dangerous or oppressive working conditions. For example, in Asia, many women migrants left their families for a more promising life in the garment industry only to experience low wages and job vulnerability. Other unemployed women and children throughout the world have been driven into the human trafficking industry and work as prostitutes on the streets, in brothels, or in massage parlours. Men are also often forced to migrate. For example, in Lesothos, Africa, many men have left their farms to work in South African mines as well as factories, kitchens, and farms, and an estimated 40 percent of these men are away at any one time (Modo, 2001).

Finally, another salient global issue is world population growth and resource sustainability. Current population statistics show that there are now twice as many people alive on Earth as there were as recently as the 1960s and that the 7 billionth person will be born in 2011 (Bartlett, 2011). Figure 3.5 provides us with an overview of this population explosion between 1750 and 2150, where it is shown that much of the growth has occurred in developing regions in Africa, Asia, and Latin America.

Figure 3.5
World Population Growth, 1750–2150

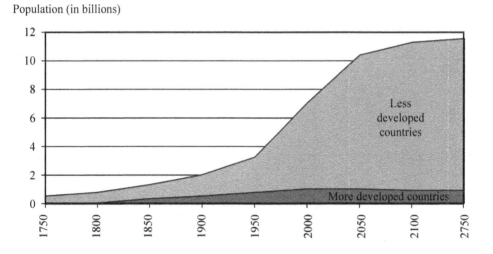

Source: United Nations World Populations, The 1998 Revision (New York: United Nations, 1998); and estimates by the Population Reference Bureau.

Some scientists worry that the human population is growing at a rate that will threaten the planet's future availability and sustainability of essential resources such as land, food, and water. They also warn that this could also create greater social inequality and war as groups vie for scarce resources. Indeed, recent data (see Figure 3.6) show that the number of hungry people recently topped one billion and that world hunger spiked sharply in 2009. This downward trend in global food security has occurred since 1996 and is also attributed to the combination of food and economic crises. For example, the significant increases in food prices in the past several years have been particularly devastating to those with only a few dollars a day to spend.

However, others suggest that population growth is not a problem because this rate is starting to decline and advancements in technology should increase the availability of food supplies and other basic resources. In other words, it is argued that since the world can easily produce enough food to feed everyone, food shortages should not be a problem. Instead, other factors than population growth per se are to blame such as harmful economic and political systems, war and conflicts that displace families, and climate change, since the latter increases drought and flooding and disrupts the conditions necessary for producing food. Further, there is also a reciprocal effect in that hunger causes

Figure 3.6
Combined Food and Economic Crisis Drove the Number of Hungry People above One Billion in 2009

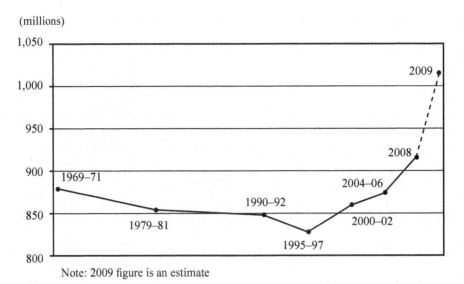

Note: 2009 figure is an estimate

Source: International Monetary Fund, Finance and Development (March 2010). "Hunger on the Rise: Number of Hungry People Tops One Billion," retrieved from www.imf.org/external/pubs/ft/fandd/2010/03.

poor health, low levels of energy, and even mental impairment. In a feedback loop, this leads to even greater poverty since it reduces people's ability to work and learn, thus leading to even greater malnourishment and hunger (World Hunger Organization, 2011).

Despite the complexity of this issue, the fact that our world population is growing has important implications for families. More families will live in cities, as evidenced by the worldwide trend of families migrating from the countryside to cities. For example, about 1.1 billion people in Asia are expected to move to cities in less than 20 years (about 137,000 every day) according to the Asian Development Bank. This rapid urbanization creates a multitude of problems related to housing and space, disease and crime, noxious pollution, overwhelmed infrastructure, and crippling congestion (Bartlett, 2011).

Moreover, we are experiencing an aging of the world's population that is unprecedented in human history. At the beginning of the 21st century, there were 600 million older people, three times the number observed 50 years earlier. With a 2 percent growth rate per year, this means that there will be more older than younger people throughout the world by 2050 (United Nations, 2002).

Underlying global population aging is a process known as the "demographic transition" in which mortality and then fertility decline from higher to lower levels. The role of international migration in changing age structures is far less important than population aging (Lesthaeghe, 2000). Over the last half century, the total fertility rate decreased globally by almost half, from five children to almost three children per woman. It is expected to fall to the replacement level (the number of people needed to keep the population at the same size) of 2.1 children per woman over the next half century. These processes reshape the age structure of the population by shifting relative weight from younger to older groups and have consequences for virtually every aspect of family life. Notably, population aging affects family composition, interaction, and functioning; housing; health care; systems of financial support; as well as overall economic growth and consumer spending.

Moreover, given that there are significant differences in population growth and aging in certain regions of the world, this will influence family life in developing versus developed countries very differently. In the developed regions, it is expected that one-third of the population will be older than 60 years of age by 2050, compared to only 20 percent in the less developed regions. Therefore, families around the world are at different stages in the aging process (Ingoldsby and Smith, 2006), and will face different life cycle demands and challenges.

Finally, it is noteworthy that a counter-movement has emerged in response to many of the world's pressing challenges. Many social activist groups are found on social media web sites and in communities, for instance, that oppose the rise in corporatization, rampant consumerism, wastage, pollution, moral apathy, and the unfair distribution of the world's wealth and natural resources. The Occupy Wall Street movement, which began in New York on September 17, 2011 is a good example of a recent international movement (that was initiated by a Canadian group called Adbusters) to protest growing economic and social inequality.

Some groups (and families) also engage in activities in an attempt to promote eco-sustainability, which is also deemed to be a significant planetary issue. "Freegans," for example, recognize that in a complex, industrial, mass-production economy driven by profit, abuses of humans, animals, and the earth abound at all levels of production and in just about every product we buy. Thus, a "freegan" individual or family might avoid buying certain products and engage in such activities as urban foraging or dumpster diving, which is a rummaging technique employed to turn garbage into useful household goods (Freegan.info, 2011). More "typical" family-related activities (with a less radical philosophy) might include the adoption of eco-behaviours within the home in an attempt to "go green" and decrease reliance on the planet's resources. This might include recycling, using fewer packaged or processed foods, reducing dependence on cars, limiting children's use of energy-consumptive entertainment, using bio-degradable cleaning products, and buying locally grown food.

Overall, these commitments to social justice and environmentalism by a relatively small but growing number of Canadian families have obvious implications for daily life. There is also the potential for effects on the division of household labour, gender equity, and marital relationships. For example, a recent study concluded that women generally perform more eco-friendly domestic labour than did their husbands, suggesting that (ironically) eco-friendly practices can actually reinforce traditional divisions of general household labour in addition to the time spent on household tasks (e.g., see Judkins and Presser, 2008).

Summary

A life course approach to the study of Canadian family life emphasizes the need to travel across temporal, geographic, and cultural boundaries to explore and appreciate the diversity of family life. Indeed, an anthropological and cross-cultural perspective on families shows that families are diverse not only in Canada and throughout the world, but also in family structure, processes, history, and social and environmental contexts (Ingoldsby and Smith, 2006). This existence of multiple family forms forces us to question notions of monogamy, two-parent heterosexual unions, rigid gender roles, and marriage as primordial to family formation. It also prompts us to critically evaluate the idea of one "traditional" family or the existence of a universal family. Moreover, another major theme is that while families are diverse in structure, they can be similar in basic functioning and values. That is, despite differing cultural traditions and opportunities, virtually all families want to feed, raise, and socialize their children in a peaceful, safe environment and make a living. In short, most families worldwide want to provide love and support to their family members to the best of their ability.

A global perspective on families also illuminates the fact that we are all connected through a world economy. In other words, we all use resources that are produced in other parts of the planet, and what occurs in one part of the world impacts the rest. Families are also all influenced by the global hierarchy and the market system under which they operate. This means that there is a pecking order with rules of domination and subordination between people. These rules specify who has access to resources, and who controls, manages, and oppresses other people. It also means that there are many distinctions among people based on their social position, such as by age, gender, race/ethnicity, and social class (Leeder, 2004). Thus, although families at first glance may look different from one another, they are all influenced by and influence similar social forces. At this point, it is difficult to predict how processes of globalization, political and economic crises, and other social changes will shape family lives worldwide. However, one thing that's certain is that economic, technological, and other changes will continue to transform family structure, roles, and relationships in significant and far-reaching ways.

Questions for Critical Reflection and Debate

1. How can a cross-cultural view of family life reduce ethnocentrism, or the tendency for us to see the world only through our own eyes so that we evaluate other cultures based on our own beliefs or ways of doing things?
2. Debate the following: Regardless of society, power and sexuality have always been linked throughout history and this determines how families are formed.
3. Choose a cultural group from anywhere in the world (preferably one that is very different from your own) and examine how family life (e.g., structure, rituals, and gender roles) is both different and similar.
4. What criticisms can be made of the manner in which the Western media have portrayed family life in non-Western societies? Does this help or hinder non-Western families? Provide specific examples to illustrate.
5. How does war, terrorism, or natural catastrophes in other countries (i.e., such as the 2004 Southeast Asian tsunami) influence Canadian family life?
6. Some futurists maintain that the forces of globalization will eventually result in a common world culture with virtually identical "Stepford" family lifestyles. Do you agree or disagree?

Glossary

Anthropology is the broad study of humankind around the world and throughout time, and is concerned with both the biological and the cultural aspects of humans.

Family-based economy includes all those activities (domestic, economic, and social) to keep a family functioning.

Globalization refers to the world scale of economic and other market activity facilitated by the expansion of telecommunications technology.

Hegemonic social groups are the more powerful groups in society that establish control (cultural, social, and moral) or domination over less powerful groups through consensus or coercion.

Neolocal residence is the tendency for a couple to establish their household in a new place, apart from their parents.

Polygamy or plural marriage is the practice of having more than one husband or wife, and consists of three forms: polygyny, polyandry, and group marriage.

Population aging occurs primarily as fertility declines and life expectancy increases.

Serial monogamy is a form of monogamy in which participants have only one sexual partner at any one time but have more than one sexual partner in their lifetime.

Further Reading

Bradbury, B. 1992. *Canadian Family History: Selected Readings*. Toronto: Copp Clark Pitman. Is a collection of articles on the history of families in Canada from New France to the 1970s. Subjects include gender relations, divorce, legal systems and the state, child labour, and the work roles of men and women.

Edgar, S. 2011. *Global Girlfriends: How One Mom Made it Her Business to Help Women in Poverty Worldwide.* New York: St. Martin's Press. An inspirational story of how one woman used her $2,000 tax return to create a socially conscious business specializing in handmade, fairly traded eco-conscious apparel and items that helped poor women in five continents feed their families and send their children to school.

Hennon, C.B., and S.M. Wilson (Eds.). 2008. *Families in a Global Context*. New York: Routledge. Explores cross-cultural diversity through a comparative analysis of family life in many countries, including: Wales, Sweden, Germany, Italy, South Africa and Kenya, Sierra Leone, Turkey, Iran, Australia, China, India, Brazil, Mexico, and Cuba.

Trask, B. 2010. *Globalization and Families: Accelerated Systemic Social Change*. New York: Springer. Offers a fresh perspective on how globalization impacts families around the world by focusing on gender ideologies, work-family relationships, and conceptualizations of children, youth, and the elderly.

Wells, K.C. 2009. *Childhood in Global Perspective*. Malden, MA: Polity Press. A unique global perspective on children's lives throughout the world, discussing wide-ranging issues such as children and war, child labour, and young people's activism around the globe.

Zontini, E. 2010. *Transnational Families, Migration and Gender: Moroccan and Filipino Women in Bologna and Barcelona*. New York: Berghahn Books. Links the experience of immigrant families with the increased reliance on cheap and flexible workers for care and domestic work within the context of globalization and transformations of Western families more generally.

Related Web Sites

Canadian Genealogy Centre facilitates the discovery of Canadian family histories and includes all physical and online genealogical services of Library and Archives Canada. It is located at www.collectionscanada.gc.ca/genealogy/index-e.html.

Early Canadiana Online provides many articles and resources on early family life in Canada, http://canadiana.org/ECO.

Freegan.info is an organization that promotes alternative strategies for living based on limited participation in the conventional economy and minimal consumption of resources and is opposed to a society based on materialism and greed.

The Project on Global Working Families, Harvard School of Public Health, is the first program devoted to understanding and improving the relationship between working conditions and family health and well-being throughout the world. Information on this project and resources can be found at: www.globalworkingfamilies.org.

United Nations Population Information Network is a centralized community of population institutions organized into global, regional, and national networks, and provides information and articles on many issues facing families worldwide, www.un.org/popin.

Women in Canada (2010–2011) is a gender-based statistical report published by Statistics Canada compiling data on family status, education, employment, economic well-being, unpaid work, health and more, www.statcan.gc.ca/pub/89-503-x/89-503-x2005001-eng.pdf.

References

Ambert, A.M. 2012. *Changing Families: Relationships in Context*, 2nd. Canadian ed. Toronto: Pearson and Allyn Bacon.

Anderson, K. 2000. *A Recognition of Being: Reconstructing Native Womanhood.* Toronto: Second Story Press.

Baker, M., and J. Dryden.1993. *Families in Canadian Society: An Introduction*, 2nd ed. Toronto: McGraw-Hill Ryerson.

Bartlett, L. 2011. "7-Billionth Person Expected This Fall," *The Vancouver Sun*, B5, Wednesday, June 22.

Bradbury, B. 1993.*Working Families: Age, Gender, and Daily Survival in Industrializing Montreal.* Toronto: McClelland & Stewart Inc.

Bradbury. 2005. "Social, Economic, and Cultural Origins of Contemporary Families." In M. Baker (ed.), *Families: Changing Trends in Canada*, 5th ed. (pp. 71–98). Toronto: McGraw-Hill Ryerson.

de Sousa Santos, B. 2006. "Globalization." *Theory, Culture, and Society* 23, no. 2/3: 393–399.

Druke, M.A. 1986. "Iroquois and Iroquoian in Canada." In R. Bruce Morrison and C. Roderick Wilson (eds.), *Native Peoples: The Canadian Experience* (pp. 61–86). Toronto: McClelland & Stewart.

Frideres, J.S. 2000. "Revelation and Revolution: Fault Lines in Aboriginal-White relations." In M.A. Kalbach and W.E. Kalbach (eds.), *Perspectives on Ethnicity in Canada* (pp. 207–237). Toronto: Harcourt Brace.

Ingoldsby, B.B., and S.D. Smith. 2006. *Families in Global and Multicultural Perspective,* 2nd ed. Thousand Oaks: Sage.

International Labour Office. 2011. *World of Work Report 2010: From One Crisis to the Next?* Geneva: International Institute for Labour Studies.

Judkins, B., and L. Presser. 2008. "Division of Eco-Friendly Household Labour and the Marital Relationship." *Journal of Social and Personal Relationship*, 25: 923–941.

Leacock, E. 1991."Montagnais Women and the Jesuit Program for Colonization." In V. Strong-Boag and A. Clair Fellman (eds.), *Rethinking Canada: The Promise of Women's History,* 2nd ed. Toronto: Copp Clark Pitman.

Leeder, E.J. 2004. *The Family in Global Perspective: A Gendered Journey.* Thousand Oaks: Sage.

Lesthaeghe, R. 2000. "Europe's Demographic Issues: Fertility, Household Formation, and Replacement Migration." IPD Working Paper 2000-6, Interface Demography, VU Brussels.

Mandell, N., and J. Momirov. 2005. "Family Histories." In N. Mandell and A. Duffy (eds.), *Canadian Families: Diversity, Conflict, and Change* (pp. 31–63). Toronto: Thomson Nelson.

Modo, I.V.O. 2001. "Migrant Culture and Changing Face of Family Structure in Lesotho."*Journal of Comparative Family Studies* 32: 443–452.

Nett, E.M. 1988. *Canadian Families Past and Present.* Toronto: Butterworths.

Otobe, N. 2011. *Global Economic Crisis, Gender and Employment: The Impact and Policy Response.* International Labour Office, Employment Sector Working Paper No. 74, Geneva, Switzerland.

Parr, J. 1990. *The Gender of Breadwinners: Women, Men, and Change in Two Industrial Towns 1880–1950.* Toronto: University of Toronto Press.

Rank, M.R., and G.N. Yadama. 2006. "Poverty and Family Policy in Global Context." In B.B. Ingoldsby and S.D. Smith (eds.), *Families in Global and Multicultural Perspective,* 2nd ed. (pp. 379–404). Thousand Oaks: Sage.

Roopnarine, J.L., and U.P. Gielen (Eds.). 2005. *Families in Global Perspective.* Toronto: Pearson.

Seccombe, K., and R.L. Warner. 2004. *Marriages and Families: Relationships in Social Context.* Toronto: Thomson Wadsworth.

Smith, S.D. 2006. "Global Families." In B.B. Ingoldsby and S.D. Smith (eds.), *Families in Global and Multicultural Perspective,* 2nd ed. (pp. 3–24). Thousand Oaks: Sage.

Statistics Canada. 2003a. *Labour Force Historical Review 2003.* Catalogue no. 71F0004XCb. Ottawa: Statistics Canada.

Statistics Canada. 2003b. *Aboriginal Peoples of Canada: A Demographic Profile.* Catalogue no. 96F0030X1E2001007. Ottawa: Statistics Canada.

The International Centre for Research on Women. 2011. *Child Marriage Facts and Figures,* retrieved June 19, 2011 from www.icrw.org/child-marriage-facts-and figures.

United Nations. 2002. *World Population Aging: 1950–2050.* New York: United Nations Departments of Economic and Social Affairs.

United Nations Development Programme. 2003. *Human Development Report 2003.* New York: Oxford University Press.

Wilson, S.J. 1991. *Women, Families and Work,* 3rd ed. Toronto: McGraw-Hill Ryerson.

World Hunger Organization. 2011. *2011 World Hunger and Poverty Facts and Statistics,* retrieved from ww.worldhunger.org/articles/Learn/world hunger facts 2002.htm.

Chapter 4

Aboriginal Families, Immigration, and the Changing Ethnic Mosaic of Canadian Families

Learning Objectives

In this chapter, you will learn that ...
- the ethnocultural composition of Canadian families has changed over time
- the ethnic mosaic is influenced by changing government and immigration policies
- Aboriginal and immigrant families have not always had the right to live in a family context of their own choosing
- ethnic groups are diverse such that assumptions of homogeneity can lead to racist outcomes
- there are sources of generational conflict and solidarity among Aboriginal, immigrant, and visible minority families
- the current Canadian ethnic mosaic is undergoing profound transformation

Introduction

Canadian society is internationally renowned for its embrace and tolerance of multiculturalism with its associated imagery of an ethnic mosaic. This term is used to denote a rich tapestry of families whose distinctive cultures give colour and texture to the whole. It also reflects a condition that symbolizes the reality of ethnic diversity, which has been increasingly characteristic of Canada over time (Agocs, 1992). While Aboriginal peoples constitute the "First Nations" of our land, family life has increasingly become ethnically and culturally diverse as a growing number of immigrants and refugees arrive from Asia, Latin America, Africa, and the Middle East. The majority of these individuals (approximately 73 percent) belong to what is euphemistically known as the "visible minority population" (see Box 4.1 for a critique of this term), and is defined by the Employment Equity Act as "persons, other than Aboriginal peoples who are non-Caucasian in race or non-white in colour."

Although Aboriginal, immigrant, and visible minority populations have very different or unique cultural and migration histories—Aboriginal groups have the longest history of living on this land whereas other ethnic groups have moved here from other parts of the world—an examination of diverse social groups within the same chapter highlights some common issues with respect to the changing cultural mosaic of Canadian families. Notably, these groups share the experience of having to struggle to maintain their family life and cultural heritage in the face of numerous obstacles and challenges. These conditions can place strains on these families with respect to availability and access to resources (e.g., state and family-based), patterns of family and generational support over the life course, and their health and well-being.

In recognition of these issues, this chapter will focus on Aboriginal, immigrant, refugee, and visible minority groups and provide an overview of how ethnicity and government policy shapes and constrains family life in Canada. Several emergent patterns

Box 4.1
The Imperative of Minority Construction

Canadian official records refer to racialized peoples as visible minorities or racial minorities. This raises the obvious questions of what we mean by minorities, and why they are accorded that status. Minorities are socially constructed entities in societies, and the label implies the imposition of an inferior status. They are often set apart by the majority group as incompetent, abnormal, or dangerous because of differences pertaining to race, gender, culture, and religion. Majority or dominant groups use these differences to distance themselves from minorities for the purpose of acquiring or maintaining privilege and power. In the process, the minority group becomes the "other," an outsider, sometimes dangerous and sometimes a pariah. Although in the Canadian case some argue that minority refers to the numerical status of the groups, the concept of minority is often extended to numerical majorities such as women (or with the majority Black population in South Africa under the apartheid regime). In the case of race, as a determinant of minority status, imposing the label suggests that race is the most distinguishing feature in the experience of racialized people in Canada—not class or gender or religion. It also fixes their identity for all time within that imposed silo, suggesting that the racialized groups will always be the "other" in Canadian society.

Source: Galabuzi, G.E. 2006. *Canada's Economic Apartheid: The Social Exclusion of Racialized Groups in the New Century.* Toronto: Canadian Scholars' Press (p. 31).

will be identified, as well as some selected generational opportunities and challenges for these selected ethnic groups. Ethnicity refers to "cultural, organizational (tribe, nation), and ideational (religion) values, attitudes and behaviours" that have to do with "social, socio-psychological, cultural, and organizational dimensions of human interaction" (Driedger, 2003: 9). We will begin with a brief historical overview of Aboriginal families and how colonization by the French and British, as well as other immigration patterns, have contributed to the current ethnic mosaic.

Aboriginal Families under French and British Colonization

The Aboriginal First Nations were the first families to inhabit what was later to become Canada and numbered about 200,000 when Europeans first "discovered" the Americas in the 1490s. At that time, the most densely populated regions were along the St. Lawrence River and the Great Lakes, as well as in some regions of future British Columbia. As discussed in the previous chapter, these families were primarily hunter-gatherers and horticulturalists and lived in settled villages and engaged in some trade. And as the term "First Nations" suggests, more than 300 nations existed, each possessing unique histories, dialects, languages, cultures, laws, and levels of economic development. Yet, they had common features such as a preference for communal living and the sharing of resources and responsibilities, from child-rearing to food (Ambert, 2012). Aboriginal families include status (registered) and non-status Indians, Métis, and Inuit, and there is considerable diversity within each of these groups.

In the 1500s, the history of Canadian families began to change when the French established the colony of New France at what is now Quebec City. Within a nuclear family structure and very high rates of child-bearing, the population rate exploded. Also, many French male colonists took First Nations women as wives, called *les femmes du pays,* in unions outside of the Church. Many factors influenced family life at this time, such as economic and political forces, as well as the expanding authority of the Roman Catholic Church. The Church developed a gender-specific curriculum, such that girls were taught to be good wives, mothers, and servants of the Church (Nett, 1993).

The British also brought unique family institutions to Canada. During British colonial rule (which lasted until 1867), rapid population growth and industrialization fuelled the emergence of major towns and the development of social stratification as classes of merchants, professionals, artisans, farmers, and labourers (MacDonald, 1990). Most families were nuclear and founded upon the same legal patriarchy as those in England. Although there was no central religious power similar to the Roman Catholic Church in New France, there were several Protestant religious authorities that strongly shaped family life. The Christian notion that fathers and husbands owned property and should be the legal head of their families prevailed, yet women's work played a critical role in the development of British Canada and the expansion of the economy (Errington, 1995).

Contact with both the French and British brought great changes to Aboriginal families. As mentioned in the last chapter, settlers brought disease, such as small pox and tuberculosis. They also brought alcohol, which created an economic dependency among the Aboriginal peoples on the colonizers. The colonists also set out to destroy their culture, since they wanted to assimilate these peoples (assimilation is the process by which a group or individual becomes more like the dominant group with respect to cultural elements) into a Euro-Canadian society. One primary instrument for social control was the imposition of a European educational system, with the primary intention of solving what was deemed as "the Indian problem" without cultural or parental influence (see boxes 4.2 and 4.3 for an example of this rationale provided by a missionary and an adult woman's experience at a residential school). In order to meet this objective, residential schools were built during the 1840s. At their peak, there were 82 residential schools operating in Canada, with the last school closing in 1996 (Assembly of First Nations, 2006).

When Aboriginal children were placed in these Church-run residential schools (primarily Roman Catholic, Anglican, United, and Presbyterian), they were taken away from their families and reserves and stripped of their culture. Forced to take Christian names and forbidden to practise their spiritual beliefs or speak in their mother tongue, their hair

---

Box 4.2
"Children's Best Interests"

Missionaries often placed pressure on the federal government to fund schools for Indigenous children, given that their attempts to convert children were often unsuccessful. Below find an excerpt from the writings of Father McGuckin of St. Joseph's Mission in 1878, who thought that a residential school would be the solution to the missionaries' problems:

In a few years hence all our boys and girls will speak English, mix with the whites and lose all of their original simplicity. To resist them the temptations that will be placed in their way nothing less than a thorough religious education will suffice. This they will never acquire in their own language. Not as children, for during childhood there is no opportunity so long as they remain with their parents. Not during boyhood or girlhood, for then they are too busy and can be found for a short time in the winter, and often then unwilling to occupy their spare time at religious institutions. Hence, if we will preserve the faith amongst them, and provide them with arms to resist temptation, we must endeavor to get them into school and keep them for a certain number of years.

Source: Furniss, E. 1995. *Victims of Benevolence: Discipline and Death at the Williams Lake Indian Residential School, 1981–1920*. Williams Lake, B.C.: Cariboo Tribal Council (p. 11).

---

was cut and their clothes were replaced with uniforms. Many were physically and sexually assaulted, as illustrated in Box 4.3, and some tried to commit suicide or run away. Sadly, these children had little contact with their parents, since "the physical isolation of children from their families and communities was a central ingredient in the residential school system" (Furniss, 1995: 14). When these children returned home as young adults, they were expected to recommence "normal family life, now among kin that they had been taught to be ashamed of. One former student stated, 'many of us raised our children the way we were raised at the schools. We disciplined our children with physical force, and we called them stupid, dumb, and lazy. We showed little or no emotion, and we found it hard to say we love them'" (Timpson, 1995: 535).

Not surprisingly, these residential school experiences decreased the children's own capacity to care for their own children later in life and perpetuated a cycle of family breakdown and dysfunction. When many of these young adults formed their own families, usually in economically and socially depressed communities, they themselves experienced the removal of their own children through cross-cultural foster placement and adoptions (Albanese, 2009). As noted by Das Gupta (2000: 152), "Generations of depression, alcoholism, suicide, and family breakdown are the legacy of such traumatic experiences and are described as the 'residential school syndrome' by native people themselves."

Box 4.3
The Residential School Experience

An adult woman describes her experience and the reality of punishment as a child in a residential school:

I remember those horrifying years as if it were yesterday. There was one nun, Sister Gilberta, she always passed out the punishment. Every day, she would take me to the bathroom and lock the door. She would then proceed to beat me 30 times on each hand, three times a day, with a strap. She would count to 30, out loud, each time she hit me. It's an awful way to learn to count to 30. My older sister, Grace, learned to count to 50.

I never understood why I had to get those beatings, but at this age of 37, I realize it had to be because I spoke my language. To this day, I can't speak my language very well, but I do understand when I am spoken to in Micmac.

Why was our language and culture such a threat that it had to be taken away from us with such vengeance?

To be taught your language with respect and kindness by your people, then to have the White Man pull it from your heart with meanness and torture. Some people wonder why we are so tough, because we had to, we had no choice.

I have polio and it affected my bladder and as a child, I wet my pants a lot. I received extra beatings for that too.

Once I was thrown across the dorm floor by Sister Gilberta. At the age of six, it seemed far away. I bounced off the wall at the other end of the dorm. I was sore on one side of my body for a few days.

Source: Cited in Schissel, B. and T. Wotherspoon. 2003. *The Legacy of School for Aboriginal People.* Toronto: Oxford University Press (pp. 51–52).

It is also important to note that The Indian Act of 1876 had a very powerful influence on Aboriginal families. Those designated "Indians" were relegated to lands set aside for them, which put them on the margins of Canadian society and its economy. This Act was also detrimental to status Indian women who marry non-status men. Section 12 (1)(b) stated that a woman married to anyone other than an Indian was not entitled to status as an Indian, nor were her children. And if she did marry an Indian man, she then became a member of his band and lost her own band. This patriarchal law contravened the matrilineality of many Aboriginal peoples and disrupted family life. For example, if an Indian woman with children lost her status, she would have no place on the reserve if her marriage dissolved because she was no longer an "Indian." This loss of community and friends meant that her children would have limited experience of the reserve community and its Native culture (Momirov and Kilbride, 2005).

Immigration Patterns Post-Confederacy

Boyd and Vickers (2000) note that record numbers of immigrants arrived in Canada during the early 1900s. These numbers plummeted during World War One and the Depression years, but by the end of the 20th century, they had again reached those levels documented almost a century earlier. The characteristics of immigrants have changed over time and reflect many factors, such as the displacement of people by wars; changes to government policies; the cycle of economic booms and busts; and the growth of communication, transportation, and economic networks linking people globally. For example, at the turn of the 20th century, Canada's economy was rapidly expanding and immigrants were lured by the promise of good job prospects. Many found employment building the transcontinental railway, settling in the Prairies and in industrial production. Men also greatly outnumbered women immigrants at this time, reflecting labour recruitment efforts targeted at men rather than women, although there was also strong demand for female domestic workers from England, Scotland, and Wales (e.g., see Figure 4.1).

Figure 4.1
"The Last Best West": Advertising for British Domestic Workers and Photo of British Immigrant Workers, 1900–1916

A bright future awaited British domestics in western Canada, this pamphlet suggested:

"Canada has an ever growing excess of males over females of no less a number than 150,000 ... as a matter of fact, a very large percentage [of females] enter the matrimonial state shortly after their arrival, in turn become themselves mistresses requiring help in their household duties."

Source: Library and Archives Canada.

Recruitment strategies included the production of posters and pamphlets (which advertised opportunities for work in every part of Canada), sent to targeted countries.

At the beginning of the 20th century, most immigrants had originated in the United States or the United Kingdom. By the 1920s, large peasant families from the Ukraine were recruited to establish farms in western Canada, since these families had the labour power to acquire full title of the land (Satzewich, 1993). Families also began to arrive from other European countries, such as the Doukhobors and Jewish refugees from Russia. Immigration from Asia was relatively low at this time. With World War One, immigration came to an abrupt stop, and during the Depression, most immigrants came from Great Britain, Germany, Austria, and the Ukraine, with only 6 percent from a non-European origin. After World War Two, the largest numbers of immigrants were from the United Kingdom, although people from other European countries were increasing.

The time period from the 1970s through the turn of the 21st century represents an era in which immigration numbers fluctuated. The proportion of Canadian immigrants born in Asian countries (including the Middle East) and other regions of the world began to rise, especially during the 1980s, as shown in Figure 4.2. By 2006, Canada's largest group of recent immigrants was from Asia, accounting for 58 percent of immigrants in 2006. Europe accounted for 16 percent, compared with 61 percent in the 1971 Census,

Figure 4.2
Recent Immigrants to Canada, by Region of Origin

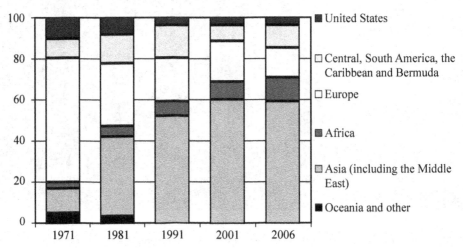

Note: 'Recent immigrants' refers to landed immigrants who arrived in Canada within five years prior to a given census. 'Other' includes Greenland, Saint Pierre and Miquelon, the category 'other country,' as well as a small number of immigrants born in Canada.
Sources: Statistics Canada, censuses of population, 1971 to 2006.

Source: Statistics Canada. Canada Year Book 2008, Chart 13.1, p. 159, retrieved June 9, 2011 from www.statcan.gc.ca.

while Central and South America and the Caribbean comprised 11 percent, and 11 per-cent originated from Africa (Canada Year Book, 2008). As a result, the visible minority population has grown substantially in the last two decades.

In 2006, the five leading Canadian ethnic groups (which were self-identified by Cana-dians and more than one origin could be reported) were: "Canadian;" English; French; Scottish; and Irish. As further shown in Table 4.1, the top 10 ethnic origins by generational status reveal interesting differences related to changing immigration patterns. Among first generation Canadians—a term used to mean either the person who immigrated to Canada or their children who were born in Canada—the top three ethnic groups are: Chinese (15 percent), East Indian (10 percent), followed by the English (8.9 percent). By way of con-trast, among third generation (or more) Canadians, 46.6 percent reported being "Canadian," followed by English (24.4 percent), and French (22.7 percent) (Statistics Canada, 2010).

Table 4.1
Top 10 Ethnic Origins* by Generational Status for People Aged 15 and Over, Canada, 2006

First generation			Second generation			Third generation or more		
Ethnic origin	number	%	Ethnic origin	number	%	Ethnic origin	number	%
Total population	6,124,560	100.0	Total population	4,006,420	100.0	Total population	15,533,240	100.0
Chinese	916,845	15.0	English	1,035,145	25.8	Canadian	7,236,370	46.6
East Indian	612,460	10.0	Scottish	635,600	15.9	English	3,794,250	24.4
English	547,865	8.9	Canadian	613,445	15.3	French	3,530,505	22.7
Italian	366,205	6.0	German	524,645	13.1	Scottish	2,865,800	18.4
German	352,805	5.8	Irish	496,990	12.4	Irish	2,755,420	17.7
Filipino	288,515	4.7	Italian	439,275	11.0	German	1,604,225	10.3
Scottish	271,545	4.4	French	284,900	7.1	North American Indian	813,405	5.2
Irish	230,975	3.8	Dutch (Netherlands)	253,325	6.3	Ukrainian	642,955	4.1
Polish	213,715	3.5	Ukrainian	212,860	5.3	Dutch (Netherlands)	376,555	2.4
Portuguese	195,480	3.2	Polish	203,725	5.1	Polish	364,980	2.3

* Table shows total responses. Because some respondents reported more than one ethnic origin, the sum of the total responses is greater than the total population, or 100%.

Source: Statistics Canada, Census of Population, 2006.

State Policies, Immigration, and Family Life

The preceding discussion highlights how government policy can significantly influence family life, as was shown in the federal government's attempt to assimilate Aboriginal peoples into "mainstream" culture. Throughout Canadian history, we can find many other examples of how policies have created both opportunities and difficulties for ethnic families. Historically, one of the major goals of immigration policy has been to populate the country and contribute to our labour force and economic production. This is because from the time of the Confederation (1867), Canadian families have never been capable of maintaining population growth. However, in spite of efforts to increase our population of workers, the government has often used specific recruitment tactics and admission policies to keep out those deemed "undesirable" (Albanese, 2005).

When the supply of American and British immigrants was insufficient at the turn of the 20th century, Canada began to recruit immigrants from "desirable" parts of Europe. Oftentimes, the government employed a number of initiatives to recruit and maintain fit, permanent settlers to populate certain regions. For example, in order to attract Mennonites, an Anabaptist sect committed to a simple life and pacifism, the government promised them freedom from military service, the right to exercise their religious principles, and the right to avoid swearing the oath of allegiance. Conversely, equally necessary migrant labourers were deemed "undesirable" for permanent settlement, as well as those deemed "unfit" (Albanese, 2005).

In this way, policies have often affected people's ability to form and live in family situations of their own choice. Many contend that from the earliest period, the government tried to exclude non-Whites from entering Canada. Yet, when visible minority migrants were needed as ready sources of labour, the government would create transitional "bachelor" communities, as formed among Chinese and East Indian male migrants. Women and families were discouraged from migrating in order to deter the creation of permanent communities. For example, thousands of young Chinese males were allowed to enter the country in the late 19th century, with the provision that they return to their homeland after working on the railway. Thus, the government's goal was to have an abundance of cheap labour to work in dangerous conditions, while also deterring mass migration from Chinese families. Indeed, the Canadian government levied a head tax of $50 per migrant, which was raised to $500 by 1903, such that it made it very difficult for Chinese men to bring their families to Canada. As a result, there were relatively few Chinese families in Canada before 1950 (Albanese, 2005; Satzewich, 1993).

Countless other examples of how government policy made large-scale restrictions in relation to colour, immigration, and family life can be found throughout the last century (see Das Gupta, 2000 and Albanese, 2005 for full overview). However, it should be recognized that overt discrimination against non-traditional, particularly non-White source countries and groups has technically been abolished. Instead, the emphasis has been on filling gaps in the economy, resulting in the upsurge of immigration from Asian and developing countries. Notably, the point system established in 1967 opened the door for families from non-traditional countries, since it favoured immigrants with skills. As a

Figure 4.3
"The Undesirables," 1910–1911

"Undesirable" immigrants were sent back to their departure points at the expense of the steamship company that brought them. Those barred included people suffering from a range of mental and physical afflictions, and prostitutes and their procurers.

Source: Canadian Museum of Civilization Corp.

result, those from middle- and upper middle-class backgrounds are now overrepresented in the immigrant population, which has also facilitated the reunion of immigrants with their relatives (Satzewich, 1993).

Yet recent research by McLaren and Black (2005) suggests that prevailing discourses that view family-class immigrants (versus economic-class immigrants), especially parents of immigrants, as undesirable burdens on society contributes to the recent decline of sponsored parents' immigration. They note that these discourses are "legitimated by the growing influence of human capital theory on the immigration point system, which establishes criteria for selecting skilled workers." From this perspective, immigrant parents are easily set up as "antagonistic" to taxpayer interests, to society, and to their own families. Thus, rather than being neutral, the point system reinforces and produces social exclusions and inequalities. As a result, officially inscribed distinctions between desirable and undesirable immigrants and the resulting exclusionary policies continue and have important consequences for families.

For example, McLaren and Black (2005) note that immigration policy does not consider parents and grandparents to be "immediate family," despite the fact that they are often essential child-care providers and supports. This means that they need to be sponsored, despite an immigration policy that has dramatically reduced support for sponsorship over the past decade by setting low target levels. A preference for economic immigrants—that is, those who are highly educated and prepared for the labour market—gives priority to economic over family concerns and family traditions. In short, these official and routine practices have far-reaching implications for Canadian family life.

Contrary to popular opinion, relatively few individuals are admitted to Canada as refugees. This term refers to individuals who have been judged by a refugee tribunal (according to the United Nations' definition of refugee) as having a well-grounded fear of persecution or danger on specified grounds. The most common grounds relate to ethnicity, race, religion, and gender. Many of these individuals are in refugee camps operated by the United Nations High Commissioner for Refugees (UNHCR). Canadian officials visit refugee camps and interview those who apply for acceptance into Canada. It should also be noted that the laws affecting refugees are different from immigration laws.

Since 1979, approximately 20,000 people per year have been admitted to Canada as refugees. Other individuals arrive in Canada as refugee claimants or asylum seekers, who have not yet been adjudged to be refugees, but who come to claim refugee status (Momirov and Kilbride, 2005). Most (70 percent) refugees originate from non-European countries, specifically conflict zones in Africa, the Middle East, and the Pacific region (Ali et al., 2003), and like other arrivals, they tend to settle in Canada's major urban centres.

Selected Ethno-cultural Family Trends and Issues

It is well established that family patterns are influenced by norms, values, expectations and traditions, immigration history, and language. As such, expectations of "appropriate" gender and family-related roles, responsibilities, living arrangements, and family practices often vary by ethnic group. For example, preferences for certain kinds of food, music, style of clothing, and the observance of certain religious holidays are commonly associated with specific ethnic groups (i.e., Italian and Indian food and restaurants). Moreover, many differences between traditional Aboriginal and non-Aboriginal, and Eastern and Western cultures are observed. Aboriginal cultures are often revered for an emphasis on sharing, extended family, and respect for elders. Concepts of health and well-being are also seen to include balance in physical, emotional, mental, and spiritual dimensions. In addition, there is a deep appreciation for the natural environment and the interconnectedness of individuals, families, communities, and nations with the spiritual order of the universe (Castellano, 2002).

Similarly, Eastern cultures are noted to have cultural histories and traditions that emphasize family-centredness, the collectivity, extended family, and holistic views of health. Respect for one's elders is based on the notion of filial piety, and can be traced to Confucian, Buddhist, or other religious principles of moral obligation, honour, and respect for one's ancestors. Conversely, "Canadian" or Western cultures are often associated with more individualistic goals and pursuits.

Yet, in keeping with a life course theoretical perspective and empirical studies, it is important not to over-generalize or to stereotype groups since there can be considerable heterogeneity (diversity in wealth or economic resources, for example) or "social capital" within subgroups. Social capital inheres in the structure of relationships, and can be found in strong supportive families and in communities. Further, the quality of family relationships and level of contact are paramount, and they can transcend cultural traditions. There is also a need to consider immigration histories and age-related changes in family behaviours and support at particular transitional points in the lifespan, such as during childhood or during old age. Thus, although it may be fruitful to understand basic cultural differences across ethnic groups, it should not be assumed that all "ethnics" are the same. This can lead to misguided assumptions or even racism, an ideology that regards racial or ethnic categories as natural social or genetic groups. Accordingly, certain groups are associated with social or biological traits that are seen as either inferior or superior. Indeed, social groups that commonly report being victims of racism and discrimination are Aboriginal, visible minority, and immigrant families.

Aboriginal Families

The Aboriginal population has fluctuated over time but rose significantly between 1971 and 1996. Today, people reporting an Aboriginal ethnic identity represent about 3 to 4 percent of the total population of Canada, with the largest number living in Ontario and British Columbia (Statistics Canada, 2001). The proportion of this population living off reserve has significantly increased over time. By 2001, over 50 percent of registered Aboriginal Canadians lived off reserves, particularly in industrial areas and cities (Statistics Canada, 2001). Many Aboriginal peoples (regardless of where they live) have difficulty finding employment due to discrimination and lower educational attainment than in the general population. As a result, continuing poverty is an important cause of problems in families.

Sources of Generational Conflict and Solidarity in Aboriginal Families

The Royal Commission on Aboriginal Peoples has reported on the serious social and economic conditions among many Aboriginal peoples, including low life expectancy, inadequate education, high teenage pregnancy rates, high levels of alcohol and substance abuse, overcrowded housing, poverty, and family breakdown. Aboriginal children are four to six times more likely than other Canadian children to come into the care of child welfare agencies and are the fastest-growing segment of the Canadian population (e.g., see Trocmé et al., 2004).

As a result of these trends, parent-child relations can be significantly impacted, since poverty and contact patterns affects the flow of generational transfers and quality of life. One area of growing concern is on grandparent-grandchild relations. Grandparents often provide care for grandchildren in response to crisis, such as alcohol and drug addiction or imprisonment of the grandchildren's parents. This can create a number of challenges and vulnerabilities between the generations. For instance, grandparents raising their grandchildren are more likely to be living in poverty and in overcrowded conditions and to have a disability or depressive symptoms. As a result, many custodial elders face substantial financial, emotional, and physical costs, which trickle down to their grandchildren (Fuller-Thomson, 2005).

On the positive side, care from grandparents can provide continuity among the generations, since it allows Aboriginal children to learn traditional ways and receive guidance from their elders. Indeed, elders have traditionally played key roles as wise advisers and keepers of their cultural legacy. This has historically helped to socialize and instruct their grandchildren, since they have often played an important role in their physical care (Castellano, 2002; Fuller-Thomson, 2005).

Overall, despite certain challenges, it is important to keep these issues in perspective since research shows that only a small minority of Aboriginal children, for instance, are raised by their grandparents. Also, it is relatively common for children to report that they experience positive ties with their families and communities. To illustrate, a recent study showed that most Inuit living in the North report having "strong" or "very strong" ties with their families, with only a minority reporting that their ties were "weak" or "very weak" (Canadian Council on Learning, 2009).

In short, it is important to consider the many positive features of Aboriginal family life and the fact that many families are doing relatively well. In other words, it should not be taken for granted that all Aboriginal families are poor and have alcohol- or other family-related problems. For instance, we should not assume that sniffing gas is the norm among Aboriginal youth, as was suggested by recent media broadcasts of Innu youth in Davis Inlet. Aboriginal communities, both rural and urban, are becoming increasingly diverse, with significant variability in education, income, health, and longevity. Yet, on average, the relative chances that Aboriginal peoples have with respect to attaining a higher socio-economic status and good health are more limited than those of the general Canadian population (Castellano, 2002).

Immigrant and Visible Minority Families
Many ethnic groups comprise the visible minority population and the immigrant population. Statistics Canada typically includes the following groups in the visible minority population: Blacks, South Asians, Chinese, Koreans, Japanese, Southeast Asians, Filipinos, Arabs and West Asians, Latin Americans, and Pacific Islanders, although members of some of these groups (i.e., Blacks) may have originated from many countries. Moreover, only two-thirds of visible minorities are foreign-born, and there is considerable diversity within this group, as well as the ethnic groups classified as visible minority. Yet, there are a number of worrisome trends with respect to current and future ethnic-related patterns of family life. Statistics Canada data show that racialized, immigrant, and Aboriginal children are more likely to live in poverty, a topic that will be further discussed in Chapter 13. Boyd (2000) also finds that living in households or families with poor economic resources is particularly likely for immigrant offspring whose ethnic

origin is Arabic, Black/Caribbean, Latin/Central/South American, Spanish (born in the Americas), Vietnamese, and/or West Asian.

Recent visible minority immigrants are also more likely to experience a trajectory of long-term disadvantage over the life course, since they tend to leave home and school early, and experience disadvantage in the labour force compared to those born in Canada. There is also concern that many visible minority immigrants face discrimination in the labour market (especially women), and that their educational qualifications from other countries are not given the recognition that they deserve.

Refugee families can also encounter numerous and unique challenges in their efforts to integrate into Canadian society. Similar to many newcomer families, some of these challenges include language barriers, finding employment commensurate with their educational credentials (underemployment), securing affordable and safe housing, cultural loss, mental health problems, the loss of an extended family support system, and for radicalized groups, racism (Este and Tachble, 2009). Refugees may also have the added challenge associated with having experienced tragedy and trauma (e.g., rape and torture), including war, persecution, dangerous escapes, witnessing violence, and in some cases, having served as child soldiers (Beiser et al., 1999). Relationships within the family can also change, including situations whereby family members are absent or role reversal occurs between family members (e.g., between husband and wife, or parent and child).

Sources of Generational Conflict and Solidarity in Immigrant and Visible Minority Families

Generational conflict can occur in immigrant or visible minority families, especially when the older generation is foreign-born and holds traditional norms and values. Also, many studies find that older individuals (especially immigrant parents) tend to assimilate or acculturate (when individuals from one cultural group, through contact with another, learn and internalize the cultural traits of the other group) less quickly than children or young people, which can create intergenerational conflict (McPherson, 2004). Common reasons for disagreement between parents and children are clashing norms and values (e.g., religious differences), schoolwork, peer group influences, and dating issues (Mitchell, 2005).

Immigrant and visible minority groups can also experience social exclusion due to the psychosocial stress of discrimination, which can also contribute to family and health problems. Visible minority youth can also encounter significant challenges coping with the school system. Factors underlying these problems include pressure from their parents to succeed in school (Momirov and Kilbride, 2005), school policies, and teachers' discriminatory attitudes. Moreover, recent studies also show that newcomer immigrant youth are twice as likely to suffer from depression than other individuals aged 35 and older (Beiser, 1999). As a result of some of these pressures, some young people may join peer groups that provide social support but that are destructive. For example, there has been growing concern that many visible minority youth are lured into gang and drug violence.

Furthermore, many elderly immigrant visible minority people experience poverty and do not qualify for pensions. Some must rely on other family members for food and shelter, which can potentially create strain, overcrowding, and dependency issues (Mitchell, 2005). Others may lack both financial and family support, in particular, women as seniors, African men, and single mothers from Africa, Latin America, and the Caribbean. Also, while most visible minority families live in nuclear families, women from Latin America and the Caribbean are more likely to be single parents, creating a different set of issues (Thomas, 2001).

With respect to refugee families, limited Canadian research has focused mainly on women or children. A notable exception is a recent study on refugee fathers conducted by Este and Tachble (2009) in Calgary. These researchers conducted in-depth interviews with Sudanese refugee men, which focused on their perceptions and experiences as fathers. Major areas of concerns revolved around a perceived loss of cultural background for their children, underemployment, lack of social support, social isolation, gender role changes, the need for greater involvement in parenting, and the discipline of children. For example, one father in the study believed that there was too much freedom given to children in Canada, "… too much freedom for somebody who does not know what is right and what is bad." This father also thought that this freedom contributed to young people in his community dropping out of school. This was echoed by another father who stated, "When we came to this country things began to change a bit because of the culture of Canadian freedom and then children can be free, they can do whatever they want and children can even go against the regulations of their families" (quoted on p. 463).

Apart from refugees—who can also immigrate without their families—there are many instances in which nuclear families are forced to live separately across national borders. Ambert (2012) asserts that with more international trade and exchange fuelled by globalization, these kinds of families—often referred to as multi-local or transnational families—have become more commonplace. Consequently, many men and women now cross nation-state boundaries to live and work without their children (in addition to other family members) at the time of settlement, which can present unique family and intergenerational issues. For example, some parents and children may drift apart due to a long and/or unanticipated separation, or children may become resentful for having been left behind.

There is also a growing phenomenon of "astronaut families" in Asian families whereby one or both parents spend much of their time abroad (e.g., in Hong Kong or China) while their young adult children are left to complete their education in Canada (with some being "satellite" children since they may return to their country of origin after immigration). These experiences can dramatically shape family interactions, identities, and relationships.

Yet, immigrant and visible minority families can also experience high levels of generational solidarity through fresh starts in a new country, the sharing of goals and resources, and the retention of their traditional culture. Sharing a new hope for the future, for example, can promote family unity (Albanese, 2009). Some ethnic groups may also have the opportunity to become even more institutionally complete, a term that refers to "parallel institutions that either inhibit or serve as alternatives to participation in the broader society" (Rosenberg and Jedwab, 1992). For example, living in a vibrant "ethnic" enclave or neighbourhood in an urban area with good social and economic opportunities, access to ethnic foods and newspapers, social networks, and religious institutions can help individuals and families to retain and reinforce their ethnic heritage and religious traditions. These conditions can also bridge bonds across generations, strengthen family solidarity, and provide opportunities for families to experience a familiar and high quality way of life.

Future Trends: The Invisibility of Visible Minorities in the Future?

In 2005, Statistics Canada produced a report with the main goal to "paint a portrait of Canadian diversity in 2017." This report produced estimates of the visible minority and immigrant populations and subgroups between 2001 and 2017, based on micro-simulation techniques. Five scenarios were produced based on differing assumptions of immigration, fertility, mortality, and internal migration. It was concluded that:

1. The population of visible minority persons in Canada will increase from about 4 million in 2001 to between 6.3 and 8.5 million in 2017. This means that about one in five Canadians would be a visible minority in 2017 compared to one in eight in 2001. And, approximately one in four Canadians would be foreign-born (immigrants). In 2017, about half of all visible minority people will be South Asian or Chinese, while Blacks will remain the third largest group (see Figure 4.4). The fastest-growing groups are the West Asian, Korean, and Arab groups, more than doubling over that time period, as revealed in Figure 4.4.
2. In 2017, the visible minority population will have a median age of 35.5, about eight years younger than the Canadian population.
3. With respect to fertility, recent immigrants have higher fertility rates than other women. In particular, Black, Arab, and Filipino groups have the highest fertility, whereas Chinese, Korean, Japanese, and West Asian groups have lower rates.
4. It was also projected that by 2017 between 21 percent and 25 percent of the total population of Canada will have mother tongues that are neither English or French, compared to 17 percent in 2001. The religions with the fastest growth during this time period will be Islam (145 percent increase), Hinduism (92 percent increase), and Sikhism (72 percent increase).
5. In 2017, Ontario will have 57 percent and B.C. will have 20 percent out of the total visible minority population of Canada, or 77 percent combined. According to projections, almost 75 percent of all visible minority people will be living in Toronto, Vancouver, and Montreal in 2017. At this time, more than half (51 percent) of the Toronto Census metro area will belong to a visible minority group, followed by Vancouver (49 percent), as shown in Table 4.2. Moreover, more than half of Canada's South Asians will be living in Toronto, while Montreal will be mainly comprised of Blacks (27 percent) and Arabs (19 percent).

Overall, these projections point to a dramatic alteration of the composition of Canada's population as the visible minority population grows faster than the total population.

Table 4.2

Visible Minority Groups Could Comprise Half the Population of Toronto and Vancouver by 2017

	Number of Visible Minority Persons ('000)		Percent of Total Population	
	2001	2017	2001	2017
Canada	4,038	7,121	13	21
Census metro area				
Toronto	1,753	3,194	37	51
Vancouver	741	1,261	36	49
Montreal	454	749	13	19
Ottawa-Gatineau*	139	316	17	28
Calgary	166	295	17	24
Edmonton	136	211	14	18
Hamilton	64	125	9	15
Winnipeg	84	115	12	16
Windsor	40	97	13	23
Kitchener	45	79	10	15
Rest of Canada	418	679	3	4

Note: Projections are based on the reference scenario, which uses assumptions based on trends observed in the 2001 Census and the preceding years.
*Ontario part only.

Source: A. Belanger and E.C. Malenfant, "Ethnocultural Diversity in Canada: Prospects for 2017," in Canadian Social Trends (Ottawa: Statistics Canada, 2005), Catalogue no. 11-008, Winter, p. 21, based on Statistics Canada, Catalogue no. 91-541-XIE.

These trends will undoubtedly have a major impact on Canadian family life in the future. They also raise a number of provocative questions about how family life will look in the future, given the relationship between certain ethnic traditions and the adoption of family-related behaviours. A continued adherence to these practices could touch upon many realms such as gender roles, socialization, religious practices, living arrangements, and family support patterns over the life course. Further, an increasing tendency for families to adopt "traditional" behaviour could counter the general movement toward individualization and secularization in our society. It could also pressure governments to revisit the relationship between religion and state, such as the recent controversy over the use of *sharia* law (a law used in some Muslim countries) in civil arbitrations in Ontario dealing

Figure 4.4

Chinese and South Asians Will Remain the Largest Visible Minority Groups in 2017

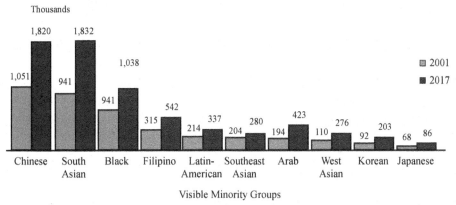

Note: Projections are based on the reference scenario, which uses assumptions based on trends observed in the 2001 Census and the preceding years.

Source: Statistics Canada, Catalogue no. 91-541-XIE, cited in A. Belanger and E.C. Malenfant, "Ethnocultural Diversity in Canada: Prospects for 2017," in *Canadian Social Trends* (Ottawa: Statistics Canada, 2005), p. 20, Catalogue no. 11-008.

with such matters as property, marriage, divorce, and custody, provided that both parties consent (Wente, 2004; see also Box 9.4 in Chapter 9 for more detail).

Summary

This chapter explores the changing ethnic composition of the Canadian population, with a focus on themes of diversity, continuity, power relations, and social change. Various challenges of Aboriginal, immigrant, and visible minority families are highlighted. Indeed, the current struggles of Aboriginal families are rooted in a history of domination and the attempts of colonial governments to assimilate them into Euro-Canadian society. Similarly, many immigrant and visible minority families have found it challenging to achieve a family of their own choosing as a result of government policies and other systemic barriers. Common problems include discrimination and racism, language difficulties, constricted employment and housing choices, poverty, and social exclusion (e.g., Momirov and Kilbride, 2005).

Within this context, the role of government policy in shaping and constraining family life was reviewed since it has played a critical role in creating the ethnic composition of our population, as well as the lived experiences and everyday lives of families. Fortunately, government policies appear to be less racist and discriminatory than in the past and victims of previous abuse are now stepping forward for compensation (for example, see the Assembly of First Nations' web site for the latest details on these claims). Yet, these past mistakes highlight the need for policy makers to carefully examine both the intended and unintended consequences of their policies (a theme to be further explored in Chapter 15), which may not be good for Canadian families in the long run. Overall, these policies raise moral, political, social, and cultural issues about who defines the "worth" of Aboriginal people and immigrants and how policy reflects prevailing discourses.

Finally, future trends with respect to the changing ethnic mosaic of the Canadian family was presented, in recognition of projected patterns and the rapidly increasing "invisibility" of the visible minority population, especially in large urban areas.

Questions for Critical Reflection and Debate

1. Is ethnic identity fluid over time and place? Provide examples from the Aboriginal, immigrant, and non-immigrant community.
2. Debate the following: Ethnic youth join gangs as a result of racism and discrimination.
3. How did the residential school experience of Aboriginal children result in devastating consequences for children, their families, and communities and reverberate through successive generations?
4. Critically evaluate how immigration policy can marginalize "other" immigrant women and their extended families because of their skin colour, cultural and linguistic characteristics, age, and lack of human capital.
5. What challenges do immigrant families face in trying to maintain and reproduce their traditional customs and mores upon their arrival to Canada? How might their area of settlement (i.e., community and neighbourhood) facilitate or hinder this process?
6. To what extent should the federal government develop policies and programs to redress many of the problems created by earlier policies?

Glossary

Acculturation occurs when individuals from one cultural group, through contact with another, learn and internalize the cultural traits of the other group.

Assimilation is the process by which a group or individual becomes more like the dominant group with respect to cultural elements.

Ethnicity refers to the cultural, organizational, and collective values, beliefs, attitudes, and behaviours of individuals who share or identify with a distinct culture or are descendants of those who have shared a distinct culture.

Institutional completeness is the extent to which an ethnic or social group develops its own institutions and formal organizations, such as religious or spiritual places of worship.

Racism is the practice of assuming that racial or ethnic categories are natural, social, or genetic groups associated with social or biological traits that are seen as either inferior or superior.

Refugees are individuals with a well-grounded fear of persecution or danger on specified conditions related to ethnicity, race, religion, gender, and political affiliation.

Visible minority population is a Statistics Canada classification that refers to those Canadians who are not White, Caucasian, or Aboriginal in their descent and includes: Blacks, South Asians, Chinese, Koreans, Japanese, Southeast Asians, Filipinos, Arabs and West Asians, Latin Americans, and Pacific Islanders.

Further Reading

Cannon, M.J., and L. Sunsert (Eds.). 2011. *Racism, Colonialism, and Indigeneity in Canada*. Toronto: Oxford University Press. This collection of works by Indigenous scholars explores the interplay of racism and colonialism and how it has shaped the lives of Indigenous peoples in such areas as family relations, criminal justice, territorial rights, and relations with settler colonialists.

Epp, M. 2008. *Mennonite Women in Canada: A History*. Studies in Immigration and Culture 2. Winnipeg: University of Manitoba Press. This book traces the multifaceted history of Mennonite women in Canada by documenting their experiences as migrants, mothers, missionaries, citizens, and workers. Using a variety of sources, from diaries and letters to memories and oral histories, Epp examines the rich diversity of their settlement experiences.

Furniss, E. 1995. *Victims of Benevolence: Discipline and Death at the Williams Lake Indian Residential School, 1981–1920.* Williams Lake: Cariboo Tribal Council. Provides a deeply moving and troubling study of two tragic events that took place at a residential school.

Highway, T. 2008. *Kiss of the Fur Queen*, 3rd ed. Norman: University of Oklahoma Press. This is a passionate story about the lives of two young Cree brothers from Northern Manitoba who are taken from their families and sent to residential school and follows the brothers as they become adults. It also explores issues around (homo) sexuality, relationships, and culture.

Simmons, A.B. 2010. *Immigration and Canada*. Toronto: Canadian Scholars' Press. Presents readers with a vital introduction to the field of international migration studies and offers up-to-date information on Canada in an evolving global-transnational system. Many key issues and debates are covered, such as transnational citizens, diasporas, emerging identities and refugees, temporary workers, and foreign visa workers.

Tastsoglou, E., and P.S. Jaya. 2011. *Immigrant Women in Atlantic Canada*. Toronto: Canadian Scholars' Press. An in-depth exploration of immigrant women's experiences in the labour force, family, and broader community in Atlantic Canada from a feminist, gender-based perspective that focuses on the intersection of gender with race, ethnicity, and class.

Wright, R.H. Jr., C.H. Mindel, T. Van Tran, R.W. Habenstein. 2012. *Ethnic Families in America: Patterns and Variations*. Toronto: Pearson Canada. This edited volume examines the multicultural diversity in the United States. Extensive coverage of historical background, family life styles, traditions, values, and adaptations of 17 ethnic groups is provided.

Related Web Sites

Aboriginal Affairs and Northern Development Canada provides information on the Indian Act, including past and recent amendments, in addition to statistics and trends on such aspects as housing, family structure, and income, www.ainc-inac.gc.ca/.

Assembly of First Nations provides links to other resources, as well as information on residential schools, legal claims, and other related material, www.afn.ca.

Canadian Heritage oversees national policies and programs dealing with multiculturalism, and is devoted to strengthening connections among various ethnic groups, www. pch.gc.ca.

Citizenship and Immigration Canada includes a number of useful resources, such as government policies and regulations on immigration, www.cic.gc.ca/english/index.asp.

Health Canada has a section that deals with immigrant and refugee health. It also provides research publications on numerous topics such as immigrant women, family violence, and older immigrants, http://www.hc-sc.gc.ca/index-eng.php.

Metropolis is an international network for comparative research on public policy development on migration, diversity, and immigrant integration in cities in Canada and around the world, http://www.metropolis.net.

References

Agocs, C. 1992. "Race and Ethnic Relations." In J.J. Teevan (ed.), *Introduction to Sociology: A Canadian Focus*, 4th ed. (pp. 237–280). Scarborough: Prentice-Hall.

Albanese, P. 2005. "Ethnic Families." In M. Baker (ed.), *Families: Changing Trends in Canada*, 5th ed. (pp. 121–142). Toronto: McGraw-Hill Ryerson.

Albanese, P. 2009. *Children in Canada Today*. Toronto: Oxford University Press.

Ali, M., with S. Taraban and J. Gill. 2003. "Unaccompanied/Separated Children Seeking Refugee Status in Ontario: A Review of Documented Policies and Practices." Toronto: Joint Centres of Excellence for Research on Immigration and Settlement, CERIS Working paper No. 27.

Ambert, A.M. 2012. *Changing Families: Relationships in Context*, 2nd ed. Toronto: Pearson Education Canada.

Assembly of First Nations. 2006. Fact Sheet: Residential Schools. Retrieved January 19, 2006 from http://www.afn.ca/article.asp?id=766.

Beiser, M. 1999. *Strangers at the Gate: The "Boat People's" First Ten Years in Canada*. Toronto: University of Toronto Press.

Belanger, A., and E.C. Malenfant. 2005. "Ethnocultural Diversity in Canada: Prospects for 2017." *Canadian Social Trends*, Catalogue no. 11-008, Winter: 18–20. Ottawa: Statistics Canada.

Boyd, M. 2000. "Ethnicity and Immigrant Offspring," In M.A. Kalbach and W.E. Kalbach (eds.), *Perspectives on Ethnicity in Canada* (pp. 137–154). Toronto: Harcourt Publishing.

Boyd, M., and M. Vickers. 2000. "100 Years of Immigration." *Canadian Social Trends*, Catalogue no. 11-008, Autumn: 2–12. Ottawa: Statistics Canada.

Canadian Council on Learning. 2009. *The State of Aboriginal Learning in Canada: A Holistic Approach to Measuring Success*. Ottawa, Ontario. Retrieved May 30, 2011 from www.ccl-cca.ca/sal2009.

Castellano, M.B. 2002. *Aboriginal Family Trends: Extended Families, Nuclear Families, Families of the Heart*. Ottawa: The Vanier Institute of the Family.

Das Gupta, T. 2000. "Families of Native People, Immigrants, and People of Colour." In N. Mandell and A. Duffy (eds.), *Canadian Families: Diversity, Conflict, and Change*, 2nd ed. (pp. 146–187). Toronto: Harcourt Brace.

Driedger, L. 2003. *Race and Ethnicity: Finding Identities and Equalities*, 2nd ed. Don Mills: Oxford University Press.

Errington, E.J. 1995. *Wives and Mothers, Schoolmistresses and Scullery Maids: Working Women in Upper Canada, 1790–1840*. Montreal: McGill-Queen's University Press.

Este, D.C., and A. Tachble. 2009. "Fatherhood in the Canadian Context: Perceptions and Experiences of Sudanese Refugee Men." *Sex Roles* 60: 456–466.

Fuller-Thomson, E. 2005. "Canadian First Nations Grandparents Raising Grandchildren: A Portrait in Resilience." *International Journal of Aging and Human Development* 60: 331–342.

Furniss, E. 1995. *Victims of Benevolence: Discipline and Death at the Williams Lake Indian Residential School, 1891–1920*. Williams Lake: Cariboo Tribal Council.

MacDonald, M.A. (1990). *Rebels and Loyalists: The Lives and Material Culture of New Brunswick's Early English-Speaking Settlers, 1758–1783*. Fredericton: New Ireland Press.

McLaren, A., and T. Lou Black. 2005. "Family Class and Immigration in Canada: Implications for Sponsored Elderly Women." Research on Immigration and Integration in the Metropolis, Working Paper Series, no. 05-26. Vancouver: Vancouver Centre of Excellence.

McPherson, B. 2004. *Aging as a Social Process: Canadian Perspectives*. Don Mills: Oxford University Press.

Mitchell, B.A. 2005. "Canada's Growing Visible Minority Population: Generational Challenges, Opportunities, and Federal Policy Considerations" (pp. 51–62). In *Canada 2017: Serving Canada's Multicultural Population for the Future*, Policy Forum

Discussion Papers. Gatineau: The Multiculturalism Program, Department of Canadian Heritage.

Momirov, J., and K.M. Kilbride. 2005. "Family Lives of Native Peoples, Immigrants, and Visible Minorities." In N. Mandell and A. Duffy (eds.), *Canadian Families: Diversity, Conflict, and Change* (pp. 87–111). Toronto: Thomson Nelson.

Nett, E. 1993. *Canadian Families: Past and Present*, 3rd ed. Toronto: Butterworths.

Rosenberg, M.M., and J. Jedwab. 1992. "Institutional Completeness, Ethnic Organizational Style and the Role of the State: The Jewish, Italian, and Greek Communities of Montreal." *Canadian Review of Sociology and Anthropology* 29: 266–287.

Satzewich, V. 1993. "Migrant and Immigrant Families in Canada: State Coercion and Legal Control in the Formation of Ethnic Families." *Journal of Comparative Family Studies* 24: 315–338.

Statistics Canada. 2001. "Aboriginal Peoples in Canada." Ottawa: Minister of Industry.

Statistics Canada. 2005. "Population Projections of Visible Minority Groups, Canada, Provinces, and Regions, 2001–2017." Catalogue no. 91-541-XIE. Ottawa: Minister of Industry.

Statistics Canada. 2006. "E-Stat: Tracking Immigration Trends." Retrieved August 3, 2006 from www.statcan.ca/english/Estat/guide/track.htm.

Statistics Canada. 2010. Visual Census. 2006 Census. Ottawa. Retrieved May 25, 2011 from www.recensement2006.ca/census-recensement/2006.

Thomas, D. 2001. "Evolving Family Living Arrangements of Canada's Immigrants." *Canadian Social Trends* 61 (Summer): 16–22.

Timpson, J. 1995. "Four Decades of Literature on Native Canadian Child Welfare: Changing Themes." *Child Welfare* 74, 3: 525–546.

Trocmé, N., D. Knoke, and C. Blackstock. 2004. "Pathways to the Overrepresentation of Aboriginal Children in Canada's Child Welfare System." *Social Service Review* (December): 577–600.

Wente, M. 2004. "Life under Sharia in Canada?" Retrieved January 25, 2005 from www.youmeworks.com/sharia_canada.html.

Chapter 5

More Than a Labour of Love

Gender and the Cult of Domesticity

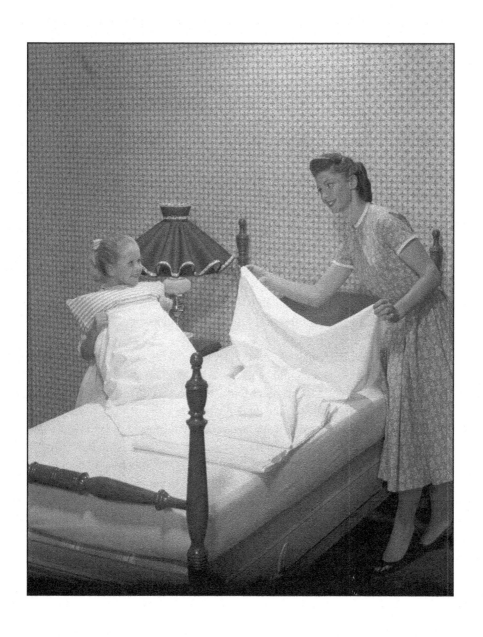

Learning Objectives

In this chapter you will learn that ...
- contemporary patterns of work reflect transformations in the economy and ideologies of motherhood and gender
- unpaid work, such as housework and child care, is a largely invisible, undervalued shadow economy, although critical to the functioning and well-being of society
- patterns of domestic work continue to be highly gendered despite technological advancements, increased male participation, and gains made by women
- the cult of domesticity, with related notions of ideal womanhood, continue to be powerful and pervasive throughout society and solidifies a gender-based power structure
- many families struggle with balancing their family and home life

Introduction

Imagine a situation whereby a full-time housewife and mother attends a corporate social function with her husband. She is asked by one of his co-workers, "Do you work?" What do you think would be her most likely response? Many of us would assume that she would reply with some degree of ambivalence, such as, "Well, I stay at home with my children." Yet, in reality, she does work (and probably more hours than her partner), since when you actually detail what has to happen within any given household to make it run smoothly, it is striking just how much work must actually be done. Indeed, work performed for wages, no matter how menial, is almost always regarded as "work," whereas work performed in the home is often not regarded as "real work" since it is generally taken for granted and invisible.

As you will learn in this chapter, domestic labour is "work" and more than "a labour of love" (Luxton, 1980). It is also highly valuable to families and society—so valuable that the economy would collapse in its absence (Wilson, 1986). It will also be shown that the people who perform most of the unpaid work are women and that they provide a crucial service to society by physically and emotionally nurturing the next generation of workers. In fact, Salary.com has valued the "Mom job" or "Mom's market value" at an annual salary of $138,095, which is well over the average pay of a full-time male worker. This salary encompasses pay for the time that mothers spend performing 10 typical job functions for their families, such as child care, errands, cleaning, laundry, cooking, transportation, and bill paying (Mom.salary.com, 2007). In light of these issues, this chapter will explore the changing and ideological meanings, practices, and work roles of women and men in relation to paid and unpaid labour. Moreover, given men's increasing participation in unpaid work, we will examine the changing division of labour with respect to gendered processes.

Patterns in Labour Force Participation and the "New Economy"

The changing economic role and decision-making power of women is one of the most significant changes in the lives of families over the past century. This transformation is reflected in popular culture and in changes in labour-force participation rates. For example, many of us have seen reruns of two very popular 1950s TV shows called *Leave It to Beaver* and *I Love Lucy*, an era in which it was not normative for married women to work outside the home. While "The Beav's" mother was a seemingly happy housewife, a repeated theme on *I Love Lucy* was Lucy trying to trick her husband Ricky to permit her to work in the paid labour market since she was totally dependent on him for money and status. In one episode, Ricky spanked her (he put her over his knees and hit her on the buttocks) because she had bought some furniture without his permission. Afterwards, he promptly returned the furniture to the store. Ironically, she was the majority owner and power behind the company that produced the show (Liazos, 2004).

Although women have always worked and a proportion has always worked outside their homes, female labour force participation has sharply risen over time. The greatest changes began to occur in the late 1970s when, for the first time, large numbers of married women, including mothers, entered the paid labour force (see Figure 5.1). In 1931, only 3.1 percent of married women had paid jobs, in contrast to 45 percent of the single, divorced, separated, or widowed. Since 1984, married women have been more likely than single women to be in the paid labour force (Crompton and Vickers, 2000). By 2003, 80 percent of married women were in the paid labour force, with the greatest increase among those aged 25–44, or among women most likely to have children at home (Beaujot, 2000; Statistics Canada, 2003). Furthermore, as detailed in Figure 5.2, the employment rate of women with children experienced a large increase between 1976 and 2009, especially among women with children under six years old. In 2009, the employment rate for women with children under six years old was 66.5 percent, up from 31.4 percent in 1976, and 78.5 percent for women with children from 6 to 15 years old, up from 46.4 percent in 1976.

Several reasons are cited for this striking socio-demographic shift. Economic growth in the postwar decades saw a rise in available jobs. The growth of the service sector and public service also expanded opportunities in jobs such as nursing, teaching, and "supportive" clerical and secretarial work, jobs that conformed to the workplace and roles that were historically associated with the home (Ranson, 2005). Further, Baker (2001a) notes that the cost of living increases of the 1960s necessitated two incomes. This was partly due to the economic growth that was accompanied by the availability of new products and the rise of a consumer-oriented culture. It also was a consequence of changes in thinking about how people should be rewarded for their work, whereas before World War Two, men's wages were usually based on their family status, with increases awarded with marriage and the birth of children. During the 1960s and 1970s, unions, professional associations, and feminist groups challenged the practice of not having pay scales based on individual merit. It was also argued that a "family wage" often needed to be earned by more than one person, given changes in the new global economy.

Figure 5.1
Percentage of Canadian Women in the Paid Labour Force, 1931–2003

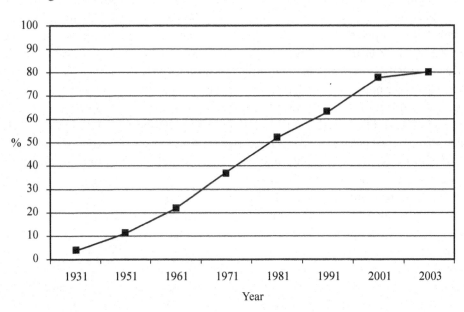

Source: Statistics Canada, "Labour Force Historical Review 2003" (Ottawa: Statistics Canada, 2003). Catalogue no. 71F0004XCB.

Changing ideas about women's roles in society also contributed to the rise in their labour force participation. Women continued to gain political rights throughout the 20th century (e.g., they were allowed to voted federally for the first time in 1921). Also fuelled by the feminist movement, access to paid work, employment equity, and higher education became more available, as well as the right to take a maternity leave and then return to paid work. Dramatic improvements in birth control also occurred when "the pill" was legalized in 1969; the year after Pierre Elliott Trudeau became prime minister. Prior to that time (beginning in 1961), doctors could only "legally" prescribe it to regulate women's menstrual cycle. The increasing tendency for women to remain in paid employment after they had children also contributed to these new patterns (Baker, 2001a; McLaren and McLaren, 1997; Ranson, 2005).

The demands of the new economy also played a role in women's labour force participation. After the 1970s, the service sector expanded, a large segment of which offered only low-paying and part-time jobs, such as in the retail, hotel, and restaurant industry. In 1951 these jobs made up only 18 percent of the labour force, but employed 37 percent by 1995 (Glenday, 1997). Many of these part-time positions are held by women, are less secure and well paid, and do not provide any health or pension benefits and ultimately contribute to poverty. In 2011, approximately one out of five of all Canadian workers aged 15 and over

Figure 5.2
Employment Rate for Women (in Percent), by Age of Youngest Child, 1976–2009

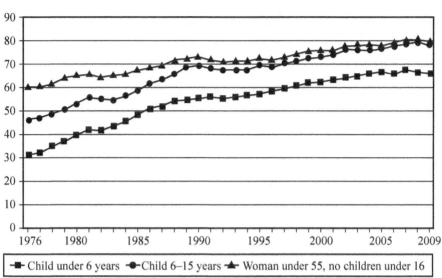

Source: Human Resources and Skills Development Canada (2011). "Women with Children," retrieved from http://www4.hrsdc.gc.ca/.3ndic.1t.4r@-eng.jsp?iid=13.

were employed part-time—28 percent of employed women and 12.1 percent of employed men. Women tend to choose part-time work in order to accommodate family responsibilities, although a significant proportion would prefer full-time jobs (Ambert, 2006). For example, in Table 5.1 we observe that among women aged 25–44 (those most likely to have young children living at home), 34.4 percent report that they work part-time because they also care for children, compared to only 3.5 percent of men in the same age range.

Yet, statistics on unpaid work mask another important type of kin or domestic work termed "spousal career support" (Haas, 1999). This refers to a situation whereby a wife or partner is not formally employed part- or full-time but is very actively involved in supporting the career of her partner. For example, wives may be unpaid "support," "auxiliary," or "enabler" workers in their husbands' careers. This may entail doing some of the same work that the partner is doing or work that would otherwise be hired out by their partner's business, such as bookkeeping, scheduling, or maintaining an office. Wives may also provide emotional support when times are tough, as well as other types of enabling assistance such as volunteering or entertaining their husbands' colleagues in order to bring prestige to their work reputation (Seccombe and Warner, 2004). They may also run their own home businesses in order to better accommodate their family and work roles, including their husbands' careers.

Table 5.1
Reasons for Part-Time Work by Sex, Ages 25–44, 2011

	Total	Males	Females
Own illness	2.8	4.5	2.2
Caring for children	26.5	3.6	34.4
Other personal/family responsibilities	3.5	1.9	4.1
Going to school	11.8	20.5	8.8
Personal preference	15.1	15.2	15.1
Other voluntary	3.4	5.3	2.7
Other*	36.9	49.0	32.6
Total employed part-time (thousands)	928.9	238.6	690.3
% Employed part-time**	12.4	6.1	19.5

*Includes business conditions and unable to find full-time work.

**Expressed as a percentage of total employed.

Source: Adapted from Statistics Canada, CANSIM (2011): Table 282-0014 and 282-001 and Catalogue no. 89F0133XIE, retrieved January 29, 2012 from http://www40.statcan.ca/l01/cst01/labor63a-eng.htm.

Furthermore, some women may find themselves in complex "marriage contracts" in which they engage in family household labour that is heavy or extends to a wide variety of activities. For example, Machum (2002) documents the situation of farm wives who perform a triple day of work compared to their urban counterparts' double day. These wives work at jobs off the farm, directly on the farm for production, and do the reproductive work of child-bearing, child-rearing, and domestic chores. These domestic activities might include growing, canning, and freezing vegetables and raising animals such as chickens, tasks that subsidize the farm unit by reducing the cash needs of the family. Yet, state policy has tended to reinforce the inequity of their situation by treating this work as not "real work," since traditionally it was considered a domestic service to their husbands.

Unpaid Work, the Shadow Economy, and the Ideology of Separate Spheres

While paid work is easy to identify and define, Beaujot (2000) and Luxton (1997) observe that the concept of unpaid work involves a diversity of meanings and forms, making it difficult to measure (see Box 5.1). The work that goes into creating a special family occasion—such as baking a birthday cake, for instance—can be seen as having no special monetary value because it comes with no monetary reward. It can also be viewed as a form of love, enjoyment, or caring work that has strong sentimental value. Yet, it can also be perceived as a type of drudgery that is valued as the material that "makes family."

Although there is a lack of consensus as to what should constitute unpaid work, many individuals and organizations have tried to give it a monetary value by estimating its replacement or fair market value (i.e., what these services would cost to purchase if hiring a third person). For example, some have estimated that in Canada, unpaid work is worth up to $319 million in the money economy or 41 percent of GDP (gross domestic product). Globally, the numbers skyrocket to $11 trillion U.S. (Waring, 2006).

Box 5.1
Measuring Unpaid Work

Meg Luxton, author of the classic work, *More than a Labour of Love: Three Generations of Women's Work in the Home* (Toronto: The Women's Press, 1980), has examined the ways in which unpaid work is measured and valued, as well as the implications for women, families, and any social policies based on them. Below find an excerpt from a journal article based on her research, which highlights the difficulty in measuring unpaid work:

In contrast to paid employment where the divisions of labour and the hours of work are clearly (and usually contractually) known, domestic labour is task-oriented and the tasks involved can vary significantly in the amount of time they take each time they are done and in the frequency with which they are done. Because it is an informal work process that is often done alone, with no standards regulated and enforced by an employer, and because it encompasses the activities of making a home and caring for the people who live there, domestic labour is difficult to measure. Where restaurant workers may be told exactly what motions to use and how much time to spend producing a drink for a customer…, making a cup of tea at home may vary quite a bit each time so that a respondent may be unable to give anything more accurate than a rough guess … Because it is unregulated, people doing domestic labour have no reason to pay close attention to the amount of time tasks take and they often underestimate time spent in familiar activities. They may be relatively unaware of even doing some tasks, either because they are so automatic, like locking the door at night, or because they do not really feel like work— for example when a woman associates preparing a meal with time-consuming effort and so dismisses the act of preparing cereal, milk, and toast (Luxton, 1980, p. 142).

Source: Luxton, M. 1997. "The UN, women, and household labour: Measuring and valuing unpaid work." *Women's Studies International Forum*, 20: 434.

It has taken many years for governments to measure the hours dedicated to unpaid work. The 1996 Canadian Census was the first to collect data on unpaid work in response to mounting pressure that women's contributions to society were overlooked and devalued (see Box 5.2). The collection of these data marked a major breakthrough for feminists across the country and provided an example for other countries around the world. And more recently, Statistics Canada recognized and measured unpaid work that is not paid (but does not include volunteer work) by dividing it into three categories: housework, care of children, and care and assistance for seniors. Yet, although unpaid work is increasingly recognized as critical to the functioning and well-being of our society, many critical theorists and feminists argue that much unpaid work remains taken for granted, invisible, and undervalued.

It is suggested that an ideology of separate spheres operates in the designation of paid activity in the public sphere of work or the formal economy such that it is perceived as real "work." Whereas this work is highly valued (and enumerated), activities pursued in the private domestic sphere—activities that reproduce, support, and sustain others—are usually overlooked and not counted in labour force statistics or other economic indicators. This is illustrated in the case of "two typical working women" (see Box 5.3). As a result, patterns of normative thought or social ideology obscure the extent and value of these contributions. And since women perform most of these activities, they are particularly disadvantaged.

Box 5.2
The Canadian Census and Unpaid Work

Debate over the devalued perception of domestic work created quite a stir in Canada a few years back. In 1991 a Canadian housewife took issue with a question on her census questionnaire that asked, "How many hours did you work in the last week, not including volunteer work, housework, [home] maintenance or repairs?" (Smith, 1996). She had run her household for 19 years, raising three children in the process, and she was furious that her hard work was considered irrelevant. So she refused to fill out the questionnaire, a crime according to Canadian law. Under threat of prosecution, she embarked on a protest campaign, which eventually drew in women from all over the country. She formed a group called the Canadian Alliance for Home Managers, which threatened to boycott the next census if unpaid work remained uncounted. Five years later, Canada became the first country in the world to count on its national census the hours spent performing household labour and child care without pay.

Source: Cited in Newman, D.M. and L. Grauerholz. *Sociology of Families*, 2nd ed. Thousand Oaks: Pine Forge Press (p. 310).

Box 5.3
Two Unpaid Working Women: Let's Meet Two "Typical" Women

Tendai
Consider Tendai, a young girl in the Lowveld, in Zimbabwe. Her day starts at 4 a.m. when, to fetch water, she carries a thirty-litre tin to a borehole about 11 kilometres from her home. She walks barefoot and is home by 9 a.m. She eats a little and proceeds to fetch firewood until midday. She cleans the utensils from the family's morning meal and sits preparing a lunch of sadza for the family. After lunch and the cleaning of the dishes, she wanders into the hot sun until early evening, fetching wild vegetables for supper before making the evening trip for water. Her day ends at 9 p.m. after she has prepared supper and put her younger brothers and sisters to sleep. Tendai is considered unproductive, unoccupied, and economically inactive. According to the international economic system, Tendai does not work and is not part of the labour force.

Cathy
Cathy, a young, middle-class North American housewife, spends her days preparing food; setting the table; serving meals; clearing food and dishes from the table; washing dishes; dressing her children; disciplining children; taking her children to day-care or school; disposing of garbage; dusting; gathering clothes for washing; doing the laundry; going to the gas station and the supermarket; repairing household items; ironing; keeping an eye on or playing with the children; making beds; paying bills; caring for pets and plants; putting away toys, books, and clothes; sewing or mending or knitting; talking with door-to-door salespeople; answering the telephone; vacuuming, sweeping and washing floors; cutting the grass, weeding, and shovelling snow; cleaning the bathroom and the kitchen; and putting her children to bed. Cathy has to face the fact that she fills her time in a totally unproductive manner. She…is economically inactive, and economists record her as unoccupied.

Source: Waring, M. 2006. "Women and unpaid work." *Women and the Economy.* Retrieved February 10, 2006 from www.unpac.ca/economy/unpaidwork.html.

It is also asserted that women's greater participation in unpaid work results in a state of "lesser citizenship" or marginalization such that they are more likely to live in poverty and have their own health compromised (Angus, 1994). For example, full-time stay-at-home mothers may suffer from low self-esteem because their tremendous social contributions are devalued. Also, since unpaid work is unpaid, many women must take on paid work, which can be highly stressful, yet it is also recognized that there are many benefits of unpaid work that outweigh monetary gain. Taking time to raise one's own children, for instance, is an experience that many women find thoroughly rewarding and satisfying.

From the Washboard and Broom to Kenmore and Hoover: The Evolution of Housework Over Time

The role of homemaker is commonly described as a woman's "traditional role" in society, yet this is a misperception since it was only during a relatively short time period (from about 1920–1960) that most married women were, or wanted to be, full-time housewives. Indeed it was not until the middle of the 20th century that the word "housework" came into existence. During this era, most households had some labour-saving appliances, such as washing machines, vacuum cleaners, and refrigerators. Prepared food, including canned food, was usually available, saving many hours of preparation time. For the first time in history, women could spend time on child care and household management (Eshleman and Wilson, 2001). Prior to the advent of "labour-saving devices," housework was physically demanding and labour-intensive. For example, swollen joints, sprained wrists, skin rubbed raw, and eternally chapped hands were some of the "joys" of doing a heavy wash on washboards and in tubs and of wringing clothes by hand (Horsfield, 1997).

At the turn of the 19th century, most Canadian families lived in rural areas, and relied on farming or a combination of paid employment (e.g., lumbering or mining) and farming. A strong sense of interdependence characterized pre-industrial family life, and family members worked together to produce much of what they needed. During industrialization and urbanization, many families were drawn away from rural life and into cities. Women continued the time-consuming and physically taxing work of feeding, clothing, and caring for family members. However, whereas many of these activities had been shared on farms (albeit still gendered), household jobs increasingly became a woman's sole duty (Wilson, 1986). In short, industrialization minimized women's involvement in the market economy and "converted them into dependent homemakers with their home-based work confined to the domestic realm" (McDaniel and Tepperman, 2004: 240).

"Housework" and "housewife" became synonymous by the middle of the 20th century and cultural ideologies supported the view that women were "naturally" suited for housework and motherhood. This perpetuated a *cult of domesticity*. As Eshleman and Wilson (2001: 69) note, "these jobs became thought of as part of what women *were*, not what they *did*." Advertising industries played an influential role in reinforcing a traditional division of labour in the home. Magazines were strongly affected by the rising growth of these industries and began to actively promote consumption; the "model" or "Stepford" housewife; and the immaculate home, prominently featuring the latest in home appliances. These new devices also fed into the increasing paranoia about domestic cleanliness that emerged in the early decades of the 20th century. This "scientization" of housework also occurred in response to a better understanding of germs and disease, improved sanitation, and attention to hygiene (Horsfield, 1997; McDaniel and Tepperman, 2004; Wilson, 1986).

Ironically, the term "labour-saving device" turned out to be an oxymoron. Although these devices altered the nature of work and made it less physically taxing on some levels, many sources document that they have not dramatically reduced the overall amount of work spent on housework. It is also observed that housekeeping standards have gone up. With respect to washing machines, some studies show that the time devoted to laundry actually increased over time. In many pioneer or pre-industrial households, for instance, laundry was done only four times per year (Eichler, 1983). It is purported that time usage rises because the machines make it possible to have clean sheets once (or twice) a week if we so choose, to do laundry daily, to wear clothes once—all practices that would have been unheard of in previous times.

Similarly, vacuum cleaners allow us to achieve dust-free wall-to-wall carpets, a task that when taken on regularly and seriously is just as time-consuming as the sweeping of floors and beating of rugs was for earlier generations. According to an article in *Ladies' Home Journal* in 1930, "Because we housewives of today have the tools to reach it, we dig every day after the dust that grandmothers had left to a spring cataclysm" (cited in Horsfield, 1997: 136).

The Changing Nature and Perceptions of Child Care
Child care, which is often subsumed under the label "housework," has also changed in dramatic ways. Up until the 1970s, women had more children (and usually at an earlier age) as well as at shorter intervals than they do now. In other words, we have moved from baby boom to baby bust. Moreover, an increasing number of preschool children receive some form of child care, defined by Statistics Canada as care not from their mother, father, or guardian. Slightly more than half (53 percent) of all Canadian children aged six months to five years are in some form of child care, such as daycare centres, or are cared for by a relative (Statistics Canada, 2005). This trend represents a shift in social attitudes toward women's work, since there had been a long-standing assumption that children are "best off at home, looked after by their mothers." In fact, daycare centres were established only when it was seen to benefit society and to accommodate the need for mothers to join the paid workforce (Ward, 2002: 263).

Despite the greater need for, and availability of child care services, many Canadians complain that our current system of daycare is ineffective. Public concerns often focus on long waiting lists, a lack of regulation standards, few options for parents in non-standard employment (e.g., shift work) or with special needs children, and inadequate government subsidization. Sitter care, for instance, is unregulated by any level of government, yet it remains the most prevalent type of care for employed parents. And while since the 1960s governments have subsidized child-care spaces for low-income and single-parent families, there are often insufficient spaces for eligible families and two-parent families with high incomes must pay the full cost. A notable exception is Quebec, which, unlike other provinces, offers heavily subsidized child care for all parents who need it, regardless of their household income or work status, at a cost to parents of only $7 per day (Baker, 2008).

Many advocacy groups and organizations (e.g., Code Blue) assert that that we need a universal early childhood education and care system that is available to all parents, regardless of their work status, income, ethnicity, ability/disability. A national, universal system would entail federal leadership, including making this a central election issue combined with legislation setting out the principles of high-quality, affordable public and non-profit

Box 5.4
Statement on Child Care: REAL Women of Canada

REAL Women of Canada is concerned about women and the care and well-being of the family. We believe the ideal situation, even in a changing world, is that every family, who so chooses, would be able to look after their children in their own home. This means that women should have a genuine choice, financially and socially, to remain at home as full-time mothers, if they so choose, especially when their children are young.

In our policy on tax reform, we have proposed specific changes to the tax base to offer this choice to women. A full-time mother makes a magnificent contribution to society and this must be recognized and acknowledged by society, both socially and financially.

We do **not** support the premise that women who stay at home to raise their children are not being fulfilled. On the contrary, for those women who choose this career choice, being a full-time mother is a long-term investment in the well-being of their children and in the future stability of the next generation. A full-time mother makes a significant contribution to society by contributing psychologically and emotionally to the well-being of her children and also economically in that her full-time care of the child negates the need and costs of outside daycare services.

REAL Women of Canada recognizes that today, because of economic necessity and social pressures, paid child care is often an essential and invaluable service. Therefore, we propose that, whenever and wherever parents require paid child care, it be of the highest possible quality. We believe that it should be the parents' right to choose the kind and location of child care that best accommodates their family value system and the particular needs of their child, whether it is government-subsidized or not. Furthermore, for many women it is a challenging, creative and rewarding career.

REAL Women of Canada does not support the concept of universally available, government-subsidized daycare. Universal daycare is an imposed government plan of institutional care for children. Studies show that for young children, the family setting is usually preferable.

We do **not** believe that it is a "fundamental right" for all women, regardless of circumstances, to have universal daycare, but rather daycare should be available according to need.

We believe, therefore, that child care funds should be paid **directly** to the parents to allow them to choose the kind of care of their children, whether home, private or institutional care. **Equal** child care tax credits should be paid to parents regardless of which type of care they choose— whether home care or substitute care.

Child care funds should provide for a flexible system. A flexible plan should, however, reject a policy of so-called "national standards" which would result in the elimination of private arrangements such as family members or church-based or neighbourhood arrangements which may be preferable for some families. Government-funded satellite child care should be made available to provide supervision,

and learning facilities (toys, equipment, books) to small neighbourhood arrangements. Neighbourhood drop-in centres could be available to provide after school
supervision and activities, or to accommodate parents on shift work. It could also
serve as a resource centre to provide educational and social support for families.

Source: Retrieved from REAL Women of Canada: Canada's Alternative Woman's Movement,
Statement on Child Care, 2011, http://www.realwomenca.com/page/statechildcare.html.

services that meet both parents' and children's needs (Code Blue, 2011). Yet, other groups
(e.g. REAL Women of Canada; see Box 5.4) do not support the concept of a universally
available, government-subsidized daycare, which they view as an imposed government
plan of institutional care for children. Instead, they argue that parents should be able to
more freely choose the kind of care they need. In particular, they support the idea of direct
payments to the family. These would provide the flexibility of keeping its child support
monies for a parent to stay in the home or to spend on daycare, whether government- or
community-operated or private (such as a nanny or relative), or a combination of the above.

Furthermore, many would assume that the trend toward having fewer children and
the growing popularity of daycare translate to a reduction in this type of domestic work.
However, many studies find that the nature of child care has altered and the time spent on
each child has expanded. This is partly because mothers have been increasingly "advised"
by experts on the crucial and extensive nature of their parenting activities. Consequently,
women spend more time keeping children's teeth clean, driving their children around,
making their beds and lunches, and worrying about the emotional consequences of their
toilet-training techniques, reward systems, or sugar intake (Armstrong and Armstrong,
1984; Luxton, 1980). And in a consumer-oriented society, children are less likely to
economically contribute to the household than in the past, which means more time spent
trying to meet children's needs for a vast array of goods and services (Ward, 2002).

You've Come a Long Way, Baby? Contemporary Patterns of Domestic Work
Studies document that women continue to do most of the housework and child care, regardless of their rising labour force participation, as illustrated in Table 5.2. Ironically, this shift
toward maternal employment has occurred at a time when the care of small children has
become more labour intensive and the pressure on women as mothers has risen (Hays, 1996).
According to Ambert (2006), the net result of this trend is what sociologist Arlie Hochschild,
with Machung (1989), calls the second shift. In other words, although society has become
more liberal with respect to women's status and role in the workplace, this development has
not been accompanied by a similarly liberating one on the home front (also see Box 5.6 for
a discussion on beliefs versus feelings with respect to gender ideology and the second shift).

In the "second shift," women arrive home from work, only to continue to work, doing
chores such as cooking, cleaning, laundry, and preparing school lunches for the next

Box 5.5 and Photo
Code Blue Statement for Child Care: Good Child Care Makes Canada More Democratic

Released Tuesday, April 5, 2011
A national child care program is fundamental to a democratic Canada, says Code Blue for ChildCare, a cross-Canada campaign to make child care a central issue in this federal election. The Code Blue coalition will join with other groups to support the Day for Democracy activities on Wednesday, April 6. "Good child care promotes and exemplifies democracy in action," said Shellie Bird, Ottawa coordinator of Code Blue. "A universal, public early childhood education and care system provides an environment where children and adults practice respect for diversity and social inclusion. It is also a community institution in its own right, and critical to women's equality."A key principle that unites the groups in the Code Blue campaign is that Canada's national child care system must be built on publicly managed, democratically controlled services.

"Child care is not a business," said Sue Delanoy of the Child Care Advocacy Association of Canada. "When child care is run as a business, decisions are made by owners and shareholders—not by the community and parents. The priority is making a profit—not quality services or children's well-being. This flies in the face of democratic participation and the public interest." Code Blue says a national child care program is not only the "smart thing" for a society to put in place but also the "right thing"—a human right and a child's right. The coalition's goal is to elect a federal government that will commit to developing an early childhood education and care system available to all families of young children in Canada. Code Blue brings together national and provincial/territorial child care organizations, labour and women's organizations, and social justice and anti-poverty groups— Canadians from all walks of life.

Source: Code Blue Statement for ChildCare, retrieved from: www.womensequality.ca/Images%20 PDFs%202011/Day%20for%20Democracy%20CB%20statement%20final.pdf; photo from Code Blue web site homepage, "About Code Blue for Childcare," buildchildcare.ca/about (note: photo not copyrighted).

Box 5.6
The Second Shift, Gender Ideology, and Feeling Rules

When I began this research, I naively imagined that a person's **gender ideology** (or a set of beliefs about men and women and marital or partnership roles) would cohere as a cognitive and emotional "piece." I imagined a man's gender ideology would "determine" how he wanted to divide the second shift. Couples with more egalitarian ideas about men and women would share more, those with less traditional ideas, less. But I discovered that the set of ideas a person has about gender are often fractured and incoherent. Peter Tanagawa supported his wife's career "a hundred percent," but grew red in the face at the idea that she would mow the lawn, or that his daughters, when teenagers, would drive a car to school. Many men like Evan Holt ideologically supported the idea of their wives working. They pointed out that they wanted their wives to work. It made their wives more interesting, and it gave the couple more in common. But when it came to a man's part in the work at home, the underlying principle changed. For Robert Myerson the principle seemed to be that a man should share the work at home "if his wife asks him." Peter Tanagawa seemed to say a man should share the work at home if he's as good at it or as interested in it as his wife.

  More important than the surface fractures in gender ideology, though, were the contradictions between what a person said they believed about men and marital roles and what they seemed to feel about them. Some people were egalitarian "on top" and traditional "underneath" like Seth Stein or traditional on top and egalitarian underneath like Frank Delacorte...In each instance, what's involved is a person's gender ideology...and the emotional meanings it evokes, which in turn reinforces or undermines that ideology...All told, what John thought (his gender ideology) was only one small part of the explanation of why he divided the work at home as he did. His gender ideology gave coherence and reason to his biographically derived feelings and his social opportunities, even as it also cloaked these.

Source: Hochschild, A.R. with Machung, A. 1989. *The Second Shift.* New York: Avon (pp. 198–200).

day. And while many women actively adopt strategies to change gender roles in the household or by "supermoming," many men continue to alternate between periods of co-operation and resistance. For example, Hochschild, with Machung, (1989: 211) illustrates how some men used a resistance strategy of "needs reduction." This is shown in the case of a salesman and father of two, who explained that he never shopped because "he didn't need anything." He also didn't need to take his clothes to the laundry to be ironed because he didn't mind wearing a wrinkled shirt. Through his reduction of needs, this man created a great void into which his wife stepped with her "greater need" to buy important items, see him wear an ironed shirt, and so on.

Table 5.2
Average Time Spent per Day on Child Care Activities, Canada, 2010*

Respondent's child's age group and employment status	Primary activities			Primary and simultaneous activities		
	Both sexes	Male	Female	Both sexes	Male	Female
	Hours and Minutes					
Children 12 years old or under	2:05	1:23	2:43	3:31	2:18	4:34
Full time work	1:38	1:20	2:04	2:44	2:14	3:28
Part time work	2:39	1:21 E	2:50	4:42	2:25 E	5:01
Other	3:23	1:58	3:45	5:38	3:10	6:16
Youngest child is less than 5 years old	2:49	1:51	3:35	4:52	3:07	6:33
Full time work	2:13	1:46	3:02	3:46	2:59	5:13
Part time work	3:20	F	3:38	6:09	2:41 E	6:43
Other	4:25	2:51	4:46	7:36	4:42 E	8:15
Youngest child is 5 to 12 years old	1:16	0:48	1:38	1:59	1:18	2:32
Full time work	1:00	0:46	1:17	1:37	1:16	2:02
Part time work	1:47	F	1:53	2:54	2:00 E	3:01
Other	2:01	1:04 E	2:18	2:59	1:37 E	3:25

E = use with caution
F = too unreliable to publish
Note: Average time spent is the average over a 7-day week
Source: Statistics Canada, General Social Survey, 2010

*Refers to population aged 15 and over with children aged 12 years or under, by primary and simultaneous activities, sex, child's age group, and employment status

Source: Statistics Canada (2011). "Highlights, Paid Work and Related Activities," Table 2, retrieved from http://www.statcan.gc.ca/pub/89-647-x/2011001/tbl/tbl2-eng.htm.

Although women generally perform more domestic labour than men, it is important to recognize that fathers have always been involved in certain domestic tasks, such as household and car maintenance and repairs and mowing the lawn. Men are also participating more in non-traditional tasks than in the past, particularly in core household activities such as cooking, cleaning, and daily child care (Sayer, 2005). For example, in Figure 5.3 we see that the proportion of Canadian men and women doing some house-work increased from 72 percent in 1986 to 79 percent in 2005. This increase is largely attributable to men, whose participation rose from 54 percent to 69 percent, whereas women's rate remained steady at about 90 percent. It is also interesting to note that while women are more likely to perform these tasks, their time spent doing them has declined slightly since 1996. And, not surprising, higher personal income (for either sex) is related to spending more time at a job and less on housework. Wives with incomes of $100,000 or more also tend to split housework equally with their husbands (Marshall, 2006).

Moreover, men are also increasingly likely to become custodial parents or to co-parent in the case of separation or divorce (Ward, 2002). In particular, when mothers are employed, fathers tend to do more around the house and play a greater role in the care of children. Yet, while important progress has occurred, fathers are shown to have more leisure time per day than married and single mothers also employed full-time (Daly, 2000). For example, mothers on average spend about three more hours per day on unpaid work

Figure 5.3
Gender Differences in Unpaid Work* (Housework), 1986 and 2005

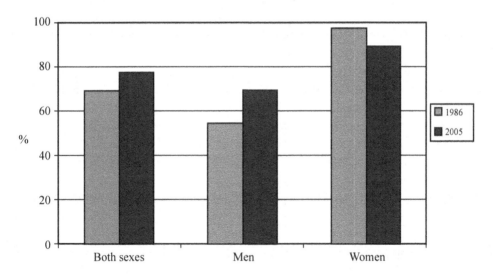

*Proportion (in percentage) of those who did some housework (e.g., meal preparation, meal cleanup, indoor cleaning, laundry, taking out garbage); based on Statistics Canada, General Social Survey data.

Source: Adapted from K. Marshall, "Converging Gender Roles," Perspectives on Labour and Economics 7, no. 7: Chart C. Retrieved August 3, 2006, from www.statcan.ca/english/freepub/75-001-XIE/10706/art-1.htm.

and three hours less per day on paid work than fathers (Fast et al., 2001). Furthermore, women are more likely than men to take maternity leave and to take time off work for family reasons (Ambert, 2006).

"A Woman's Place Is in the Home": Gender Ideologies, Stepford Wives, and the Cult of Domesticity

Despite considerable change and functioning of Canadian families, certain ideas about women's domesticity remain entrenched in the public mind. These ideas are also reflected in the way that social scientists have theorized the gendered division of labour. Many classical theorists, such as Durkheim and Marx, generally ignored the interrelationship of the private and public spheres of work and women's contributions to society. For Marx, the sphere of economic production structured the totality of social relations. As a result, the reproductive or family sphere was the subordinate sphere, including the domestic or unpaid work that occurred in families (Beaujot, 2000).

Sociologists did not study unpaid work in the household systematically until the 1970s. This interest was also prompted by such books as Betty Friedan's *The Feminine Mystique* (1963). This classic work contributed to the second phase of the feminist movement since it identified the isolation of the suburban housewife and her lack of meaningful work as major causes of women's malaise and oppression (Baker, 2001b).

Traditionally, sociologists assumed a sexual division of labour was a necessary feature of family life because it established a mutual dependency among family members. As covered in Chapter 2, structural-functionalist Talcott Parsons was particularly influential in this regard, and his analysis of American middle-class family life had an enormous impact on the way that sociologists (who were predominantly men) thought about family interaction (Wilson, 1986). Parsons assumed that because of their early biological tie with children, women were better suited to provide affective support or the expressive function. Conversely, because men were more experienced in the public sphere, they were better suited to perform the task of relating the family to society or the instrumental role.

There have been many variants of "anatomy-as-destiny"–type theories, all of which assume that sex differences are rooted in the biological tie between mothers and infants. Yet, many of these ideas have been strongly criticized by feminists, who argue that these explanations ignore the economic dependence of women on men and other dimensions of power relations and sexual inequality. Moreover, these "explanations" are ideological in the sense that they support a belief system that rationalizes women's secondary status in the paid labour force (Wilson, 1986). They also justify (rather than explain) men's resistance to do more unpaid work because women are deemed "better suited" to perform certain kinds of work (e.g., daycare, secretarial work), which also tend to be low-paid.

Furthermore, these theories ignore how socialization processes, including systems of indoctrination and patriarchy, contribute to create a gendered division of labour and the "cult of domesticity." The expectation that mothers willingly remain the primary caretakers of their children at all costs is an example of one societal-wide norm. According to Gustafson (2005), this deeply entrenched assumption advantages fathers by removing restrictions on their parental obligations, thus allowing them more flexibility, freedom, and control. Moreover, many structural barriers continue to exist that prevent men from equal parenting or splitting domestic work 50/50. For example, men who choose to take paternity leave, become stay-at-home dads, or who do housework may be teased or ridiculed by co-workers, friends, or spouses, as commonly depicted in popular media (see Figure 5.4). As a result, they may not feel competent enough to take on these responsibilities as a result of gender stereotyping.

Figure 5.4
A Media Depiction of Men and Housework

Source: CartoonStock.com

Summary

This chapter has examined a fundamental feature of daily life for Canadians—work, and the paid and unpaid work that it takes to sustain families. Although unpaid work remains a "shadow economy," it is necessary for the functioning of the rest of society. Although largely invisible, our monetary economy is dependent on this reproductive and caregiving work for the health, well-being, and very existence of the paid workforce. Moreover, these two categories of work entail both "earning and caring" and decisions about "who does what" are influenced by expectations of appropriate roles for men and women (Beaujot, 2000). These expectations about gender operate on many levels, beginning with the individual and ending with societal institutions (Ranson, 2005). In the words of one (anonymous) woman, "Society views domestic labour as women's responsibility and assumes that it is a donation they should make to the economy" (cited in Waring, 2006). Thus, work is more than the performance of basic tasks—it is also a symbolic expression of gendered relations in society.

It is shown that work roles are changing and becoming more demanding. They are also strongly influenced by opportunities (and constraints) for alternative behaviours, such as the pay structure of the formal labour market, workplace support, child care availability, and government programs and policy, such as parental leave (Beaujot, 2000; Ranson, 2005). This contributes to gendered inequities such as the wage gap, a term that refers to the lower overall earning power of women relative to men, resulting in the need for women to work longer hours than men to earn the same amount.

Furthermore, during times of economic restructuring and cutbacks in globalizing Western democracies, privatization of care and primacy to intergenerational relations means that women do even more of the "dirty work" (as well as child care and emotional work). Ironically, this additional unpaid work further devalues paid caregiving. Consequently, women are serving as "ambulance attendants," picking up the bits and pieces of caring and intergenerational continuity as they "tumble out" of contemporary changes (McDaniel, 2002). Therefore, for women to move to full citizenship, the conditions by which men and women share responsibilities as social and political actors will need significant transformation (McDaniel, 2002; Voet, 1998).

In conclusion, thinking about how families divide their labour is a good way to understand the interrelationships among domestic life, ideologies, practices of "doing gender," and the economy. Although women have made significant gains in the labour market, the division of work remains unequal and inequitable. In short, this domain reflects a "stalled revolution" (Hochschild, with Machung, 1989). Indeed, the economy continues to rely heavily on women to volunteer their time by "picking up the slack"—that is, by mopping floors, cooking, caring for children, husbands, the elderly, and so on. Yet, despite the significance of this caring work, these contributions keep women "looking through the kitchen window" and on the margins of the public sphere.

Questions for Critical Reflection and Debate

1. Debate the following: Earnings outside the home should determine who does the housework and child care.
2. Critically analyze the popular notion that women are "naturally inclined" to cook, clean, and raise children with respect to how this ideology is used to justify gender inequality.
3. How are families portrayed on prime-time television with respect to the division of labour, and how has this changed over time? Do these portrayals influence gender role socialization and workplace inequality?
4. Discuss linkages among gendered patterns of family work and other societal institutions, such as religion, politics, and education.
5. Do you think that men and women will ever share paid and unpaid work equally? Outline barriers to "equal parenting," or the idea that couples should split child care and other household responsibilities 50/50.

Glossary

Cult of domesticity developed as the family lost its function as an economic unit and supports the ideology that a woman's place was in the home and she should therefore tend the "home sweet home."

Family work includes all of the tasks and activities required to maintain and reproduce families, such as child-rearing, child care, and housework, as well as coordinating paid and unpaid work activities.

Gender ideology is a set of beliefs about men and women and marital or partnership roles.

Ideology of separate spheres relates to the idea that paid activity in the public sphere is viewed as "work," whereas activity in the private sphere tends to remain invisible and undervalued.

Second shift is a term used to refer to the household and child-care tasks that working women perform after a day of paid work.

Unpaid work, according to Statistics Canada, is work that is not paid (but does not include volunteer work), and is divided into three categories: housework, care of children, and care and assistance for seniors.

Wage gap refers to the lower overall earning power of women relative to men, resulting in the need for women to work longer hours to earn the same amount as men.

Further Reading

Antonopoulos, R., and I. Hirway. 2010. *Unpaid work and the Economy: Gender, Time Use and Poverty in Developing Countries*. New York: Palgrave. Investigates the intersections of income poverty, unpaid work, and women's overtaxed time with a focus on Africa, Latin America, and Asia.

Hochschild, A. 2012. *The Second Shift: Working Families and the Revolution at Home*, 3rd ed. New York: Penguin Books. A newly revised version of Hochschild's classical study on the challenges that women in dual-career households continue to face in combining paid work with unpaid work.

Ranson, G. 2010. *Against the Grain: Couples, Gender, and the Reframing of Parenting*. Toronto: University of Toronto Press. Based on qualitative interviews with 32 families across Canada, this book explores the experiences of mothers and fathers who have adopted unconventional gender scripts, household responsibilities, and parenting roles.

Romeo, M. 2011. *The Maid's Daughter: Living Inside and Outside the American Dream*. New York: New York University Press. The moving story of Olivia, the Mexican daughter of a live-in maid to a wealthy American family who is raised alongside the other children of the family. Reveals the hidden costs of paid domestic labour that are transferred to the families of private household workers and nannies.

Sangster, J. 2010. *Transforming Labour: Women and Work in Postwar Canada*. Toronto: University of Toronto Press. Using case studies from across Canada, this book examines a range of themes, including women's experiences within unions, Aboriginal women's changing patterns of work, and the challenges faced by immigrant women. Challenges the stereotype of the postwar era as one of conformity, domesticity for women, and feminist inactivity.

Smith, J.A. 2009. *The Daddy-Shift: How Stay-at-home Dads, Breadwinning Moms, and Shared Parenting are Transforming the American Family*. Boston: Beacon Press. Explores the meanings and social/economic developments that have made it possible for fathers to become more involved in the raising of their children.

Treas, J., and S. Drobnic (Eds.). 2010. *Dividing the Domestic: Men, Women and Household Work in Cross-National Perspective*. Palo Alto, Calif.: Stanford University Press. Investigates how culture and country characteristics permeate our households and private lives and influence family and gender relations, inequality, and the division of household work.

Related Web Sites

Canadian Council on Social Development offers research and resources on policy aspects related to families and the economy, www.ccsd.ca.

Centre for Work, Families, and Well-Being is a research centre at the University of Guelph that offers statistics on work, family, and well-being, www.worklifecanada.ca.

Childcare Resource and Research Unit is at the University of Toronto, and provides national and international studies and resources on child care and family leave, in addition to other work-related material, www.childcarecanada.org. Facebook: Childcare Resource and Research Unit

National Council of Women in Canada, founded in 1893, provides policy briefs and reports and works to improve the conditions of life for women and families, www.ncwc.ca. Facebook: National Council of Women in Canada

Statistics Canada's web site contains summary trends on labour force participation and unpaid work patterns by gender (search under "The People," Canada e-book), www.statcan.gc.ca.

Women and the Economy provides statistics and information on several topics germane to unpaid work, www.unpac.ca/economy.

References

Ambert, A.-M. 2006. *Changing Families: Relationships in Context*, 2nd ed. Toronto: Pearson.

Angus, J. 1994. "Women's Paid/Unpaid Work and Health: Exploring the Social Context of Everyday Life." *Canadian Journal of Nursing Research* 26: 23–42.

Armstrong, P., and H. Armstrong. 1984. *Labour Pains: Women's Work in Crisis*. Toronto: The Women's Press.

Baker, M. 2001a. "Paid and Unpaid Work: How Do Families Divide Their Labour?" In M. Baker (ed.), *Families: Changing Trends in Canada*, 4th ed. (pp. 96–115). Whitby: McGraw-Hill Ryerson.

Baker, M. 2001b. *Families, Labour, and Love: Family Diversity in a Changing World*. Vancouver: University of British Columbia Press.

Baker, M. 2008. "Families and Intimate Relationships." In L. Tepperman, J. Curtis, and P. Albnese (eds.), *Sociology: A Canadian Perspective,* 2nd ed. (pp. 220–243). Toronto: Oxford University Press.

Beaujot, R. 2000. *Earning and Caring in Canadian Families*. Peterborough: Broadview Press.

Crompton, S., and M. Vickers. 2000. "One Hundred Years of Labour Force Participation." *Canadian Social Trends* (Spring): 2–13. Catalogue no. 11-008. Ottawa: Statistics Canada.

Daly, K. 2000. *It Keeps Getting Faster: Changing Patterns of Time in Families*. Ottawa: The Vanier Institute of the Family.

Eichler, M. 1983. *Families in Canada Today: Recent Changes and Their Policy Consequences*. Toronto: Gage Publishing.

Eshleman, J.R., and S.J. Wilson. 2001. *The Family*, 3rd Canadian ed. Toronto: Pearson Education.

Fast, J., J. Frederick, N. Zukewich, and S. Franke. 2001. "The Time of Our Lives ..." *Canadian Social Trends* (Winter): 20–23. Catalogue no. 11-008. Ottawa: Statistics Canada.

Glenday, D. 1997. "Lost Horizons, Leisure Shock: Good Jobs, Bad Jobs, Uncertain Future." In A. Duffy, D. Glenday, and N. Pupo (eds.), *Good Jobs, Bad Jobs* (pp. 8–34). Toronto: Harcourt Brace.

Gustafson, D.L. (Ed.). 2005. *Unbecoming Mothers: The Social Production of Maternal Absence.* New York: Haworth Press.

Haas, L. 1999. "Families and Work." In M.B. Sussman, S.K. Steinmetz, and G.W. Peterson (eds.), *Handbook of Marriage and Families*, 2nd ed. (pp. 571–612). New York: Plenum.

Hays, S. 1996. *The Cultural Contradictions of Motherhood*. New Haven: Yale University Press.

Hochschild, A.R., with A. Machung. 1989. *The Second Shift*. New York: Avon.

Horsfield, M. 1997. *Biting the Dust: The Joys of Housework*. London: Fourth Estate.

Liazos, A. 2004. *Families: Joys, Conflicts, and Changes*. Boulder: Paradigm Publishers.

Luxton, M. 1980. *More Than a Labour of Love*. Toronto: The Women's Press.

Luxton, M. 1997. "The UN, Women, and Household Labour: Measuring and Valuing Unpaid Work." *Women's Studies International Forum* 20: 434.

Machum, S. 2002. "The Farmer Takes a Wife and the Wife Takes the Farm: Marriage and Farming." In G.M. MacDonald (ed.), *Social Context and Social Location in the Sociology of Law* (pp. 133–158). Peterborough: Broadview Press.

Marshall, K. 2006. "Converging Gender Roles."*Perspectives on Labour and Economics* 7, no. 7. Retrieved August 3, 2006 from www.statcan.ca/english/freepub/75-001-XIE/10706/art-1.htm.

McDaniel, S.A. 2002. "Women's Changing Relations to the State and Citizenship: Caring and Intergenerational Relations in Globalizing Western Democracies." *Canadian Review of Sociology and Anthropology* 39: 125–151.

McDaniel, S.A., and L. Tepperman. 2004. *Close Relations: An Introduction to the Sociology of Families*, 2nd ed. Scarborough: Prentice-Hall.

McLaren, A., and A.T. McLaren. 1997. *The Bedroom and the State: The Changing Practices and Politics of Contraception and Abortion in Canada, 1880–1997*. Toronto: Oxford University Press.

Mom.salary.com. 2007. "What Is Your Mom Worth? Families Can Customize Mom's Job Description and Create a 'Mom Paycheck'." Retrieved May 7, 2007, from www.swz.salary.com/momsalarywizard/htmls/mswl_momcenter.html.

Newman, D.M., and L. Grauerholz. 2002. *Sociology of Families*, 2nd ed. Thousand Oaks: Pine Forge Press.

Ranson, G. 2005. "Paid and Unpaid Work: How Do Families Divide Their Labour?" In M. Baker (ed.), *Families: Changing Trends in Canada*, 5th ed. (pp. 99–121). Toronto: McGraw-Hill Ryerson.

Sayer, L. 2005. "Gender, Time, and Inequality: Trends in Women's and Men's Paid Work, Unpaid Work, and Free Time." *Social Forces* 84: 285–303.

Seccombe, K., and R.L.Warner. 2004. *Marriages and Families: Relationships in Social Context*. Toronto: Thomson Wadsworth.

Statistics Canada. 2003. "Labour Force Historical Review 2003." Catalogue no. 71F0004XCB. Ottawa: Statistics Canada.

Statistics Canada. 2005. "Child Care." *The Daily* (Monday, February 7).

Voet, R. 1998. *Feminism and Citizenship*. London: Sage.

Ward, M. 2002. *The Family Dynamic: A Canadian Perspective*, 3rd ed. Toronto: Nelson Thomson Learning.

Waring, M. 2006. "Women and Unpaid Work." In *Women and the Economy*. Retrieved February 10, 2006 from www.unpac.ca/economy/unpaidwork.html.

Wilson, S.J. 1986. *Women, the Family, and the Economy*, 2nd ed. Toronto: McGraw-Hill Ryerson.

Part II

The Ties that Bind: Family Formation and Generational Connections

From a life course perspective, family transitional events or turning points often have a profound impact on our lives. These transitions are often key developmental phases that change as we age. For example, the transition to parenthood, which typically occurs in young adulthood, is a major developmental milestone event that alters our day-to-day individual lives in significant ways as we care for and raise our children. Moreover, the timing and nature of these transitional events have important implications for family and kinship relations (e.g., our parents now become grandparents), as well as support across the generations (e.g., grandparents may provide assistance with child care), which constitutes a secondary focus of this section. Beginning with the transition to adulthood, Chapter 6 examines the family formation patterns of young people by considering the different ways that young people search for love and the changing nature of partnership formation and parenthood. In Chapter 7, we consider families and children in the early years and the various agents of socialization (notably parents), as well as several theories used to explain how children become socialized. Chapter 8 explores fundamental text assumptions of the existence of both sameness and diversity in family composition and in family-related life course patterns by examining the family lives of lesbian, gay, and transgendered individuals.

Moreover, in recognition that transition events are not always permanent and are subject to reversibility— a theme found throughout many parts of this text, Chapter 9 specifically focuses on family dissolution (e.g., divorce) and the transition to a "new" beginning (e.g., remarriage). In Chapter 10, we examine how the transition to the empty nest can also be reversed when young people return to parental "nests" as "boomerang kids." Finally, in Chapter 11, attention will shift to transitions and intergenerational relations in later life by turning the spotlight on aging families, caregiving, and other salient issues that are commonly experienced during the "sunset" years.

Chapter 6

Close Relations in Youth and Young Adulthood

Establishing Partnerships and Starting Families

Learning Objectives

In this chapter you will learn that ...
- a life course perspective is invaluable for situating contemporary trends in intimate relations and family formation within the context of shifting gender roles and social change across the generations
- close relations are socially constructed and socially regulated and are shaped by political, economic, and technological forces
- unmarried cohabitation is likely to be the first conjugal union of most Canadian young people, and is particularly prevalent in places like Quebec
- although marriage and parenthood occur at historically unprecedented older ages, these transitions are also characterized by diversity and fluctuations over time
- many young people increasingly choose to delay or reject marriage and parenthood and are having smaller families, yet the desire to form and create family ties remains as strong as ever

Introduction

The formation and maintenance of intimate partnerships and the development of one's own family—known as the family of procreation—are key markers of the transition to adulthood. The life course perspective provides a dynamic and flexible framework for understanding the creation and changing nature of these close family ties. It also underscores the importance of situating family-related behaviours and transitions within their unique social contexts. Whereas the current generation of young people has grown up in an era of tumultuous social and economic change, the previous generation (known as the "baby boomers," born between 1946 and 1964), was raised in its own distinct historical location. These baby boomers were born during a time in which sexual expression was more constrained, young people left home relatively young to get married and have children, the nuclear "intact" family was pretty much the norm, men were the main breadwinners, and most marriages lasted a lifetime.

In this chapter, we will focus on patterns and changes in family-related transitions that occur primarily during the youth and young adult phase of the family life course. This time period covers and extends the time of life described as "emerging adulthood" (Arnett, 2000), since it constitutes a significant developmental phase that occurs between childhood and adulthood. Topics such as dating, romance, love, and sexuality will be explored, as well as shifting trends in the formation of committed couple relationships. The chapter will conclude with an overview of patterns in parenthood, including general trends in fertility behaviour.

Dating, Romance, Love, and Sexuality

As young people navigate their way to adulthood, many will look for someone special with whom to share their private time. Some of these relationships will be of a relatively short duration, while others may lead to more long-term unions, such as marriage.

The Search for Love: Going on Dates and Hooking Up

Dating behaviour and customs in Canada have varied throughout history. In the years leading up to World War One, courtship occurred mainly in community activities and in the parents' home under adult supervision. Changes began to occur on university campuses among older young adults as they began to question these traditions, and this spread to the high school population, the media, and popular culture (Nett, 1988). In the 1923 edition of Emily Post's etiquette book, there was a chapter on "The Chaperone and Other Conventions." By the 1930s, this monitor of morals was relegated to the past tense, as "The Vanished Chaperon." Going out alone without parental surveillance was also made easier as cars became a more common means of transportation.

By the 1950s, new dating practices became established, although they continued to be highly formalized. Dating typically involved a series of phases from casual to steady dating to engagement and marriage. Each of these stages was marked by an exchange or gift, which symbolized the degree of "seriousness" in the relationship. Men and women usually developed distinct attitudes and roles on these dates, reflective of a double standard. In most cases, men would initiate contact, pay for the cost of the date, and were socialized to emphasize sex, while women learned about love, romance, and marriage (Nett, 1988).

In our high-tech culture, methods of dating and mate selection have undergone a transformation. A growing number consider "traditional" dating styles as out of date, time-consuming, and inefficient. One-on-one dating is becoming less popular among young people and there is a more egalitarian approach as to who asks for and pays for "the date" (Ward, 2002). Overall, modern youth romance culture is a primarily informal one, and is reflected in language which frequently lacks a clear vocabulary to define relationship status or practices. Miller and Benson (1999), for instance, observe the popularity of terms like "hanging out," "going out," and "talking to" instead of terms like "courtship" or "dating."

One needs to only turn on the television or surf the web to quickly get the idea that popular culture is characterized by a huge transformation in how we approach intimacy and matchmaking. The proliferation in so-called reality shows devoted to helping people find mates is one such example. Beginning with the 2000 Fox show *Who Wants to Marry a Millionaire*, in which 50 women competed to marry a wealthy man whom they had never met, a number of spin-off shows have since emerged. The top-rated ABC show *The Bachelorette* recently qualified as the most-watched program on Monday nights (for its sixth straight season) among viewers and young people in 2011.

Modern technology and modifications in dating customs have also contributed to an expansion of social network sites and chat rooms, as well as Internet dating services.

These dating services cover a wide range of dating preferences and also reflect shifting norms in dating behaviours and gender roles. For example, in 2007 Mark Penn (Hilary Clinton's chief strategist for her 2008 presidential campaign) documented the emergence of a new "micro trend" in dating whereby women (typically over the age of 40) date younger men. These women were referred to as "cougars," a term popularized by the recent comedy series *Cougar Town*. Subsequently, there has been a number of recently launched web sites such as The National Association of Prime Cougars that have appeared and are geared toward professional older women who want to date younger men. Baker (2010) provides a discourse analysis pertaining to the language use of the term "cougar" and concludes that it signifies important changes in gender relations and identities. In other words, as women become more economically independent, well educated, and have more power to choose potential mates, they begin to adopt traditionally "male" dating behaviours, whereby the dating partner is considerably younger and less financially powerful in the relationship.

Turning our attention to new media technologies such as cell phones, instant messaging, texting, and social network sites, Pascoe (2011) observes that these are now a central aspect of young people's social, romantic, and sexual lives, although most young people meet their partners "offline." These new media technologies provide a wider private sphere for youth dating practices since they can expand traditional practices of meeting, dating, and breaking up. They also can provide important resources about sexual health and identities. Yet, despite these possible benefits, Pascoe argues that use and access to these media technologies often mirror the contemporary ordering of economic, racialized, and gendered power. For example, based on her multi-year, multi-site collaborative ethnographic research project, she finds that some marginalized young people (e.g., sexual minority, homeless, and other disadvantaged youth) are more likely to experience online venues as riskier spaces than more advantaged youth (i.e., online sexual predators, cyber bullying).

Pascoe also critically evaluates the pervasiveness of cautionary tales about young people's sexuality and their new media (usually aimed at parents) and how they are constantly turned into "moral panics" in the daily news cycle. These stories often feature teens posting risqué pictures of themselves on their social network sites, and sending semi-nude self portraits via their cell phones, known as "sexting." She recounts the tragic news story of Jesse Logan, a high school student who sent nude photos of herself to her boyfriend. After they broke up, he forwarded the stored photos to other girls at the high school. Sadly, Jesse was so relentlessly harassed that she later became so distraught she committed suicide. Yet, while these kinds of stories are very real and troubling, Pascoe is also quick to point out that they are relatively rare. She also argues that the tendency to focus on negative behaviours related to teen sexuality reinforce societal stereotypes that adolescents are out of control, make poor decisions about their bodies, and that new media and sexuality are a dangerous mix.

And finally, although not the norm but of sociological interest, other "novel" trends include those who try to meet potential partners through innovative activities such as "speed dating" or through "mail order bride" services as further discussed in Box 6.1.

Box 6.1
From Russia, Maybe with Love: Mail-Order Brides a Booming Business

Three to six months' worth of e-mails, a 14-day visit to Russia, and a new wife. That's the promise of Mark Scrivener, a Martensville, Sask., man who on Jan. 1 this year opened a Canadian branch of the Volga Girls mail-order bride service. Though available for 10 years via the Kentucky-based head office, Scrivener is providing Canada-specific services to men looking for a wife who is a little bit more "out of the box."

Of those single men he's counselled, he says "most men would rather have a cup of coffee and a sandwich… than a $4,000 paycheque a month brought to them," and those foreign women signed up for his service are willing to provide just that. "They are more traditional in a marriage. They still don't mind pulling up their roots and probably not pursuing their career and maybe pursuing a family. Being a stay-at-home mother," Scrivener said. His company's website provides a catalogue of such women looking for marriage to foreign men.

Take 22-year-old Natalia, who lists her interests as going to nightclubs, movies, and reading. She speaks no English, has college education, and is the chief sales-person at a store in Togliatti, in the country's western region. Prospective husbands can also learn about her height, weight, and 35-inch bustline, all with the click of a mouse. According to her bio, she hopes to travel around the world and have many children. For a fee you can purchase her address, write her letters, send her gifts, and hope to win her affection.

The website's main gallery lists more than 1,100 such profiles from women in and around Togliatti, a Russian city of approximately 710,000. Of the 60 men using the website worldwide there are approximately 14 engagements per year, says Scrivener. The process can take between nine months and one year and cost approximately $5,000, including flights, from initial correspondence "to the day you slide the ring on the ladies' hand," Scrivener said. According to the company website, there is a 75 per cent success rate with clients who become engaged on their 10- to 14-day Russian visit. The women can then apply for a visa to come to Canada. "There's no reason for them not to be approved, unless they go absolutely stupid in their interview," Scrivener said.

His own quest for a foreign bride began in 2004. Everything in his life was good, he said, except for his inability to find a wife. The search culminated in his 2006 marriage to a Ukrainian woman. It didn't work out. She returned home to take care of business, and never came back. Scrivener decided to try a different agency, and to focus on Russia, where he said women outnumber men by 10 million. Women there are also subject to the label of "old maid," said Scrivener. "If you're over the age of 26 there, you probably won't get married," he said. Scrivener believes he will be married by August, as he plans to travel to Russia soon for business and to meet with a couple of prospective brides.

But some say services such as this one are less about helping couples find love and more about exploiting a power balance between the First World and the Third World. "It becomes a way for men to access vulnerable women, women who ultimately have very high rates of turning up in battered women's shelters," said Norma Ramos, the director of the New York City–based International Coalition Against Trafficking in Women.

She said the mail-order bride phenomena takes place all over the world with men "helping themselves to women in vulnerable situations" and taking advantage of women who are desperately seeking better economic opportunities. For those women who enter a successful, loving relationship, coming to Canada as a bride is seen as a fantasy and a way out of old-world poverty. For those mail-order brides who end up in abusive, controlling relationships, the picture isn't so pretty. "The word is slavery for us," said Josephine Pallard, the Executive Director of Changing Together, a Centre for Immigrant Women in Edmonton.

In 2007, the group launched a website called Canadian Law and Modern Foreign Brides, which aims to provide legal information for women who are victims of the mail-order bride system. Pallard said Canadian men are bringing over women from Latin America, Asia, and Eastern Europe, and estimated up to 40 per cent of these women end up in controlling, abusive relationships. He said his clients are also often looking for women to provide the same life they grew up with, with mothers and grandmothers growing a garden, baking, and raising children. "It's just a known fact that in North America, a lot of women have wandered away from those traditional values," he said. "I think a lot of men really are looking for that. A woman who will stay at home and raise the kids." Yet, Pallard frames the situation differently. "It's the macho man," said Pallard. "I am the king of the family so it has to be 'my word is all.' Of course, they see the Canadian women not tolerating that."

In some cases, the women are being used to provide care to aging parents or children, or to perform labour on farms. In the worst situations, women are being held as sex slaves and sold into prostitution. "It's men from developed nations who feel they can buy anything they want. They're not looking for equality in the marriage," said Ramos. "These mail order, these Internet husbands, these buyers, they want someone who is not going to assert equality in the marriage. Someone who is going to look at this man as their ticket out."

Source: Jeanette Stewart. 2010 (March 2). *Canwest News Service.* "From Russia, maybe with love: mail-order brides a booming business," retrieved July 29, 2011 from http://www.nationalpost.com/news/story.html?id=2634201.

Love, Romance, and Sex among Singles

Whereas passion refers to the drive that leads to romance, physical attraction, and sexual consummation, love is a deep and vital emotion that involves caring and acceptance and satisfies certain needs (Reidmann et al., 2003). The idea that romantic love is the basis for marriage is a relatively new social invention. Romantic love emerged gradually from the "courtly love" tradition practised in the 12th century by feudal nobility and celebrated by poets and developed even further during the Industrial Revolution. This was a time in which an emphasis on individuality grew, such that young people began to demand the right to choose their own mates. The earliest settlers from Europe also brought their tradition of romantic love with them to North America (Ward, 2002).

Love relationships also don't necessarily happen instantly as reflected in common experiences such as "love at first sight." Instead, love relationships "ebb and flow, with false starts and continual negotiations and renegotiations" (Kollock and Blumstein, 1988: 481). And since love and romance are somewhat elusive concepts and are socially created, their meanings can vary according to the context in which they are expected or experienced. Indeed, what is desirable and sexually attractive varies from culture to culture, and from subculture to subculture. For example, some might view multiple body piercings and tattoos as sexy and erotic, while others might find this type of body adornment gross and disgusting. Further, some young adults from traditional ethnic backgrounds may not regard the pursuit of romantic love as the most important force behind a successful marriage. For example, in arranged marriages (discussed later in this chapter), love often grows in the marriage as partners get to know one another.

As previously mentioned, sexuality is a critical aspect in the formation of intimate relationships. Castells (2004) has proposed that we are undergoing a sexual revolution unlike the sexual liberation of the 1960s and 1970s. The current revolution is characterized by the "de-linking of marriage, family, heterosexuality, and sexual repression (or desire)." In other words, sexuality and desire are increasingly separate from marriage and family. And, as always, this topic draws much public and personal attention as well as considerable controversy.

Despite the controversy, all societies have social norms that grant approval or disapproval of certain sexual behaviours. For example, it is taboo in our culture for couples to engage in public sex or to have sex with certain family members, such as first cousins. Laws and customs have been established that punish certain sexual acts, and violators may face public shame, ridicule, fines, and imprisonment. In brief, sexual expression is highly regulated in a variety of ways (Eshleman and Wilson, 2001).

Living Together: Trends in Cohabitation

"Living together," "shacking up," "living in sin," and "trial marriage" are examples of expressions that have been used to describe the living arrangement that demographers refer to as cohabitation or common-law unions. Obviously, some of these terms are more value-laden than others and their meanings reflect historical and cultural contexts. For example, in Canada, "moving in together" no longer carries the same "immoral baggage" that it did prior to the 1970s, although some traditional ethnic groups continue to disapprove of this living arrangement for personal or religious reasons. And although cohabitation can refer to same-sex couples, most of the research to date has concentrated on opposite-sex partners.

The 2006 Canadian Census shows that an increasing proportion of couples choose cohabitation (more commonly referred to as "common-law" unions in Canada). From 1986–2006, the proportion of common-law families increased from 7.2 percent to 15.5 percent, and an estimated 56 percent of young adults aged 20–24 now live common-law (Statistics Canada, 2007; Vanier Institute of the Family, 2000). Thus, similar to the U.S. and many other countries, it is not surprising that for young adults in their twenties, unmarried cohabitation is likely to be their first conjugal union. Further, the Census counted a total of 1,376,865 common-law families in 2006 and these family types are more common in some areas, notably Quebec. In this province, there were 611,855 common-law families, which represented approximately 44 percent of the national total.

Table 6.1 shows the distribution of families with children aged 14 and under by proportions married, cohabiting, and one-parent across Canada, based on the 2006 Census. The prevalence of cohabitation is highest in provinces and regions such as Quebec, Northwest Territories, and Nunavut. It is also higher than in many western European countries and in the United States. As shown in Table 6.2, the proportion of common-law couples in Quebec is higher than Sweden, a country often referred to as having one of the highest incidences of non-marital unions in the world (Statistics Canada, 2007). Moreover, cohabitations are not as stable as marriages, which is true in all Western societies. More than 50 percent of all cohabitations end in dissolution within five years (Milan, 2000).

Who Cohabits and Why?
Cohabitation has become a normative part of the life course for many young people. The propensity to cohabit is influenced by a number of factors. Wu (2000) documents that heterosexual cohabitation tends to be selective of people who are younger, more liberal, less religious, and more supportive of egalitarian gender roles and non-traditional family roles. For example, women in unmarried-partner households are less likely to be in a traditional homemaking role than their married counterparts. With regard to characteristics of same-sex couples, sparse research indicates that there are slightly more male same-sex common-law couples (at 55 percent) than females. Most of these couples have higher educational attainment than either heterosexual unmarried partners or married couples (Statistics Canada, 2002).

Why do people choose to live together rather than marry? The answer to this question will probably depend upon the couple you ask. However, many young people report that it is a convenient way to gain some of the benefits of marriage and to avoid the risk of divorce. If it doesn't work out, it is easy to dissolve the union, since the couple does not have to seek legal or religious permission. Conversely, macro-level explanations tend to focus more on the large-scale trend toward secularization and individualization, including an increasing rejection of traditional institutionalization and moral authority And for same-sex couples, the choice to legally marry has only recently become an option.

Recent research indicates that many young people do not consciously plan to move in together or decide between cohabitation and marriage. Rather, the decision often seems

Table 6.1
Distribution of Children Aged 14 and under by Family Structure, Canada, Provinces and Territories, 2006

	Total	% Married parents	% Common-law parents	% Lone parents	Other*
Canada	**100.0**	**65.7**	**14.6**	**18.3**	**1.4**
Newfoundland and Labrador	100.0	65.8	12.0	21.0	1.3
Prince Edward Island	100.0	70.4	8.7	19.8	1.1
Nova Scotia	100.0	64.3	11.5	22.9	1.4
New Brunswick	100.0	62.8	13.9	21.8	1.4
Quebec	100.0	45.9	33.8	19.4	0.9
Ontario	100.0	73.8	7.9	17.1	1.1
Manitoba	100.0	66.0	9.6	21.6	2.8
Saskatchewan	100.0	63.4	11.2	22.8	2.7
Alberta	100.0	72.9	9.4	16.0	1.7
British Columbia	100.0	71.1	9.3	17.8	1.8
Yukon	100.0	52.9	18.6	25.4	3.1
Northwest Territories	100.0	46.3	27.6	22.5	3.4
Nunavut	100.0	40.9	33.2	22.2	3.7

*Includes other relatives and non-relatives.

Source: A. Milan, M. Vézina, and C. Wells, "Family Portrait: Continuity and Change in Canadian Families and Households in 2006: Findings," table 10. Census release, September 12, 2007, www.statcan.ca.

to centre on whether to remain single or cohabit (although marriage is sometimes on the horizon in the future). A recent qualitative study on 115 young adults who are currently cohabiting or recently cohabited also finds that the movement to cohabitation is often a gradual, unfolding process or a "general slide" (Manning and Smock, 2005). This makes it difficult to identify a clear beginning and ending and can raise issues of autonomy and independence, in addition to several legal/economic and relationship issues. For example, one respondent named Fiona stated, "Ah … [when] we met, he was 19. I was 20. Within that next year, he basically moved in. There wasn't a definite date. He would stay one night a week, and then two nights, then … it got to a point where he never left.

Table 6.2
Proportion of Common-Law Couples in Quebec Higher Than in Canada and in Other Selected Countries

Countries	Percentage of all couples	Reference year
Sweden	25.4	2005
Finland	23.9	2006
New Zealand	23.7	2006
Denmark	22.2	2007
Iceland	19.9	2006
Canada	18.4	2006
Quebec	34.6	2006
Other provinces and territories	13.4	2006
United Kingdom	15.5	2004
Australia	14.8	2006
Ireland	14.1	2006

Source: A. Milan, M. Vézina, and C. Wells, "Family Portrait: Continuity and Change in Canadian Families and Households in 2006: Findings," table 8. Census release, September 12, 2007, www. statcan.ca. Data from: Statistics Canada, Statistics Finland, Statistics New Zealand, Statistics Denmark, Statistics Iceland, United Kingdom Office for National Statistics, Australian Bureau of Statistics, Ireland Central Statistics Office, and Statistics Sweden.

And ... I wanted the control, of saying, uh, go home, if need be. I didn't want him to pay the rent ... to have to be entitled to be here. That was at my discretion. It was kind of like my way of maintaining some, control, independence, however you want to say it."

Studies also suggest that cohabiting women experience unique stressors and issues in cohabiting relationships because cohabitation is not a committed "formalized" agree-ment identical to a legal marriage contract. Cohabiting men, for instance, tend to be less committed to the relationship and their partner than married men (Stanley et al., 2004). As a result, some of these men remain in a permanent state of availability and are still "playing the field" (Ambert, 2006), which can leave women feeling insecure and vulner-able. The women may also be less willing to sacrifice employment opportunities and to invest as much in housework as do married women (Seltzer, 2000).

Finally, another emergent living arrangement trend in modern life that represents the flip side of living together without being legally married is the "commuter marriage" or the LAT (living apart together) relationship. This is a marriage or other intimate relation-ship between partners who live in two separate households. In Canada, one out of every

12 "partnered" individual lives separately from his or her partner (Statistics Canada, 2003). For some couples, this may be a temporary arrangement, for example, when the couple works in different cities for a brief period of time. For others, it may be a long-term lifestyle to accommodate professional careers or preferences for autonomy and independence without sacrificing a committed relationship. Other economic, cultural, or even policy pressures can be at play in why some couples choose this relationship. For instance, immigration laws and policies can make relocating to another country difficult (McDaniel and Tepperman, 2011).

"Tying the Knot": Getting Married

Marriage can broadly be defined as a socially and legally recognized relationship that includes sexual, economic, and social rights and responsibilities. This definition draws our attention to the fact that marriage is a matter of public concern and that society maintains norms and sanctions for appropriate behaviour related to marriage (Seccombe and Warner, 2004). Good illustrations of this are found in same-sex marriage debates and in the recent public outrage and controversy over the polygamous practices of the fundamental Mormons living in Bountiful, British Columbia (see Box 6.2 and Figure 6.1). In this secluded community that was formed over 50 years ago, plural marriage is practised such that some men have close to 30 wives and father up to 80 children, many of whom are underage teenage mothers.

On the one hand, many individuals and lobby groups have maintained that polygamy is a criminal offence since it is illegal to have multiple wives in Canada. On the other hand, supporters say that the law banning polygamy is unconstitutional because it infringes on religious freedom. Despite this controversy, the B.C. Supreme Court recently upheld Canada's polygamy laws arguing that while the law does infringe on religious freedom, it is justified, particularly given the substantial harm that is causes to children, women, and society and the institution of monogamous marriage. As a result, this community is currently under investigation, although Chief Justice Robert Bauman maintains that minors who end up in polygamous marriages should be exempt from prosecution (CBC News, 2011).

McDaniel and Tepperman (2011) observe two trends in contemporary marriage: a decline in marriage rates and the continuing popularity of marriage. And although these trends appear contradictory, they actually are not. From a historical perspective, more people now marry at some point in their lives than they did in the 1910s. But at the same time, there has been a decline in marriage rates since the 1970s. And despite the ever-increasing popularity of cohabitation, the institution of marriage remains highly valued in contemporary society. Indeed, the vast majority of young people in Western countries eventually marry. Yet, this majority will be smaller than in the past—approximately 75 percent will probably marry compared to the traditional 90 percent (Turcotte, 2002).

Young people tend to marry later now than they did in previous times, especially compared to individuals during the mid-20th century. This trend contributes to the dramatic rise

---

Box 6.2
The Secret Lives of Bountiful's Wives

The Fundamental Mormons in Bountiful, British Columbia believe in polygamy. But are many of the commune's celestial wives really just teenage concubines? By Daphne Bramham, *The Vancouver Sun*

BOUNTIFUL, B.C. – No one in Bountiful disputes the fact that most first-time mothers who walk into this polygamous community's midwifery clinic are younger than 18. No one disputes the fact that the fathers are often three or four times older than the mothers. And nobody disputes that many are the "plural wives"— or concubines— of men much older than them. After all, when it comes time to register the births, midwife Jane Blackmore says the fathers in this religious community near Creston in south-central British Columbia sign their names on the forms that are sent to the provincial government. They are members of the Fundamentalist Church of Jesus Christ of Latter Day Saints and they believe polygamy is the "new and everlasting covenant." It is what separates them from mainstream Mormons. Fundamentalists claim they are the true Mormons and it is the mainstream Mormon church that has broken away from Joseph Smith's teachings— in particular his directive on polygamy.

What Marlene Palmer, a plural wife and the public defender of other plural wives, disputes is whether the women and girls have a choice in becoming "celestial wives" in their teens. "Women and girls do get to choose who they marry," she says emphatically. "Most are 17, 18, and some are as old as 20 when they get married. There have been some who are 16 and occasionally some are 15... But they never marry without their parents' permission." Palmer, 45, is Winston Blackmore's sister. Blackmore, a powerful businessman and wealthy landowner, is the former bishop of Bountiful. He has 26 wives and more than 80 children. Blackmore has repeatedly said that polygamy is a religious practice and as such is protected by the Canadian Constitution's guarantee of religious freedom.

Source: Excerpt retrieved July 18, 2005 from www.polygamyinfo.com/plygmedia%2004%20 237vsun.htm.

---

in one-person households as young, independent singles delay marriage while focusing on their careers (Canadian Press, 2007). As you may recall from Chapter 1, in 2008 women were about 29 years of age on average at first marriage, and men about 31. Comparatively, in 1961, the average age of marriage was much lower for women at 22.9 and 25.8 for men. Yet, this is only one historical benchmark—in some ways young adults are reverting back to behaviours characteristic of earlier times. For example, during the Great Depression (1929–1939), marriage was often delayed because of great economic hardship.

Figure 6.1
Rights vs. Marriage: The Same-Sex Marriage Debate Continues as 55 Percent of Canadians View Same-Sex Couple Recognition as Positive, 2005

Question: Which of the following statements comes closer to your point of view?

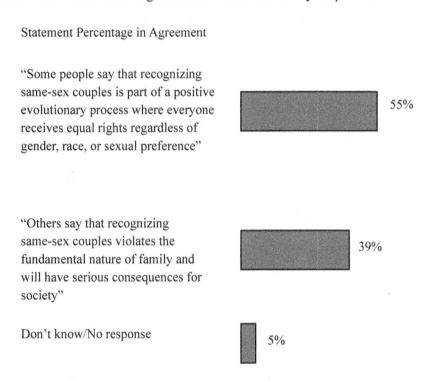

Statement Percentage in Agreement

"Some people say that recognizing same-sex couples is part of a positive evolutionary process where everyone receives equal rights regardless of gender, race, or sexual preference"   55%

"Others say that recognizing same-sex couples violates the fundamental nature of family and will have serious consequences for society"   39%

Don't know/No response   5%

Source: EKOS Research Associates, Media Release, February 12, 2005, as cited by Allison Millar, Just Research no. 13—Research in Brief, "Rights vs. Marriage: The Same Sex Marriage Debate Continues," Department of Justice Canada, retrieved Aug. 5, 2006 from http://www.justice.gc.ca/eng/pi/rs/rep-rap/jr/jr13/fig4l.html.

In contemporary times, certain factors also lead to early versus later marriage timing. Socio-economic resources generally slow down young adult's formation of intimate relationships (Amato and Booth, 2000). This is shown by the tendency for individuals from lower- and middle-class families to marry earlier than those from well-educated or privileged families. Also, the role models provided by mothers in professional occupations may reduce daughters' interest in early marriage and increase their labour force attachment (Amato and Booth, 2000). Moreover, young adults from urban areas tend to marry later than those from rural regions, and ethnic/cultural factors influence the timing of marriage.

Further, although same-sex marriage is now legal in Canada, very little research has been conducted on this topic. This should not be surprising given that a federal law—Bill C-38, or the same-sex marriage bill—was signed only on July 20, 2005. This put an official end to two years of national debate. This occurred after an event in 2003 when an Ontario court became the first to rule that the common-law limit of marriage to the union only between a man and a woman violated the Charter of Rights. However, we do know that just over half of Canadians (51 percent) support the view that same-sex marriages should be recognized by the law as valid with the same rights as traditional marriages. This is similar to Britons (52 percent), but much higher than Americans, whereby only 35 percent support this view (Millar, 2006).

The 2006 Census was the first to provide data on same-sex marital and common-law partnerships. In this survey, a total of 43,345 same-sex couples fell into this category, representing 0.6 percent of all couples (married and unmarried). Of these, 16.5 percent were married couples. Ontario has the largest number of same-sex partners (17,510), while Quebec has the largest proportion (0.8 percent of all couples). Newfoundland and Labrador had the lowest proportion of same-sex couples (0.2 percent of all couples). Male couples are more likely to live in Census Metropolitan Areas; 85 percent live in the larger urban areas of Canada, compared with 76 percent of female couples (Statistics Canada, 2002, 2007).

Finally, some Canadians continue to practise arranged marriage, which is still common to many parts of Africa, Asia, and the Middle East. For example, many Indo-Canadian young people report that their marriages are arranged (Netting, 2006). As a result, they experience two family systems—the "love marriage" taken for granted by their Western peers, and the "arranged marriage" experienced and advocated by their parents (see Box 6.3 for examples of how youth negotiate these two possibilities). Arranged marriages also entail diversity with respect to the degree of parental or family input. In a semi-arranged marriage, for example, the children have more say in decisions and may be free to express preferences or to reject a person they consider unsuitable. Potential choices are usually limited to people of the same race/ethnic group and socio-economic class, but some will also consider the importance of love and compatibility. Generally, arranged marriages support collectivist rather than individualistic goals, since they preserve family resources, protect the economic well-being of the couple, and ensure family continuity from generation to generation (Ralston, 1997; Wilson, 2005).

The Marriage Gradient

Men tend to marry women younger than themselves, although we are seeing a rise in the number of women marrying men younger than themselves. Yet, only about 12 percent of all marriages consist of wives who are two or more years older than their husbands. The phenomenon of women marrying older men is known as the mating gradient, which was first discovered by well-known sociologist Jessie Bernard in the 1970s. This gap declined steadily throughout the 20th century, such that the current gender disparity is about two years (Mitchell, 2006). Yet the fact that women continue to marry older men has important implications for women over the life course. The

Box 6.3
Some Kind of Arrangement—Arranged Marriages and Indo-Canadian Youth

A recent study by Netting (2006) explores how Indo-Canadian young people negotiate love and arranged marriages in Canada. This research finds that in some ways the Indo-Canadian marriage system is converging with standard North American practice. Some Indo-Canadian youth are rebelling against their cultural tradition, while other young people negotiate the process by winning parental consent for their own personal selections. In general, the participants in the study adopt the love-ideology and dating systems of Canada, while also drawing upon a cultural perspective that "love-conquers-all discourse" can lead to troubled marriages.

Below find some verbatim quotes based on this study that illustrates divergent perspectives of Indo-Canadian youth (all in their twenties, never married, of Indian heritage, and permanently residing in Canada):

"I would personally rank love very high up on that ladder of qualities—probably number one...For myself, I think it could be love at first sight...I can't see love taking a long time to blossom...For a love-marriage...if anything goes wrong, you'll always have love. With true love, you can pretty much get through anything." (Sohan)

"If you have an arranged marriage, then you have to learn to love that person... True love could be the girl you actually love and want to be with. But if you can't, then you have to end up loving somebody else...I may get true love if I have an arranged marriage to someone else, but...will you be able to do the same things with your wife? And if you do it with your wife, will you be thinking of your girl friend?" (Kirpal)

"I know I probably won't marry in the [Indian] culture...I want somebody in tune with nature...mountain-bike, rock-climb, hiking. I've never met one East Indian guy who ever does any of that stuff. They're too interested in fancy clothes and cars. He has to be creative because I am—do music, dance, or art, or whatever." (Ravinder)

"They saw him at his sister's wedding...For me, it was time to be with someone...my family hadn't pushed me, but I'm almost finished with my education...My brother spent a long time talking with him: he is open, broad-minded, honest, and straightforward. My brother really liked him, and called to tell me, 'he's perfect.' Then they had an engagement ceremony, because other families were after him, and they wanted to make sure we had him. I didn't know they'd done this! When they came back and told me, I was really mad...but the pictures showed this glow on his face. He was so happy. I thought he was pretty cute! I put all my faith in my brother; I said 'I put my life in your hands.'" (Nirmal).

Source: Netting, N. 2006. "Two-lives, one partner: Indo-Canadian youth between love and arranged marriages." *Journal of Comparative Family Studies*, 37(1): 129–146.

younger spouse (the wife) typically starts marriage with fewer assets, such as less schooling, less job experience, and lower income.

Over time, this disadvantage accumulates, since the husband's job will be given priority because it is deemed more important to the overall economic situation of the family. A woman will also usually be the one who quits her job (which is usually lower paid) to care for young children. In this way, the initially small economic difference becomes a substantial gap. Women's "choice" to marry at a younger age, therefore, in addition to other structural economic inequities that exist, contributes to their economic dependency. It also illustrates how gendered marital patterns have economic implications that operate in rather subtle but potent ways (Gee, 2000).

A Portrait of "Mixed" Unions

It has only been four and a half decades since Hollywood's first interracial kiss in the 1967 movie *Guess Who's Coming to Dinner?*, starring Sidney Poitier, the first Black man to ever win an Academy Award (for a previous movie in 1963). This "groundbreaking" comedy featured a set of affluent parents whose attitudes are challenged when their daughter brings home a fiancé who is Black. La Rose (2008) recalls how this movie shocked mainstream America and that it reflected how North America used to have very different attitudes toward individuals partnering with someone of a different race or visible minority group. She documents that not only was this behaviour taboo, it could potentially land someone in jail, particularly in the U.S, whereby until 1967, 16 states had laws banning interracial marriage. At this time, a Supreme Court decision ruled that banning mixed-race marriages was not constitutional. It ruled that the state of Virginia could not criminalize the marriage that Richard Loving, a White, and his Black wife, Mildred, entered into nine years earlier in Washington, D.C.

Fortunately, much has changed since then, and the latest census figures show that on both sides of the border, love is increasingly "colour blind" since mixed unions are forming at unprecedented rates. As shown in Table 6.3, in 2006, a relatively high percentage of certain visible minority group Canadians were in mixed-race unions, reflecting shifting norms of homogamy (when couples are of the same race/ethnicity, religion, social class, and age group) and endogamy (the tendency to marry within one's group). Yet, overall only 4 percent of all couples in Canada were in mixed unions, suggesting that norms of endogamy were still strong, particularly within certain ethno-cultural groups. However, since mixed unions have generally increased over the last decade or so, it is fair to assume that social norms governing appropriate relationship partners are malleable and change over time as attitudes evolve (Milan and Hamm, 2004).

Table 6.3 shows the numbers of visible minority couples and the proportions of those who marry inside and outside of their group. Japanese Canadians are more apt to marry or live with a non-Japanese person (59.7 percent), followed by Latin Americans (30.7 percent), whereas Chinese (9.5 percent) or South Asians (6.8 percent) are the least likely to form mixed unions. Further, other research establishes that well-educated, urban, and younger adults are the most likely to be in "mixed" unions. These factors are found to be related to the adoption of behaviours and attitudes that question the boundaries of prevailing social norms, as well as a greater tolerance and acceptance of diversity and social inclusion (Milan and Hamm, 2004). For example, in the mid-1970s, only 55 percent of Canadians approved of marriage between Blacks and Whites, whereas 92 percent of Canadians were in favour of such unions in 2005 (Bibby, 2007).

Table 6.3
Persons in Couples and in Mixed Unions by Visible Minority Group, 2006

Visible minority group	Persons				
	Total	In a couple		In a mixed union	
	Number	Number	Percentage	Number	Percentage
All persons belonging to visible minority groups	3,922,700	2,181,200	55.6	331,300	15.2
Chinese	1,005,600	587,500	58.4	56,000	9.5
Black	562,100	216,800	38.6	55,200	25.5
South Asian	957,600	612,800	64.0	41,500	6.8
Latin American	244,300	130,300	53.3	40,000	30.7
Filipino	320,900	179,200	55.9	35,600	19.8
Arab/West Asian	321,800	185,000	57.5	26,500	14.3
Japanese	66,400	37,200	56.0	22,200	59.7
Southeast Asian	184,600	98,200	53.2	18,100	18.4
Korean	114,600	62,800	54.8	6,800	10.8
Multiple groups or N.I.E.*	144,700	71,400	49.3	29,400	41.3

*Belonging to multiple visible minority groups means that respondents reported more than one visible minority group by checking two or more mark-in-circles, e.g., Black and South Asian. Less common visible minority groups are reported in the visible minority N.I.E. (not included elsewhere) category. This category includes respondents who reported a write-in response such as Guyanese, West Indian, Kurd, Tibetan, Polynesian and Pacific Islander.

Source: Statistics Canada, Census of Population, 2006.

Source: Statistics Canada (2010), "A Portrait of Couples in Mixed Unions," Table 2, retrieved August 10, 2011 from www.statcan.gc.ca/pub11-008-x/2010001/t/11143/tb1002-eng.htm.

"Along Comes Baby": The Transition to Parenthood

As previously mentioned, the average age of motherhood has steadily climbed over the past several decades. In Canada, the mean age of mothers was 29.3 years in 2008, up almost five years from 1970. Ontario and British Columbia had the highest average of mothers at 30 years, while Nunavut had the lowest average age at 24.4 years. Remarkably, almost half (49.6 percent) of births were to mothers aged 30 and older, whereas two decades ago, three-quarters of moms in Canada were under the age of 30.

Rates of teenage pregnancy have also been steadily declining and are at their lowest level in over 50 years. Notably, births to teenage mothers decreased from about 30 births per 1,000 teenage mothers in 1974 to 12 per 1,000 births in 2008. However, this overall rate masks some significant regional variations in the propensity to be a teenage mother. For example, in Nunuvat, out of every 1,000 female teens aged 14 to 19, 94 of them are teenage mothers (or about one out of 10). Conversely, in Quebec, only about 9 out of 1,000 female teens of this age are mothers (or about one out of 100). Additionally, more children are being born outside of traditional, legal marital unions, with Canada's extramarital birth rate calculated at approximately 30 percent of all live births (Human Resources and Skills Development Canada, 2011).

Although most women are postponing having their first child and marrying, some women—particularly those from lower socio-economic status backgrounds—may have children at a relatively young age and out of wedlock. In an ethnographic study of poor families in the United States, Edin and Kefalas (2005) explore how girls from poor families conceptualize their active choices to have children young and before marriage. They note that middle-class beliefs about the "right way to start a family" are conditioned by a social context that offers great economic rewards for those who are willing to wait to have children. For example, for a White, college-bound adolescent, each year of postponed child-bearing will likely lead to higher lifetime earnings. And if she can hold out until her mid-thirties, she'll probably earn twice as much as if she'd had a child right out of college or university. Conversely, young people from impoverished communities do not share the same prospects. As concluded by these authors:

> The centrality of children in this lower-class worldview of what is important and meaningful in life stands in striking contrast to their low priority in the view of more affluent teens and twenty-something youth, who may want children at some point in the future, but only after educational, career, and other life goals have been achieved. Putting motherhood first makes sense in a social context where the achievements that middle-class youth see as their birthright are little more than pipe dreams: Children offer a tangible source of meaning, while other avenues for gaining self-esteem and personal satisfaction appear vague and tenuous. (Edin and Kefalas, 2005: 49)

Another rising trend that has occurred as people live longer, cohabit, divorce more, and increasingly have children outside of marriage, is that of "multiple partner fertility." Also referred to as "multipartnered," this term refers to having biological children with more than one partner. For example, a woman might have three biological children from three different men, whom she may or may not have married or cohabited. While Canadian research is virtually non-existent in this area, some U.S. studies (e.g., Guzzo and Furstenberg, 2007) suggest that it is more common among the poor, unmarried parents than married parents, it varies by race and ethnicity (with Blacks having higher rates), is higher if the father has been incarcerated, and is higher if parents had their first child when young. In sum, multiple partner fertility appears to be the most prevalent among the least advantaged in our society. It also underscores the increased complexity of kin relations and raises questions about stress and conflict stemming from this complexity (Smock and Greenland, 2010).

Moreover, biology alone does not determine parenthood—one can become a parent yet never give birth to a child, for example, by "inheriting" foster or stepchildren, through surrogacy or via adoption. Statistics show that in the late 1990s, 1.2 percent of Canadian children under 12 years of age had been adopted, representing 57,300 children (Ambert, 2006). Most adoptions involve adults who are already related to the child, such as a stepparent adopting a stepchild. It is also interesting to note that public perceptions of biological mothers who make adoption plans vary according to gender and the circumstances of the mother "putting her child up for adoption." For example, men are more likely than women to consider the biological mother as uncaring (March and Miall, 2006).

International adoptions are also on the rise, which raises a number of provocative sociological and political issues (e.g., see Dorow, 2006). Canadians have recently adopted between 1,890 and 2,220 children internationally each year. Many of these children are from China, with its preponderance of girls due to a one child per family policy that favoured boys (Adoption Council of Canada, 2003). Adoption as an alternative form of family formation has been socially constructed as less "natural" than biological parenting. Regardless, studies reveal that the consequences of adoption tend to be divided between those that show no disadvantage and those that indicate small deficits. Ironically, if disadvantages do appear, they are most likely created by the less than optimal social climate surrounding adoption, particularly in children's peer groups (Ambert, 2006).

Cross-race and cross-cultural adoption is a sensitive issue that is often the source of debate and controversy. In 2006, there was a great deal of divided opinion with respect to the 48-year-old popular singer/entertainer Madonna and her adoption of a 13-month-old Malawi baby named David. Many individuals and the media questioned why she adopted a Black child from a foreign country, especially given the high number of orphans and other "unwanted" children in her home country. Similarly, in Canada, White parents who adopt babies from other countries (e.g., China, India, Russia) and Aboriginal children are often the target of criticism. In the case of Aboriginal children, White parents may be accused of being unable to provide these children with the opportunity to learn their ancestry and cultural traditions and to preserve their cultural identity (e.g., see Ambert, 2006).

Finally, similar to predictors of early and late marital timing, the age at which one becomes a parent is influenced by a number of factors such as family background, gender, age, and educational attainment. Obviously, there are a number of benefits to delayed parenthood, such as maturity and improved economic resources. At the same time, some health professionals are concerned about the unprecedented number of women extending their reproductive years into their mid-thirties and beyond. They argue that there are a number of implications for the health care system, many of which relate to the increased demand and requirement for special services that assist pregnancy and birth. This includes a greater need for assisted reproductive technologies, such as in vitro fertilization (IVF), donor inseminations, and artificial insemination (e.g., see Health Canada, 2005). These new reproductive technologies raise a number of concerns for sociologists, scientists, and ethicists and have many important ramifications for families, as discussed in Box 6.4.

The Shrinking Canadian Family and the Social Pressure to Reproduce
In demography, the crude birth rate of a population is an estimation of the number of live childbirths per 1,000 people per year. Another indicator of fertility frequently used is the total fertility rate, or the average number of live children born to each woman over the course of her life during her child-bearing years (e.g., aged 15–49). Generally, demographers prefer to use the total fertility rate rather than crude birth rates because this rate is not affected by the age distribution of the population. This also facilitates more accurate comparisons across countries. As a result, we are aware that fertility rates tend to be higher in less economically developed countries and lower in more economically developed countries.

From a historical perspective, the transition to low fertility (and reduced mortality rates) began around 1870 and is known as the first demographic transition. Since 1965, we have witnessed even more dramatic reductions in fertility, known as the second demographic transition. This means that the size of the Canadian family is shrinking. In Figure 6.2 and Table 6.4 we observe that over time the fertility rate has decreased substantially (both in Canada and in many other industrialized countries). In 1851, the total fertility rate was 6.6 and this declined to 1.53 in 2004 and it has remained fairly stable at 1.68 in 2008 (Statistics Canada, 2011). This is below the replacement level of 2.1, or the level of fertility at which a developed population exactly replaces itself from one generation to the next. In short, replacement-level fertility can be taken as requiring an average of 2.1 children per woman. Therefore, unless there is a radical shift in fertility, mortality, or immigration, our population will continue to get smaller and older during the next century.

It is also interesting to observe fluctuations or "blips" in fertility behaviour. In particular, the postwar baby boom occurred as a result of compressing two decades of births into a decade and a half as a result of postponed fertility due to World War Two.

Recent fertility intention studies (e.g., Edmonston et al., 2010) document that most Canadian young adults plan to have children, with one-half reporting that they intend to have two children. Almost one-third plan to have three or four children, and only 7 percent report that they do not want any children. These statistics support actual trends in recent behaviour, which include the overall pattern of decreasing fertility rates and postponed births. Moreover, thoughts about intended fertility have not changed that much and contemporary social norms about family size (around two children) are found to be remarkably resilient. Yet, at the same time, young people are now more

Box 6.4
Reproductive Technologies, State Regulation, and Issues for Families

Health Canada plans to regulate egg freezing: Review may result in limit on number of clinics licensed to perform service

Health Canada is reviewing the science and safety issues of freezing women's eggs for future use and says it will be among the reproductive technologies that will have to be licensed.

A Health Canada official confirmed yesterday that egg freezing would be considered a "controlled activity" under the 2004 Assisted Human Reproduction Act, and if the review suggests the science is still "somewhat risky" it could limit the number of clinics licensed to provide the service.

Francine Manseau, a senior policy analyst with Health Canada, said regulations are under development and will be implemented and enforced by Assisted Human Reproduction Canada, a federal agency created under the act to regulate the country's fertility clinics.

Only in the past few years have scientists found relatively reliable ways to freeze the human egg, making it possible for women to preserve their fertility. At the McGill Reproductive Centre in Montreal, for example, where researchers have pioneered a leading procedure, more than 50 women have frozen their eggs. Most are cancer patients undergoing treatment that would leave them sterile. But about a dozen are older women who, for personal reasons, hope to have children later than biology would naturally allow.

While safety is always a concern with new medical technology, egg freezing has just as often raised ethical and social concerns because it could allow women to have children at any age they choose. But increasingly, scientists and ethicists are seeing egg freezing as an inevitable element of motherhood in the modern era. An article published today in the journal *Science*, for example, entitled "Melting Opposition to Frozen Eggs" notes that: "A typical man has almost a lifetime to become a father, but a woman's reproductive prime lasts only a decade or so—and coincides with the critical time for getting an education and establishing a career."

Tim Caulfield, head of the Health Law Institute at the University of Alberta, agreed, saying, "I do think by and large this is a good thing, especially for women who have a medical need to [freeze their eggs for future use]. I don't see how anyone could criticize it from that point of view."

Any moves to set limits around how and when women can freeze their eggs, he said, would raise profound questions.

"To what degree does the state have a right to tell women when they can or can't have children? When does the government have a right to step in and say, 'Oh, you're too old.'"

Seang Lin Tan, director of the McGill Reproductive Centre, said society tends to be more judgmental of the prospect of older women having children than it is of older men, who routinely father children into their retirement years— former prime minister Pierre Trudeau and silent screen star Charlie Chaplin among them.

Prof. Caulfield said it could be that society views mothers as the primary care-givers, and when they reach a certain age, people debate their ability to handle the physical demands of childbearing and child rearing.

A comment posted online to *The Globe and Mail* site in response to the Wednesday story that revealed the demand for the new egg-freezing service, however, criticized women for using the procedure. With so many older children in need of adoption, a 41-year-old woman wrote, why turn to egg freezing?

"It's a shame, a real shame, that women resort to these technologies instead of looking to care for children who are already in the world," the posting read.

Montreal ethicist Margaret Somerville at the McGill Centre for Medicine, Ethics and Law is well known for her criticism of certain reproductive technologies that override what would be possible in nature.

But in this instance, Prof. Somerville said that egg freezing in general does not trouble her. For those women who have a medical need, such as cancer patients who could face sterilizing treatments, she said the technology is "fantastic."

"The broader idea [doctors] are postulating is that you'll store your eggs when you're 19 and use them when you're 50," Prof. Somerville said. "If these are your own eggs, and you are going to use them [to conceive a child later with in vitro fer-tilization], I don't have much of a problem with that."

But Prof. Somerville opposes the use of the technology in cases where the result may not be in the best interests of the child. At the McGill Centre, for example, 36-year-old Melanie Boivin has frozen her eggs for her seven-year-old daughter who has Turner's Syndrome, a genetic condition that will not allow her to have her own children.

Ms. Boivin is freezing her eggs so that her daughter may one day have the option to use them.

"We've done all of our analysis through the eyes of someone who wants to have a child," Prof. Somerville said. "I try to view it through the lens of the child."

"This young woman would give birth to her half-sister, and her genetic mother would be her grandmother."

Source: Abraham, C. *The Globe and Mail.* April 20, 2007. Retrieved April 30, 2007 from http://www.theglobeandmail.com/servlet/story/LAC.20070420.BABIE.

likely to question whether or not they really want to have children, when they should start trying to conceive, and how many children they should ideally have (Vanier Insti-tute of the Family, 2008).

Figure 6.2
Total Fertility Rate per 1,000 Canadian Women, 1851–2003

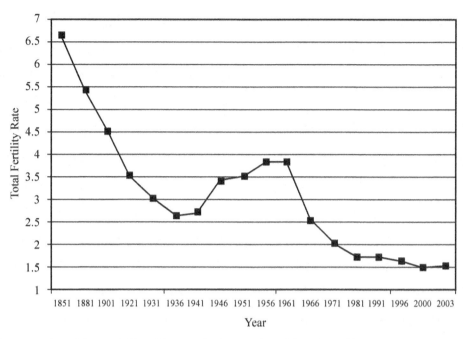

Sources: Adapted from A. Milan, "One Hundred Years of Families," *Canadian Social Trends* 56: 2–12; W.W. McVey, Jr., and W.E. Kalbach, *Canadian Population* (Toronto: Nelson, 1995); Statistics Canada, "Births, 2002," *The Daily* (April 19, 2004).

Baker (2010) points out that most parents see children as the natural outcome of adulthood and marriage rather than a conscious choice. Yet, sociological explanations—unlike biological ones, which may emphasize the role of "maternal instincts" of why people reproduce—tend to focus on two reasons: social pressures or costs and benefits. The social pressure to reproduce originates from many sources: religious, government officials, the media, family, friends, and even strangers. For example, churches have traditionally viewed the purpose of marriage as reproduction. After the wedding ceremony friends and family often symbolize this expectation by throwing symbols of fertility (such as rice or confetti) on the couple. Governments and community leaders see children as necessary because they become the future generation of taxpayers, voters, workers, and consumers. Individuals may also perceive benefits by way of reduced stigma (i.e., that the childless are selfish and immature) and for advantages such as companionship and personal fulfillment.

Turning to the topic of delayed family transitions, why are so many young adults postponing marriage, parenthood, and having fewer children? Numerous individual, sociocultural, economic, and political factors are at play. Economic conditions, education,

Table 6.4
Total Fertility Rates, Selected OECD Countries, 2004 to 2008

OECD* Countries	2004	2005	2006	2007	2008
Japan	1.29	1.26	1.32	1.34	1.37
Germany	1.36	1.34	1.33	1.37	1.38
Switzerland	1.42	1.42	1.44	1.46	1.48
Czech Republic	1.23	1.28	1.33	1.44	1.50
Canada	1.53	1.54	1.59	1.66	1.68
Netherlands	1.72	1.71	1.72	1.72	1.77
Finland	1.80	1.80	1.84	1.83	1.85
Denmark	1.78	1.80	1.85	1.85	1.89
Sweden	1.76	1.77	1.86	1.88	1.91
United Kingdom	1.78	1.80	1.84	1.90	1.96
Norway	1.83	1.84	1.90	1.90	1.96
Australia	1.76	1.79	1.82	1.93	1.97
France	1.92	1.94	2.00	1.98	2.01
United States	2.05	2.05	2.10	2.12	2.08
Iceland	2.04	2.05	2.08	2.09	2.15

*OECD = Organisation for Economic Co-Operation and Development.

Note(s): Total fertility rate is the average number of children per woman. Data sources from National Statistics Offices, National Vital Statistics Reports and Eurostat.

Source: Statistics Canada. 2008. "Births," retrieved January 26, 2012 from http://www.statcan.gc.ca/pub/84f0210x/2008000/part-partie1-eng.htm, Comparison with Low Fertility Selected Countries, Table 4.

and career factors are reported as important in women's decisions to delay marriage and parenthood. Contraceptive use and cohabitation have also risen dramatically, sex before marriage is less frowned upon, and the effects of economic conditions (e.g., cost of marriage and having children) and marital disruption also explain these trends. For example, as children increasingly remain at home and in school longer, and are thus consumers rather than producers (as was the case in pre-industrial society), it becomes very expensive to become parents and raise large families.

One can also remain unmarried or childless either for life or until one enters the older adult years. Childlessness is more prevalent now than in recent decades, and it is estimated that approximately 15 percent of Canadian women reach age 44 without having given birth to any children (Beaujot and Belanger, 2001). However, this is not a new trend and rates fluctuate over time. In fact, childlessness decreased from 15 percent among women born at the beginning of the century to a historic low of 7–8 percent among women born 1927–1936—the women who helped produce the baby boom (Rosenthal and Gladstone, 2000).

It is also important to distinguish between those who choose not to have children or the "childless by choice" from those who are childless by circumstances, such as due to infertility (e.g., Clarke, Martin-Matthews, and Matthews, 2006; Veevers, 1980). It is estimated that approximately nine out of 10 young Canadians aged 20–34 intend to have at least one child. However, a minority of Canadians do not voluntarily intend to have children because they do not want children (e.g., because of career demands) or because they are unable to because of medical problems (Stobert and Kemeny, 2003). Demographic characteristics of the voluntarily childless are relatively consistent in that these individuals tend to be well educated, live in urban areas, have little or no religious affiliation, and ascribe to non-traditional roles (Trella, 2007).

Moreover, Trella (2007) asserts that research on childless couples relies not only on traditional conceptions of marriage and family, but also upon conceptions of femininity that she labels as "hegemonic motherhood." This term refers to the perception that women are, by nature, maternal and desire children. In other words, it reflects a social discourse on motherhood that creates a taken-for-granted understanding of what is "natural" and indicative of healthy feminine identity.

In summary, research suggests that the decision to forego parenthood is linked to personal, economic, social, and political circumstances rather than "selfish" or "immature" personalities. A good example of how state policies can influence fertility decisions is the Chinese One-Child Policy, which was initiated for economic reasons in the 1970s to curb population growth. This policy was highly effective in reducing the population (albeit, many have pointed out that this policy produced many negative side effects, such as a preference for boys which resulted in a plethora of other problems). Moreover, social discourse on parenthood decision is restrictive in that it limits our understanding of why people want children in the first place. Indeed, Trella argues that the "invisible power of hegemonic parenthood operates in such a way that individuals are led to believe that they should want children, and will be unhappy and regretful if they choose not to have children" (Trella, 2007: 13).

Summary

This chapter explores the changing nature of how young people form intimate and committed family relations. Many young people are choosing to stay single longer, cohabit, and marry and have children later, and they are more likely to have children outside of legal marriage. Canadian families are also shrinking and, compared to recent decades, more young people are deciding to stay childless. However, a life course perspective reminds us that many of the trends we witness in contemporary society were also witnessed in previous times. Yet, family structures and the acceptability of certain family behaviours as "legitimate" continue to broaden and evolve in relation to changing times.

What will become of intimate relations, marriage, and parenthood in the future, given these transformations? As discussed in Chapter 1, many worry that families, in the traditional sense at least, will slowly disappear. Many researchers also emphasize that marriage generates numerous health and economic benefits (e.g., see Waite and Gallagher, 2000). For example, married individuals are more likely to maintain a healthy lifestyle and diet, and are less likely to use alcohol and drugs than non-married adults (Bachman et al., 1997). Conversely, some "radical" writers (e.g., Fineman, 1995) argue that marriage, as a legal category, ought to be abolished because it is an inherently conservative institution that places women in a subordinate position under patriarchal domination.

The recent federal law allowing same-sex couples to legally marry supports the idea that many Canadians continue to think that marriage provides greater equality and protection among citizens. It also shows that marriage remains a sacred institution. And with continuing high rates of immigration from countries in which marriage is the norm, it is difficult to imagine that it will ever disappear. Whatever the future brings, there is little doubt that family ties will continue to be diverse, sought after, and highly valued by young people. However, meanings and practices will undoubtedly undergo continued critical reflection and alteration in response to shifting socio-economic, political, cultural, and technological landscapes.

Questions for Critical Reflection and Debate

1. What advantages and disadvantages do you see with respect to meeting potential mates in "non-traditional" settings, such as through Internet dating services and chat rooms?
2. Why has cohabitation become so popular among young people? Do you think that it will eventually replace marriage?
3. Debate the following: Women who cohabit or marry men older than themselves experience a number of advantages over the course of their lives.
4. What factors do you think contribute to the decision for an individual or a couple to remain childless? To what extent is childlessness stigmatized in society?
5. Critically evaluate whether arranged marriages are more beneficial for individuals and families than "free-choice" marriages based on romantic love.
6. Same-sex and mixed unions are on the increase in Canada. Discuss the factors underlying these trends and consider other emergent patterns that will contribute to greater diversity in family life.

Glossary

Arranged marriage involves the role of an intermediary and occurs when families play a pivotal role in the choice of one's marital partner.
Endogamy is the tendency to date and marry within one's social group or social class, race, religion, or language group.

Family of procreation refers to the family that we form when we mature, apart from the family of origin, or the family that one is born into.

Fertility rate is an estimate of the average number of children that women will have in their lifetime.

First demographic transition from high mortality and fertility to low mortality and fertility began around 1870 and lasted until about 1965.

Hegemonic motherhood refers to social discourse that creates the perception that women are, by nature, maternal and desire children.

Homogamy refers to a non-random approach of selecting mates or spouses who have similar physical, intellectual, personality, and social class traits.

Marriage gradient is women's tendency to marry "up" with regard to age, education, occupation, and even height.

Multiple partner fertility is on the rise and refers to having biological children with more than one partner.

Further Reading

Beets, G., J. Schippers, and E.R. te Velde. 2011. *The Future of Motherhood in Western Societies: Late Fertility and its Consequences.* New York: Springer. Offers a holistic overview of the process of postponing the birth of a first child. Also explores issues such as: childlessness, contraception, reproductive technologies, economic rationality, women's lifestyle preferences, and delayed fatherhood.

Dorow, S. 2006. *Transnational Adoption: A Cultural Economy of Race, Gender, and Kinship.* New York: New York University Press. Presents a global framework for understanding the political economy of international adoption and presents a unique ethnographic study of China/U.S. adoption, the largest contemporary intercountry adoption program.

Edin, K., and M. Kefalas. 2007. *Promises I Can Keep: Why Poor Women Put Motherhood before Marriage*, 2nd ed. Berkeley: University of California Press. Provides a groundbreaking ethnographic study on motherhood and marriage among 162 low-income urban women. Offers an intimate look at why these women put children ahead of marriage despite the daunting challenges they know lie ahead.

Fincham, F., and M. Cui. 2011. *Romantic Relationship in Emerging Adulthood.* New York: Cambridge University Press. Presents a synthesis of cutting-edge theory and research that addresses the formation, nature, and significance of romantic relationships from an interdisciplinary perspective.

Hankeln, M.D. 2008. *India's Marriages Re-Arranged: Changing Patterns among the Middle Class.* Saarbrucken, Germany: Verlag. Covers the topic of Indian arranged marriages and investigates how globalization processes affect the Indian marriage market. Also compares the meaning of marriage from both Western and Indian perspectives.

Holland, S. (Ed.). 2008. *Remote Relationships in a Small World.* New York: Peter Lang. Covers a broad range of issues related to forging and managing intimate relationships via communication technologies, particularly for those in adolescence and in married life.

Related Web Sites

Adoption Council of Canada, an umbrella organization, raises public awareness of adoption and provides services such as a resource library, a quarterly newsletter, referrals, and conference planning, www.adoption.ca.
Canadians for Equal Marriage adopts a nationwide, bilingual campaign for the rights of same-sex families and works at the grassroots level, in the media, and in Parliament. www.equal-marriage.ca.
Sex Information and Education Council of Canada is a non-profit organization (est. 1965) to foster public and professional education about human sexuality, www.siec-can.org.
Quirky Alone explores issues of single living and cheerfully questions compulsory coupledom. www.quirklyalone.net.
Statistics Canada has a web site that provides some of the best information on family formation trends, including the latest figures on cohabitation, fertility, and marriage, www.statcan.gc.ca.

References

Adoption Council of Canada. 2003. "International Adoptions Steady: 1,891 in 2002." Ottawa: www.adoption.ca.
Amato, P.R., and A. Booth. 2000. *A Generation at Risk: Growing up in an Era of Family Upheaval*. Cambridge: Harvard University Press.
Ambert, A.M. 2006. *Changing Families: Relationships in Context*. Toronto: Pearson Allyn and Bacon.
Arnett, J.J. 2000. "Emerging Adulthood: A Theory of Development from the Late Teens through the Twenties."*American Psychologist* 55: 469–480.
Bachman, J.G., et al. 1997. *Smoking, Drinking, and Drug Use in Young Adulthood*. Mahwah, NJ: Erlbaum.
Baker, M. 2010. *Choices and Constraints in Family Life*, 2nd ed. Toronto: Oxford University Press.
Baker, P. 2010. "Discourse and Gender." In K. Hyland and B. Paltridge (eds.), *The Continuum Companion to Discourse Analysis* (pp. 199–212). New York: Continuum International Publishing Group.
Beaujot, R., and A. Belanger. 2001. "Perspectives on Below Replacement Fertility in Canada." Paper presented at the IUSSP Working Group on Low Fertility meeting, Tokyo, March 21–23.
Bibby, R.W. 2007. "Racial Intermarriage: Canada and the U.S." Retrieved August 29, 2007, from www.reginaldbibby.com/images/PC_9_RACIAL_INTERMARRIAGE_AUG2907.pdf.
Canadian Press. 2007. "Solo-dwellers on the Rise as Young, Independent Singles Delay Marriage." Retrieved September 13, 2007, from canadianpress.google.com/article.

Castells, M. 2004. *The Power of Identity*, 2nd ed. Malden: Blackwell Publisher.

CBC News. 2011. "Canada's Polygamy Laws Upheld in B.C. Supreme Court," November 23, retrieved January 17, 2011 from www.cbc.ca/news/canada/british-columbia/story/2011.

Clarke, L.H., A. Martin-Matthews, and R. Matthews. 2006. "The Continuity and Discontinuity of the Embodied Self in Infertility." *Canadian Review of Sociology and Anthropology* 43: 95–113.

Dorow, S. 2006. *Transnational Adoption: A Cultural Economy of Race, Gender, and Kinship.* New York: New York Publishers.

Edin, K., and M. Kefalas. 2005. *Promises I Can Keep: Why Poor Women Put Motherhood before Marriage.* Berkeley: University of California Press.

Edmonston, B., S. Lee, and W. Zheng. 2010. "Fertility Intentions in Canada: Change or No Change?" *Canadian Studies in Population* 37: 297–337.

Eshleman, J.R., and S.J. Wilson. 2001. *The Family,* 3rd ed. Toronto: Pearson.

Fineman, M.A. 1995. *The Neutered Mother, the Sexual Family, and Other Twentieth-Century Tragedies.* New York: Routledge.

Gee, E.M. 2000. "Contemporary Diversities." In N. Mandell and A. Duffy (eds.), *Canadian Families: Diversity, Conflict, and Change* (pp. 78–111). Toronto: Harcourt Canada.

Guzzo, K.B., and F.F. Furstenberg. 2007. "Multipartnered Fertility among American Men." *Demography* 44: 583–601.

Health Canada. 2005. "Changing Fertility Patterns: Trends and Implications." Health Policy Research Bulletin, 10 (May). Ottawa: Minister of Public Works and Government Services.

Human Resources and Skills Development Canada. 2011. "Family Life – Age of Mother at Childbirth." Retrieved January 28, 2012 from http://www4.hrsdc.gc.ca/.3ndic.1t.4r@-eng.jsp?iid=75.

Kollock, P., and P. Blumstein. 1988. "Personal Relationships." *Annual Review of Sociology* 14: 467–490.

La Rose, L. 2008. "Mixed Race Marriages on the Rise," April 2, retrieved from www.thestar.com/printarticle/409104.

Manning, W.D., and P.J. Smock. 2005. "Measuring and Modelling Cohabitation: New Perspectives from Qualitative Data." *Journal of Marriage and the Family* 67: 989–1002.

March, K., and C. Miall. 2006. "Reinforcing the Motherhood Ideal: Public Perceptions of Biological Mothers Who Make an Adoption Plan." *Canadian Review of Sociology and Anthropology* 43: 367–385.

McDaniel, S., and L. Tepperman. 2004. *Close Relations: An Introduction to the Sociology of Families,* 2nd ed. Toronto: Pearson Prentice-Hall.

McDaniel, S., and L. Tepperman. 2011. *Close Relations: An Introduction to the Sociology of Families,* 4th ed. Toronto: Pearson Prentice-Hall.

McVey, W.W., Jr., and W.E. Kalbach. 1995. *Canadian Population.* Toronto: Nelson.

Milan, A. 2000. "One Hundred Years of Families." *Canadian Social Trends* 56: 2–12.

Milan, A., and B. Hamm. 2004. "Mixed Unions." *Canadian Social Trends* 73: 2–6.

Millar, A. 2006. "Rights vs. Marriage: The Same-Sex Marriage Debate Continues." *Just Research no. 13—Research in Brief*. Ottawa: Department of Justice Canada.

Miller, B.C., and B. Benson. 1999. "Romantic and Sexual Relationship Development during Adolescence. In W. Furman, B.B. Brown, and C. Feiring (eds.), *The Development of Romantic Relationships in Adolescence* (pp. 99–121). Cambridge: Cambridge University Press.

Mitchell, B.A. 2001. "Ethnocultural Reproduction and Attitudes toward Cohabiting Relationships." *The Canadian Review of Sociology and Anthropology* 38: 391–413.

Mitchell, B.A. 2006. *The Boomerang Age: Transitions to Adulthood in Families*. New Brunswick, NJ: Aldine Transaction.

Nett, E. 1988. *Canadian Families: Past and Present*. Toronto: Butterworths.

Netting, N. 2006. "Two Lives, One Partner: Indo-Canadian Youth between Love and Arranged Marriages." *Journal of Comparative Family Studies* 37, no. 1: 129–146.

Pascoe, C.J. 2011. "Resource and Risk: Youth Sexuality and New Media Use." *Sexuality Research and Social Policy*, 8: 5–17.

Penn, M.J. with E.K. Zalesne. 2007. *Microtrends: The Small Forces Behind Tomorrow's Big Changes*. New York: Hachette Book Group.

Ralston, H. 1997. "Arranged, Semi-arranged and 'Love' Marriages among South Asian Immigrant Women in the Diaspora and Their Non-migrant Sisters in India and Fiji." *International Journal of Sociology of the Family* 27: 43–68.

Reidmann, A., M.A. Lamanna, and A. Nelson. 2003. *Marriages and Families*. Toronto: Thomson Nelson.

Rosenthal, C., and J. Gladstone. 2000. "Grandparenthood in Canada." Ottawa: Vanier Institute of the Family.

Seccombe, K., and R.L. Warner. 2004. *Marriages and Families: Relationships in Social Context*. Toronto: Wadsworth.

Seltzer, J.A. 2000. "Families Formed outside of Marriage." *Journal of Marriage and the Family* 62: 1247–1268.

Smock, P.J., and F.R. Greenland. 2010. "Diversity in Pathways to Parenthood: Patterns, Implications, and Emerging Research Directions." *Journal of Marriage and the Family* 72: 576–593.

Stanley, S.M., S.W. Whitton, and H.J. Markman. 2004. "Maybe I Do: Interpersonal Commitment and Premarital or Nonmarital Cohabitation." *Journal of Family Issues* 25: 496–519.

Statistics Canada. 2002. "Census: Marital Status, Common-Law Status, Families, Dwellings, and Households." *The Daily* (October 22).

Statistics Canada. 2003. "Couples Living Apart." *The Daily* (June 10).

Statistics Canada. 2004. "Births, 2002." *The Daily* (April 19).

Statistics Canada. 2007. "2006 Census: Families, Marital Status, Households and Dwelling Characteristics." *The Daily* (September 12, 2007)

Statistics Canada. 2011. "Births and Total Fertility Rate, by Province and Territory." CANSIM, Table 102–450S and Catalogue no. 84F0210X.

Stobert, S., and A. Kemeny. 2003. "Childfree by Choice." *Canadian Social Trends* (Summer): 7–10. Catalogue no. 11-008. Ottawa: Statistics Canada.

Trella, D. 2007. "Hegemonic Motherhood: Reconceptualizing Femininity and Family through the Lens of Voluntary Childlessness." Paper presented at the annual meeting of the Population Association of America, New York, March 31.

Turcotte, P. 2002. "Changing Conjugal Life in Canada." *The Daily* (July 11). Ottawa: Statistics Canada.

Vanier Institute of the Family. 2008. *Profiling Canada's Families*. Ottawa: Vanier Institute of the Family.

Veevers, J.E. 1980. *Childless by Choice*. Toronto: Butterworths.

Waite, L.J., and M. Gallagher. 2000. *The Case for Marriage*. New York: Doubleday.

Ward, M. 2002. *The Family Dynamic: A Canadian Perspective,* 3rd ed. Toronto: Nelson Thomson Learning.

Wilson, S. 2005. "Partnering, Cohabitation, and Marriage." In M. Baker (ed.), *Families: Changing Trends in Canada*, 5th ed. (pp. 143–162). Toronto: McGraw-Hill Ryerson.

Wu, Z. 2000. *Cohabitation: An Alternative Form of Family Living*. Toronto: Oxford University Press.

Chapter 7

Families and Children in the Early Years

Childhood, Socialization, and
Shifting Ideologies of Parenthood

Learning Objectives

In this chapter you will learn that ...
- childhood, similar to other life course stages and categories, is a social construct embedded within a particular cultural time and place
- there are key agents of socialization, such as parents, daycare providers, siblings, the media, peer groups, and the educational system
- socialization is bi-directional or reciprocal and lifelong
- theories on childhood socialization are not created in a vacuum; instead, they reflect changing assumptions about the nature and role of children in society
- gender-role socialization persists and continues over the life course in response to inequitable structural conditions and opportunities for alternative behaviour
- shifts in child-rearing advice and ideologies of parenthood have profound implications for how people interpret and do the work of parenting in their everyday lives

Introduction

From a life course framework, childhood constitutes a distinct developmental phase of the life cycle associated with young family life. As such, childhood is conceived as a category strongly related to biology, since it is associated with our physical maturation. In other words, we are all young once, and with the passage of time, we will all become old. Yet, this empirical fact hides a much wider and more complex set of issues. Notably, there is not a precise definition of concepts like "childhood," and there is social significance of such concepts in relation to the social context in which they are created and applied. Therefore, in order to understand the sociological concept of "childhood," we need to appreciate how categorizations, interpretations, and attributions are socially constructed (e.g., see Livesey, 2005). That is, we need critical social understandings about what children experience, need, and what is expected of children, as well as children's place in the larger society and how they vary by culture and historical era (Wall, 2005).

Philippe Ariès (1962) highlighted the notion of childhood as a social construct in his classical work entitled *Centuries of Childhood*. This book ignited a great deal of controversy among historians because he argued that the concept of childhood did not exist in earlier times. Through an analysis of paintings and diaries in medieval Europe, Ariès offered a picture of society in which children were not considered a unique group. He observed that children were typically not represented in art and, if so, they were usually depicted as little or "miniature" adults. And although his ideas have been attacked by historians because of his methodology and interpretations, there is general agreement that conceptions of childhood have changed over time. For example, unlike today, children in the 17th and 18th centuries often left their families at a very early age to become wage earners. As a result, they entered the adult world much earlier than Canadian children do today (Bradbury, 2005).

Cognizant that cultural conceptions of childhood vary according to time and place, this chapter will continue to investigate this theme by investigating a number of dimensions relevant to understanding contemporary childhood and families in the early years. Specifically, we will consider what socialization entails, as well as a number of theories on childhood socialization. And in recognition that socialization is lifelong and bidirectional—for instance children can socialize parents just as parents socialize their young—we will examine a number of salient issues relevant to these processes. Finally, we will conclude with a review of how child-rearing advice and ideologies of parenthood have changed over time.

What Is Socialization? What Are the Key Agents of Socialization?

Socialization is the process by which a society passes on its behaviour patterns, attitudes, values, and knowledge to the next generation. This is a complex process that also allows an individual to develop a self-identity, including the skills needed to prepare for new roles and to function effectively in a given society. Hence, the emphasis is on social learning and learning the ways of a given society rather than predetermined inherited genetic traits. For example, most of us would agree that there is nothing in the genetic endowment of children to become racists or to commit to certain religions such as Christianity or Islam. Instead, these kinds of proclivities are generated or reproduced by differences in cultural and family background and in the structure of social relations. This does not mean that biological inheritance or genetic influences are irrelevant, since human beings are also biological organisms. Indeed, a certain degree of physiological ability is needed (e.g., memory) in order for socialization to occur or to be successful.

Parents play one of the most significant roles in the socialization of their children. However, there are also many other important socializing institutions. Many parents cannot afford to stay at home to raise their children and must place them in some form of child care. Data from the National Longitudinal Survey of Children and Youth show that over half of Canadian children aged six months to five years were in some form of child care by 2000–2001 (Statistics Canada, 2005). Child care and daycare centres encompass a wide variety of forms and programs, ranging from babysitting-type services by friends or relatives to preschool environments with many educational activities (see Figure 7.1 for an overview of possible sources of child care). Also, daycare centres may have differential staffing ratios, routines, and other resources. Therefore, the effects of these experiences on children can vary tremendously.

In general, there is consensus that high-quality, stimulating daycare centres can have a number of positive benefits for children, such as improved social skills and cognitive development, yet high-quality daycare generally comes with a higher financial cost. This means that better-off families have greater opportunity than their less wealthy counterparts to provide "resource-rich" child-rearing experiences. These childhood experiences

Figure 7.1
Sources of Child Care in Canada

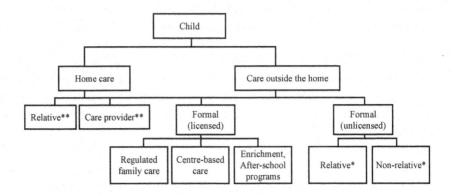

*May be paid or unpaid
**Could be a licensed care provider

Source: Social Development Canada, "The Impacts of Non-parental Care on Child Development—August 1999," retrieved August 5, 2006 from www.sdc.gc.ca/.../images/figure1_e.gif.

can also accumulate over the life course and reproduce and perpetuate class inequity through relative advantage or disadvantage.

Delegating "mother-work" to paid child-care providers, such as daycare workers, nannies, or au pairs, is an increasingly common arrangement for working mothers. Arat-Koc (1989) notes how foreign domestic workers have historically been recruited as "a solution to the crisis in the domestic sphere in Canada," a topic to be further explored in Chapter 15. These nannies and au pairs, usually hired only by wealthier families, are often characterized as "family like" and "shadow labourers" because they play a significant role in the socialization of children, yet their work is often hidden in households and in child-care centres. And while these child-care providers are "pseudo parents" and "like moms" and are often a part of the families they serve, they are also outside the dominant cultural ideology of what constitutes family (Murray, 1998). This means that these workers are continually engaged in emotional labour—that is, they must learn to mediate their emotional experiences of caregiving with others' expectations of them (Murray, 1998).

Domestic workers also experience a set of unique working conditions and interactions with the parents and children that they serve. For example, Macdonald (1998) finds that mothers and nannies "manufacture" a certain image and experience of motherhood that creates an idealized version of the mother-child relationship. As such, this "symbolic order re-defines the division of mother-work which magnifies a mother's significance and minimizes the nanny's," as depicted in Box 7.1 (Macdonald, 1998: 37).

Other key socializing agents include siblings, the peer group, the educational system, religion, and the mass media. Siblings, in particular, can be a powerful source of influence on children and adolescents. Older siblings, for instance, can be important sources

---

Box 7.1
Manufacturing Motherhood—"Maximizing and Minimizing"

The mothers I interviewed simultaneously maximized and minimized the importance of their children's bonds with paid caregivers. On one hand, mothers frequently stressed the success of the nanny-child bond, stating that their nanny and child were "really attached" and the child "really loved" his or her caregiver. On the other hand, they defined nannies as out of the family by minimizing the importance of the nanny-child bond, particularly in discussions about nanny turnover. Although the need to feel good about her childcare arrangements can lead a mother to maximize the nanny-child bond, to state that her provider is "great" and that her children "love" the nanny, this same need can lead her to minimize the effects of nanny turnover on her children's emotional well-being.

For example, Jane, a corporate vice president, described the departure of various nannies as not a problem for her sons. She said that because her older son (age eight) had been in daycare, "he deals with transitions incredibly well, so for him if a person is living here isn't that big an issue." She said that her younger son and his first nanny, who was with him from birth to 18 months, "adored each other," but at the same time described the nanny's departure as not a big deal:

"Well, he's young enough so that, you know, he talks about her all the time. I mean he understands and says that Andrea went home to be with her mommy and daddy. I think he missed her, but it doesn't seem to have had any huge impact on his overall well-being...I guess my sense has always been if family life is stable enough, that the transitions of child care people, as long as they're not constant changes, aren't going to have any terrible effects."

Jane's distinction between "family life" and "child care people" reveals how the nanny is situated in her child's life: although she spent more time with him than anyone else during the first year-and-a-half of his life, she is not an integral part of his family, psychologically or symbolically. This mother's strategy, therefore, was to simultaneously maximize the bond with the nanny in terms of how much her son benefited from it, and minimize the bond in terms of how much its loss would affect him. Not surprisingly, mothers and nannies often disagreed in their appraisals of the effects of nanny turnover.

Source: Macdonald, C.L. 1998. "Manufacturing motherhood: The shadow work of nannies and au pairs." *Qualitative Sociology*, 21: 25–53.

of information and can role model certain types of behaviour that younger children imitate. They may even play a large role in parenting or socializing younger children as babysitters and companions. Further, siblings can also be a source of conflict and competition over family resources, including parental time and attention.

Other institutions, such as religion and the media, are also key transmitters or shapers of knowledge, norms, values, and ultimately, our behaviour. It is well documented that attendance at religious services has fallen dramatically over the past several decades, a trend that has many implications for family socialization processes. Notably, religious norms influence many facets of family life such as gender roles, parent-child relations, attitudes toward moral issues (e.g., abortion), and how families celebrate rituals such as the holidays.

With respect to children from birth to aged 14, many studies show that a growing proportion of children report "no religious affiliation." Moreover, the age group with the largest proportion of those reporting "no religion" is aged 25–44 at 35 percent, an age range that encompasses the prime child-bearing/rearing years. Thus, it is likely that many of these parents are not exposing their own children to any particular formal, organized religion on a regular basis. And of those Canadians (of all ages) who do identify with a particular religion, seven out of 10 are Roman Catholic or Protestant. Yet, religions such as Islam, Hinduism, Sikhism, and Buddhism have increased substantially as the result of the changing sources of immigrants. Taken together, these patterns contribute to a more diverse religious profile of Canadian families (Statistics Canada, 2001), and suggest that despite overall declining religiosity among children and families, many families continue to adhere to traditional religious beliefs and practices.

Turning to the socializing effects of the mass media, studies reveal that children spend a large part of the day exposed to, and engaged in various mediums, including TV, music, computers, and video games. In Figure 7.2 we observe that on average, 8–10 year olds report almost one-third of their day (7:51 hours) exposed to media, and almost 1/4 of the day (5:29 hours) using these media. Interestingly, this figure also shows that both exposure and use increase as children become teenagers. This high degree of media exposure raises many issues and controversial concerns for parents and experts alike.

On one hand, educational television shows such as *Teletubbies* and *Reading Rainbow* are deemed to positively mould socialization processes because they help children's imagination and mental skills to grow. Conversely, some television programming is shown to promote less desirable socialization by encouraging behaviours such as aggressiveness and unhealthy eating habits (e.g., see Box 7.2), as well as consumerism through targeted advertising. The world of television also perpetuates gender roles, sexism, and racism since it is largely a "White man's domain" with male characters outnumbering non-White and female characters, particularly in more dominant roles. Women also still tend to play roles in which they are "more ornamental" and in which they are portrayed as young, attractive, and sexy (Côté and Allahar, 1994). Music videos and other types of media, such as video games, Internet sites, and magazines, are also commonly criticized for portraying women as sexual objects and victims of violence, as illustrated in Table 7.1.

Figure 7.2
Average Amount of Time Spent with Each Medium in a Typical Day, 8- to 18-Year-Olds

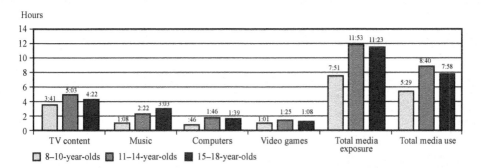

Source: Victoria J. Rideout, Ulla G. Foehr, and Donald F. Roberts. 2010. *Generation M²: Media in the Lives of 8- to 18-Year-Olds*, A Kaiser Family Foundation Study, January 2010, p. 5, Menlo Park: California. Retrieved from www.kff.org/entmedia/upload/8010.pdf.

Children can also participate in many social networks that can impact their learning, sense of social connectedness, and their health and well-being. These social networks can also instill certain societal and subgroup values, such as co-operation and competition, as well as norms related to socially acceptable "masculine" and "feminine" behavior. A good example of this is the popularity of sports participation, as shown in Table 7.2. This table reveals that in 2005, 51 percent of children aged 5 to 14 regularly took part in sport during the previous year, with soccer the most common sport for both boys and girls. Most children are first introduced to sports through the family, who strongly influence their children's sports involvement by investing time, emotional support and financial resources. In short, "sporty parents" tend to have "sporty kids," with a majority of parents being involved in some way with sports as participants, spectators, coaches, referees, and so on (Clark, 2011).

Not surprising—given the cost of equipment, facility rentals, transportation to sports events, club memberships, and completion entry fees—Clark (2011) documents that sports participation is most prevalent among children from high-income households, as well as in two-parent families in which the father works full-time and when the mother works part-time. Boys are also more likely to participate in sports than girls the same age, although this gap is narrowing. Finally, children of recent immigrants are less likely to participate in sports due to financial barriers. This occurs even in sports like soccer, an internationally popular sport that can offer a familiar place to integrate into Canadian society.

Furthermore, even though most books on socialization focus on the young child, socialization is a never-ending, lifelong process that does not end in childhood, a

Table 7.1
Content Analysis of Video Game Magazine Character Gender-Role Stereotypes*

Characterization	Male (%)	Female (%)
Aggressive	82.6	62.2
Sexualized	0.8	59.9
Scantily Clad	8.1	38.7
Sex Role Stereotype**	33.1	62.6
Portrayal of Aggression		
Military	4.1	0.0
Fighting	33.2	16.2
Glamorized Violence***	31.6	30.6
Wearing Armor	41.9	35.6

*Video game magazines analyzed were those ranked by Amazon.com as their six top sellers (on sale January 2006)

**Sex role stereotype refers here to the beauty stereotype for the female characters and to the hypermasculine stereotype (i.e., exaggeration of "macho" characteristics) for the male characters

***Refers to posing with a weapon

Source: Data drawn from Karen E. Dill and Kathryn P. Thill. 2007. "Video Game Characters and the Socialization of Gender Roles: Young People's Perceptions Mirror Sexist Media Depictions." *Sex Roles*, 57: 851–864 (Table 1, p. 858).

theme to be further discussed later on in this chapter. A growing number of studies show that socialization is also very powerful during the adolescent and teen years, as well as the influential role of the peer group in shaping these experiences. At this time, many adolescents become actively engaged in gender-role identification and learning the norms and expectations of the opposite sex. It is also during this developmental phase that many begin to separate from their parents and develop more self-reliance.

Overall, socialization is also a bi-directional or reciprocal process, a tenet that also helps to explain why children raised in the same family or in different historical locations can have very different experiences and outcomes. Indeed, children play a role in shaping the behaviour of their parents just as parents can shape the behaviour of their children. An example of this is when adolescent children (or "tweens" aged between eight and 14) want to buy the latest consumer goods that they have seen on television or that have been purchased by their peer group, such as iPods, cellphones, or trendy fashion accessories. This demand (and thanks to allowances, birthday money, and generous

Box 7.2
Television's Impact on Kids

Below is an abbreviated excerpt from the Media Awareness Network:

Television is one of the most prevalent media influences in kids' lives. According to the *Young Canadians in a Wired World Survey* (MNet, 2001), almost 80 percent of Canadian kids watch at least one hour of TV each day.

How much impact TV has on children depends on many factors: how much they watch, their age and personality, whether they watch alone or with adults, and whether their parents talk with them about what they see on TV...some areas of concern include:

Violence—Three potential responses to media violence in children include: increased fear, known as the "mean and scary world" syndrome; desensitization to real-life violence; and increased aggressive behaviour.

Effects on Health Development—Television...cuts into the time kids need for activities crucial to mental health and physical development such as reading, playing, exploring nature, learning about music, playing sports...sedentary activity has been proven to be a significant factor in childhood obesity....TV contributes to obesity by aggressively marketing junk food to young audiences. According to the Canadian Pediatric Society, most food advertising on children's TV shows is for fast foods, candy, and pre-sweetened cereals. Commercials for healthy food make up only four percent of those shown.

A Scientific American article entitled "Television Addiction" examined why children and adults may find it hard to turn their TVs off...researchers finds that viewers feel an instant sense of relaxation when they start to watch TV—but that disappears just as quickly when the box is turned off.

Sexual Content—Kids are bombarded with sexual messages and images in all media...While television can be a powerful tool for educating young people about the responsibilities and risks of sexual behaviour, such issues are seldom mentioned or dealt with in a meaningful way in programs containing sexual content.

Source: Retrieved May 5, 2009 from http://www.media-awareness.ca/english/parents/television/tv_impact.

relatives) influences parental and family spending patterns both subtly and directly. As a result, children are playing an increasingly powerful role in household purchases and as "agents of materialism" (see Box 7.3). In short, our current generation of children and "tweens" have been raised and socialized as sophisticated, savvy, and influential consumers and their buying behaviour is purported to be in the billions of dollars (Sutherland and Thompson, 2003).

Table 7.2
Top 10 Organized Sports of 5- to 14-Year-Olds in 2005

	1992	2005
	Percentage of 5- to 14-Year-Olds Participating	
	%	%
All Sports	57	51*
Soccer	12	20*
Swimming	17	12*
Hockey	12	11
Basketball	6	8*
Baseball	13	5*
Volleyball	5	3*
Gymnastics	4	2
Karate	2E	2
Skiing, downhill	6	2*
Track & Field (Athletics)	2E	2E

E = use with caution

*Statistically significant difference from 1992 (p<.05)

Source: Statistics Canada, General Social Survey, 1992 and 2005, retrieved from http://www.statcan. gc.ca/pub/11-008-x/2008001/article/10573-eng.htm#a3.

Theories on Childhood Socialization

Learning/Behaviourist Frame of Reference

Learning theory, which has its roots in behaviourism, assumes that the same concepts and principles that apply to animals apply to humans. Although there are many variations of this theory, learning or socialization as applied to the newborn infant involves changes that result from maturations that may include classical or instrumental conditioning. Classical conditioning, for instance, links a response to a known stimulus. A common example is Pavlov's dog experiment, in which a hungry dog is placed in a soundproof room and hears a tuning fork (a conditioned stimulus) before receiving some meat. After this situation is repeated several times, the dog begins to salivate upon hearing the tuning fork. Similarly, the same principles are assumed to hold true with an infant upon hearing his or her mother's voice or approaching footsteps.

Operant or instrumental conditioning, however, focuses attention on the response, which is not related to any known stimuli. Instead, it functions in an instrumental

Box 7.3
Parenting in a Culture of Consumption

Given the proliferation of goods on the marketplace, our almost constant exposure to commercial messages, and the energy we invest in acquiring consumer goods, one could argue that consumption activities dominate much of our everyday lives. Globalization, on-line shopping and the proliferation of specialty stores have created a world of unlimited options…As advertising is increasingly directed to children, their needs and wants have also come to shape the organization of time and money in the household. As Schor (1989) has suggested, children are "agents of materialism" bringing their consumerist values into the home through their wants and shopping lists. Cook's (2004) work on the commodification of childhood argues that children's development is increasingly being defined by their stage of consumption (the kinds of clothes, the types of toys) and that rather than seeing children as in some way tangential to the culture of consumption, they are the very core of it. Many of our largest corporations (Nike, Sony, Nabisco) have found that the key to their success is in marketing to children. Not only do children develop brand loyalty early on in their lives, but these loyalties last well into adulthood.

There are indications that children are playing an increasingly powerful role in family household purchases. Not only do children have an influence over the small stuff that is brought into the home (e.g., cereal, games, clothing), they are influencing the bigger consumer choices such as cars, computers, and holiday destinations. Smaller family size, increased family income, and a shift from authority and obedience to negotiation and decision-making participation has meant that children are more market savvy and powerful than they have ever been (Valkenburgand Cantor, 2002). The result, according to some, is that parents have become more indulgent with children, wanting to ensure that they do not lack for material goods (McNeal, 1992).

Source: Daly, K. 2004. *The Changing Culture of Parenting.* Contemporary Family Trends, Ottawa: The Vanier Institute of the Family.

manner, in that one learns to make a certain response on the basis of the outcome that response produces. According to Skinner (1963), it is the response that correlates with positive reinforcement or a reward. For example, imagine that a baby is picked up after saying "da-da-da" because the father is convinced that the baby is saying "Daddy." Consequently, the baby begins to say "da-da-da" all day long because there may be lots of rewards. As children grow older, different reinforcements (e.g., praise, candy, allowance) are used as deliberate techniques to teach children approved forms of behaviour.

Some argue that while there is some usefulness to this theory, there may be limited applicability of generalizing animal behaviour to socialized humans. For instance, it is asserted that humans, unlike animals, have the capacity to share symbolic meanings and symbols in ways that animals cannot.

Psychoanalytic Frame of Reference

Developed by Sigmund Freud (1856–1939) and his followers, psychoanalytic theory stresses the importance of biological drives and unconscious processes. Beneath the surface of each individual's consciousness is the repressed unconscious, a storm of contradictory impulses controlled only by the individual's gradual internalization of societal restraints. Parents, therefore, play a key role and are mainly responsible for their child's "impulse taming" (Strong and DeVault, 1992).

Socialization consists of a number of precise and overlapping stages of development. These stages occur between birth and age five or six, and are called the *oral, anal,* and *phallic stages*, followed later by a period of *latency* and then a *genital phase*. Three principal erogenous zones—the mouth, the anus, and the genitals—are of great importance in the socialization process because they are the first significant sources of irritating excitations with which a baby has to contend and upon which the first pleasurable experiences occur. For example, during the oral stage, which occurs during the first year of life, the earliest erotic gratifications come from the mouth. As a result, the child forms a strong emotional attachment to the mother, who supplies the source of food, warmth, and sucking.

Overall, Freudian ideas have received mixed empirical support and many of these ideas have been discredited. For instance, such practices as breastfeeding and bowel and bladder training (which have been so strongly emphasized in the psychoanalytic literature) have been found to be almost completely insignificant in terms of how they affect personality and psychosocial adjustment. Moreover, it should be noted that Freud's work was highly controversial at the time of his writings, particularly since he often focused on sexuality during a repressive Victorian era in which this topic was rarely discussed openly. Indeed, Freud thought that sexuality was a primary motivating force not only for adults, but also for children, an idea that sparked public outrage at the time.

Child Development Frames of Reference: Erikson and Piaget

Similar to Freud, both Erikson and Piaget emphasize the early stages of childhood development. Unlike Freud, both extended their stages beyond the early years and focused more attention on social structure and reasoning. Erikson, who was one of Freud's students, viewed socialization as a lifelong process that continues into old age. He developed the well-known "eight stages of human development." These stages and related issues range from *trust versus mistrust* (first year of infancy) to *integrity versus despair* (old age). As individuals create solutions to developmental concerns, those solutions become institutionalized in our culture. Swiss social psychologist Jean Piaget, who wrote during the 1920s, was also interested in maturational stages. However, his interest was more in cognitive development and characterizing this as the ability to reason abstractly, to think about hypothetical situations logically, and to organize rules into higher-order, complex operations or structures.

Piaget also developed four major cumulative stages of intellectual development, which include the sensorimotor period (birth to two years), pre-operational period (two to seven years), concrete operational period (seven to 11 years), and the formal operational period (age 11 through adulthood). In Piaget's view, children develop their cognitive abilities through interaction with the world and adaptation to their environment. They adapt by assimilating, which means making new information compatible with their understanding of the world. In addition, they accommodate by adjusting their cognitive framework to incorporate new experiences as they become socialized into adults (Strong and DeVault, 1992).

So far, we have reviewed frames of reference that emphasize overt behaviour (i.e., behaviourism, learning theory), the unconscious role of motives and emotions (i.e., the Freudians), and motor skills, thought, reasoning processes, and conflicts (i.e., child developmentalists). Next, we will review the symbolic interactionist frame of reference, a sociological perspective that shares many assumptions of Erikson and Piaget in relation to language, reasoning, and societal influences of behaviour.

Symbolic Interactionist Frame of Reference

From the symbolic interactionist perspective (e.g., Mead, Cooley, Blumer), socialization is viewed as a lifelong process. Central importance is placed on interactions with others and the internalized definitions and meanings of the work in which one interacts (Charon, 1979). Basic assumptions include:

1. *Humans must be studied on their own level*. This means that we must be careful in not making inferences from non-human forms of life or animals. Social life involves sharing meanings and communicating symbolically via language, which enables humans alone to deal with events in terms of past, present, or future. In other words "lower animals," such as mice and dogs, do not have a culture or a system of beliefs, moral codes, values, and ideas that is shared and symbolically transmitted.

2. *An analysis of society is the most valuable method in understanding society*. In order to best understand social behaviour, we need to contextualize individual behaviour within macro-level processes, or the structure of society. For example, when one is born into a given society, one learns the language, customs, and expectations of that culture. Thus, behaviour that is appropriate in one culture (e.g., spanking a child) may not be appropriate in others.

3. *At birth, the human infant is asocial*. Newborns are born with impulses and needs, and with the potential for social development and to become a social being. For example, a newborn does not cry all night to punish parents, or sleep all day to please parents. Thus, behaviours and expectations do not begin to take on meaning until babies begin to learn to channel their behaviours in specific directions via training and socialization from their parents.

4. *A socialized being is an actor as well as a reactor*. Humans do not simply react to one another in robotic fashion. Rather, humans are minded beings, responding to a symbolic environment that involves responses to interpreted and anticipated

stimuli. In this way, they can feel guilt over past behaviours, assess new ways of responding, and dream of future possibilities. This suggests that humans can take the role of others, or that we can place ourselves "in someone else's shoes."

There are also a number of other key concepts. The first is the idea of the development of a social self, which is developed in interaction with others. For example, a young adult may occupy the status of child, student, sister, athlete, and many others. These statuses have expectations (roles) assigned to them, and are organized and integrated into the social self. In this way, the social self is never fixed, static, or in a final state. Family members not only play an important role in the development of the social self, but also in feelings of self-worth, which do not exist at birth but are learned (e.g., Felson and Zielinski, 1989).

Also of central importance in understanding child development and modifications of the social self are the role of significant others and reference groups. Although parents, particularly mothers, are usually the most significant socializers, other people or groups can also be important. These individuals can be other family members such as siblings, grandparents, aunts, or uncles, or even role models presented in the media, such as the pop stars Justin Bieber or Miley Cyrus. These significant others influence children's behaviour by what they do and what they say. Reference groups, on the other hand, constitute a source of comparison that operates in a similar fashion. These groups serve as a point of reference and standard for conduct, such as a religious group, a hobby club, peer groups, or a company (e.g., The Gap, Nintendo).

Finally, another central concept of the symbolic interactionist perspective is the notion of George Herbert Mead's generalized other. This concept signifies how individuals are often consistent and predictable in their behaviour, and how people learn to view themselves from the perspective of others who are either physically or symbolically present. As such, behaviour results less from drives and needs, unconscious processes, and biological forces and more from interaction processes and internalized meanings of self and others. Interactions are also situated within socio-cultural context, including schools, peers, the mass media, and day-to-day living in particular social environments.

Gender-Role Socialization

Gender roles refer to the expectations associated with being masculine or feminine, which may or may not correspond with one's sex, whereas sex roles can be defined as the expectations related to being biologically of one sex or another. Formation of these roles and one's identity (i.e., how one defines or perceives oneself in terms of these roles) is a developmental process that unfolds over time (Greenglass, 1982). There is also little denying that males and females differ in these processes, and that gendered divisions are found in virtually all societies.

For many centuries, it was assumed that "anatomy is destiny" and these differences were largely innate or inborn. However, many feminists argue that this belief provides a major ideological justification for a system of stratification that privileges men and subordinates women. Instead, they argue that we must also consider socialization processes and the organization and practices of society. Fundamental differences in sex-role socialization and gender-role stereotypes continue to exist, and this begins at birth and continues throughout one's life. This is illustrated in the media (as previously discussed) and the kinds of toys and games that continue to be manufactured, marketed, and bought for children. Gender-specific toys are thought to perpetuate activities directed toward appearance, romance, and the home for girls. Conversely, "rugged" and aggressive activities directed away from the home are encouraged for boys (Greenglass, 1982). Moreover, many studies show that little boys experience greater pressure to behave in a gender-appropriate way, and that this pressure is enforced more harshly.

For example, traditionally, little girls are given dolls, sewing machines, and makeup, while little boys are often presented with toy guns, action figures, cars, and computer games that contain violent content. And while the ever-popular Barbie doll (introduced by Mattel in 1959) has transformed over time to represent the "career woman" and other professions as well as non-White ethnic identities, many feminists continue to bemoan Barbie's unrealistic connotations and body measurements, cultural ideals that, they claim, are imposed on little girls by a patriarchal society. For example, in reality, the probability of a girl obtaining Barbie's body shape in adulthood is estimated at less than one in 100,000. Conversely, "Ken"—Barbie's "boyfriend"—is more realistic to achieve at about one in 50 (Nortons, Old, Olive, and Dank, 1996).

Another example of how institutions are highly gendered is our educational system, which also plays an important role in the formation of gender identities through curriculum and its local culture. Connell (1996) maintains that each school has its own "gender regime," which contributes to the ongoing negotiation and renegotiation of femininity or masculinity. By way of illustration, a school's style of dress can act as a power signifier of social acceptability, expression of identity, and a signifier of fashion that separates "the girls from the boys." For instance, at some schools, "the look for boys" is to appear somehow connected to sports, athleticism, strength, and power and this becomes the hegemonic norm (Swain, 2004).

Fox (2001, 2009) reveals other structural sources of gender differences and how these can resurface beyond childhood (i.e., in young families). Her research uncovers how parenthood can produce a more conventional division of labour in the home. From this perspective, gender inequity and gender-role behaviour arise out of the gendered division of paid and unpaid work, and these conditions further shape and constrain our options and behaviour. In contemporary society, a shortage of outside community supports and the privatization of parenthood mean that women continue to have the ultimate responsibility for their babies' welfare. This creates women's dependence on men or other family members (e.g., on their own mothers), and strengthens gendered divisions between men and women.

In short, gender socialization is lifelong and does not end in childhood. It continues (and can even deepen) through certain institutional practices and discourses that produce gendered adults and identities. As a result, despite feminist efforts over the past 30 years to challenge gender-role socialization and conventional gender divisions, many inequities remain in families. And while many couples negotiate the changes in their lives, women in a materially strong position (whose bargaining power tends to be relatively good before motherhood) may be better able to resist dynamics that place them in an unequal position within the family (Fox, 2009).

Furthermore, despite gender-role socialization, some scholars argue that empirical research actually shows more variation *within* genders than *between* the two groups. For example, while many of us would imagine two non-overlapping groups with respect to traits such as aggressiveness or math scores, in reality, the overlap between males and females is far greater than the difference, as depicted in Figure 7.3. This means that two normal bell-shaped curves on math scores would be virtually identical if we removed the tiny percentage of males who are "prodigies" from the sample (Travis, 1992). This finding calls into question popular conceptualizations such as "sugar and spice and everything nice ... that's what little girls are made of." It also beckons us to move away from the narrow and limited questions of "Do girls and boys differ and, if so, who's better or worse?" and ask instead: "Why is everyone so interested in differences?" and "What functions does the belief in differences serve?" (Travis, 1992: 43).

Cultural Shifts in Child-Rearing Advice and Ideologies of Parenthood

It is also valuable to track changes in child-rearing advice and the culture of parenting, since these shifts also reflect changing conceptions of childhood as well as theoretical and hegemonic ideologies on childhood socialization. For example, Wall (2005) notes that child-rearing advice emerged in tandem with the growing authority of medical science in the late 19th and 20th centuries. At this time, advice in Canada focused on medical concerns over high rates of infant mortality. This was also an era of poor refrigeration

Figure 7.3
Overlapping Normal Curves and Gender: Distribution of Math Scores

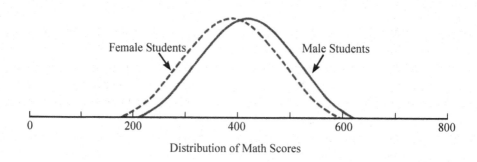

Source: C. Travis, *Mismeasure of Woman: Why Women Are Not the Better Sex, the Inferior Sex, or the Opposite Sex* (New York: Touchstone, 1992), p. 42.

and poor sewage/water systems, as well as high rates of contagious diseases. However, while a war was waged on infant mortality—a war that included government funding for milk depots, well-baby clinics, and a major educational campaign aimed at mothers—it did not include a battle against poverty or unsafe living conditions.

Rather, mothers' behaviour and lack of knowledge was targeted, which spurred the growth of advice literature (Arnup, 1994; Wall, 2005). In particular, this advice, which shows the early influences of behaviourism, focused heavily on personal hygiene, breast-feeding, and proper food preparation. Mothers were expected to rely on "science" and "experts" for advice in all areas. Many of these experts (who, ironically, were often men) came from medicine and psychology backgrounds, and strongly encouraged "scientific management" of children. As a result, they tried to promote self-discipline and good habits through behaviours such as rigid scheduling and early toilet training (Wall, 2005).

Many researchers (e.g., Coontz, 1992; Wall, 2005) observe that following World War Two, a distinct shift in child-rearing advice could be seen. Hay (1996: 9, 69) further notes that during this time, "the ideology of intensive mothering" became a widely accepted belief system. In other words, this set of child-rearing guidelines supported the view that child-rearing should be "child centered, expert guided, emotionally absorbing, labour intensive, and financially expensive." This was also an era in which many families wanted security and comfort. The favourable economic conditions of the time also allowed many families to live in middle-class, traditional family structures with distinct gender roles. In particular, mothers, who had been increasingly encouraged in the first part of the century by medical science to view motherhood as a full-time occupation (Arnup, 1994), now had the time and the means to do so. As a result, child-rearing literature began to focus more on the social context of mother-child relationships and its role in psychological health, rather than on medical concerns such as children's physical health. In particular, Bowlby's theory of mother-child bonding, which inspired subsequent attachment theory, strongly affected expert advice. This theory emphasized the importance of the continual presence of a warm, loving, and responsive mother from birth onward (Wall, 2005).

Wall (2005) also finds that there has been a wider expansion of educational material targeted at parents stressing the importance of secure attachment, in addition to ample stimulation in a child's early years (usually up to three to five years). This advice pro-liferated in the early 1990s and was based on the purportedly "new" brain science. This body of research "evidence" suggests that the amount and type of synaptic connections made in the young child's brain will affect the manner in which the child's brain will become wired. It is assumed that once the connections are made (or not made), brain wiring becomes almost impossible to undo. However, critics charge that there is very little evidence to prove that the years before five are as critical as the expert would suggest (e.g., see Brunner, 2000). Yet, despite this criticism, the new brain research has become part of the taken-for-granted discourse with respect to children's needs and "proper" parenting behaviour. Interestingly, this research also spilled over into the pre-birth period, which focuses on how expectant mothers can give their children a competitive advantage by beginning to stimulate and educate them while they are still in the womb (Wall, 2005).

It is also important to note the legacy of Dr. Spock's pioneering book entitled, *Baby and Child Care*, which was printed in 1946. Advice in this book was very different from the kind of advice offered in earlier times, such as the 1920s (see example in Box 7.4). As Wall (2005) notes, his approach fit within, and helped to define, a more permissive and child-centred style of parenting. This is reflected in his opening words: "Trust yourself. You know more than you think you do." Thus, Spock's conception of children was more innocent than the child of past expert advice. Furthermore, the needs of the child took precedence over those of the mothers. Therefore, by implication, mothers became more blameworthy when something went wrong.

Indeed, Gustafson (2005) asserts that "master discourses" about mothering continue in today's society. These master discourses refer to those overarching social narratives that organize women's way of thinking about, interpreting, and performing motherwork, thereby creating social expectations for women's connection with their children. As elaborated in Box 7.5, mothers continue to be blamed for children's negative experiences and behaviours and a "good mother/bad mother" binary with oppositional categories is socially created.

Finally, it is also important to recognize how family life and the practice of mothering children has historically been monitored and regulated through government policy in tandem with

---

Box 7.4
Changing Advice on Children and Pacifiers

These excerpts illustrate interesting differences in child-rearing advice with respect to the use of pacifiers on children:

The "pacifier" habit—the habit of sucking a rubber nipple—is an inexcusable piece of folly for which the mother or nurse is directly responsible. The habit when formed is most difficult to give up. The use of the "pacifier," thumb-sucking, finger sucking, etc., make thick baggy lips, on account of the exercise to which the parts are subjected. They cause an outward bulging of the jaws, which is not conducive to personal attractiveness.

Source: Department of Public Health, *The Care of the Infant and Young Child* (Toronto: Author, 1922, cited in Ward, 2002).

A pacifier is helpful for fretfulness or to prevent thumb-sucking…A baby who has periods of mild irritability can often be entirely quieted by having a pacifier to suck. We don't know whether this is because the sucking soothes some vague discomfort or simply kept the baby's mouth busy…Most of the babies who use a pacifier freely for the first few months of life never become thumb suckers, even if they give up the pacifier at three or four months.

Source: Dr. Benjamin Spock, *Baby and Child Care*, p. 286, 1945, 1946, 1957, 1968, 1976.

Box 7.5
"The Bad Mother"

In the discourse of binary polarization, the opposite of the good mother is the bad mother. Marked as different, undeserving, and Other, the bad mother is the woman who fails to reproduce white, middle-class, Judeo-Christian family values in appearance, the espousal of beliefs, and the performance of motherwork. Poor women, Aboriginal women, immigrant women, lesbians, and other marginalized women tend to be positioned as Other mothers on a short downward slide to the embodiment of a bad mother.

The bad mother is imagined to ignore, trivialize, or reject her child's need for love, caring, and nurturance both as an intellectual understanding and as a lived practice. She is regarded as unloving and uncaring. The stereotypical image of the bad mother that springs to mind is the woman who neglects, abuses, or fails to protect her child. A woman who is unwilling or unable to perform her motherly duties is thought to be motivated by selfishness, self-absorption, and self-indulgence—all individual defects. Finally and germane to this discussion, the bad mother is the absent mother—absent emotionally or absent physically from her children. Given these ways of thinking and talking about mothering, a woman who lives apart from her birth children would seem to be the epitome of the bad mother—an unnatural, aberrant woman.

In this passage drawn from the case study, the polarization of the good mother/ bad mother is evident in this woman's recollection of the day she told her work colleagues that her children were living with their birth father and his new wife:

Colleagues who had not previously engaged me in discussions of a personal nature were intrigued by my decision. The questions were variously phrased but the implications were clear. Why weren't the children living with me? Had the courts awarded custody to the father? Had I abused them? Had I neglected them? Was I unfit for some other reason? Did I have a "problem" with alcohol? Did I have a history of drug abuse? When I denied these causes for a change in custody, their questions took on a different tone. If there were no grounds for removing the children from my care, then why weren't they still with me? My simple answer was that the children wanted to live with their dad. Children want to do lots of things, I was told, but that doesn't mean that they get to decide where to live. Clearly I was abdicating my motherly duty to raise my children. Or perhaps, came the insinuation, there was a more ugly explanation. Was I using my children's feelings as a cover for my own deep-seated desires to be childless and carefree? Was I putting my own needs before those of my children? What other reasons could I have for downloading the care of my children to another woman? In any case I was unfit to parent and the children were better off with their father.

Source: Gustafson, D.L. 2005. "The social construction of maternal absence," in D.L. Gustafson (ed.), *Unbecoming Mothers: The Social Production of Maternal Absence.* New York: Haworth Press (pp. 27–29).

the growth of other medical and social service institutional practices. For example, Donzelot (1979) draws upon data from European countries to show how governments deliberately set out to "police" mothers and how this continues in contemporary social work practices. In the case of "the troubled child," the true locus of illness is seen as the family rather than certain conditions, such as poverty or a lack of social support. Treatment, therefore, might consist of sending a child to a psychiatrist or to a foster home and by regulating his or her behaviour under juvenile law. In this way, the agency workers become "rivals" with the judicial system. In short, the politics of the family become, in fact, the business of official agencies, such as psychiatry or social work. Similarly, Gubrium (1992) illustrates how parenting and domestic troubles are embedded in organizational activities and institutional images by focusing on a common venue of "domestic repair," the treatment facility. From this perspective, he highlights how family therapy workers come to see family troubles as they do, and how they get family members to accept their version of family troubles.

In sum, we have witnessed some significant changes in the type of expert advice presented to parents over the last century. We can also see the emergence of the ideology of motherhood. This set of beliefs highlights the powerful and persistent way of thinking that a woman's primary responsibility is to care for her biological offspring. Indeed, child-care labour, like all forms of caring labour, is highly gendered (Gustafson, 2005), yet change is slowly occurring in this area as fathers begin to participate more in child care, as previously covered in Chapter 5.

Summary

This chapter underscores the problems inherent in viewing childhood as an essentially definable social position. Instead, childhood is a fluid social construct such that meanings of children and experiences of childhood and parenting change over time. For example, the emergence of adolescence as a "new" and separate developmental phase places new demands on parents and family consumption practices. From a life course framework, this idea illuminates how life course developmental stages are embedded within unique socio-historical, political, and geographical locations and reciprocally influence "linked lives." Notably, conceptualizations of children and how they become socialized shift in tandem with changing ideologies of childhood and the changing culture of parenting.

Socialization is defined as a lifelong, bi-directional process that teaches and prepares children to become functional members of society. The child's initial and most enduring social interactions are in the family, making parents one of the most significant agents of socialization. In addition to this intergenerational influence, other institutions also play important roles in moulding children's behaviour, such as daycare, the mass media, the educational system, the peer group, and religion. Several competing and complementary theories on childhood socialization were presented, and it was noted that these socialization processes are gendered and contribute to masculine or feminine identities.

And while theories often share some basic assumptions, similar to social constructions of childhood, they are also created within a particular historical time and location and in reaction to the scientific and political thoughts of the day. Child-rearing advice has also transformed in relation to these new developments, particularly in psychology and medicine, but also in relation to shifting and emergent ideologies of parenthood that occur at the societal and state level. In particular, the pervasive ideology of motherhood fosters discourse, practices, and the belief that mothers are most naturally suited to raising and socializing their children. This ideology has considerable consequence for child-rearing practices, gender socialization, and our day-to-day experiences of family life in Canada.

Questions for Critical Reflection and Debate

1. Debate the following: As life expectancy continues to increase, childhood will become extended as a social category.
2. Recall the last time that you visited a toy store. What kinds of toys and games seemed specifically targeted to little boys and girls? How might this affect the kinds of toys and games that parents buy for their children and how they are socialized into gender-specific roles?
3. Why are siblings raised in the same family environment often very different from one another? Consider the role of both genetics and socialization processes.
4. Present an argument for and against the following statement: Parental care is superior to daycare.
5. What kinds of challenges might a recent immigrant child face in trying to become socialized in Canadian society?
6. How do the popular media (e.g., films, TV, printed material) perpetuate specific ideologies of motherhood and fatherhood? Provide specific examples relative to other socialization agents (e.g., educational and religious institutions).

Glossary

Attachment theory is based on the premise that a strong attachment to a warm, loving, and responsive mother is necessary for emotional, psychological, and cognitive development.

Childhood as a social construct refers to how social understandings about what children experience, need, and what is expected of them in larger society vary by time and location.

Classical conditioning is rooted in learning theory and links a known response to a stimulus, as illustrated in Pavlov's dog experiment.

Generalized other is the internalized moral "self" and the social controls that the individual develops from interacting with significant others.

Ideology of motherhood refers to the belief system that women are "naturally" suited to take on the primary responsibility for the care and nurturance of children.

Operant or instrumental conditioning focuses on the response, which is not related to any known stimuli. Instead, it functions in an instrumental manner, in that one learns to make a certain response on the basis of the outcome that response produces.

Significant others are those individuals or role models who take on special importance to children, such as parents, other relatives, TV heroes, or friends.

Socialization is a lifelong process of learning to become a capable, functioning member of society and is shaped by institutions such as the family, peer groups, schools, religion, and the mass media.

Further Reading

Albanese, P. 2009. *Children in Canada Today*. Toronto: Oxford University Press. The first in-depth work of childhood sociology in this country. Covers the key social theories and agents of socialization, as well as various social policies designed to improve their lives.

Berson, I.R., and M.J. Berson. 2010. *High-Tech Tots: Children in a Digital World*. Charlotte, N.C.: Information Age Publications. Examines the interface between young children and information and communication technology from a global perspective and several related issues, such as cybersafety and cybercitizenship.

Fox, B. 2009. *When Couples Become Parents: The Creation of Gender in the Transition to Parenthood.* Toronto: University of Toronto Press. Using data from longitudinal, in-depth interviews with both male and female partners in 40 heterosexual Canadian couples over the course of a year, this book explores the ways in which gender is "produced" and "reproduced" in the transition from singlehood to parenthood.

Handel, G., S. Cahill, and F. Elkin. 2007. *Children and Society*. Los Angeles: Roxbury. Presents a comprehensive sociological portrayal of children and childhood. It emphasizes the tension between children's active agency and other primary socializing influences, primarily from a symbolic interactionist perspective.

Lauster, N., and G. Allan (Eds.). 2011. *The End of Children? Changing Trends in Childbearing and Childhood*. Vancouver, B.C.: University of British Columbia Press. A timely examination of the causes and consequences of declining fertility rates and modern parenting practices.

Thelen, T., and H. Haukanes. 2010. *Parenting after the Century of the Child: Travelling Ideas, Institutional Negotiations and Individual Responses*. Burlington, VT: Ashgate. Drawing on research conducted in the U.S., Africa, and South East Asia, this book provides insights into the dynamics and ambivalences involved in the reframing of childhood and parenthood.

Related Web Sites

Canadian Childcare Federation is a national organization dedicated to providing Canadians with the information on early learning and child care knowledge and best practices, http://www.cccf-fcsge.ca/home_en.html.

Invest in Kids Foundation is a national charitable organization dedicated to ensuring the healthy social, emotional, and intellectual development of children from birth to age five by strengthening parenting knowledge, skills, and confidence, http://fnih.investinkids.ca/.

Kids Health (est. 1995 by The Nemours Foundation's Centre for Children's Health Media) is the largest and most visited site on the web, providing health information about children from before birth and through adolescence, www.kidshealth.org.

Mombian is a site offering social support links on LGBT parenting, starting a family, raising children, law and politics and other topics, www.mombian.com. Facebook: Mombian. Twitter: Mombian

National Parenting Centre, founded in 1989, dispenses valuable information and advice to parents from some of the world's most respected authorities in the field of child-rearing and development, http://tnpc.com.

References

Arat-Koc, S. 1989. "In the Privacy of Our Own Home: Foreign Domestic Workers as a Solution to the Crisis in the Domestic Sphere in Canada." *Studies in Political Economy* 28: 33–55.

Ariès, P. 1962. *Centuries of Childhood: A Social History of Family Life*. New York: Vintage Books.

Arnup, K. 1994. *Education for Motherhood: Advice for Mothers in Twentieth-Century Canada.* Toronto: University of Toronto Press.

Bradbury, B. 2005. "Social, Economic, and Cultural Origins of Contemporary Families." In M. Baker (ed.), *Families: Changing Trends in Canada*, 5th ed. (pp. 71–98). Toronto: McGraw-Hill Ryerson.

Brunner, J. 2000. "Tot Thought."*New York Review of Books* XLVII, no. 4: 27–30.

Charon, J.M. 1979. *Symbolic Interactionism: An Introduction, an Interpretation, an Integration*. Englewood Cliffs: Prentice-Hall.

Clark, W. 2011. "Kid's Sports," retrieved January 24, 2011 from http://www.statcan.gc.ca/pub/11-008-x/2008001/article/10573-eng.htm#a3.

Connell, R.W. 1996. "Teaching the Boys: New Research on Masculinity, and Gender Strategies for Schools."*Teachers College Record* 98: 206–235.

Coontz, S. 1992. *The Way We Never Were: American Families and the Nostalgia Trap.* New York: Basic Books.

Côté, J.E., and A.L. Allahar, 1994.*Generation on Hold: Coming of Age in the Late Twentieth Century*. Toronto: Stoddart.

Donzelot, J. 1979. *The Policing of Families*. New York: Random House.

Felson, R.B., and M.Z. Zielinski. 1989. "Children's Self-Esteem and Parental Support." *Journal of Marriage and the Family* 51: 727–735.

Fox, B. 2001. "The Formative Years: How Parenthood Creates Gender." *The Canadian Review of Sociology and Anthropology* 38: 373–390.

Fox, B. 2009. *When Couples Become Parents: The Creation of Gender in the Transition to Parenthood*. Toronto: University of Toronto Press.

Greenglass, E.R. 1982. *A World of Difference: Gender Roles in Perspective*. Toronto: John Wiley & Sons.

Gubrium, J. 1992. *Out of Control: Family Therapy and Domestic Order*. Thousand Oaks: Sage.

Gustafson, D.L. (Ed.). 2005. *Unbecoming Mothers: The Social Production of Maternal Absence*. New York: Haworth Press.

Hay, M.S. 1996. *The Cultural Contradictions of Motherhood*. New Haven: Yale University Press.

Livesey, C. 2005. "Family Life: Childhood." Retrieved September 13, 2005 from Chris Livesey: www.sociology.org.uk.

Macdonald, C.L. 1998. "Manufacturing Motherhood: The Shadow Work of Nannies and Au Pairs." *Qualitative Sociology* 21: 25–53.

Murray, S.B. 1998. "Child Care Work: Intimacy in the Shadows of Family-Life." *Qualitative Sociology* 21: 149–168.

Nortons, K., T. Old, S. Olive, and S. Dank. 1996. "Ken and Barbie at Life Size." *Sex Roles: A Journal of Research* 34: 287–294.

Skinner, B.F. 1963. "Operant Behavior." *American Psychologist* 18: 503–515.

Statistics Canada. 2001. "Religions in Canada." Retrieved December 11, 2006, from www12.statcan.ca/English/census01/Products, 96F0030XIE2001015.

Statistics Canada, 2005. "Child Care." *The Daily* (February 7).

Strong, B., and C. DeVault. 1992. *The Marriage and Family Experience*, 5th ed. New York: West Publishing Co.

Sutherland, A., and B. Thompson. 2003. *Kidfluence: The Marketer's Guide to Understanding and Reaching Generation Y—Kids, Tweens and Teens*. Toronto: McGraw-Hill.

Swain, J. 2004. "The Right Stuff: Fashioning an Identity through Clothing in a Junior School." In M. Webber and K. Bezanson (eds.), *Rethinking Society in the 21st Century: Critical Readings in Sociology* (pp. 81–92). Toronto: Canadian Scholars' Press Inc.

Travis, C. 1992. *Mismeasure of Woman: Why Women Are Not the Better Sex, the Inferior Sex, or the Opposite Sex*. New York: Touchstone.

Wall, G. 2005. "Childhood and Childrearing." In M. Baker (ed.), *Families: Changing Trends in Canada*, 5th ed. (pp. 163–180). Toronto: McGraw-Hill Ryerson.

Chapter 8

All Our Families

Diversity, Continuity, and Challenge in Lesbian, Gay, and Transgendered Families

Learning Objectives

In this chapter you will learn that …
- the ideological use of The Family and the assumption of difference in lesbian and gay families is problematic
- it is difficult to arrive at accurate estimates of lesbian and gay individuals and families in the Canadian population
- there are both similarities and differences between lesbian and gay couples and heterosexual couples with respect to life course patterns of support and family relationships
- children of lesbians and gays fare as well as children of heterosexual parents—socially, economically, and health-wise—despite assumptions to the contrary
- many challenges remain ahead with respect to social and legal rights and acceptance of lesbian and gay families

Introduction

We are all aware of the fact that not all intimate partnerships are "opposite sex," that is, comprised of one heterosexual man and one heterosexual woman. Indeed, many Canadians identify themselves as gay, lesbian, bisexual, or "transgendered"—the latter which is a blanket term used to describe someone who does not conform to social roles based on their biological sex—yet the family lives of gay and lesbians have remained largely invisible until fairly recently. This partly stems from the methodological problems inherent in studying a sensitive topic area. Gay and lesbians must also be willing to disclose a status that is sometimes met with anti-homosexual prejudice. Therefore, many of these individuals may not wish to share the intimate details of their lives with researchers for fear of being further victimized or categorized (Nelson, 1996: 10).

While research on this topic continues to grow, much remains to be learned about gay and lesbian families and how the very idea of assuming "difference" shapes our contemporary ideas and knowledge about diverse family lifestyles. The fact that same-sex marriage became legal only in recent years, for instance, means that we do not know much about same-sex legal unions or divorce, for that matter. Moreover, there is growing awareness of the pitfalls associated with characterizing gay and lesbian families as homogeneous and deviant relative to the "standard North American family" ideological code (or SNAF, as discussed in Chapter 1). From this perspective, these families constitute a "social problem" rather than a legitimate family lifestyle that biases how and what we know about diverse family arrangements (Hicks, 2005; Kinsman, 2006—see boxes 8.1 and 8.2).

In light of these important research gaps and methodological issues, this chapter will explore a variety of trends and issues relevant to the lives of gay and lesbian families. This will include a focus on the historical and ideological positioning of gay and lesbians

Box 8.1
Is Gay Parenting Bad for Kids? Responding to the "Very Idea of Difference" in Research on Lesbian and Gay Parents

...I do not support the view that we live in a society in which lesbians and gay men are "just different." Instead, we live in one that organizes sexual discourse to produce hierarchies in which traditional and heteronormative family forms are dominant, and this is reinforced through a series of textual, legal, social, and cultural practices...if we start from the baseline that differences between gay and straight families exist, then such ideas can play into the hands of the Christian right because they do not question the very system of sexual knowledge that organizes contemporary ideas about sexuality. That is, the "idea of difference" shapes our practices of knowing (Seidman, 1997), so that we start to ask whether and how the children of lesbians and gay men turn out different, instead of asking how contemporary discourses organize "sexual identities" into discrete groupings.

Source: Hicks, S. 2005. "Is gay parenting bad for kids? Responding to the 'very idea of difference' in research on lesbian and gay parents." *Sexualities*, Vol. 8: 153–168.

in opposition to The Family. In addition, an overview of socio-demographic trends with respect to prevalence and partnership formation will be provided, as well as the wider network of kin and friendship relations of lesbian and gay couples. Finally, social and legal recognition in relation to rights, entitlements, and benefits, and challenges to reduce discrimination and homophobia will be highlighted.

Changing Attitudes toward Same-Sex Partnerships

Contemporary attitudes toward same-sex partnerships have religious, legal, and moral historical roots. Before the High Middle Ages, homosexual acts appear to have been widely tolerated or ignored by the Christian Church throughout Europe, although this changed by the 13th century (Hereck, 2005). Negative sentiments continued into the 19th and early 20th centuries, such that public opinion was that all sex not intended to produce children could lead to "degeneration because precious bodily fluids were wasted" (Ward, 2002: 95). Yet, it is interesting to note that some Aboriginal peoples had complex systems of sex and gender in which some individuals were perceived to combine the spirits of male and female. These "two-spirited" people were thought to be very fortunate and blessed with power, generosity, and good luck (O'Brien and Goldberg, 2000; Williams, 1992).

By the mid-19th century, the notion that homosexuality was a mental illness came to be widely accepted in North American society, although it was not universally viewed as

---

Box 8.2
Homosexuality as a "Social Problem"

Heterosexual hegemony is produced on many fronts—from family relations that often marginalize and sometimes exclude gays and lesbians, to the violence we face on city streets, to state policies, to the medical profession, to sociology, sexology, and psychiatry, to the church, the school system, and the media. These forms of sexual regulation (which do not develop in a linear fashion) interact with the social relations we live to produce heterosexist "common sense." There exist also conflicts between and within various agencies over definitions of homosexuality and jurisdictional disputes over who can best deal with the sexual deviant.

The entry of heterosexual hegemony into public "common sense" involves many variants of heterosexist discourse, each of which merits its own analysis...These include homosexuality as a sin (in religious discourse); as unnatural (in both religious and secular discourse); as an illness (in medicine and psychiatry and, in a new sense, with the current AIDS crisis); as a congenital disorder or inversion (in sex psychology and sexology); as deviance (in some sociological theory); homosexuals as child molesters, seducers, and corruptors (in certain sexological studies, the law, and the media); as a symptom of social or national degeneration (in Social Darwinist and eugenic discourse): homosexuals as communists, "pinkos," and a national security risk because of the potential for blackmail (rooted in McCarthyism, military organization, the Cold War and 1950s/1960s security regime practices); as tolerated only when practiced between consenting adults in "private" (the Wolfenden strategy of privatization); and as a criminal offence or a social menace (in police campaigns, "moral panics," and the media).

Source: Kinsman, G. 2006. "The creation of homosexuality as a 'social problem,'" in A. Glasbeck (ed.), *Moral Regulation and Governance in Canada: History, Context, and Critical Issues.* Toronto: Canadian Scholars' Press (pp. 103–104).

---

a "degenerative sickness." For example, Sigmund Freud's basic theory of human sexuality was that all individuals were innately bisexual and that they became heterosexual or homosexual as a result of their experiences with parents and others (Freud, 1905). Therefore, Freud argued that homosexuality should not be viewed as an unnatural form of pathology. It is also noteworthy that homosexuality was not removed from the American Psychiatric Association's *Diagnostic and Statistical Manual of Mental Disorders* (DSM) until 1973 (Hereck, 2005), although transgenderism and transsexualism continue to be classified as "gender-identity disorders," as discussed in Box 8.3.

It was not until 1969 that the Canadian Criminal Code was reformed so that acts in private between consenting adults were no longer criminal. However, this change in law did not completely erase a (continuing) popular stereotype that homosexuality represents

Box 8.3
Gender Identity Disorder Reform Advocates Contest Gender Identity Disorder

"Difference is not disease;
non-conformity is not pathology;
uniqueness is not illness"

GID Reform Advocates are medical professionals, caregivers, scholars, researchers, students, human rights advocates, and members of the transgender, bisexual, lesbian, and gay communities and their allies who advocate reform of the psychiatric classification of gender diversity as mental disorder.

What is GID?
"Gender Identity Disorder" (GID) is a diagnostic category in the *Diagnostic and Statistical Manual of Mental Disorders* (DSM), published by the American Psychiatric Association. The DSM is regarded as the medical and social definition of mental disorder throughout North America and strongly influences *The International Statistical Classification of Diseases and Related Health Problems* published by the World Health Organization. GID currently includes a broad array of gender variant adults and children who may or may not be transsexual and may or may not be distressed or impaired. GID literally implies a *"disordered"* gender identity.

Source: GID Reform Advocates. 2006. "Gender identity disorder reform," retrieved August 8, 2006 from www.transgender.org/didr/index.html.

a deviant kind of "perversion" (Ward, 2002). Fortunately, at the turn of the 21st century, attitudes are continuing to liberalize as the government, scholars, and the general public are increasingly likely to recognize and accept same-sex individuals and families as "legitimate" and equally deserving of respect, rights, and entitlements. Since the introduction of the Civil Marriage Act (introduced by Paul Martin's Liberal government as Bill C-38 and enacted on July 20, 2005), same-sex couples can now legally wed.

Worldwide, same-sex marriages are currently performed in Belgium, the Netherlands, Spain, South Africa, and the state of Massachusetts. New York State legalized same-sex marriages only just recently, in 2011 (see Table 8.1 for a summary table). However, many other countries and U.S. states permit some type of civil union, contract, or domestic partnership. For example, since 2001, same-sex couples in Germany can register for "lifetime partnerships," although they cannot legally wed. France also introduced a civil contract called the Pacs in 1991, which gives some rights to cohabiting couples regardless of sex (BBC News, 2006).

Table 8.1
Examples of Gay Marriage Legalization around the Globe

Country/State	Year Recognized
Belgium	2003
Canada	2005
Massachusetts, U.S.A.	2004
New York, U.S.A.	2011
Netherlands	2001
South Africa	2005
Spain	2005

Source: Partly adapted from BBC News, "Gay Marriages around the Globe," retrieved December 18, 2006, from www.newsvote.bbc.co.uk/mpapps/pagetools/print/news.bbc.co.uk.

The Canadian Census only recently began to collect data on same-sex couples, and researchers are also increasingly likely to include same-sex couples in studies of courtship, marriage, and other types of family studies. However, data and research focus almost exclusively on same-sex relationships such that we do not know much about bisexuality. Therefore, most of this chapter focuses on the family lives of gays and lesbians, with the recognition that some individuals may also be bisexual.

Ideological Positioning of Gays and Lesbians and "The" Family

The 1960s represents a decade distinguished for the formation of many social groups devoted to civil rights and greater equality for oppressed and disadvantaged groups. The Stonewall Riots (as shown in Figure 8.1) are frequently cited as a defining moment in North American history when people in the homosexual community fought back against what they perceived as a government-sponsored system that persecuted sexual minorities. Taking place in New York City, these spontaneous, violent demonstrations heralded the start of the gay rights movement in the United States and around the world. In Canada, many social activist groups began to form and numerous protests occurred (such as the one depicted in Figure 8.2). For example, Pride Toronto came into existence in the 1970s and this group has been very active in many events (e.g., parades, picnics, marches) and in raising public awareness of queer issues.

Overall, since the 1960s gays and lesbians have formed a massive social movement aimed at improving their social recognition, as well as a complete reorganization of gen-

Figures 8.1 and 8.2
The Gay Rights Movement in North America

In 1969, during the final weekend in June, drag queens and queer street kids rioted at the Stonewall Inn, a gay Club in New York City, as shown in the top photo. This event sparked a series of riots and is commonly cited as the beginning of the gay liberation movement. Subsequently, many protests and demonstrations occurred throughout the rest of the world, including Canada, such as the one shown in the bottom photo, which took place at the Vancouver Courthouse, August 28, 1971.

der, family, and sexuality. For example, some radical feminist lesbians and gays rejected traditional family values and motherhood because they saw these institutions as inherently oppressive. Indeed, some activists could be seen carrying banners that read "Smash the Family" and "Smash Monogamy" at public protests (Stacey, 1998). However, it is recognized that "lesbians and gays are not, and never have been, a unified group with one collective agenda for social change" (Clarke and Kitzinger, 2005: 139).

Many activists also fought against the tendency of heterosexual writers and researchers to characterize lesbian and gays as "outside relationships" and as unhappy, hedonistic, and alone as objects of pity and fear. Their concern was that as a result of this practice, "family" came to mean the opposite of homosexuality, with its presumed stability and as the natural source of happiness and caring. Yet, as argued by O'Brien and Goldberg (2000: 117), "this characterization of families is ridiculously wrong." In support of this assertion, they point to how heterosexual families are often sites of violence and abuse, as well as change, instability, and discomfort, themes that are also echoed throughout this textbook.

In today's society, many social groups continue to denounce this population, which further sets up an ideological divide between lesbian/gay and heterosexual families. These so-called defenders of "family values" (e.g., Focus on the Family, REAL Women) tend to attack groups that supposedly menace and undermine The Family. Moreover, family sociology has traditionally displayed a heterosexist bias that reproduces an ideology that places gay men and lesbians outside of and as hazardous to family relations. For example, many previous studies on lesbian/gay families have fallen into the category "sociology of deviance" or "social problems." Also, little original work has been done in a number of areas popular in sociology more generally, such as gender, social class, the effect of partner separation on children, ethnicity, and in areas of social policy and service delivery (Ambert, 2005). Notably, sociological research related to gender tends to assume that gender identity is a subjective and fixed sense of being either male or female, resulting in the usage of only two "legitimate" categories.

In sum, definitions and meanings given to The Family by social groups and researchers have significant repercussions for the lives of lesbian/gay families. In particular, they can undermine claims for greater measures of social justice. Indeed, ideological usages of The Family against gays and lesbians are homophobic since they spread an irrational fear and hatred of people who are not heterosexual. As a result, heterosexuality is politicized as the only valid form of sexual behaviour and as superior to any other family structure. Yet, as O'Brien and Goldberg further remind us, "there is no valid reason for refusing to call them families. They fall under every conceivable sociological criterion for identifying families" (2000: 133). Like all families, these individuals form close relations, pool material resources, socialize children, engage in emotional and physical support, and make up part of a larger kin network, topics that will be explored in further depth throughout this chapter.

Prevalence of Lesbian and Gay Individuals and Families

Ambert (2005) notes that in terms of a definition, there is not always a clear-cut distinction between homosexual and heterosexual self-identity. Some homosexuals may self-identify only at certain points in their life, rather than throughout their entire adult years. Also, some individuals may have had a homosexual past, but may identify as a heterosexual. And some individuals may identify as heterosexual, yet display or experiment with behaviours (e.g., cross-dressing, having same-sex sexual fantasies) that do not conform to societal norms of what is considered "gender appropriate." As Golden stated, "sexuality may be an aspect of identity that is fluid and dynamic as opposed to fixed and invariant" (1987: 19). Thus, coupled with a variety of other methodological issues, it is difficult to know exactly how many Canadians are gay, lesbian, bisexual, or transgendered individuals.

However, it is fairly well established that gays and lesbians constitute a significant but fairly small minority of the population. A recent Statistics Canada survey found that among Canadians aged 18–59, 1 percent reported that they considered themselves to be homosexual and 0.7 percent considered themselves bisexual, for a total of 1.7 percent of the population (see Table 8.2). Approximately 1.3 percent of men considered themselves homosexual, about twice the proportion of 0.7 percent among women. Women were slightly more likely to report being bisexual (0.9 percent) than men (0.6 percent). Moreover, as shown in Table 8.2, there appear to be variations in prevalence across Canada, although, as previously mentioned, a number of challenges exist with respect to gathering accurate data on this subject. Other carefully designed studies suggest that at the upper limit, approximately 5 percent of men identify as gay and fewer than 3.5 percent of women identify as lesbian, estimates that match other research studies (e.g., see Ambert, 2005, for review). These rates are lower than the well-publicized Kinsey Report, conducted in 1948, which suggested that 10 percent of the population was gay, a report that was later criticized for its non-representativeness and the self-selection of respondents.

Although previous national Census surveys have not asked individuals their sexual orientation, in Canada, the 2001 Census was the first to provide data on same-sex partnerships, although these data probably underestimate actual prevalence. In this survey, same-sex couples reflect people who identified themselves as living in a same-sex common-law union. A total of 10,360 same-sex couples fell into this category, representing 0.5 percent of all couples (married and unmarried). Of these unions, the Canadian Census counted about 19,000 male same-sex couples, or 55 percent of the total. Also, 6,455 lived in the Census metropolitan area of Montreal, while an additional 1,140 lived in the Quebec Census metropolitan area. Ontario has the largest number of same-sex partners (12,505), while Newfoundland and Labrador had the lowest proportion of same-sex couples (0.1 percent of all couples).

Male couples are more likely to live in Census metropolitan areas; 85 percent live in the larger urban areas of Canada, compared with 76 percent of female couples (Statistics Canada, 2001). In addition, female same-sex couples were five times as likely to have children living with them compared to male same-sex couples. Approximately 15 percent of the 15,200 female same-sex couples were co-residing with their children, compared with only 3 percent of male same-sex couples (Statistics Canada, 2002).

Table 8.2
Sexual Orientation in Canada, 2003

	Homosexual or Bisexual	
	Number	% of Total Population
Total	316,800	1.7
Newfoundland and Labrador	4,100E	1.3E
Prince Edward Island	F	F
Nova Scotia	5,900E	1.1E
New Brunswick	7,200E	1.6E
Quebec	103,400	2.3
Ontario	107,200	1.5
Manitoba	9,600E	1.5E
Saskatchewan	6,600E	1.2E
Alberta	23,400E	1.2E
British Columbia	47,700	1.9
Male	172,600	1.8
Female	144,300	1.5
18–34	139,200	2.0
35–44	101,900	1.9
45–59	75,700	1.2

E = Use with caution
F = Suppressed due to high sampling variability

Source: Statistics Canada, "Canadian Community Health Survey," *The Daily* (June 15, 2004): 8, retrieved from www.statcan.ca.

Gay and Lesbian Couple Relationships and Patterns of Support

O'Brien and Goldberg (2000) argue that the ideological positioning of gay men and lesbians in opposition to the The Family leads to the stereotype that these individuals lead lonely lives characterized by casual sexual encounters. However, similar to heterosexual couples, lesbian/gay couples can form a variety of relationships, from casual dating to cohabitation to, more recently, legal marital unions. Breakup rates between lesbian/gay and heterosexual couples are also found to be relatively the same, and research on older gay men and lesbians indicates that relationships lasting 20 or more years are not uncommon (Peplau, 1991). Moreover, most gay men and lesbians are satisfied with their relationships, despite the stresses of life in a heterosexist society (Peplau, 1991).

And, similar to heterosexual couples, partner abuse (covered in Chapter 14) can also be a problem in some intimate relationships (O'Brien and Goldberg, 2000).

Interestingly, lesbian and gay couples tend to report a more egalitarian division of labour than married couples (Patterson, 2000). It is suggested that unlike heterosexual relationships in which each gender is automatically given duties and rights, lesbians and gay couples negotiate a division of labour based upon skill, preference, and energy related to age and ability (e.g., see O'Brien and Goldberg, 2000 for review of studies). Gay couples also often report more autonomy from each other in terms of activities, friendships, and decision making than heterosexual married couples. Lesbian partners also tend to state that they enjoy greater relationship satisfaction and more intimacy, autonomy, and equality than married couples (Ambert, 2005). It is also suggested that greater equality and satisfaction found in gay and lesbian partnerships may be related to the tendency for couples to be dual wage earners and therefore have a high level of "material self-sufficiency" (Weston, 1991).

Linked Lives: Intergenerational Relations, Friendship Networks, and Children

The family of origin—or the family that one is born into or grows up in—can also play an important role in the lives of lesbians and gays. Relations between families and gays and lesbians, similar to heterosexual families, can be fairly unproblematic, or they can be fraught with tensions and ambiguity. In particular, young people may struggle with coming out (that is, to publicly acknowledge their sexuality) and try to challenge their family for acceptance, as depicted in Box 8.4 (Gibson, 1989). Unfortunately, families can mirror societal homophobia and this can be particularly troublesome if youth are living at home and are dependent on parents. And for those who decide to leave home to escape family- or school-related non-acceptance, many may find themselves caught in a vicious circle of homelessness and other social problems due to their young age, vulnerability, and lack of family support.

Research documents that gay and lesbians commonly experience shame, self-hatred, social isolation, verbal and physical harassment, suicide, and rejection by their families and other societal institutions. A recent highly publicized example of some of these challenges is voiced by Chaz Bono (formerly known as Chastity and the child of the famous entertainers Sonny and Cher) who recently published the book *Transition: The Story of How I Became a Man* (2010). In this candid account of a 40-year struggle to match his gender identity with his physical body and his transformation from female to male, Chaz tells his story of his painful but eventually joyful coming out and his ultimate state of self-acceptance.

Other research mirrors many of the same struggles that the LGBT population can experience. Suicide has been documented as a serious social problem among gay and lesbian youth, with family rejection and harassment at school cited as root causes (O'Brien and Goldberg, 2000). In addition, research documents that homosexuals and bisexuals

Box 8.4
Coming Out in the 905

I grew up in Thornhill, a fairly wealthy suburb of Toronto that forms part of the "905 belt" (so named because of the area code) surrounding the city...Growing up in this bubble, I had the warped perception that because my friends' families often seemed to have more disposable income than mine, I wasn't well off. I later realized that most of us were steeped in class privilege...Although there was a large Jewish population and a significant degree of racial diversity, many kinds of difference were superficially flattened out and glossed over with a veneer of shared class privilege and the language of liberal multiculturalism...I fit into my community in many ways: I was White, middle class, and Jewish. Still, from an early age I felt excluded in other respects. I was never interested in sports and had a terrible fear of gym class and of competing athletically in the schoolyard....And I remember being teased often...On several occasions I was mistaken for a girl.

In retrospect, I see the early signs of queerness in my young self. I idolized handsome actors and musicians, going through various crushes and later rationalizing that I didn't want these men but wanted to be like them. I don't recall consciously considering my own sexuality until about grade eight, which is when I developed a very tight friendship with M.W....I had such a strong desire to be with him that I would walk over to his house almost every day, hoping he might be outside playing basketball on the driveway...I also started to have the inkling that my feelings for M.W. and for other boys might mean that my sexuality was somehow different. I had never met any queer people—no relatives, teachers, friends or acquaintances—so I had to search discreetly for role models.

I looked first to media for information. I read anything I could get my hands on that dealt with LGBTQ people or issues. I rented queer movies. This was before *Will & Grace* and *Queer as Folk*, so Ellen DeGeneres's coming out was about the extent of a queer presence on TV...As I learned more and found role models, a swirling mass of thoughts and emotions began to resolve into a coherent expression of identity. If others were living their lives with openness and integrity, then perhaps I, too, could feel pride in being different. I tentatively attached a new label to myself—gay—and secretly wore it around for awhile...It wasn't until about six months later that my pride in my gay identity and an eagerness to share my desires and frustrations prompted me to come out. I chose Audrey as the first person to tell. She was my closest friend, and I knew that at the very least, I could trust her not to reveal my secret....When I was seventeen, I decided to come out to my parents, which remains the hardest thing that I've ever had to do. I told my mother first, and let her relay the news to my dad...But she was in no way prepared for what I had to say. She was shocked and went through several stages of understanding and accepting of my news...My father had lots of rational objections. He told me that same-sex attraction was an experience common to most boys…One of the things my parents and I argued about was my intention to come out to other people. I had visions of raising hell as a gay high-school activist, but for a long time my parents were very uncomfortable with the thought of my coming out to anyone else, because they didn't want people to judge me and have doors closed to me because of my sexual orientation…For a few months we didn't discuss it much, but when we started talking again after that silence, they had come to a much deeper understanding. Since then, I have felt comfortable being completely open about my life and sharing my thoughts and values with them.

Much of coming out is about coming into language—identifying ourselves with words and ideas, and choosing which words we will use to make ourselves coherent and legible to others. Our stories—and sometimes our memories—are therefore shifting and malleable. We trim and amend them in order to turn messy life experiences into a meaningful narrative of becoming, but the beginnings and endings are never fixed. And like all versions, this retelling of my coming out is incomplete. The story was heavily edited long before it reached this volume…. In the future, I'm sure the language and means of communication I use to tell my story will change many times. But the memory of struggling across language to put my desires and identity into words for the first time will remain with me.

Source: Collins, A. "Coming Out in the 905." In Project of Planned Parenthood of Toronto. 2004. *Hear Me Out: True Stories of Teens Educating and Confronting Homophobia*. Toronto: Second Story Press (excerpt from pp. 38–49).

are more likely to have unmet health care needs. For example, in 2003, the Canadian Community Health Survey found that 21.8 percent of homosexuals and bisexuals aged 18–59 reported that they had an unmet health care need, nearly twice the proportion of heterosexuals (12.7 percent). They are also more likely than heterosexuals to find life stressful, as shown in Figure 8.3. Moreover, youth not living in large urban centres may be particularly disadvantaged, since they may not have access to the same type of organizational support (e.g., in the educational system) and access to health and social services.

With respect to family reactions to gay and lesbian cohabitation, in comparison with opposite-sex cohabitation, research suggests that parents can have problems with acceptance and ambivalence. For example, in one study, a woman described being referred to in a joking manner by her partner's family as the "aunt" or "live-in-nanny" (Espstein, 2003). Indeed, the concept of intergenerational ambivalence, defined as "the experience of contradictory emotions toward the same object" (Weigert, 1991: 21), has utility in furthering our understanding of "institutionally incomplete" (Cherlin, 1978: 634) family relationships, including lesbian/gay family relationships across the life course. This line of thinking suggests that contemporary family life is characterized by a multiplicity

Figure 8.3
Variations in Health-Related Measures for Heterosexuals, Homosexuals, and Bisexuals

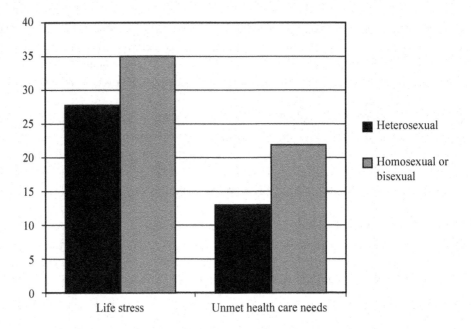

Source: Statistics Canada, "Canadian Community Health Survey," *The Daily* (June 15, 2004): 8, taken from table, retrieved from statcan.ca.

of forms yet to be "institutionalized," with well-established guidelines and norms for behaviours. This includes gay and lesbian unions, such that family relationships may be characterized by a polarization (i.e., positive to negative) of simultaneous feelings (Luescher, 2000).

Generally, the concept of intergenerational ambivalence can be conceptualized as structurally created contradictions in relations between parents and adult offspring. This term also highlights how intergenerational solidarity is not a one-dimensional concept because ambivalence is both a variable feature of structured sets of social relationships and a catalyst for social action, since actors can negotiate and renegotiate relationships over time. In this way, ambivalence represents a valuable "bridging concept" because it allows a conceptual link between social structure and individual agency (Connidis and McMullin, 2002; Lowenstein et al., 2003).

With regard to the impact of cohabitation among gay and lesbian partners on linked family lives, there is ample evidence to suggest that families can experience more ambivalence in their attitude toward same-sex cohabitation than heterosexual cohabitation. This may be partly due to a general lack of social acceptance toward this type of union (because of homophobia or fear of homosexuality), which in turn can make family acceptance more challenging. As a result, there may be more resistance from family members than in heterosexual partnerships (Nock, 1998). Some young adults may even be led to conceal the "true" nature of their partnership from their parents and other family members in an effort to avoid conflict and stress.

However, similar to the research on heterosexual cohabitation, the reactions and support from family members (particularly parents) is shown to vary according to a number of factors such as religion, race and ethnicity, parental education, and pre-existing relationship quality. For example, many religious orientations support only heterosexual unions and some racial/ethnic groups are less supportive in their attitudes (Morales, 1990). Ambivalent or negative reactions are also more evident among older parents, those with less education, and those who had strained relationships with their children prior to learning of their gay or lesbian identity (Savin-Williams, 2001).

Yet, research shows that over time, family members who initially disapproved often become more accepting and supportive of the relationship (Bernstein, 1995). This lends support to the idea that familial ties can involve more or less ambivalence at different points in the life course (Connidis and McMullin, 2002). However, in general, gay and lesbian individuals and cohabiting couples are found to receive more social support than non-gay couples from friends and their subculture than from their parents and their family of origin (Kurdek, 1998).

Turning to the children of lesbian/gay couples, studies on family relationships in these households is relatively sparse but generally indicate more similarities than differences (e.g., Patterson, 2000). For example, home environments are as conducive to psychosocial growth among family members, including children, as are those of heterosexual couples. Also, the daily routine and family life cycle is largely similar for both same-sex and opposite-sex families—children arrive, need love and supervision, grow up, and parenting flows accordingly. Lesbian and gay parents may also create a network of fictive kin or chosen family (such as a mixture of gay and non-gay friends and relatives) for social and emotional support. This network can provide their children with social support to compensate for a lack of family of origin support, or may constitute an additional network of supportive relations (Ambert, 2005).

With respect to the consequences of gay parenting, three main issues tend to surface at the societal level. These issues tend to be motivated by fears that: (1) children will grow up to be maladjusted because of social stigma; (2) that offspring will be sexually molested by their parents or associates; and (3) that the children will grow up to become homosexual (e.g., because of a lack of proper role models). Yet, none of these concerns has received empirical support. For example, children of same-sex couples tend to show few psychosocial differences than other children, despite the existence of societal homophobia. Moreover, children are not at a higher risk of being molested; in short, homosexuality is not synonymous with pedophilia. In fact, the vast majority of child molestors are heterosexual men (Ambert, 2005; Epstein, 2003). Also, children of homosexual partners tend to develop heterosexual identities, although they may be more tolerant of same-sex experimentation than children of heterosexual parents (Stacey, 1998).

The Battle Continues: Rights, Entitlements, and Challenges Ahead

Gay and lesbian social and legal rights, entitlements, and benefits continue to remain among the most hotly contested social and political issues, as illustrated in Box 8.4. Among these issues is social recognition, since a lack of this can place unique stresses upon lesbian/gay individuals and families. For example, some lesbian/gay individuals may not be able to "come out" in their families, workplaces, or communities. This can deny them the right to reveal their partner's existence, censor their conversations about their activities, and silence their pain and grief when a partner is ill or dies, or when a significant relationship has dissolved. And at social gatherings, such as during holidays or family events, they may have to bear the pain and stress of separation from their lovers, or they may have to downplay their verbal and physical expression of affection (e.g., see O'Brien and Goldberg, 2000, for an overview of studies).

With respect to legal and other social issues, dramatic shifts in same-sex relationships and parenting rights occurred during the late 1990s and early 2000s. Until recently, for instance, the homosexuality of a parent was deemed sufficient "proof" to deem a person "unfit" to have custody of a child (Epstein, 2003). In fact, as recently as the early 1990s, a study conducted for the Royal Commission on New Reproductive Technologies revealed that 76 percent of medical practitioners would refuse donor insemination to women even in a stable lesbian relationship (Rayside, 2002). Since that time, medical practitioners have become less discriminatory and laws have broadened to allow lesbians and gays to adopt children.

Yet, on a legal level, many lesbian/gay individuals continue to face discrimination even though they have successfully fought for the inclusion of sexual orientation as a prohibited ground of discrimination in the human rights code of all provinces and territories (with the exception of the Northwest Territories). Some gays and lesbians continue to be ineligible for the same tax breaks and work-related benefits, such as pensions, survivor's benefits, and parental leave. Yet, gay men and lesbians have successfully challenged official forms of discrimination in a number of different ways, and recent changes to same-sex marriage legislation show future progress. Overall, with the rising acceptance of lesbian/gay families and specific policies to support these families, it is likely that these discriminatory behaviours will continue to be reduced (Epstein, 2003; O'Brien and Goldberg, 2000).

Summary

This chapter explores the lives of lesbian/gay families, beginning with the recognition that it is problematic to assume difference and that it is imperative to ask how our societal discourse organizes "sexual identity" into discrete groupings. A major theme is that traditional meanings and interpretations of "family" are non-inclusive and need to be challenged. These definitions tend to reflect heteronormativity and result in social, institutional, and legal practices that reinforce heterosexuality as the only "normal" sexuality (Kitzinger, 2005). This creates a wedge between family types deemed not natural and legitimate and therefore not deserving of social recognition. Indeed, biology often becomes a more important component than emotional or social relationships as defining characteristics of a family (Epstein, 2003).

Studies establish more similarities than differences between same-sex and heterosexual couples and families. This observation further highlights how treating gender and sexuality as measurable outcomes is problematic (Hicks, 2005). At the same time, conducting research on social processes and challenges (such as on unmet health care needs) unique to gay/lesbian families has the potential to dispel homophobic stereotypes and improve lives (e.g., Benson, Silverstein, and Auerbach, 2005). For example, some recent research on how gay fathers work to challenge traditional cultural norms for fathers, families, and masculinity helps to reconceptualize family and "de-gender" parenting. From this lens, gay fathers are shown to expand role norms in novel ways that may serve as alternative models for all families (Schacher, Auerbach, Silverstein, 2005). Similarly, a previous study on lesbian mothering in Alberta highlights the importance of a positive social milieu for successfully raising their children (e.g., see Nelson, 1996).

Several social and legal challenges are outlined with respect to individual and family rights, entitlements, and benefits. Overall, it is clear that while progress has been made in reducing homophobia, we need to collectively address the systemic roots of oppression that are still faced by lesbians and gays at the turn of the 21st century. These experiences and conditions of subordination and injustice continue to be supported by many of our dominant institutions, including our families, the educational system, religious organizations, the media, and the legal system. Thus, until widespread social and cultural transformation occurs within these key institutions, greater equality for all families—regardless of sexual orientation—will not be achieved.

Questions for Critical Reflection and Debate

1. Rates of youths' disclosure that they are lesbian, gay, and bisexual vary widely. Explore how ethnicity, religious orientation, and other factors might affect the propensity to disclose one's sexual orientation.
2. Public opinion remains divided on whether same-sex marriage should be legal. Provide an argument for and against this issue.
3. Research documents that lesbian and gay couples tend to report a more egalitarian division of labour than married couples. Explore some possible reasons for this finding.
4. Outline some strategies (national, local, community) for reducing homophobia and discrimination for lesbian/gay families in Canadian society.
5. Do you think that the Canadian government has the right to request that individuals reveal their sexual orientation in Census surveys? What could be some possible uses and misuses of these data?

6. Imagine that you are a researcher studying transgendered families. Which topic areas do you think require more attention? What challenges might you face in trying to collect these data?

Glossary

Coming out is the public act of declaring oneself as a gay man or lesbian, as in "coming out of the closet."

Gender identity is the subjective sense or self-labelling as either male or female.

Heteronormativity results in social, institutional, and legal practices that reinforce heterosexuality as the normal, natural, taken-for-granted sexuality.

Heterosexist bias is the tendency to assume that families and households consist of partnerships between men and women, and that heterosexuality is the only normal form of sexual expression.

Homophobia refers to the fear of homosexuality or homosexuals and the tendency to label certain kinds of LGBT (an acronym for lesbian, gay, bisexual, and transgendered) behaviour as social problems.

Intergenerational ambivalence refers to contradictory emotions or the coexistence of both positive and negative feelings within generational relationships.

Transgendered is a term used to describe someone who does not conform to social roles based on his or her biological sex.

Further Reading

Duder, C. 2010. *Awfully Devoted Women: Lesbian Lives in Canada, 1900–65*. Vancouver: University of British Columbia Press. From a historical perspective, this book examines the social worlds of lesbians in Canada and the sexual relationships between women in an era of heteronormativity.

Feinberg, L. 1993. *Stone Butch Blues*. Ithaca: Firebrand Books. This is a deeply troubling novel that forces us to recognize the violence inflicted on those who do not fit stereotypes of heterosexual, male/female divisions. Within this context, the novel forces the reader to re-evaluate sexual stereotypes and medicine's role in their perpetuation.

Fruhauf, C., and D. Mahoney (Eds.). 2009. *Older GLBT Family and Community Life*. New York: Routledge. Covers a variety of issues older GLBT face within their families and communities such as family relationships and physical and mental health.

Goldberg, A. 2010. *Lesbian and Gay Parents and their Children: Research on the Family Life Cycle*. Washington, DC: American Psychological Association. Integrating both quantitative and qualitative approach and an interdisciplinary perspective, this book covers a wide range of family-related issues and research on lesbian and gay parents and their children.

Moore, M. 2011. *Invisible Families: Gay Identities, Relationships, and Motherhood among Black Women*. Berkeley, Calif: University of California Press. Drawing from interviews and surveys on Black gay women in New York City, this book explores how race and class influence understandings and experiences of lesbian family life.

Murray, H.A. 2010. *Not in this Family: Gays and the Meaning of Kinship in Postwar North America.* Philadelphia: University of Pennsylvania Press. Shows how kinship ties have been a strong force in gay culture and gives voice to gays and their parents through the use of introspective writings, including personal correspondence and diaries, published memoirs, fiction, poetry, song lyrics, movies, and visual and print media.

Powell, B. 2010. *Counted Out: Same-Sex Relations and Americans' Definitions of Family.* New York: Russell Sage Foundation. Explores the question "Who counts as family?" through an examination of diverse viewpoints and issues such as gay marriage, adoption, and social policy (e.g., child custody laws, end-of-life issues, estate rights).

Related Web Sites

Canadian Lesbian and Gay Archives was established in 1973 and preserves lesbian and gay history in Canada and other parts of the world. It offers public access to collected records, photographic collections, posters and artifacts, www.clga.ca.

Children of Lesbians and Gays Everywhere (COLAGE) is a support and advocacy organization for daughters and sons of lesbian, gay, bisexual, and transgender parents, http://www.colage.org. Facebook: COLAGE Twitter: COLAGENATIONAL

Family Equality Council is a national online resource centre (e.g., searchable library) related to lesbian, gay, bisexual, and transgendered families, http://www.familyequality.org/site/PageServer. Facebook: Family Equality Council, Twitter: family_equality

Lesbian and Gay Immigration Task Force—Canada (LEGIT/ICGL) is an all-volunteer organization that provides Canadian immigration information and support for same-sex partners, http://www.legit.ca/. Facebook: LEGIT: Canadian Immigration for Same-Sex Partners

Parents, Families, and Friends of Lesbians and Gays (PFLAG) has several chapters across Canada, http://www.pflagcanada.ca/en/index-e.asp.

References

Ambert, A.M. 2005. *Same-Sex Couples and Same-Sex Parent Families: Relationships, Parenting, and Issues of Marriage.* Ottawa: The Vanier Institute of the Family.

BBC News. 2006. "Gay Marriages around the Globe." Retrieved December 18, 2006, from www.newsvote.bbc.co.uk/mpapps/pagetools/print/news.bbc.co.uk.

Benson, A.L., L.B. Silverstein, and C.F. Auerbach. 2005. "From the Margins to the Center: Gay Fathers Reconstruct the Fathering Role." *Journal of GLBT Family Studies* 1: 1–29.

Bernstein, R.A. 1995. *Straight Parents, Gay Children: Keeping Families Together.* New York: Thunder's Mouth Press.

Cherlin, A. 1978. "Remarriage as an Incomplete Institution." *American Journal of Sociology* 84: 634–650.

Clarke, V., and C. Kitzinger. 2005. "We're Not Living on Planet Lesbian: Constructions of Male Role Models in Debates about Lesbian Families." *Sexualities* 8: 137–152.

Connidis, I.A., and J. McMullin. 2002. "Sociological Ambivalence and Family Ties: A Critical Perspective." *Journal of Marriage and the Family* 64: 558–568.

Epstein, R. 2003. "Lesbian Families." In M. Lynn (ed.), *Voices: Essays on Canadian Families*, 2nd ed. (pp. 76–102). Scarborough: Thomson Nelson.

Freud, S. 1905. "Three Essays on the Theory of Sexuality." In J. Strachey (ed. and trans.), *The Standard Edition of the Complete Psychological Works of Sigmund Freud* (vol. 7, pp. 123–245). London: Hogarth Press.

Gibson, P. 1989. "Gay Male and Lesbian Youth Suicide." In M.R. Feinleib (ed.), *Report of the Secretary's Task Force on Youth Suicide* (vol. 3, pp. 109–142). Washington: U.S. Dept. of Health and Human Services.

Golden, C. 1987. "Diversity and Variability in Women's Sexual Identities." In Boston Lesbian Psychologies Collective (ed.), *Lesbian Psychologies* (pp. 18–34). Urbana: University of Illinois Press.

Hereck, G. 2005. "Facts about Homosexuality and Mental Illness." Retrieved December 6, 2005, from http://psychology.ucdavis.edu/rainbow/html/facts_mentalhealth.

Hicks, S. 2005. "Is Gay Parenting Bad for Kids? Responding to the 'Very Idea of Difference' in Research on Lesbian and Gay Parents." *Sexualities* 8: 153–168.

Kinsman, G. 2006. "The Creation of Homosexuality as a 'Social Problem.'" In A. Glasbeck (ed.), *Moral Regulation and Governance in Canada: History, Context, and Critical Issues* (pp. 103–104). Toronto: Canadian Scholars' Press Inc.

Kitzinger, C. 2005. "Heteronormativity in Action: Reproducing the Heterosexual Nuclear Family in After-Hours Medical Calls." *Social Problems* 52: 477–498.

Kurdek, L.A. 1998. "Relationship Outcomes and Their Predictors: Longitudinal Evidence from Heterosexual Married, Gay Cohabiting, and Lesbian Cohabiting Couples." *Journal of Marriage and the Family* 60: 553–568.

Lowenstein, A., R. Katz, D. Prilutzky, and D. Melhousen-Hassoen. 2003. "A Comparative Cross-National Perspective on Intergenerational Solidarity." *Retraite et Societe* 38: 52–80.

Luescher, K. 2000. "A Heuristic Model for the Study of Intergenerational Ambivalence." Arbeitspapier no. 29. Konstanz: University of Konstanz.

Morales, E.S. 1990. "Ethnic Minority Families and Minority Gays and Lesbians." In F.W. Bozett and M.B. Sussman (eds.), *Homosexuality and Family Relations* (pp. 217–239). New York: Harrington Park.

Nelson, F. 1996. *Lesbian Motherhood*. Toronto: University of Toronto Press.

Nock, S.L. 1998. *Marriage in Men's Lives*. New York: Oxford University Press.

O'Brien, C.A., and A. Goldberg. 2000. "Lesbians and Gay men inside and outside Families" In N. Mandell and A. Duffy (eds.), *Canadian Families: Diversity, Conflict, and Change*, 2nd ed. (pp. 115–145). Toronto: Harcourt Canada.

Patterson, C.J. 2000. "Family Relationships of Lesbians and Gay Men." *Journal of Marriage and the Family* 62: 1052–1069.

Peplau, L.A. 1991. "Lesbian and Gay Relationships." In J.C. Gonsiorek and J.D. Weinrich (eds.), *Homosexuality: Research Implications for Public Policy*. Newbury Park: Sage.

Rayside, D. 2002. "The Politics of Lesbian and Gay Parenting in Canada and the United States." Paper presented at the 2002 Annual Meeting of the Canadian Political Science Association.

Savin-Williams, R.C. 2001. *Mom, Dad, I'm Gay. How Families Negotiate Coming Out.* Washington: American Psychological Association.

Schacher, S.J., C.F. Auerbach, and L.B. Silverstein. 2005. "Gay Fathers Expanding the Possibilities for Us All." *Journal of GLBT Family Studies* 1: 31–52.

Stacey, J. 1998. "Gay and Lesbian Families: Queer Like Us." In M.A. Mason, A. Skolnick, and S.D. Sugarman (eds.), *All Our Families: New Policies for a New Century* (pp. 117–143). New York: Oxford University Press.

Statistics Canada. 2001. Profile of Canadian Families and Households: Diversification Continues. Catalogue no. 96F0030XIE2001003. Ottawa: Statistics Canada.

Statistics Canada. 2002. "2001 Census: Marital Status, Common-Law Status, Families, Dwellings, and Households." *The Daily* (October 22).

Ward, M. 2002. *The Family Dynamic: A Canadian Perspective*, 3rd ed. Toronto: Nelson Thomson.

Weigert, J. 1991. *Mixed Emotions: Certain Steps toward Understanding Ambivalence.* Albany: State University of New York Press.

Weston, K. 1991. *Families We Choose: Lesbian, Gays, Kinship*. New York: Columbia University Press.

Williams, W.L. 1992. "Benefits for Nonhomophobic Societies: An Anthropological Perspective." In W.J. Blumenfield (ed.), *Homophobia* (pp. 509–517). Boston: Beacon.

Chapter 9

Family Dissolution and the Brady Bunch

Separation, Divorce, and Remarriage

Learning Objectives

In this chapter you will learn that …
- there are shifting trends in divorce and remarriage
- there are important predictors of divorce and remarriage at individual, family background, and societal levels
- divorce and custody laws have changed over time and changes are proposed to the Divorce Act, highlighting the "best interests of the child"
- there are consequences of divorce and remarriage for adults in areas such as socio-economic status and social-psychological well-being
- it is necessary to critically evaluate popular perceptions of the consequences of divorce and remarriage for children, such as the cultural stereotype of the "wicked stepmother"

Introduction

For most us, marriage symbolizes a relationship that should ideally last a lifetime or until "death do we part." Realistically, many of us know that not all marriages will last forever, and that many Canadian families will experience marital disruption and possibly remarriage. More than one-third or approximately 40 percent of Canadian (first) marriages end in divorce (Vanier Institute of the Family, 2011). Although this rate is relatively high, it is lower than the common assumption that 50 percent of all marriages will end in divorce; a statistic that is usually based on American trends and perpetuated by sensationalistic media reports. Moreover, given that many divorced individuals will eventually re-partner, numerous opportunities and challenges arise for families "the next time around." And while many will go on to experience successful and positive relationships, others will face stress and strain. Indeed, the sociological conceptualization of remarriage as an incomplete institution (Cherlin, 1978) reflects the idea that remarriage is often characterized by ambiguity and confusion in role and status boundaries as well as divided loyalties.

From a life course perspective, a family member's decision to separate, divorce, or remarry carries significant implications for one's life, as well as for other transitional behaviours and for "linked lives." This is because the effects of experiences that occur at a later point in the life course often depend on earlier events. For example, children who experience parental divorce while growing up are more likely to see their own marriages dissolve than those from intact families (Mitchell, 2006). Also, divorcing at a relatively young age may carry different short- and long-term consequences compared to divorcing in later life. Indeed, it may be more difficult to remarry in mid or later life because of a narrowing pool of eligible mates (Clark and Crompton, 2006).

It is also recognized that transitions to divorce or remarriage are "long-term processes that result in a qualitative reorganization of inner life and external behaviour" (Cowan, 1991: 5). These transitions can also create a counter-transition—that is, a transition produced by the life changes of others—which can add or remove social roles and relation-ships. For example, previous in-laws may be replaced with new in-laws in the case of remarriage. Furthermore, if children are involved, divorce creates a counter-transition for at least two generations—the parents and children of the divorcing couple (Downs, Coleman, and Ganong, 2000).

In this chapter, we will consider how formal relationship dissolution and remarriage affect the lives of both adults and children in a number of realms. Before we consider the aftermath of divorce and remarriage for families, an overview of socio-demographic trends in divorce and remarriage will be presented. Explanations of why divorce rates have generally risen over time and research on who is likely to divorce and remarry will also be reviewed. Finally, selected issues with respect to divorce law and the division of property, as well as custody and the notion of "best interests" of children, will also be highlighted.

Trends in Separation, Divorce, and Remarriage

There are many means that couples can use to try and get out of an unsatisfactory mar-riage, such as desertion, legal separation, informally agreed-upon separation, and annul-ment. Desertion can be defined as the willful abandonment of one's spouse, children, or both, while a legal separation refers to people who are living apart with the intention of obtaining a divorce. Informal separations, on the other hand, entail an arrangement that has been called "the poor man's divorce," since the couple is separated but legally mar-ried and occurs mostly among low-income families who cannot afford a divorce. Annul-ments occur when the marriage contract is considered void due to particular causes that existed before the marriage, such as being underage, one partner was already married, or the couple was involved in an incestuous relationship. And while most of these actions are stepping-stones to divorce, it is possible (particularly in the case of marital separa-tion) that some couples will use this time to work out a reconciliation in order to end their marital difficulties (Eshleman and Wilson, 2001).

Divorce can be defined as the formal dissolution of a valid marriage by judicial decree. Prior to 1867, divorce was not allowed in Canada with the exception of the Maritimes. Throughout that era, marriage was viewed as "a divine institution ordained by God." As a result, divorce in Canada was very rare before 1900 at less than two per million population. By 1921, divorce rates climbed up to 6.4 per 100,000 population (Eshleman and Wilson, 2001). These rates have steadily increased over time, particularly follow-ing the liberalization of divorce laws in 1968 and 1985. Before 1968, adultery, cruelty, and desertion of 10 years were the only grounds for obtaining a divorce. After 1968, it became possible to get a divorce following a separation of three years. The Divorce Act of 1985 further amended these changes. Notably, parties to the divorce no longer had to show fault and the waiting period on the grounds of marriage breakdown was reduced to one year (Ward, 2002).

Crude divorce rates, calculated as the number of divorces in a given year divided by the mid-year population, also show that rates have generally risen over time. And although this method of reporting is often criticized (i.e., they may be measured in populations that have not aged enough to face the risk of divorce), some interesting patterns are worth highlighting, both nationally and internationally. In Figure 9.1 we observe that in 1921 the divorce rate was relatively low (at approx. 6.4 divorces per 100,000 population) and it steadily rose until 1968 to 54.8 divorces per 100,000 population. In 1969, following reforms to the divorce laws, the divorce rate almost doubled to 124.2 divorces, which is relatively low in comparison to the more recent 2003 rate (at approximately 224 divorces per 100,000 population). Since that time (and as you will note in Table 9.1), divorce rates have remained fairly stable at 220 divorces per 100,000 in 2008. However, there are striking fluctuations over time, or peaks and valleys in divorce rates. Contrary to public opinion that divorce is at an all-time high, the peak year for divorce was in 1987, when the rate was 362.3 divorces per 100,000 population. Moreover, in 2008, women and men were, on average, 41.9 and 44.5 years old, respectively, when they divorced, although divorce is most likely to happen after four or five years of marriage. Also, the average duration of a marriage before a divorce is now 14.5 years (for marriages ending in divorce in 2008), which is about two years longer than a decade ago. This may stem from the fact that men and women increasingly marry at later ages (Vanier Institute of the Family, 2011).

Figure 9.1
Divorce in Historical Perspective, Canada, per 100,000 Population, 1921–2003

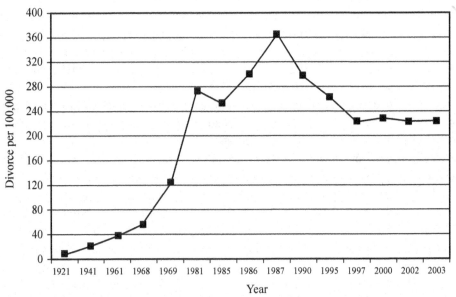

Source: Statistics Canada data, adapted from A.M. Ambert, *Divorce: Facts, Causes, and Consequences* (Ottawa: The Vanier Institute of the Family, 2005), p. 4.

Crude Canadian divorce rates are also similar to those observed in other Western industrialized countries, such as the United Kingdom, France, and Germany, as shown in Table 9.1. Yet, these rates are relatively low compared to the United States. Canadian rates are also much higher than countries such as Chile, Vietnam, Mexico, and Italy. In general, worldwide divorce rates tend to be associated with factors such as socio-economic development. For instance, although not shown in this table, other developing countries of Latin America (e.g., Nicaragua, Peru) and Asia (e.g., Thailand, Sri Lanka) typically have substantially lower divorce rates than more developed countries (Newman and Grauerholz, 2002). Strong traditional or religious forces (e.g., Catholicism) in countries can also influence divorce laws, attitudes, and behaviours, such as in Italy or in Ireland, where divorce was not legal until fairly recently.

The overall trend toward increased divorce is typically explained by fundamental social, cultural, and legal shifts, as well as changes in the ties that bind family members to one another. Whereas family bonds once rested on strong economic interdependence, today they rest more often on voluntary emotional ties. Economic development also stimulates individualism and secularization by changing the values, norms, and preferences in the larger society. Women's economic independence, for instance, makes them less dependent on a male breadwinner. Sociologists also focus on how laws governing divorce have liberalized over time, making divorce relatively simple to obtain. Indeed, rates quickly rose after the liberalization of divorce laws in 1968 and 1985. Yet, many researchers are quick to point out that laws only reflect ideological change. In this vein, liberal divorce laws have been described as "merely tools for the ready user" (McDaniel and Tepperman, 2004).

The Second (or Third) Time around: Patterns in Remarriage
Following divorce, many individuals will find a partner with whom to date, cohabit, or remarry. With respect to remarriage, the rate of this behaviour among divorced men and women has fallen, particularly for men. Most of this can be explained by the corresponding increase in cohabitation. Yet, approximately 70 percent of divorced men and 58 percent of divorced women remarry in Canada, excluding Quebec, probably due to a preference for cohabitation in this province (Ambert, 2009). Moreover, it is extremely rare for someone to marry three or more times. In 2001, 137,500 Canadian adults had been married more than twice. This represented less than 1 percent of the ever-married population aged 25 and over, and virtually all of them had tied the knot three times (Clark and Crompton, 2006). In other words, it would be very difficult to locate someone who has experienced more than three marriages, contrary to the well-publicized remarriage behaviour found on television among celebrities like the late movie star legend Elizabeth Taylor (eight times to seven husbands) and previous CNN talk-show host Larry King (seven times to six wives).

Studies also establish that remarriages are also more likely than first marriages to end in divorce. This may be due to several factors. "Serial" brides and grooms may be more accepting of divorce. They may also have more "emotional baggage" due to the unfulfilled expectations of the prior relationship, which can strain remarriages. Also, the presence of stepchildren, ex-spouses, and ex-in-laws, and a general lack of social support can create forces that divert the couple's task of building their relationship (Ambert, 2006).

Table 9.1
Selected International Divorce Rates per 1,000 Population, 2008*

Country	Rates per 1,000 Population
Australia	2.20
Canada	2.20
China	1.60
Chile	.10
Cuba	3.20
France	2.10
Germany	2.59
Japan	2.30
Italy	.90
Iran	1.40
Mexico	.80
Singapore	1.90
Spain	2.40
Sweden	2.40
Turkey	1.40
United Kingdom	2.40
United States	3.50
Vietnam	.20

*Rates are the number of final divorce decrees granted under civil law per 1,000 mid-year population for the latest data available between 2007 and 2008.

Sources: United Nations, *Demographic Year Book* (New York: UN Publications, 2008) (http://unstats.un.org/unsd/demographic/products/dyb/dyb2.2008.htm, table 25), except for Canadian and U.S. data, which are from Statistics Canada (2008). Table 101-6501 – *Divorce and Crude Divorce Rates, Canada, Provinces and Territories*, annual, CANSIM. Retrieved from www5.statcan.gc.ca/cansim/a01?lang=eng.

Centers for Disease Control and Prevention; National Center for Health Statistics (2011). *National Marriage and Divorce Rate Trends; Provisional Number of Divorces and Annulments and Rate: United States, 2000–2009*. Retrieved from www.cdc.gov/nchs/nvss/marriage_divorce_tables.htm.

The Divorcing and Remarrying Kind: Who Is Likely to Divorce and Remarry?

Age at marriage is consistently found to be the strongest predictor of divorce in the first five years of marriage. People who enter marriage at the youngest ages, particularly during their teenage years, do so with the greatest risk for marital dissolution. Also, people with a university degree are at less risk for marital dissolution compared to those with less than high school. Those who cohabit prior to marriage are also more likely to divorce, possibly due to adverse selectivity. That is, cohabitation may attract some who are less keen on commitment and stability, although as cohabitation becomes more normative, this effect may be diminishing (Mitchell, 2006).

People who attend religious services also have a lower risk of dissolution than those who do not attend at all, showing that religious belief can have a protective factor. Moreover, the relationship between premarital child-bearing and the likelihood of divorce is overwhelming. Yet, couples who divorce tend to have no children, or fewer on average, than those with more children, an observation that is found across most societies and cultures. In addition, the longer a couple has been married, the greater the likelihood of staying together. Moreover, the attitudes and religiosity of serial marriers are different than those who have not married multiple times. For example, research shows that serial marriers are less likely to say that in order to be happy it is very important to have a lasting relationship, and that married couples facing problems should stay together for "the sake of the children." They are also more likely to report no religious affiliation and less likely to attend religious services (Clark and Crompton, 2006).

With regard to family background factors, researchers have found that children who experience the disruption of their parents' marriage are more likely to see their own marriages dissolve (Amato, 1996; Wolfinger, 2000). It is postulated that parental divorce affects the risk of offspring divorce through three mediating mechanisms: life course and socio-economic variables (i.e., early marriage, lower socio-economic origins); commitment and attitudes toward divorce; and patterns of interpersonal behaviour that are detrimental to marital stability (Amato, 1996). Children born out of wedlock (and who did not experience parental divorce or death) are as likely, if not more likely, to have their own marriages dissolve (Teachman, 2002). Cultural background or ethnicity can affect the probability of divorce. For example, divorce is less common among people from certain ethnic backgrounds, such as Chinese and Indo-Canadians (Mitchell, 2006).

Figure 9.2 shows geographical locale and regional factors are also related to the risk of divorce. The lowest divorce rates are found for the Maritimes and the highest rates are found in the Yukon Territories and in Quebec. In 2008, the Yukon had the highest proportion (59.7 percent) of marriages expected to end in divorce before the 30th wedding anniversary, while Newfoundland and Labrador had the lowest (25 percent). Lower rates in the Maritimes may be due to the fact that, despite economic pressure, there may be a higher level of social integration or demographic factors such as a smaller number of married couples or an older population. Conversely, higher divorce rates may be reflective of less "traditional" family values or regional conditions that prevent marital stability. For example, in Quebec, higher divorce may occur from a combination of variables such as widespread cohabitation before marriage, lower religiosity, and more individualistic or liberal attitudes (Ambert, 2005).

Finally, it is also important to consider the personal reasons that people give for divorce. These include such problems as different values and interests, domestic abuse/violence,

Figure 9.2
30-Year Total Divorce Rate, by Province and Region, 2008 (per 1,000 Marriages)

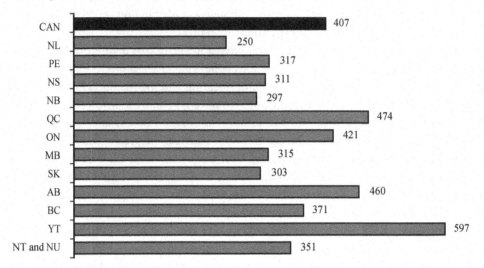

Note: The total divorce rate represents the proportion of new marriages that can be expected to end in divorce before the 30th wedding anniversary if the divorce rates by marriage duration observed in a given year are repeated in the future.

Source: Canadian Vital Statistics, Divorce Database and Marriage Database. Ottawa: Statistics Canada, 2011.

drug or alcohol abuse, adultery, career-related conflict, and money problems (Ambert, 2009). Regarding individual perceptions for divorce, a recent study of 274 divorcees in response to the question, "What do you think caused the divorce?", resulted in some general tendencies. The three most common answers were: infidelity (18.4 percent), incompatibility (16.4 percent), and drinking or drug use (9 percent). Gender differences were also found, with women more likely than men to cite infidelity and drinking or drug use as the major reason. And in general, former wives are more likely than former husbands to cite a cluster of negative partner behaviours, including physical and mental abuse, substance use, going out with "the boys," and neglect of home and children (e.g., see Amato and Previti, 2003).

With respect to motivations for remarriage, from a historical perspective, in earlier times, this typically involved widows or widowers. Due to lower life expectancies, men and women often died at relatively young ages and the surviving spouse often needed a new partner. Now, with increased divorce, remarriages are more prevalent and usually involve younger people. And, as previously noted, men are more likely to remarry than women. It is postulated that men may have more advantages in their chance to remarry than women, partly due to age factors (e.g., see Sweeney, 1997). Also, men may have a greater need and interest in remarrying than women, who generally have stronger support networks and domestic skills that can support independent living. Remarriage is also more common among immigrants than Canadian-born (Ambert, 2005). It is also more likely for those who have no children or only a small number of children in their first marriage. In addition, remarriage is more likely among women who are not in the paid labour force, for those with less education, and for women (but not men) with lower incomes (Eshleman and Wilson, 2001). This suggests that some economically marginalized women are "pushed to partner" in order to attain a basic standard of living.

Consequences of Divorce and Remarriage for Adults

There is little doubt that divorce can be an emotionally painful and devastating experience for individuals and families and that remarriage introduces a new layer of complexity into family life (e.g., see Box 9.1 for Patti Posner's story). Consequently, mandatory pre-divorce information sessions for couples have been introduced, such as in Ontario, as shown in Box 9.2. These sessions are attended by couples before ending their marriage in court in an effort to reduce pressure on the family court system and to encourage mediation over litigation. From a symbolic interactionist perspective, family members must now renegotiate new relationships and meanings in their daily lives. Some of these relationships will deteriorate or vanish, and this can affect relationships between other extended family members, such as those between former in-laws or friends with whom the couple shared time together. Also, new strains can also be placed on immediate and extended family networks, such as a greater need for assistance from the divorcing couple's parents.

Most of us would agree that making a valiant attempt to save a marriage is a worthwhile effort, especially when children are involved. However, if these efforts are not successful, many of us would also agree that divorce may be the best decision since it can provide the opportunity to build a healthier life. Indeed, recently there has been a plethora of books published that focus more on some of the positive experiences that individuals have following their marital breakdown. In her book entitled, *Happily Ever After Divorce: Notes of a Joyful Journey*, radio commentator Jessica Bram (2009) shares with readers how she maintained a sense of self and humour during a most difficult time and how she emerged triumphant. She also discusses how she handled everything from everyday tasks to earning a living with newly discovered talents, the delightful aspects of single-parenthood, to eventually finding love all over again. Overall, her story is consistent with others who maintain that, all things considered, their divorce was the right decision for them and that they have few regrets overall.

Yet other studies establish that divorce can also have a strong negative effect on adults' social-psychological well-being, particularly in the short term. Some degree of anger toward the ex-spouse is a relatively common sentiment, and this hostility can last for 10 or more years (Seccombe and Warner, 2004). Moreover, other research shows that there

Box 9.1
Family Narratives—One Family's Journey to Healing

I was divorced in 1986, when my daughter was eight years old. When I started dating and realized that one day I would remarry, I remember thinking that I would like to marry a man who already had children. I never thought about what it would mean to be a part of a step or blended family, and just how that would impact my life.

In 1990 I married a man who had two children. My husband also has an ex-wife, ex-in-laws, plus his ex-wife's live-in significant other. The coming together of my daughter and myself, my husband, his children, his ex-wife, her significant other, and her parents has been a very difficult task.

It is very difficult to form a blended and extended family. Part of the dilemma of blending families is that there are few, if any, cultural guidelines to follow. For example, we know how to behave and what is expected of us when we become in-laws. But we really do not know what our role is with our spouse or ex-spouse. There is no language for these new members of our extended family, nor do we think of them as friends. They may actually be seen as intruders, and a relationship built on this type of foundation can be very draining.

My own story is probably not all that different from the many other women who have married men who have previously been married. It took over eight years for the adults to come together. For years I felt in the midst of an angry tug of war. My husband's relationship with Jane (ex-spouse) was based on anger and fighting. I was hurt when my husband was unable to set boundaries for himself and for letting Jane manipulate him. I felt that Jane was trying to control her children in ways that were interfering with my life with my new husband. It seemed that no matter what my husband and Jane did, I had to enter into the picture and would become angry and frustrated as well. The two main issues that I was confronted with were control and anger. And then I had to learn to deal with issues of jealousy. I had no role model, and I was very confused by all the emotions because of having Jane in my life.... There were no road maps for any of us to follow. The difficulties between the three of us kept growing, and none of us were capable at the time to make the necessary adjustments. I could no longer take having Jane call our home, because most times an argument would ensue. I did not know how to pull myself out of the turmoil. I did something that may sound radical; I sent a note to Jane asking her not to call our home and explained that I could no longer deal with the arguing.

A year later I came to a halting revelation: I can choose to be married to my husband, and if I do, then his ex-wife must be part of the picture. I sent another note, this time asking her to simply put the past aside and to begin again as friends. I give Jane much credit because she has been able to do this with dignity.

Our first meeting was for her son's college graduation. The whole family went, myself, my husband, all our children, Jane and her boyfriend, and her parents. Our first few minutes were a bit awkward, and then we eased into a relationship. Her boyfriend and I have an inside take on "our family," as we share the sense of being "the in-laws." In the past two years we have shared several family events. Having been able to succeed at this relationship has been and continues to be a very gratifying experience.

Source: Extract from Posner, P. 2007. "One family's journey to healing." Stepfamily Network Inc., www.stepfamily.net.

may be a gender difference in the experience of divorce, in that people (especially men) who are divorced tend to be less happy and healthy than people who are married (Waite and Gallagher, 2000).

In addition to emotional or social-psychological effects and changes to social networks, there are usually economic repercussions of divorce. Virtually all studies report a decline in economic well-being for women (and children) in the immediate post-divorce period. In particular, women's economic standing is altered, usually because their spouses earned more money in the paid labour force. Women also tend to take primary responsibility for children, if children are involved. One obvious outcome of divorce involving children is the formation of single-parent households. Although there is more than one path to single-parenthood (i.e., the parent never married), we have witnessed a general rise in the number of single parents over the past several decades. As noted in Chapter 1, by 2006, 16 percent of Canadian children were living in single-parent families, with the majority (81 percent) with female parents (Statistics Canada, 2006).

Many single parents (particularly mothers) live well below the poverty line. It is estimated that half of female lone parents are at risk of applying for welfare following marital separation and divorce (Gorlick, 2005). Single parents may also have difficulty in achieving a good social life, particularly if there is a lack of money or support systems to help with child care. This is easy to understand if you calculate the cost of going out—for example, going to a movie—which would entail paying for admission, snacks, babysitting, and transportation (Ward, 2002).

In summary, it is obviously too simplistic to picture the aftermath of divorce for individuals in completely positive or negative terms. It is also misleading to emphasize either negative outcomes or greater personal-growth opportunities following divorce because it "places the onus for adaptability solely on the individual" (Gorlick, 2005). In particular, this practice overlooks the complexity of the process and the differing concerns, resources, and capacities of individual family members, and how these can change over time. When women leave a physically or emotionally abusive relationship, for instance, many simultaneously experience more challenges with respect to their economic standing and finding affordable housing. At the same time, these women can experience relief and improved mental and physical functioning as well as enhanced self-worth.

Box 9.2
Pre-Divorce Talks Mandatory in Ontario

TORONTO – All Ontario couples seeking a divorce will now be required to attend a mandatory information session before ending their marriage in court, ushering in a program aimed at unclogging the family court system and encouraging mediation over litigation.

Divorcing couples must attend a two-hour session run by volunteer lawyers and social workers whose goal is to educate parents about the effects of divorce on both their bank accounts and their children.

"We're trying to take some of the emotional and financial cost out of separation and divorce," Attorney General Chris Bentley said. "We want to help them resolve their issues so they can get on with the rest of their lives as quickly as possible."

Although the concept is not new in Ontario—as part of a pilot program, 17 courts already offer the mandatory information session—the latest move expands the requirement to more than 50 provincial courts at a total cost of $7.2 million per year. The province, which is paying for the program through savings elsewhere, will also fund on-site mediation for couples who are willing to forego litigation.

Grant Gold, immediate past chair of the Canadian Bar Association's family law branch, which launched its program within the Superior Court system several years ago, has led mandatory information sessions for both applicants and respondents in Toronto and runs the evening sessions each week.

"On applicants night, they're all kind of gung-ho because they started the whole thing and they want the divorce," Gold said. "On respondents night, you see people who are all uptight and cranky that they have to be there. But by the end of the two-hour session, you can see people's shoulders go down. You hear people saying their eyes were opened to different processes."

Bentley said the program will make the family justice system more affordable, more efficient, and less confrontational. "Some cases involve a long court fight," he said, adding that spouses will ideally attend the session before they even file for divorce.

But while family lawyers and mediators say they welcome the new rules, some among the divorce community feel the regulations do not go far enough. "There might be some people who say, 'I didn't know those services were available,' or 'They're putting it right in my face so I'll spend the time and try to settle some of the issues of the case,'" Toronto-based divorce lawyer Brian Ludmer said.

Source: Kathryn Carlson (Postmedia News), Ontario: "Pre-Divorce Talks Mandatory," cited in *The Vancouver Sun*, Tuesday, July 19, 2011, p. B3.

The Brady Bunch or Wicked Stepmother? Consequences of Divorce and Remarriage for Children

Contrary to the popular 1970s sitcom *The Brady Bunch*, which depicted a happy suburban stepfamily with six precocious and well-adjusted children from previous marriages, research on this topic has generally assumed a host of negative consequences for children. Many of these outcomes centred on finding short- and long-term behavioural problems and emotional trauma, problems that were purported to be due to the missing father or "deadbeat dad" and the "emotionally overwrought mother." Generally, it is assumed that children are living in an "aberrant" single-parent family or a troublesome "blended" or remarriage family (Gorlick, 2005). In the case of single parents, it has been especially common for sociologists and other professionals in the past to refer to these families as "broken," as if something were missing or faulty (Ward, 2002).

Empirical research on this subject reveals more mixed findings. Although there are many ways to become a single parent, children living in single-parent homes are often found to be at risk for developing certain kinds of problems. On average, children from single-parent homes tend not to do as well in school as children in two-parent families. They are also more likely to marry and cohabit at earlier ages, both of which are connected to higher divorce. Moreover, many young adults (particularly if parents separated before they were five) are more likely to have long-term emotional difficulties—known as the sleeper effect—as well as to have committed serious crimes, or to have children outside of marriage (Ward, 2002).

Many of these problems can be traced to a lack of financial resources and a lack of outside supports rather than the family structure per se. Moreover, some research shows that many single parents and their children develop very strong, supportive, and close-knit relationships to compensate for the lack of an additional adult in the home (Seccombe and Warner, 2004). Moreover, in light of the fact that stepfather-stepchild relationships are more common than stepmother-stepchild relationships (because children typically remain with their mothers), the "wicked stepmother" myth remains strong (Cheal, 1996). This cultural stereotype of the "wicked stepmother," which emerged from folk tales and children's stories such as "Cinderella" and "Snow White," however, has not been supported empirically. For example, Cheal (1996) found that stepmothers were not harsher or more inconsistent in their interactions with their stepchildren than were biological/adopted mothers with their biological/adopted children.

Yet, children exposed to stepfamily environments are found to leave home earlier due to conflict at home (e.g., Mitchell, 2006) than those raised in intact families, and children are faced with more complex relationship structures and processes (e.g., Ferri and Smith, 1998). For example, if there are step-siblings, there may be tension if they now have to share a bedroom or other possessions. Problems can also result if the "baby of the family" suddenly has to contend with younger step-siblings (Newman and Grauerholz, 2002).

Research generally supports the view that it is important to consider a number of characteristics and circumstances that can influence the aftermath of divorce and remarriage, such as who the child lives with, the age and gender of the child, the level of parental conflict, visitation patterns and parental involvement, socio-economic status, and outside support networks. For example, sometimes parents use the children as a weapon to hurt the ex-partner or try to get children to take sides in a dispute. They may also communicate their anger and hurt toward each other to their children and demean or ridicule their ex-spouses. As a result, children experience tremendous stress. Conversely, if parents can co-operate or at least try to minimize overt conflict in front of them, children tend to have fewer emotional and behavioural problems (Seccombe and Warner, 2004).

Demo and Fine (2010) further demonstrate the highly dynamic nature of the divorce process and the complex set of factors that affect adult and child adjustment. Their integrated model (as shown in Figure 9.3) outlines the key processes influencing outcomes. In particular, this conceptual model highlights the importance of marital and family relationship trajectories beginning in the pre-divorce years and evolving through the post-divorce period. This includes consideration of individual and interpersonal skills and resources, socio-economic changes accompanying and following divorce, reconfigurations in family structure over time, and alterations in family processes following divorce. Overall, this model is consistent with a life course approach, in that it situates adjustments within a variety of contexts (e.g., socio-historical, economic) and considers the highly fluid and variable nature of individual adjustment.

Figure 9.3
The Divorce Variation and Fluidity Model

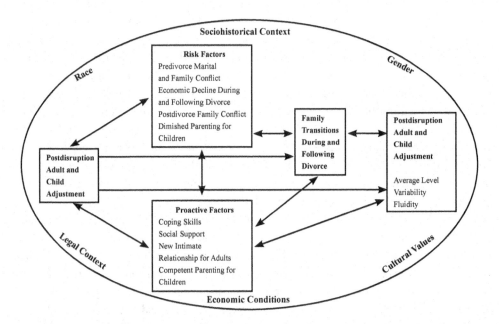

Source: D.H. Demo and M.A. Fine, *Beyond the Average Divorce* (Thousand Oaks, Calif.: Sage Publications, 2010), Figure 2.1, p. 17.

Finally, it is important to acknowledge the limitations of divorce and stepfamily research. Notably, many researchers argue that the literature on single or stepfamilies uses a nuclear "intact" measuring stick to compare blended family experiences. This tendency assumes that non-intact families are "deviant," which glosses over the tremendous variability that can occur within families regardless of structure, as well as changes over time. For instance, research documents that children who grow up in intact but conflict-ridden families may suffer more than children whose parents divorce but maintain a friendly family relationship. In addition, some family environments are transitional (i.e., single-parent homes), such that remarriage may improve the financial well-being of children whose parents divorced, and provide the child with an additional caretaker (Newman and Grauerholz, 2002).

Selected Issues in Divorce: The Law, Property Division, and Custody

Divorce entails the division of property and assets, as well as the responsibilities and care of children, if children are involved. However, many feminists argue that since legislatures and courts have historically been dominated by men, family law has been more protective of men's than of women's interests. A good example of this argument can be found in the *Murdock vs. Murdock* case (see Box 9.3). This case rested on the assumption that a wife had no claim on matrimonial property (property acquired during marriage) even though she worked very hard to acquire it.

The obvious injustice of this case led to revisions in matrimonial property laws in all of the provinces by the early 1980s. Both federal and provincial family laws now stipulate that the division of property will be governed by the principle of equalization. As a general rule, all family assets are to be shared equitably, although not necessarily equally (e.g., see Chunn, 2005). There also remain variations in provincial laws, particularly with respect to guidelines specifying the conditions under which the court may order an unequal division of business assets. And, as discussed in Box 9.4, increased immigration to Canada from other countries presents new challenges to the Canadian legal system. This is illustrated by the emergence of Islamic law (*sharia*) in Canadian legal institutions.

Apart from the division of property, another significant consequence of divorce is the children's custody and child support, which is under federal control. In Canada, the governing principle is that custody awards should be based on the "best interests of the child," regardless of the wishes of the parents. Currently, there are a number of proposed changes to the Divorce Act (Bill C-22) to avoid presumptions regarding which parental arrangement is in the best interests of the child. This Child-Centred Family Justice Strategy bases recommendations for change on a number of issues. These include changes in the following areas: parental responsibilities (e.g., to replace the terms "custody" and "access"); best interests criteria (e.g., greater emphasis on the child's well-being and safety); contact orders (e.g., better provision between the child and other family members such as grandparents); expansion of lawyer's roles (e.g., through non-adversarial dispute resolutions and interventions); and attempts to address parents living in different provinces or territories.

Box 9.3
Murdock vs. Murdock

The Murdocks were Alberta ranchers who separated in 1968 after 25 years of marriage, during which time Irene Murdock had worked alongside her husband to the extent that he did not have to hire a hand. However, when she sued for half-interest in their property, cattle, and other assets, the Alberta courts and, ultimately, the Supreme Court of Canada decided that Mrs. Murdock was entitled to alimony and had no claim on the value of the property because she had not made "a direct financial contribution" to the ranch; the work she had carried out for 25 years was "the work done by any ranch wife." In short, Mr. Murdock held the title to the property, and Irene Murdock "was expected to hoe, mow, dehorn, brand (and cook, clean, and bear and raise children)" with no hope of a share of it when the marriage ended.

Sources: Kieran, 1986; Morton, 1988 (cited in Chunn, 2005: 288).
Kieran, S. 1986. *The Family Matters: Two Centuries of Family Law and Life in Ontario.* Toronto: Key Porter (p. 142).
Morton, M.E. 1988. "Dividing the wealth, sharing the property: The (re)formation of 'family' in law in Ontario." *Canadian Review of Sociology and Anthropology*, 25: 254–75.
Chunn, D.E. 2005. "Politicizing the personal: Feminism, law and public policy," in N. Mandell and A. Duffy (eds.), *Canadian Families: Diversity, Conflict and Change*, 3rd ed. Toronto: Thomson Nelson (pp. 276–310).

In order to implement these proposals, the federal government will offer $16.1 million for 62 new judges and will expand the Unified Family Courts to promote "a holistic approach to each family's situation" (*Family Justice Newsletter*, 2003).

And since most children have two parents and the child's welfare is strongly affected by the conditions of access, a number of issues can arise with respect to legal custody (the authority to make long-term decisions about how the child is to be raised), physical custody (who is responsible for the child on a daily basis), and joint custody (legal custody is shared equally, although it may not mean sharing physical custody). For example, children in joint custody are now in a bi-nuclear family (see Figure 9.4), since they continue to have two parents, but in two separate residences.

Given the impact of these various custody, guardianship, access and support issues on children and families, many local governments have created programs to assist parents who have recently separated. For example, in British Columbia, a "Parenting after Separation" program has been developed by the family justice government branch. This program is a free, three-hour information session for parents and other family members, such as grandparents or guardians. It is intended to help parents make careful and informed decisions and to resolve any conflicts that may result in order to facilitate the best interests of their children.

Box 9.4
The Emergence of Shariah Law in Canadian Legal Institutions

Because Canadian society now consists of individuals from many places and cultures, it is not possible to generalize about how Canadians actually live out their pair bonding and dissolution experiences. What we all experience in common is the law. Whether or not religious rules apply is now strictly a matter of individual choice, in striking contrast to earlier periods when the demands of religious edicts were sometimes harsh and imposed with considerable force. Some cultural practices that newcomers to Canada might otherwise be inclined to follow are ruled out by law, as is multiple marriage, or are granted not standing in law, as is religious divorce. One striking departure from this pattern has begun to emerge, however.

The gradual and subtle introduction of Islamic law (shariah) in Canada has raised some difficult and troubling questions. In the normal course of events, countries have one universal system of civil and criminal codes. Indeed, it is one of the elemental aspects of democracy that all citizens be accorded the same rights and privileges under law. Canada has always been an exception to this rule by the acceptance of the Civil Code system in Quebec, an integral part of the historic bargain that brought Quebec into Confederation. Other slight departures of a purely optional nature have existed for some time. Among these are the orthodox Jewish requirement for a religious *get* or divorce before remarriage can occur, and a similar Roman Catholic requirement for a religious annulment. The *get* has been an especially vexing problem for some divorcing wives because it is granted (or not) exclusively by the husband of the failed marriage. Lawsuits of the common civil variety to compel the delivery of a *get* are not unknown.

But the introduction of shariah principles in recent years is a qualitatively different initiative. In reflection of the growing diversity of cultural origins present in Canadian society, disputes involving Muslim women's dowries, divorce, inheritance, and property ownership have actually been arriving in civil court.

In Ontario until very recently, judges might choose to refer such cases to an Islamic tribunal for binding arbitration, provided the parties were willing. However, the matter of parallel justice systems in Ontario came to a head in early 2006 when the government of Ontario ultimately decided against continuing this practice. The Family Statute Law Amendment Act, passed 14 February 2006, ensures that only Ontario family law can be used in binding arbitrations in Ontario. According to Attorney General Michael Bryant, "the bill reaffirms the principle that there ought to be one law for all Ontarians."

In British Columbia, a judge recently upheld a Muslim woman's *maher*, a form of prenuptial agreement that defines in advance the amount of payment to be made upon subsequent marriage termination. Acknowledging that a *maher* has force and effect in Canadian courts as a contract (even though it has purely religious legitimacy) is a step in the direction of parallel legal systems, which is completely alien to the Canadian legal context. Although it does have some resonance with sentencing circles and restorative justice initiatives carried out in Aboriginal communities across Canada with the blessing of the courts, the fact remains that some few separation and divorce proceedings in Canada are now taking place in purely religious context, with judgments only subsequently confirmed (as in "rubber-stamped") in a conventional civil law document. Actions such as that of the province of Ontario in disallowing the use of religious-based tribunals in the settlement of civil disputes may simply drive these activities underground.

Source: McKie, C. 2007. "Separation and divorce: Fragmentation and renewal of families," in D. Cheal (ed.), *Canadian Families Today: New Perspectives.* Toronto: Oxford University Press (pp. 83–100).

Figure 9.4
The Bi-nuclear Family

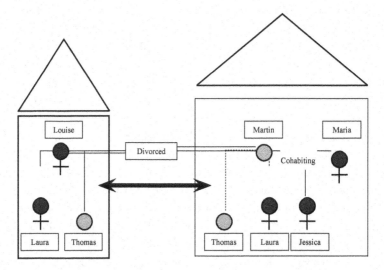

Source: H.D. Juby, "Canada's Step-families," *Transition Magazine* 33, no. 4 (Ottawa: Vanier Institute of the Family, 2003), retrieved August 8, 2006, from www.vifamily.ca/library/transition/334/334.html.

While mothers continue to primarily have primary custody of children (and children of recently divorced or separated parents are most likely to live in lone-mother households compared to lone-father parents), men are increasingly likely to apply for either solo or joint custody, the latter of which is soon to be called co-parenting (McDaniel and Tepperman, 2004). In 2004, 46.5 percent of all court-determined divorce cases resulted in a joint-custody settlement, more than double the figure in the mid-1990s and four times that of the late 1980s (Statistics Canada, 2006). These trends reflect changing norms and ideologies that a mother's care is necessarily "best." Yet, there is concern that with the increasing emphasis on "the best interests" of children and the increasing political strength of the fathers' rights movements, mothers' rights will become less visible. This appears to be particularly pronounced for women dealing with substance abuse, mental health issues, and family violence (Greaves et al., 2002).

Furthermore, the "deadbeat dad" stereotype is a common figure in today's news media. These fathers are often pictured as cold and heartless, living the high life, while their former families live on welfare and visit food banks. There are even web sites dedicated to assisting families in the recovery of unpaid court-ordered child support. For example, the non-profit web site "Deadbeat Dads and Moms," which is operated and maintained by an army of "concerned citizens" (e.g., parents, bill collectors, lawyers) features "most-wanted" posters in their hall of shame. A "web detective" helps individuals locate "deadbeat" family members.

Although relatively recent, most jurisdictions and ministries in Canada have created family maintenance and enforcement programs to ensure that child and spousal support payments are paid on time and in full. If enforcement is necessary, federal and provincial laws are used such as the Family Responsibility and Support Arrears Enforcement Act, passed in 1996 in Ontario. Under this legal authority, measures such as garnishing wages, tax returns and bank accounts, making liens against real estate or personal property, and/or withholding driver's licences can be instilled to monitor and enforce court-ordered support payments.

Table 9.2
Living Arrangements of Recently Divorced or Separated Mothers and Fathers

New Household Living Arrangement	Fathers (%)	Mothers (%)
Living alone	25	6
With new partner—no kids	7	4
Step family with common kids	1	4
Step family without common kids	17	16
With new partner and new kids	5	1
Lone parent	30	66
With parent(s)	8	1
Other	8	3
Total	100	100

Source: Vanier Institute of the Family (2008). "Families Apart," *Transition* (Autumn), p. 10, Table 3 (using Statistics Canada 2006 General Social Survey microdata).

Indeed, statistics appear to support the fact that non-payment of child support is a serious problem. The national default rate (including late payment, partial payment, and full default) is estimated at ranging between 50–75 percent, and in only 43 percent of cases is it paid regularly (Richardson, 2001). However, not all of these "deadbeats" are uncaring or unsupportive in principle—at least some of those parents in arrears over child support are members of the working poor whose low incomes may be based on seasonal or part-time employment (Gorlick, 2005).

Summary

This chapter explores family relationships following separation, divorce, and remarriage. Contrary to popular perception, it is noted that although divorce rates have generally risen over time, they are not at an all-time high, nor are Canadian rates the same as the 50 percent failure rate found in the United States, although more than one in three first Canadian marriages will end in divorce. Macro- and micro-level factors associated with divorce are also considered, such as the effects of secularization, individualization, divorce law reform, and the changing role of women in families. Several consequences of the effects of divorce on individuals and children are also discussed. In particular, given the low pay structure for many women, divorced single mothers often face poverty and struggle financially to support and raise their families (Pulkingham, 1995). A lack of economic resources and state supports can produce stress and vulnerability for parents and children alike. It is also interesting to note that many studies indicate that a sizable proportion of divorces are salvageable, and that some ex-spouses are not happier or better off after the divorce (Ambert, 2005).

Trends in serial marriage are reviewed, as well as the consequences for both adults and children. While remarriages can be successful like the 1970s *Brady Bunch* TV sitcom, remarried couples face a higher probability of divorce than first-married couples. Step-families often face vague and confusing expectations, obligations, and rules because it is an "incomplete institution." As a result, family members face additional complexity and unique challenges. Despite these general tendencies, it is important to acknowledge that stepfamilies are diverse, and that not all children in stepfamilies face major problems. Indeed, negative views of stepfamilies as deficient or problematic ignore the fact that children from divorced families can experience a new beginning and go on to lead happy, well-adjusted, and successful lives in their new family settings.

Questions for Critical Reflection and Debate

1. Debate the following: Despite difficulties, married couples with children should remain together for the sake of the children.
2. Why are remarriages less stable than first marriages? Do you think that this will change in the future as remarriage becomes a more complete institution?

3. What are some of the ways in which gender, ethnicity, sexual orientation, and social class can affect the divorce experience of individuals and families?
4. From a life course perspective, discuss fundamental similarities and differences between newly separating and divorcing families with young children and divorcing families with teenaged children.
5. Why are power and control issues often at the root of many of the problems that are caused following divorce? Also discuss this issue in the context of property division, using the *Murdock vs. Murdock* case as an example (Box 9.3).
6. Following divorce, some couples may opt for joint custody of the children. What are the advantages and disadvantages of this arrangement, from the perspective of both generations? Also, what is your opinion of "parallel parenting" (as described in Box 9.1)?

Glossary

Bi-nuclear family is created when both the mother and father act as parents to their children following divorce, although they maintain separate residences.

Counter-transition is a transition produced by the life changes of others (e.g., remarriage creates new in-laws).

Crude divorce rate is calculated as the number of divorces in a given year divided by the mid-year population.

Joint custody is defined as the legal right and responsibility of both parents to make decisions and care for their child(ren) following a divorce.

Legal separation occurs when married couples separate with the intention of obtaining a divorce.

Remarriage as an incomplete institution refers to a lack of normative guidelines for solving problems and can result in disagreement, division, and conflict among family members.

Sleeper effect manifests itself as a problem or set of problems that emerge long after a stressful or traumatic event is experienced, such as divorce.

Further Reading

Allan, G., G. Crow, and S. Hawker. 2011. *Stepfamilies*. New York: Palgrave Macmillan. Combining published studies with original fieldwork, this book provides a sociological review of stepfamily life and the internal dynamics of their households and relationships.

Ambert, A.M. 2009. *Divorce: Facts, Causes, and Consequences*, 3rd ed. Ottawa: The Vanier Institute of the Family. Provides a succinct summary of trends and issues in divorce and remarriage and the consequences for parents and children.

Celello, K. 2009. *Making Marriage Work: A History of Marriage and Divorce in the Twentieth Century United States*. Chapel Hill: University of North Carolina Press. Offers an insightful and wide-ranging account of marriage and divorce, focusing on the development of the idea of marriage as "work."

Das, C. 2011. *British-Indian Adult Children of Divorce*. UK: Ashgate Publishing. High-lights the particular challenges that British-Indian children face from these communi-ties and makes a strong case for culturally competent and culturally sensitive practices for those working with this community.

Demo, D.H., and M.A. Fine. 2010. *Beyond the Average Divorce*. Thousand Oaks, Calif: Sage. Proves a rich depiction of how children and adults of all ages respond to divorce experience rather than "average" or typical outcomes. Also offers a dynamic theoreti-cal model and discusses policy implications.

Harvey, J.H., and M.A. Fine. 2010. *Children of Divorce: Stories of Loss and Growth.* New York: Routledge. Valuable in providing the diverse voices and narratives of chil-dren experiencing divorce as well as various theoretical perspective and methodologi-cal orientations.

Metz, T. 2010. *Untying the Knot: Marriage, The State, and the Case for their Divorce*. N.J.: Princeton University Press. Provides a liberal theory of marriage and the state.

Related Web Sites

Canada Focus on the Family is a charitable organization that provides care, advice, support, and encouragement to families at every stage of life (e.g., step-parenting), http://www.focusonthefamily.ca/.

Canadian Equal Parenting Groups Directory is a not-for-profit definitive directory of Canadian groups concerned with the continued support of children's relationships with both parents after divorce, separation, or for fathers and mothers who never lived married or lived in a common-law relationship, http://www.canadianequalparenting-groups.ca/default.aspx.

Department of Justice Canada offers questions and answers on divorce law, http://www.canada.justice.gc.ca/eng/index.html.

Duhaime's Canadian Family Law Centre offers a wealth of information on separations and divorce in Canada and has an informative section on the treatment of matrimonial property and spousal support in Canada, www.duhaime.org/family/default.aspx.

Supporting Families is an initiative by the Department of Justice of Canada that pro-vides information to adults and children experiencing family dissolution. Notable are the documents providing information and guidance to children, http://www.justice.gc.ca/eng/pi/fcy-fea/lib-bib/pub/book-livre/index.html.

References

Amato, P.R. 1996. "Explaining the Intergenerational Transmission of Divorce." *Journal of Marriage and the Family* 58: 628–640.

Amato, P.R., and D. Previti. 2003. "People's Reasons for Divorcing: Gender, Social Class, the Life Course, and Adjustment." *Journal of Family Issues* 24: 602–626.

Ambert, A.M. 2005. *Divorce: Facts, Causes, and Consequences*. Ottawa: The Vanier Institute of the Family.

Ambert, A.M. 2006. *Changing Families: Relationships in Context*. Toronto: Pearson.

Ambert, A.M. 2009. Divorce*: Facts, Causes, and Consequences*, 3rd ed. Ottawa. The Vanier Institute of the Family.

Bram, J. 2009. *Happily Ever After Divorce: Notes of a Joyful Journey*. Deerfield Beach, Florida: Health Communications.

Cheal, D. 1996. *Growing up in Canada*. National Longitudinal Survey of Children and Youth, no. 1. Ottawa: Statistics Canada and Human Resources Development Canada.

Cherlin, A.J. 1978. "Remarriage as an Incomplete Institution." *American Journal of Sociology* 84: 634–651.

Chunn, D.E. 2005. "Politicizing the Personal: Feminism, Law, and Public Policy." In N. Mandell and A. Duffy (eds.), *Canadian Families: Diversity, Conflict, and Change*, 3rd ed. (pp. 276–310). Toronto: Thomson Nelson.

Clark, W., and S. Crompton. 2006. "Till Death Do Us Part? The Risk of First and Second Marriage Dissolution."*Canadian Social Trends*, Catalogue no. 11-008, 81: 25–31.

Cowan, P.A. 1991. "Individual and Family Life Transitions: A Proposal for a New Definition." In P.A. Cowan and M. Hetherington (eds.), *Family Transitions*, 3rd ed. (pp. 3–30). Hillsdale: Erlbaum.

Downs, J.M., M. Coleman, and L. Ganong. 2000. "Divorced Families over the Life-Course." In S. Prince, P.C. McKenry, and M.J. Murphy (eds.), *Families across Time: A Life Course Perspective* (pp. 24–36). Los Angeles: Roxbury Publishing.

Eshleman, J.R., and S.J. Wilson. 2001. *The Family*, 3rd Canadian ed. Toronto: Pearson.

Family Justice Newsletter. 2003. Vol. 1 (Spring): 1–4. Department of Justice Canada. Retrieved December 19, 2006, from www.canada.justice.gc.ca/en/ps/pad/news/052003.

Ferri, E., and K. Smith. 1998. *Step-Parenting in the 1990s*. Family and Parenthood. Policy and Practice Series. London: Family Policy Studies Centre.

Gorlick, C.A. 2005. "Divorce: Options Available, Constraints Forced, Pathways Taken." In N. Mandell and A. Duffy (eds.), *Canadian Families: Diversity, Conflict, and Change*, 3rd ed. (pp. 210–238). Toronto: Harcourt.

Greaves, L., C. Varcoe, N. Poole, M. Marrow, J. Johnson, A. Pederson, and I. Irwin. 2002. *A Motherhood Issue: Discourses on Mothering under Duress*. Ottawa: Status of Women Canada.

McDaniel, S., and L. Tepperman. 2004. *Close Relations: An Introduction to the Sociology of Families*, 2nd ed. Scarborough: Prentice-Hall.

Mitchell, B.A. 2006. *The Boomerang Age: Transitions to Adulthood in Families*. New Brunswick: Aldine Transaction.

Newman, D.M., and L. Grauerholz. 2002. *Sociology of Families*, 2nd ed. Thousand Oaks: Pine Forge Press.

Pulkingham, J. 1995. "Investigating the Financial Circumstances of Separated and Divorced Parents: Implications for Family Law Reform." *Canadian Public Policy* XXI: 1–19.

Richardson, C.J. 2001. "Divorce and Remarriage." In M. Baker (ed.), *Families: Changing Trends in Canada*, 4th ed. (pp. 208–237). Toronto: McGraw-Hill Ryerson.

Seccombe, K., and R.L. Warner. 2004. *Marriages and Families: Relationships in Social Context.* Toronto: Nelson.

Statistics Canada. 2003. "Profile of Canadian Families and Households: Diversification-Continues." 2001 Census Analysis Series. Ottawa: Statistics Canada.

Statistics Canada. 2004. "Divorces." *The Daily* (May 4).

Statistics Canada. 2006. *Women in Canada*, 2005, 5th ed. Catalogue no. 89-503-XIE. Ottawa: Minister of Industry.

Sweeney, M.M. 1997. "Remarriage of Women and Men and Divorce: The Role of Socio-economic Prospects." *Journal of Family Issues* 1: 479–502.

Teachman, J.D. 2002. "Childhood Living Arrangements and the Intergenerational Transmission of Divorce." *Journal of Marriage and the Family* 64: 717–729.

Vanier Institute of the Family. 2011 (October 26). "Four in Ten Marriages End in Divorce." *Fascinating Families*, Issue 41.

Waite, L.J., and M. Gallagher. 2000. *The Case for Marriage*. New York: Doubleday.

Ward, M. 2002. *The Family Dynamic: A Canadian Perspective*, 3rd ed. Toronto: Nelson.

Wolfinger, N. 2000. "Beyond the Intergenerational Transmission of Divorce: Do People Replicate the Pattern of Marital Instability They Grew up with?" *Journal of Family Issues* 21: 1061–1086.

Chapter 10

Families in the Middle and the Launching of Children

Home-Leaving, Boomerang Kids, and the Empty Nest

Learning Objectives

In this chapter you will learn ...
- to situate contemporary patterns of transitions to adulthood and child launching within the context of social and economic change
- that there is not one singular institutionalized life course with respect to mid-life family development
- how mid-life family living arrangements are socially structured by factors such as gender, ethnicity, region, and social capital
- to understand the reciprocal effects of mid-life family co-residence on "linked lives"
- to critically evaluate popular stereotypes that co-resident adult children are "too close for comfort" and that mothers experience the "empty nest syndrome" when children leave home

Introduction

What is your current living arrangement? Have you left your parental household to go to school and are you living alone or with a roommate, partner, or in a dorm? Or, like many other Canadian post-secondary students, are you still living at home with your parents while you attend school? And if you have left the "parental nest," do you plan to return home as a boomerang kid once you complete your studies? Leaving the parental home and establishing a separate residence is obviously a significant and meaningful milestone for most Canadian mid-life parents and their children. As previously noted, dramatic transformations have occurred in the child-launching phase of family development. And, unlike previous times—particularly prior to World War Two when there was an absence of state supports to assist the older generation—young people continue to live at home for economic and housing support, rather than to provide such assistance to their aging parents.

Table 10.1 presents a comparison of three generations—late baby boomers (born 1957 to 1966), Generation X (born 1969 to 1978), and Generation Y (born 1981 to 1990). This table highlights how today's young adults (Generation Y, currently between 20 and 29 years of age) grew up during a period of changing family dynamics and family formation. Notably, their baby boomer parents, born and raised after the Second World War, were predominantly dual earners and a substantial number of mothers were primary earners. Moreover, during Generation Y's childhood, some of their fathers were likely to have taken parental leave, a program that was introduced and offered to fathers for the first time in 1990. Overall, this profile shows that several socio-economic characteristics have changed considerably from one generation to the next, themes that appear throughout many other chapters of this book. In particular, data show that more Generation Y young adults are living at home with their parents and that they are staying in school longer. Living as a married or common-law couple and having children is also less common for Generation Y compared to earlier generations (Marshall, 2011).

Table 10.1
Profile of Late Baby Boomers and Generations X and Y at Ages 20 to 29

	Late baby boomers (born 1957 to 1966)	Generation X (born 1969 to 1978)	Generation Y (born 1981 to 1990)
	thousands		
Total population	4,552	4,186	4,663
	percentage		
Sex			
Men	51	50	51
Women	49	50	49
Age			
20 to 24 years	50	48	49
25 to 29 years	50	52	51
Marital Status			
Married/common-law	48	37	33
Single	50	61	67
Other	F	F	F
Has children	29	22	19
Employment rate			
Both sexes	73	72	74
Men	78	76	75
Women	68	69	72
Student			
Both sexes	15	18	19
Men	16	20	19
Women	13	17	20
Lives at home with one or both parents			
All ages (20 to 29 years)	28	31	51
20 to 24 years	43	46	73
25 to 29 years	12	17	30
Immigrant	11	16	18
Reports no religion	14	25	35

F = too unreliable to be published

Source: Statistics Canada, General Social Survey and Labour Force Survey, 1986, 1998 and 2010.

Cited in: Marshall, K. (2011). "Generational Change in Paid and Unpaid Work," *Canadian Social Trends*, Catalogue no. 11-008-X, Table 1, p. 16.

Thus, if you remain at home, have returned home, or plan to return at some future time, you are certainly not alone and are characteristic of Generation Y. Moreover, not only are Gen Yers postponing final departure from the parental home without ever having left, they are increasingly likely to refill parental households. This has led to the popular conceptualization of boomerang kids, who are viewed as members of the "boomerang age" (Mitchell, 2006). Statistics Canada, based on Census data (2002), show that 28 percent of young women aged 20–29 and 33 percent of young men aged 20–29 have returned home at least once after an initial departure. Therefore, once children leave, they are not necessarily gone for good, which suggests a number of emergent trends and issues for mid-life family development. This phenomenon also sensitizes us to the fact that life course and living arrangement transitions are diverse and flexible in modern society.

In light of these important trends, this chapter evaluates contemporary research on the child-launching phase of mid-life family development, with an emphasis on extended home-leaving processes. The focus will be on macro- (e.g., changing economic and cultural conditions) and micro-level factors (e.g., gender, family background) shaping this transition. Moreover, since patterns of home-leaving and intergenerational co-residence have profound implications for mid-life family development, attention will also be paid to examining the effects of these trends on intergenerational relations.

Who Is a Home-Leaver? A Mature Co-resider? A Boomerang Kid?

Child launching is a mid-life developmental phase whereby young adult children leave home, which usually entails a process of separation. Young adults can physically separate from the parental home, although they can continue to be financially or social-psychologically dependent upon their families and/or on parental household resources. This illustrates Goldscheider and DaVanzo's (1985) concept of semi-autonomous living arrangements. For example, a young adult may move into a dorm or an apartment with a roommate but continue to have daily emotional contact and support from one or both parents; receive food, money, or gifts; and continue to rely on many of their parents' household utilities (e.g., to do laundry, use the family car).

Ideally, home-leaving should be conceptualized as a multidimensional behaviour that entails physical as well as non-physical dimensions of separation and autonomy. However, researchers usually measure home-leaving as a discrete transitional event in the form of a physical residential move (of at least four months) from the parental home. Remaining at home past the usual age of approximately 19–20 is generally conceptualized as "home staying" or intergenerational co-residence, while co-residing past the age of 25 is coined "mature co-residency" (e.g., see Mitchell, Wister, and Gee, 2002). Similarly, in order to be considered a boomerang kid, home returning usually requires a leave and return of at least four or more months, since shorter stays have very different causes and consequences.

The Timing of Home-Leaving and Pathways Out of the Parental Home

A large proportion of young adults aged 18 and over reside in parental homes, and there is an increasing propensity for older-aged young people to live at home as "mature co-residers." In 2006, 60.3 percent of Canadian young adults aged 20–24 and 26 percent of those aged 25–29 were living in a parental home, rates that have risen over the last few decades. For instance, 43.5 percent of Canadian young adults aged 20–29 lived with their parents in 2006, a jump from 32 percent in 1986 (Statistics Canada, 2007). Previous Census data also shows that most young people leave home for school-related reasons (43 percent), followed by "independence" (29.5 percent), employment (11 percent), to form a partnership (9 percent), conflict at home (5.5 percent), or "other" reasons (2 percent).

Although these trends highlight key pathways out of the parental home, more detailed analyses find that specific characteristics of young people and their families shape these processes. Females tend to leave home earlier than males in all industrialized countries, although overall timing conceals wide gender differences in the likelihood of leaving home by a given pathway. Women tend to marry at earlier ages than men and are also more likely to begin a non-traditional family, either through cohabitation or single parenthood. It is also speculated that young women leave earlier than young men because they are subjected to higher levels of parental supervision and monitoring while living at home. They also tend to have better domestic skills to facilitate independent living (Boyd and Pryor, 1989).

Figure 10.1
More Young Adults in Their Twenties Live in the Parental Home in 2006

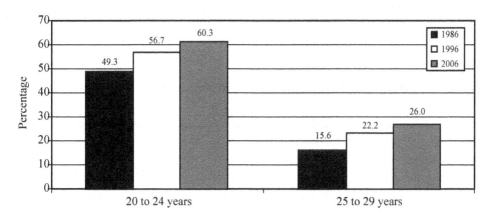

Source: A. Milan, M. Vézina, and C. Wells, "Family Portrait: Continuity and Change in Canadian Families and Households in 2006: Findings," figure 15. Census release, September 12, 2007, www. statcan.ca.

A variety of family background factors are also found to affect home-leaving. Living in non-intact households is found to lead to early home-leaving. In particular, exposure to a stepfamily is found to lead to early home-leaving and more often due to conflict (Mitchell, 1994; Turcotte, 2006; Zhao, Fernando, and Ravanera, 1995). It is also interesting to note that children are more likely to leave home later when their parents left home after the age of 21 (Turcotte, 2006). Moreover, there may be a positive selection factor in the propensity to remain home until later ages; that is, adult children who get along better with their parents are more likely to do so (Mitchell, Wister, and Gee, 2004). Thus, social capital—an "intangible" resource that inheres in the structure of relational bonds such as close, supportive parental relations—can make the family home a very comfortable "feathered nest" and decrease the probability of early home-leaving.

With respect to parental socio-economic status, previous research found that social class matters in the timing of home-leaving, in that more highly educated parents can purchase privacy and independence, which reduces the probability of later home-leaving (e.g., see Goldscheider and Goldscheider, 1999). However, Turcotte (2006) finds that overall, the effects of socio-economic status is no longer influential per se. Instead, what matters most is the type of dwelling the parents live in. Generally, parents with more space (e.g., living in a single detached home versus an apartment) increases the likelihood of later home-leaving. Having more siblings also promotes earlier home-leaving because of household crowding (Mitchell, 2006).

Race/ethnicity is a factor that significantly affects the timing and routes out of the parental household. Turcotte (2006) finds that the parents' place of birth influences the likelihood that parents will live with an adult child. Parents born in Europe (other than the U.K.), South America, and Asia have much higher predicted probabilities (at 35 percent, 50 percent, and 60 percent, respectively) than Canadian-born parents (only 22 percent). This may partly be explained by the tendency for young adults from certain ethnic backgrounds to remain at home until they get married. In some cultures, it is also normative to remain at home to care for an aging parent (i.e., in Chinese families), while in some Southeast Asian societies it is still very common for newlyweds to live with the husband's parents. Moreover, many recent immigrants may find intergenerational doubling-up an attractive lifestyle choice, particularly when extended family living is a cultural tradition and housing is very expensive in large cities (Mitchell, 2006).

Youths with greater financial resources and those who are employed generally leave home earlier than those with less income and the unemployed (Boyd and Norris, 1999). Conversely, young adults who are looking for work have a tendency to remain at home longer than those who are attending post-secondary school or who are in the paid labour force (Goldscheider and Goldscheider, 1999; Mitchell, Wister, and Gee, 2004). Place of residence can also greatly affect opportunities related to employment and the location of educational institutions. For example, remaining at home to attend college or university may not be an option for rural youth who live far away from the school. "Local culture" can also affect family-related norms and preferences, as well as expectations related to dependency and autonomy. In short, regional variations can be viewed as an important social or community context that can shape family relationships and family behaviours.

In Canada there are striking differences by region, especially by province/territory in the propensity of young adults aged 20–29 to live in parental homes. Notably, about half of young adults from Newfoundland and Labrador and Ontario were living with their parents in 2006 compared to less than one-third in provinces such as Saskatchewan and Alberta. Moreover, the proportion of young adults in the parental home is highest in metropolitan areas such as Toronto (57.9 percent) and Vancouver (50.6 percent), but is relatively low in cities such as Saskatoon (28.4 percent) and Sherbrooke (25.3 percent) (Milan, Vézina, and Wells, 2007).

Leaving the Nest "Early" or "Late": Factors Contributing to Premature or Postponed Home-Leaving

A life course perspective emphasizes how the age at which one leaves home can set up a chain reaction of consequences that reverberate over the life course. Early home-leaving (e.g., under the age of 18), particularly when not in conjunction with attending school away from home, has been shown to create a host of negative repercussions for the trajectory of young people into successful career patterns and stable families (Goldscheider and Goldscheider, 1999). Many early leavers (especially "runaways") have lower educational attainment and are at a higher risk of poverty, homelessness, street prostitution, drug addiction, and other problems. This can seriously limit their life chances and opportunities, as well as their health and well-being. Moreover, many of these young people do not have the option of returning home because of a history of problematic family relations (Mitchell, 2006). As a result, intergenerational ties and family relations can be compromised or severed, in both the short- and long-term.

At the other end of this age spectrum, living at home well past the "normal" age of emancipation (e.g., past age 25) as a "mature co-resider" also has important consequences for both adult children and their parents. Late home-leaving can delay the empty-nest period for parents, which can affect mid-life marriages, plans to downsize, retirement planning, leisure activities, or other post-parental plans. Yet, the benefits of "home" can provide a myriad of benefits for young adults and make the transition to adulthood much easier. For example, young adults can use parental and household resources to expand educational training, save money, and acquire consumer goods while continuing to live in a supportive family setting.

What factors promote early or late home-leaving? One of the strongest sets of findings is that family disruption in the parental household can promote premature home-leaving. Children who have experienced a great deal of household change while growing up or are exposed to stepfamilies have a higher risk of early home-leaving (Goldscheider and Goldscheider, 1999; Mitchell, 1994; Zhao, Fernando, and Ravanera, 1995). As a result, young people will often try to escape these stressful environments or move because of conflict at home. Research on "mature co-residency" also finds that there are factors that increase the likelihood of remaining at home until later ages. Not surprisingly, those with more social capital in the form of supportive intergenerational ties (especially with moms) are more likely to remain at home past the age of 25. For example, a recent national Canadian study by Mitchell, Wister, and Gee (2002) find that emotional closeness to parents (while growing up) plays a strong role in the determination to live at home as "mature co-residers," controlling for other factors. Other key predictors include a younger age (25–29 vs. 30–34), being male, unemployed, having higher levels of education, and being unmarried.

Back Home Again: Contemporary Patterns of Home Returning

The trend of adult children moving back to the parental home has been rising since the 1970s and contributes to the dramatic increase in the number of young adults who live with their parents. From an international perspective, home returning is also popular in many industrialized countries such as Britain, Japan, Australia, France, and Germany (Mitchell, 2006). It is especially common in the U.S. where it is estimated that about 40 percent of American young adults return home (Goldscheider and Goldscheider, 1999). In part, this is due to higher rates of military service among young people. Indeed, Goldscheider and Goldscheider (1999) observe that "the leaving home transition has become more renewable, less of a one-way street and more like a circular migration."

Why are young adults increasingly likely to flock back to the parental nest? According to Paul (2001), the rise in the homeward bound signifies not only the changing transition to adulthood, but also a fundamental shift in how parents and adult children view their roles and identities within the family. Prior to the mid- to late 1990s, having an adult child back at home was not generally perceived as a desirable living arrangement. This is because it was assumed to violate parental (and Western cultural) expectations for independence and autonomy. This theme was reflected by the North American media and the scholarly literature on the subject by books such as *Boomerang Kids: How to Live with Adult Children Who Return Home* (Okimoto and Stegall, 1987). This book counselled parents about thorny issues like charging children rent, the move toward eventual eviction, and negotiating household chores, and the general tone was that parents should work hard to "let the children move on."

However, with changing times, parental roles have shifted such that some point the finger at the older generation for facilitating longer periods of residential stays and their children's "bouncing back and forth" from the parental home. For example, a recent (and controversial) article in *Psychology Today* entitled, "The PermaParent Trap" (Paul, 2003) discusses how many parents in today's society are unable to "let go when they ought to" and that this is partly to blame for the high numbers of boomerang kids. Whereas previous generations emphasized educational and financial independence, baby boomer parents are the first generation for whom their children's emotional fulfillment is a primary goal. As a result, some suggest that there is more of a tendency to "hyper-invest" in children, and one manifestation of this is the reluctance of some parents to want to empty the nest during mid-life. Another manifestation is the phenomenon of "helicopter" parents. Indeed, as shown in Box 10.1, many college administrators across North America are expressing concern over what they claim is a growing trend of "over-involved" baby boomer parents. These parents are unable to "let go," which, they claim, interferes with campus life and student learning and does not facilitate the transition to independence.

Figure 10.2
Boomerang Kids: A Popular Trend in Today's Families

"I'm here to update your census form. Since you mailed the
form in, have any of your children moved back in with you?"

Source: CartoonStock.com

At a more macro-economic level, researchers usually emphasize factors that in turn affect opportunity structures and delay adult transitions and statuses. In this way, family-related change in union formation among young adults has also helped to fuel the trend of home returning. Transitions out of the parental home have become increasingly unstable since the 1950s, when leaving home for marriage during an era of low divorce was generally fairly permanent. As you will recall from Chapter3, marriage has become increasingly delayed and cohabitation is a popular living arrangement for many young adults. Yet cohabitation is considerably more fragile than legal marital partnership. The need for post-secondary attendance has also increased, with enrolment levels skyrocketing in the 1990s in North America and many European countries. This can make the parental home a convenient "home base" when one is single and during "transitional periods."

Moreover, returning home has become a popular and expected lifestyle choice for many young adults, especially after college or university. Low starting salaries in expensive housing markets, fewer career jobs, and high student loan debt, in conjunction with rising

Box 10.1
"Mommy, Tell My Professor He's Not Nice!" (Over)Involved Baby Boomer Parents—and Cell Phones—Redefine Adulthood

Parents of University of Florida students log on to their children's personal Gator-Link accounts to check grades, then call deans when they don't like what they see. University of Central Florida parents call administrators to complain when their kids can't get into classes they want. At Florida State University, parents of graduating seniors haggle with job recruiters. They want to make sure Junior gets a good salary and work schedule.

University administrators have a name for these baby boomer moms and dads who hover over their offspring's college lives. "Helicopter parents," says Patrick Heaton, FSU's assistant dean of student affairs. The worst of them—those who do unethical things, like write their kid's term papers—are branded "Black Hawks," a nod to the souped-up military helicopters. "I also call them tether parents," says Heaton, who directs FSU's freshman orientation program. "It's like a leash. Students are afraid to make decisions about classes or anything without calling home."

Good luck finding a parent who admits to being a helicopter, much less a Black Hawk. But across the nation, college administrators are struggling with what they say is a growing phenomenon, a product of the unique relationship between many boomer parents and their millennial-generation children. Administrators say they know these parents mean well. But their frequent phone calls and unreasonable demands stunt student development and test the patience of college officials. "Where parent behavior becomes a challenge for us is when they encourage dependence, and they become too involved because they are afraid their son or daughter will make a mistake," says Tom Miller, a University of South Florida dean of students. "Our students are graduating," says Jeanna Mastrodicasa, associate dean of the UF honors college. "But they are not ready to go into the real world." Administrators noticed the hovering problem a few years ago, when the first members of the so-called millennial generation entered college. Millennials are the children of baby boomers, born between the early 1980s and 2000. Sociologists and higher education officials say this generation is unlike any other, thanks to the child-rearing approach of their parents and the unprecedented influence of technology.

Many boomer parents carefully planned and fiercely protected their children, according to *Millennials Rising: The Next Great Generation*, by Neil Howe and William Strauss. They saw their youngsters as "special," and they sheltered them. Parents outfitted their cars with Baby on Board stickers. They insisted their children wear bicycle helmets, knee pads and elbow guards. They scheduled children's every hour with organized extracurricular activities. They led the PTA and developed best-friend-like relationships with their children, says Mastrodicasa, co-author of a book on millennials. Today, they keep in constant touch with their offspring via e-mail and cell phones. And when their children go off to college, parents stay just as involved. Sometimes the attention is healthy and supportive. But in some cases, administrators say, their hovering is intrusive.

"The biggest change is technology," says Robin Leach, interim dean of students at FSU. "Where students in the past might just write home, now they're on the phone with their parents all day, every day. If something goes wrong or right, parents know about it very quickly." An online survey in March by College Parents of America, an advocacy group formed two and a half years ago for the parents of college children, found that one out of three parents communicates with their child two to three times a day, typically via cell phone. More than half of the 839 parent respondents said their involvement with their children is "much more" than what they experienced with their own parents during their college years. "When I went to college in the 70s, contact with my parents was standing at a pay phone on Sunday afternoon," says James Boyle, College Parents of America president. "And there was no expectation beyond that." Freedom High School graduate Ashton Charles, 18, will attend UF in the fall. She says her mother is supportive but "not ridiculously overprotective." They take yoga classes together. They watch *Grey's Anatomy* and *Desperate Housewives*. They use their cell phones to chat and send text messages. Ashton figures their close relationship will continue even when she moves to Gainesville this fall. "I'm sure I'll call her all the time when I'm here," Ashton says....Today universities expect a full house of moms and dads and other guardians, and many colleges are refashioning their programs with parent-only talks that politely convey the message: "Back off, your kid's not a kid anymore." "We talk about the value of letting go," USF's Miller said. UF officials separate students from parents for much of the two-day orientation. If not, "Mom will take notes and want to make decisions," Mastrodicasa says. FSU students and parents also attend separate sessions, but that doesn't stop students from text messaging their parents for help before scheduling their first semester of classes, Heaton says.

At UCF, "we have parents who come and stay the whole first week of class, just to 'make sure they're okay,'" said spokeswoman Linda Gray, shaking her head. "They didn't use to do that." In a recent online survey, "Helicopter Poll," by the career services provider Experience Inc., 38 percent of more than 400 college students admitted their parents participate in meetings with academic advisers. One-quarter of the students polled think their parents are "overly involved" to the point of embarrassment or annoyance.

But Boyle, of College Parents of America, thinks concerns about helicopter parents are "overblown." "It's better than the alternative, them not being involved at all," he says. "In every generation of parents, there are those that get too involved. I think it's a small percentage of parents who do things like try to personally intervene in a roommate dispute." He says "smart schools" accept that parental involvement is higher with the millennial generation and respond by "catering to the parents." "They are paying a large part of the tuition bill, and it's just good customer service," he says. That is USF's approach, Miller said. USF, like an increasing number of universities, has a parents association. Other colleges are hiring parent "advocates." This is the new reality, Miller said. "When I was in college, if my parents actually called the dean, I would have been mortified. Now, it's very common."

http://www.sptimes.com/tpc/TC.Copyright.html

Source: Colavecchio-Van Sickler, Shannon. St. Petersburg Times Online, Tampa Bay, June 19, 2006. Retrieved February 3, 2007 at www.sptimes.com/2006/06/19/news_pf/State/Mommy.

tuition fees, are common reasons for the decision to move back home (Mitchell, 2006). Indeed, neo-liberal government policies that treat post-secondary education as a private consumer good enormously impacts Canadian families. And not only are young people's lives affected, but these economic policies shift responsibility for financial support back onto the shoulders of the families of post-secondary students and recent graduates.

The 2001 General Social Survey finds that 34.7 percent of all boomerang kids return for school-related reasons, whereas 24 percent refill the nest for financial reasons. Almost one in 10 (10.5 percent) return because a relationship ended, and 9.3 percent because their job ended or other work-related reasons. In 4.5 percent of the cases, young people returned due to parental need (e.g., parental health or financial problems) or due to their own health issues (4 percent). Thirteen percent returned because of "other" reasons (e.g., returned after travelling abroad).

Moreover, recent research based on a sample of almost 500 parents living in the Greater Vancouver area (a region with very expensive housing) shows that unlike recent cohorts who experienced severe recessionary periods in the early 1980s and 1990s, many young people do not return out of dire economic circumstances (Mitchell, 2011). Instead, living at home is often a means to save money and pay off debts while living in a comfortable home setting. Thus, many young people are willing to sacrifice some independence to maintain their parents' standard of living. This has been called an intergenerational taste effect, whereby the luxuries of one generation become the necessity of the next generation (Crimmins et al., 1991). This study also reveals increasing de-stigmatization and acceptance of intergenerational co-residence, which also helps to fuel its popularity.

Other personal-level and family background factors affect the propensity to return home in North America. Generally, sons are slightly more likely to return than daughters (Mitchell, Wister, and Gee, 2004). This trend is partly explained by the fact that females tend to marry at younger ages. Marital status also affects the propensity of young adults to return. Generally, the vast majority of returnees are single, although a small percentage is divorced/separated and married. Only a small minority return with children, and race/ethnicity is not found to affect the likelihood of returning home (Goldscheider and Goldscheider, 1999; Mitchell, Wister, and Gee, 2004).

Linked Lives: Implications of Leaving Home and Co-residence for Intergenerational Relations

There is a growing body of literature that documents how nest leaving and intergenerational co-residence affects mid-life parental experiences and parent-child relations. For example, as discussed in boxes 10.2 and 10.3, most parents (particularly moms) do not seem to experience the empty nest syndrome, although there may be gender and cultural differences in how this event is experienced. Furthermore, it should be recognized that relationships with parents usually continue long past the time when children leave home, and most young adults find that parents are a continuing source of companionship and support. Yet some young people, after leaving home, have little contact with parents,

Box 10.2
The Empty Nest Syndrome: Fact or Fiction?

One pervasive belief used to be that middle- and older-aged parents—particularly stay-at-home mothers—suffer severe emotional crises when all their children grow up and leave home (Newman and Grauerholz, 2002). Commonly dubbed "the empty nest syndrome," some psychiatrists claim that this syndrome is a clinically diagnosable condition, and medical journals used to run full-page advertisements for anti-depressants that can be prescribed as treatment (Harkins, 1978). Why should parents experience the empty nest syndrome? Many theorize that during middleage and the transition to old age, individuals experience "loss" events. These loss events include the loss of work, the departure of children, the death of a partner, and the loss of autonomy. Therefore, on one level, the empty nest syndrome makes some intuitive sense, since the roles people occupy provide meaning and behavioral guidance in their lives. And since most women have devoted a significant portion of their lives to raising children, one might expect women to suffer when their children leave because an important part of their identity and motherhood role has gone. Yet according to many researchers, such an explanation rests on some dubious assumptions such as the idea that being a parent is the individual's only pertinent social role; that when children are gone, they are gone for good; and that when children leave, parenting abruptly stops (Newman and Grauerholz, 2002).

In reality, and contrary to popular belief, research on the "empty nest syndrome" finds that, for most parents, the departure of children is a positive experience. Parents can find freedom, relief from responsibilities, and time for themselves. For example, sociologist Lillian Rubin (1992) found that the stereotype of the painful empty nest is largely a myth. In fact, many of the mothers that she interviewed experienced feelings of accomplishments that they had done their "job" well and were ready to move on to the next stage of life. Moreover, many seemed guilty about feeling happy. Such guilt illustrates the pervasiveness of gender-based expectations in parenting and the stereotype that women are supposed to be unhappy when their children leave. However, Rubin did not study cultural differences in these processes, although she did notice some class differences in the way mothers respond to their children leaving home. Notably, working class parents could not take for granted that their children would attend college, and this made preparation for the empty nest more difficult. Yet, the difficulty is generally brief and does not constitute clinical depression.

Source: Mitchell, B.A. 2006. *The Boomerang Age: Transitions to Adulthoods in Families.* New Brunswick, NJ: Aldine-Transaction Publishers (pp. 81–82).

and others can harbour feelings of resentment toward parents because of childhoods that were less than idyllic (Amato and Booth, 2000). Thus, the nature of these relation-

Box 10.3

The Midlife Parenting Project: Cultural and Gendered Aspects of the Empty Nest Syndrome

A recent SSHRC-funded study entitled "The Parenting Project" (2006–2009) conducted by Principal Investigator Barbara Mitchell from Simon Fraser University surveyed 490 Metro Vancouver parents of young adult children aged 18 and 35 who self-identified as belonging to one of four primary Canadian cultural groups: Chinese, South Asian, Southern European and British. In-depth telephone interviews (35–55 minutes) were conducted with these respondents primarily using random sampling techniques in the preferred language of their choice. Parents were asked many questions (both open- and close-ended) about the relationships they had with their children, spouses, and other family members, as well as their health and well-being. Follow-up face-to-face interviews (1.5 hours) were also conducted with a sub-sample of 40 parents who agreed to be re-interviewed.

In the survey, parents (with a mean age of 58) were asked the question, "Generally speaking, do you feel that this [the empty nest syndrome/ENS, previously defined as a situation whereby mothers become very depressed when their children leave home] is something you experienced when your study child left home?" Parents were also asked, "How difficult was it for you on an emotional level to see your (study) child leave home (for the first time, if left more than once)?" and were given the opportunity to elaborate their answers.

The results of this mixed-methods study reveal some interesting findings. The quantitative analyses (conducted with a sub-sample of 316 parents who had at least one homeleaver) show that only a minority of parents reported experiencing the empty nest syndrome. Most parents reveal positive psychological consequences after children leave, such as increased personal growth, improved marital relations and leisure time, and feelings of mastery in successfully raising and launching their children.

However, cultural background and other sociodemographic and relational processes are found to increase the likelihood of reporting this condition, which was mainly of a temporary duration. Below find the emergent themes based on the qualitative analysis of why parents reported ENS:

1.   **Attachments Matter in Cultural and Social Context**
     These parents tended to report difficulties because they perceived a loss of cultural tradition or a severed relationship. This was particularly pronounced in the South Asian community and among parents with ambiguous attachment ties to their child. For example, in the South Asian community, some parents expected that their oldest son would remain at home, given the cultural traditions (and their later wives) would provide

an important source of help in a multigenerational or extended house-hold. As one father states (aged 59), "I'm not used to the son's leaving home." Other parents (regardless of ethnic background and especially mothers) had difficulty because they mourned the loss of their parental identity or the day-to-day contact/companionship of their child and experienced great loneliness.

2. **Unfinished Business: Off Time Launches and Violations of Social Scheduling Expectations**

    Parents experienced ENS if they felt that the departure occurred too early or too late, based on their cultural and social lens. For example, as one Southern European (Italian) mother reported, "I thought he could have stayed with us, that being 25, it was pretty early for him to leave." Conversely, a British mother (aged 64) was depressed over her son's departure because of his reluctance to "launch on time": "I bloody well had to get a team of oxen to pull him out of the house. I have to move to a one bedroom apartment to force him out. This was hard on me." Parental personal experiences of their own homeleaving timing also influenced normative expectations with respect to their children's timing of homeleaving.

3. **Parental Anxiety or Worry and the Real World: Flying the Coop and Unfeathered Landings**

    Many parents expressed ENS because they had deep-seated worries about their child's health and well-being and the child's ability to maintain independence. These concerns were less likely to be tied to cultural background and gender, although some cases supported a cultural interpretation and mothers generally worried more than fathers. For instance, daughters who left home for arranged marriages in the South Asian community sometimes contributed to ENS for parents. Conversely, when children were perceived to be "looked after" the emotional difficulty was less prevalent. As one Chinese mother (aged 58) states, "My eldest son had gone to Hong Kong for work before my other child left. I thought they could take good care of each other, if needed."

Perhaps these concerns over safety, security and well-being are not surprising given our culture of fear, for example, the media increasingly saturates today's parents with a constant barrage of possible threats, ranging from terrorism, road rage, health epidemics, environmental disasters, and predatory behaviour from strangers.

Source: Adapted from Mitchell, B.A. 2010. "The empty nest syndrome in midlife families: A multimethod exploration of parental gender differences and cultural dynamics." *Journal of Family Issues*, 30: 1651–1670.

ships has important implications over the life course, as feelings of affection facilitate exchanges of assistance between parents and adult children.

The Effects of Delayed Home-Leaving on Intergenerational Relations: Feathered Nest or Gilded Cage?

On a broad level, the trend toward delayed home-leaving suggests that mid-life and aging parental roles and responsibilities have become restructured in modern society. Now, many parents must modify prior expectations and resume their day-to-day "in-house" parental roles to facilitate their children's transition to adulthood. This has led researchers to comment that parenthood has become a more unpredictable and complex role and experience (Ambert, 1994). This issue is particularly salient for mothers, since they are more bound to caregiving and domestic roles than fathers.

However, there are fundamental differences in caregiving experiences among women linked to their time and their economic, socio-political, cultural, and physical locations, as well as to their health and their abilities (Armstrong and Armstrong, 2002). Therefore, the effects of extended co-residence on mothers will depend on the unique circumstances and resources of the particular family. For example, "sandwich-generation" mothers (that is, those faced with demands from competing generations, to be addressed in the next chapter), who are trying to juggle work and family roles with few economic and social supports, are more vulnerable to adverse consequences (Kobayashi, 2010).

In a similar vein, the trend of home staying has several distinct implications for family socialization over the life course. When adult children remain at home, mid- and later-life parents are confronted with carrying out extended or "additional" socialization. This occurs, in part, because parents must continue to impart the expertise, skills, and knowledge necessary for their children to become independent adults. Young people living at home may also adopt their parents' behaviour more thoroughly (Boyd and Pryor, 1989). Since co-residency is an experience lived through a network of family relationships, it follows that there are unique processes of reciprocal socialization that occur. One outcome of mutual influence may be greater intergenerational monitoring, whereby parents monitor adult children and children monitor middle-aged and elderly parents (Boyd and Pryor, 1989). It is also possible that parents and their children develop more peer-like orientations toward each other at this time.

Moreover, staying at home until later ages has the potential to either increase intergenerational solidarity or to weaken it (e.g., create intergenerational conflict). While traditional life course theory predicts general dissatisfaction with "mature co-residence" or the return of an adult child, Elder (1994) emphasizes the interplay of human lives and socio-historical context. During the postwar period between the 1950s and 1990s, social scientists and the popular press usually portrayed extended home-leaving as something aberrant or abnormal. Home returning was assumed to signal family dysfunction or individual pathology, and social scientists frequently offered conceptualizations fraught with negative connotations such as "the returning adult syndrome" and the "cluttered nest." Indeed, it was not uncommon for researchers to assume that when young adults live at home, "everybody loses" (Bibby and Posterski, 1992: 221).

Media images of families with co-resident children continue to be sympathetic to a White, middle-aged, middle-class readership. In particular, grown adult children (especially men over the age of 25) living with their parents continue to be portrayed in movies, newspapers, magazines, or on daytime talk shows as "adultescents" and their parents as victims of greedy or lazy children. Afflicted with what has been termed the "Peter Pan Syndrome" (Goldscheider, 1997), these adult children living at home continue to be stereotyped as immature adults or "mamma's boys" who are unable or unwilling to let go of "the apron strings." Indeed, a recent series of *Dr. Phil* shows featured the theme, "The New Generation of Moochers," while Paramount recently released the 2006 movie called *Failure to Launch* with the tagline, "To leave the nest, some men just need a little push." This movie portrayed a White, middle-class family with a 30-something co-resident son who is a successful boat salesman and drives a Porsche. Their "slacker son" refuses to leave the comforts of home, so the parents resort to hiring an attractive private detective to lure him out of the nest. And while this movie is obviously an extreme version of real life, it does represent a popular cultural stereotype that continues to persist.

Studies generally find that the vast majority of parents and their children are relatively satisfied with the living arrangement, although a minority report significant stress and conflict. This is possibly due to "positive selection factors." Close families tend to stick together, such that unhappy co-resident living arrangements would likely dissolve before the typical four-month spell needed to be considered a home returner. This selection process can also inhibit the formation of co-resident living arrangements among less compatible family members (Mitchell, 2006). However, most parents do not want it to be a permanent situation.

What are some of the direct effects on intergenerational relations when young adults live with their parents? As previously noted, in the past, it was assumed that the presence of adult kids in the household was problematic because it can create intrafamilial conflict and tensions. Mid-life parents, faced with the day-to-day presence of returnee children, were speculated to experience disruption and to think that this situation reflects badly on their parenting skills. Similarly, children were assumed to feel like social and economic failures due to their inability to maintain residential independence and adult roles and responsibilities. As a result, stress associated with a mutual intergenerational mindset of "Where did I go wrong," combined with the extra dependency and responsibility, was speculated to create a host of negative side effects for family functioning and well-being.

Despite these alleged negative effects, research shows that overall, intergenerational relations tend to be characterized by mutual interdependence and reciprocity. Although children tend to receive more instrumental and financial support than parents receive, children attempt to maintain reciprocity by exchanging a variety of helping behaviours. Some of these exchanges are non-tangible, yet may be perceived as an adequate "reward" for instrumental and financial contributions. Parents of co-resident children, for example, commonly report that they receive benefits such as companionship and satisfaction in helping their children to become more successful adults, as shown in Table 10.2. However, parents are the most satisfied when their children reciprocate support and show definitive signs of moving toward adult roles and statuses (Mitchell, 1998). Young adults also reveal that they enjoy the day-to-day companionship and emotional support of their parents, in addition to the comforts of home. However, children are more likely than their parents to report economic benefits, such as "It is cheaper to live at home to save money."

It is also not surprising that while both generations report mainly positive experiences, they are also able to cite several aspects that they don't like about living together under one roof, which are also covered in Table 10.2. From the parental perspective, the most commonly cited problem of "boomerang kids" includes a lack of privacy and independence. This finding is hardly surprising, given the long-standing Western cultural ideal of "intimacy at a distance." That is, most aging parents want to maintain close contact with their adult children, but they generally do not want to live with them. Parents also

Table 10.2
Parental Appraisals of "Boomerang Kid" Living Arrangements by Gender

	Fathers		Mothers	
	Percent	N	Percent	N
Aspects Like				
Companionships/friendship	47.5	29	72.5	108
Having family together	36.1	22	17.4	26
Child helps out/emotional support	6.6	4	4.7	7
Other	9.8	6	5.4	8
Total	100.0	61	100.0	149

Chi Square = 11.9, 3df, p.<.01
Missing observations = 7

	Fathers		Mothers	
Aspects Don't Like				
Child messy/does not help	6.5	4	11.9	18
Lack privacy/independence	17.7	11	24.5	37
Child's personality/attitude	16.1	10	9.9	15
Child's lifestyle	8.1	5	10.6	16
Fights/arguments/stress	6.5	4	6.6	10
Child's dependence	1.6	1	8.6	13
Other	11.3	7	8.6	13
No answer	32.3	20	19.2	29
Total	100.0	62	100.0	151

Chi Square = 11.57, 7df, Not statistically significant
Missing observations = 4

Source: B.A. Mitchell, "Too Close for Comfort? Parental Assessments of 'Boomerang Kid' Living Arrangements," *Canadian Journal of Sociology* 23 (1998), no. 1: 16.

often complain about the following aspects: child is messy or does not help out; child's personality, attitude, or lifestyle; and child's dependence. Additional research on this topic also finds that while home returners do not negatively affect mid-life marriages, returning home multiple times can negatively affect parental relationships (Mitchell and Gee, 1996). Notably, the child's "bouncing back and forth" can create frustration and spill over to a marital relationship by creating problems such as divided loyalties and financial stress. And when grandchildren are present (which is relatively rare), this can add more complexity with respect to child-care issues and financial expenses.

Similarly, adult children commonly cite a number of aspects they like and don't like about living with their parents after the age of 19 (see Box 10.4 for examples).

Box 10.4
Young Adults' Personal Views on Living at Home with Parents

What I like about living at home with my parents...
"I get emotional support from my parents and I can concentrate on my school." (19-year-old Chinese-Canadian male, student)

"Everyone is close by. I get courage and strength from my family. I have a strong bond between me and my other family members." (25-year-old Canadian Southern-European female, employed)

"...free room and board...clean clothes and stuff...cozy and comfortable. It's home." (21-year-old Canadian Southern-European female, student)

"Family support more than anything else and I like the security." (21-year-old Canadian Southern-European female, student)

"It's nice being around the family. [I like] The sense of unity and teamwork to achieve a common goal." (24-year-old Indo-Canadian male)

What I don't like about living at home with my parents...
"[my parents]...they are very annoying and love to ask me questions." (20-year-old Chinese-Canadian female, student)

"My parents are nagging me a little and this makes me feel like I am in high school." (22-year-old British-Canadian female, student)

"I miss the freedom to do as I please...plus there is no privacy." (22-year-old British-Canadian male, employed)

"I can't blast my music, and [I don't like] the feeling of being dependent....at my age I should be out on my own." (23-year-old British-Canadian male, looking for work)

"I dislike having rules about what I'm allowed to do. I'm not free to do many things." (24-year-old Indo-Canadian female, employed)

Source: Mitchell, B.A. 2001. "Preliminary findings: The culture and coresidence study." Unpublished findings from a SSHRC-funded study, Simon Fraser University.

Positive advantages often include the ability to save money and emotional and social support, whereas a "lack of privacy and independence" is often perceived as a negative drawback. Other disadvantages of co-residence commonly reported by young people include conflict and stress, parental rules and regulations, feelings of dependency, and having to subject themselves to the popular parental dictum: "As long as you are under my roof, you'll do what I say." This can be particularly difficult for those young people who have returned home after having lived on their own (Mitchell, 2006).

Summary

This chapter highlights one important aspect of mid-life family development by focusing on the process of child launching. Generally, this rite of passage has become delayed in most Westernized countries due to significant transformations in economic, schooling, state policies, and family-related realms. As a result, middle-generational parents are increasingly responsible for providing housing, economic, and social support for their children. This prolongation of adult transitions raises a number of important implications for contemporary families, society, and economic policy, as discussed by two prominent sociologists in boxes 10.5 and 10.6.

From a historical or cross-cultural perspective, however, parent-child co-residence is not something new. For example, high rates of co-residence between an aging parent and an unmarried adult child were observed in earlier parts of the 21st century, particularly during recessionary periods (White, 1994), as well as during the economic recessions of the early 1980s and 1990s. Moreover, many cultures throughout the world and in Canada prefer and continue to practise some form of extended family living for economic or practical reasons.

Leaving home is also not necessarily a one-time event, and the current high rate of home returning (which is unprecedented from a historical perspective) is a trend that may be here to stay. Refilling parental nests has become a popular strategy for many young adults to maximize their economic and social well-being during the transition to adulthood, given changing patterns of family formation and social and economic opportunity structures. Implications of the timing and nature of home-leaving and intergenerational co-residence also have considerable consequences for young adults and their linked lives. Generally, research on parent-child co-residence reveals positive experiences for mid-life families, contrary to popular media stereotypes. These stereotypes are shown to be ideological in the sense that they tend to reflect one ethnocentric view of how families ought to live, rather than embracing ideas of cultural or family diversity and incorporating the changing social and economic realities of youth.

This chapter also considers how intergenerational "doubling-up" adds new roles and responsibilities for mid-life families. Notably, many Canadian mid-life mothers are increasingly confronted with additional (unpaid) caregiving responsibilities and a delay in their

Box 10.5
On a New Schedule: Transitions to Adulthood and Family Change

That the passage to adulthood has become more protracted and the sequence of transitions less orderly and predictable is well documented...Social scientists, having relied for too long on anecdotal reports from the mass media about the direct effects of the later transition to adulthood, are now conducting their own independent research. So far, though, researchers still know far more about the demography and economics of the change than about its implications for family life and practices. Recent evidence from the General Social Survey shows that families generally accept that it now takes their children longer to pass the milestones that mark economic independence and social maturity. How parents and their young adult offspring are managing this longer period of co-residence and economic dependency remains less well understood. More fine-grained information on daily routines, rules and understandings, and exchanges of time, money, and support among co-resident parents and children should make it possible to chart how this new timetable for growing up affects the family. It also remains to be seen whether and how this period of semi-autonomy (or semi-dependency, if the glass is seen as half empty) changes the path of psychosocial development. Using new and more discriminating measures of development during the early adult years, analysts will be able to examine more directly whether and how the experience of adult transitions fosters psychological development, a topic that has remained largely unexplored.

The new schedule of adulthood has complicated family formation itself, particularly for the less-advantaged members of American society. Moving out of the natal household has become precarious for those with limited means. Unlike the not-so-distant past, when marriage provided an easy (though not always a successful) route out, fewer young adults today are willing to commit to a permanent union, in part because they lack the resources and the mind-set to settle down and in part because they lack confidence that marriage provides the security that it once did. These conditions help to explain why parenthood now often precedes marriage for many young adults growing up in disadvantaged households. By contrast, for youth from advantaged families who are able to complete college, the extended period of growing up brings few costs and many benefits. The longer educational process provides greater opportunities for self-exploration, including the search for stable life partners. Delaying marriage and parenthood, it appears, results in wiser marriage choices and consequently more stable family situations and more positive environments for childbearing and childrearing. This class divide in the early adult transition risks reinforcing social advantage and disadvantage in family formation in the next generation.

The body of research on the connections between young adults and their parents across households is growing. Clearly, parents continue to channel support and economic assistance to their adult children after they leave home. But exactly how, when, and why do parents extend help, and how is it reciprocated in both the short term and the long term? Much also remains to be learned about how such family assistance affects both the givers and the receivers of help. How intergenerational exchange is affected by the distribution of resources in the larger society also requires more investigation. I have argued that the United States, with its relatively underdeveloped welfare system, relies more on the family to invest in young adults than do many nations in Europe. The heavy burden placed on families may come at a price if young adults begin to regard childbearing as too onerous and perhaps not sufficiently rewarding. Although there may be no immediate policy prescription for addressing this problem, it is essential to recognize the importance of strengthening the family nest and reducing the immense and competing demands that are being placed on today's parents.

Source: Furstenberg, F.F. 2010. "On a new schedule: Transitions to adulthood and family change." In *The Future of Children, 20,* 1. *The Future of Children* is a collaboration of The Woodrow Wilson School of Public and International Affairs at Princeton University and The Brookings Institution, retrieved August 16, 2009 from CYC-Online, Issue 137, July 2010, from www.cyc-net.org/cyc-online/cyconline-july2010-furstenberg.html.

Box 10.6
Delayed Life Transitions: Trends and Implications

The delay in early life course transitions cannot be separated from the rest of the life course, which means that there are significant implications for individuals and societies. As with other changes that are central to life, there are both positives and negatives, and significant adjustments are necessary....In many regards, the implications of these delays are positive. By leaving home later, children are receiving more transfers from the parents; by staying in education longer, youth is better prepared for a world where the labour force is growing much more slowly and we need to depend on the quality of workers. Two-worker families reduce the dependence of women on men and reduce the exposure of women and children to the risks associated with family instability.

At the individual level, the most negative implication is that people will not have saved enough during a shorter work life, partly because they entered full-time work later, partly because children have spent more time in education and have been slow at establishing their financial independence and leaving home. The accommodations here are obvious, to work longer while one is still healthy and productive, turning at least part of what we have called the troisième age (60–79) into a longer period of post-reproductive productivity. The stronger negatives are at the societal level, because delayed early life transitions bring lower fertility and population aging.

Source: Beaujot, R. 2006. "Delayed life transitions: Trends and implications," in K. McQuillan and Z.R. Ravanera (eds.), *Canada's Changing Families: Implications for Individual and Society.* Toronto: U of T Press (pp. 123–124).

own transition to the empty nest. And while many may not see this extra caring work as a huge burden for Canada's wealthier families, there is little doubt that it creates more challenges for families who struggle in weaker economic, social, or physical positions.

Questions for Critical Reflection and Debate

1. Debate the following: Leaving home is strictly an individual decision.
2. Critically evaluate the advantages and disadvantages of prolonged home-leaving for parent-child relations from a life course perspective.
3. Returning to the parental home most commonly occurs during young adulthood. Do you think that the reasons for returning would be different at later ages? Consider the changing needs of both generations in your answer.
4. Do you agree or disagree that today's parents are unable to let go compared to parents in previous generations? Evaluate how changing socio-demographic, economic, political, and technological advances influence changing patterns of middle-generation parenting styles.
5. Further consider how cultural background, gender, and socio-economic status can influence parental reactions to empty-nest transitions.
6. Discuss how globalization, technological change, and population aging will affect mid-life families, household living arrangements, and intergenerational relations in the future.

Glossary

Boomerang kids are young adults who return to live in the parental home, usually after an absence of four or more months, for a stay of at least four months.

Child launching is the mid-life developmental process of children leaving parental homes, which typically takes place during young adulthood.

Empty nest syndrome refers to the grief that many parents feel when their children move out of the home, and is more common in women since they are more likely to have had the role of primary caregiver.

Intergenerational taste effect is the phenomenon whereby the luxuries of one generation become the necessity of the next generation.

Mature co-residency refers to adult children, usually over the age of 25, who continue to live in the parental home.

Semi-autonomous living arrangements occur when young adults physically leave the parental home, but continue to live in family-like settings (e.g., dorms) and draw upon parental resources.

Social capital is a non-tangible resource that inheres in the quality of relationships. It can be found in strong, supportive families or other social networks and facilitates certain goals or objectives (e.g., the opportunity to remain at home during a transitional period).

Further Reading

Krauss-Whitbourne, S., M.J. Sliwinki, and M.M. Sliwinski. 2012. *The Wiley-Blackwell Handbook of Adulthood and Aging*. West Sussex, UK. From a human development perspective, this collection of papers covers a wide range of topics relevant to aging families, including transitions to the empty nest and retirement.

Mitchell, B.A. 2006. *The Boomerang Age: Transitions to Adulthood in Families*. New Brunswick, NJ: Aldine Transaction. Reviews the literature on patterns of home-leaving and intergenerational co-residence (including the "boomerang kid" phenomenon) from a life course, historical, and international perspective. Implications for intergenerational relations, mid-life/aging families, and social policy are also discussed.

Newman, K. 2012. *The Accordion Family*. Boston: Beacon Press. From a social, economic, and political lens, this book explores relationships between parents and their adult children, with a particular focus on boomerang kids.

Settersten, R., and B. Ray. 2010. *Not Quite Adults: Why 20-Somethings are Choosing a Slower Path to Adulthood, and Why It's Good for Everyone*. New York: Bantam Books. Offers a fresh and compelling view of why it is taking this generation longer to make career and family decisions. Draws upon a decade of research and nearly 500 interviews with young people.

Stabiner, K. 2008. *Empty Nest: 31 Parents Tell the Truth about Relationships, Love and Freedom after Kids Fly the Coup*. New York: Voice Publishers. A highly readable and engaging collection of insightful essays that focus on diverse parental experiences (both mothers and fathers) and the process of separating from their grown children.

Trish, G. 2010. *Motherhood, Absence and Transition: When Adult Children Leave Home*. Surrey, UK: Ashgate Publishers. From a feminist critical lens, this book is about women's perspectives and experiences of their adult children leaving home and how it impacts their sense of identity.

Related Web Sites

AARP (American Association for Retired Persons) provides a webpage on how parents cope with the empty nest in addition to other issues that aging parents face in relation to child launching (e.g., retirement and family careving). http://www.aarp.org/relationships/parenting/info-09-2010/goyer_empty_nest.html.

Aging Hipsters: The Baby Boom Generation offers a humorous look at many of the issues that aging parents currently face and provides a source for trends, research, comment, and discussion of, and by, people born from 1946–1964. http://www.aginghipsters.com/.

Empty Nest Advice, from the Berkeley Parents Network, illustrates the stories and experiences of parents faced with the empty nest, parents.berkeley.edu/advice/parents/emptynest.html.

Older Women's Network presents the executive summary and recommendations of this network and reports on the challenges that mid-life women face with respect to economic security. www.olderwomensnetwork.org/publications/research security of midlifewomen.htm.

Statistics Canada has published data on parents with adult children living at home, http://www.statcan.gc.ca/pub/11-008-x/2005004/article/9124-eng.pdf.

References

Amato, P.R., and A. Booth. 2000. *A Generation at Risk: Growing up in an Era of Family Upheaval.* Cambridge: Harvard University Press.

Ambert, A.M. 1994. "An International Perspective on Parenting: Social Change and Social Constructs." *Journal of Marriage and the Family* 56: 529–544.

Armstrong, P., and H. Armstrong. 2002. *Thinking It through: Women, Work, and Caring in the New Millennium.* Halifax: Nova Scotia Advisory Council on the Status of Women.

Bibby, R.W., and D.C. Posterski. 1992. *Teen Trends: A Nation in Motion.* Toronto: Stoddart.

Boyd, M., and D. Norris. 1999. "The Crowded Nest: Young Adults at Home." *Canadian Social Trends* (Spring): 2–5. Catalogue no. 11-008. Ottawa: Statistics Canada.

Boyd, M., and E. Pryor. 1989. "The Cluttered Nest: The Living Arrangements of Young Canadian Adults." *Canadian Journal of Sociology* 15: 462–479.

Crimmins, E.M., R.A. Easterlin, and Y. Saito. 1991. "Preference Changes among American Youth: Family, Work, and Goods Aspiration, 1976–86." *Population and Development Review* 17: 115–133.

Elder, G.H., Jr. 1994. "Time, Human Agency, and Social Change: Perspectives on the Life Course." *Social Psychology Quarterly* 57: 4–15.

Goldscheider, F. 1997. "Recent Changes in U.S. Young Adult Living Arrangements in Comparative Perspective."*Journal of Family Issues* 18: 708–724.

Goldscheider, F., and J. DaVanzo. 1985. "Semiautonomy and Leaving Home in Early Adulthood." *Social Forces* 65: 187–201.

Goldscheider, F., and C. Goldscheider. 1999. *The Changing Transition to Adulthood: Leaving and Returning Home*. Thousand Oaks: Sage.

Harkins, E. 1978. "Effects of Empty Nest Transitions on Self-Reports of Psychological and Physical Well-being." *Journal of Marriage and the Family* 40: 549–556.

Kobayashi, K. 2010. "'Mid-life Crises': Understanding the Changing Nature of Relationships in Middle-Age Canadian Families." In D. Cheal (ed.), *Canadian Families Today: New Perspectives,* 2nd ed. (pp. 84–95). Toronto: Oxford University Press.

Milan, A., M. Vézina, and C. Wells. 2007. "Family Portrait: Continuity and Change in Canadian Families and Households in 2006: Findings." Census release, September 12, 2007, www.statcan.ca.

Mitchell, B.A. 1994. "Family Structure and Leaving Home: A Social Resource Perspective." *Sociological Perspectives* 37: 651–671.

Mitchell, B.A. 1998. "Too Close for Comfort? Parental Assessments of Boomerang Kid Living Arrangements." *Canadian Journal of Sociology* 23: 21–46.

Mitchell, B.A. 2006. *The Boomerang Age: Transitions to Adulthood in Families*. New Brunswick, NJ: Aldine Transaction Publishers.

Mitchell, B.A. 2011. "Preliminary Findings: The Midlife Parenting Project." Unpublished findings based on SSHRC-funded project #31-635133, Simon Fraser University.

Mitchell, B.A., and E.M. Gee. 1996. "Boomerang Kids and Midlife Parental Marital Satisfaction." *Family Relations* 45: 442–448.

Mitchell, B.A., A.V. Wister, and E.M. Gee. 2002. "There's No Place Like Home: An Analysis of Young Adults' Mature Coresidency in Canada." *International Journal of Aging and Human Development* 54: 1–28.

Mitchell, B.A., A.V. Wister, and E.M. Gee. 2004. "The Family and Ethnic Nexus of Homeleaving and Returning among Canadian Young Adults." *Canadian Journal of Sociology* 29: 543–575.

Okimoto, J.D., and P.J. Stegall. 1987. *Boomerang Kids: How to Live with Adult Children Who Return Home*. Boston: Little, Brown and Co.

Paul, P. 2001. "Echo Boomerang." *American Demographics* 23: 44–50.

Paul. 2003. "The Permaparent Trap." *Psychology Today*. Retrieved October 11, 2003, from http://www.psychologytoday.com/thdoscs/prod/PTOArticle/Pto-2003.

Rubin, L. 1992. "The Empty Nest." In J.M. Heaslin (ed.), *Marriage and Family in a Changing Society*. New York: Free Press.

Statistics Canada. 2002. *2001 Census: Profile of Canadian Families and Households: Diversification Continues*. Census release, October 22, 2002, www.statcan.ca.

Statistics Canada. 2007. "2006 Census: Families, Marital Status, Households and Dwelling Characteristics." *The Daily* (September 12, 2007).

Turcotte, M. 2006. "Parents with Adult Children Living at Home." *Canadian Social Trends* 80: 2–9. Catalogue no. 11-008.

White, L. 1994. "Coresidence and Leaving Home: Young Adults and Their Parents." *Annual Review of Sociology* 20: 81–102.

Zhao, J.Z., R. Fernando, and Z.R. Ravanera. 1995. "Leaving Parental Homes in Canada: Effects of Family Structure, Gender, and Culture." *Canadian Journal of Sociology* 20: 31–50.

Chapter 11

Aging Families and the Sunset Years

Caregiving and Support across the Generations

Learning Objectives

In this chapter, you will learn that ...
- many inaccurate stereotypes and myths about aging families and the elderly exist
- there are many difficulties inherent in defining aging families and the elderly
- key socio-demographic patterns shape generational relations and aging families
- exchanges of support across the generations tend to be reciprocal and are influenced by a number of factors
- there are many pressing issues facing today's aging families and the elderly

Introduction

What images come to your mind when you think of aging families and the elderly? Some of you may conjure up warm, fuzzy memories of nostalgia based upon your own childhood family experiences with your older relatives at family gatherings or during visits. Others may envision grey-haired grandparents with mobility or cognitive problems that require constant care. And while our conceptions often arise from our personal experiences, the media and other socializing agents are also highly influential in the formation of many images and stereotypes. Fortunately, many favourable gains in this area have been made—in particular, we are seeing a growing number of positive age-related images portrayed in society and the media, such as in the movies and in print sources. The recently launched Canadian lifestyle magazine entitled *Zoomer*, which targets "baby boomers with zip" is a good example of changing trends and attitudes toward aging. Affiliated with the Canadian Association of Retired Persons (CARP), this new magazine is directed at older adults and regularly features photos and articles that show the positive side of aging.

Unfortunately, however, other scholarly and popular media continue to grossly exaggerate and negatively depict aging individuals and family-related experiences. A recent study by Blakeborough (2008) published in the *Canadian Journal on Aging*, on representations of aging, for example, shows that cultural stereotypes abound that portray elderly people as senile, feeble, useless, and sites of some other social problems. Blakeborough illustrates this point through a critical analysis and deconstruction of dialogue and scenes between some of the main characters of the highly popular show *The Simpsons*:

HOMER: Hmmm....sorry, Dad. You're too old.
ABE: [Stammers] Too old? Why that just means I have experience. Who chased the Irish out of Springfield village in aught four [sic]? Me, that's who!
IRISH MAN: And a fine job you did too.

HOMER: Aw, Dad. You've done a lot of great things, but you're a very old man now, and old people are useless. [Tickles Abe]. Aren't they? Aren't they? Huh? Yes they are! Tee hee—
ABE: Stop it! That's a form of abuse.

(Swartzwelder, 1994, cited in Blakeborogh, 2008, p. 57).

Blakeborough cites additional instances of how irony, parody, and satire are used on the show with overt references to negative portrayals of aging and to stereotypes associated by age. For example, he describes how the family drops Grampa off at the retirement home where he resides. The sign out front reads, "Springfield Retirement Castle—Where the Elderly can Hide from the Inevitable." After dropping off Grampa, the family speeds off, and the discussion turns to what Grandpa smells like. Bart feels that he smells "like that trunk in the garage where the bottom's all wet," while Lisa thinks Grampa smells more like a "photo lab."

Many argue that these negative stereotypes originate from a culture that worships youth and "ableness" and that also has a growing and powerful "anti-aging" industry. Hence, aging is seen as something undesirable but that can be easily reversed or "fixed" if one only buys the proper products and services, such as expensive skin creams, facial fillers, and Botox. Demographically, there is also widespread focus on population aging (the growing proportion of elderly over the age of 65) and its associated disability and dependency, as well as the popularity of such terms as "caregiver burden." Yet, in reality, the majority of older adults are healthy and only a relatively small percentage suffers from serious health problems. Consequently, this practice perpetuates ageism, as well as alarmist demographic views of a "caregiving crunch" for sandwich-generation parents (e.g., see Gee and Gutman, 2000).

Moreover, imagery of older adults as frail, unproductive, and dependent are often accompanied by an equally disturbing, contradictory, and inaccurate societal myth about older adults. This stereotype depicts them as wealthy, jet-setting "snowbirds" or "greedy geezers." From this viewpoint, the elderly are seen as taking a disproportionate share of society's resources (including paid jobs) and disrupting intergenerational relations in the process (Zimmerman, 2000). In reality, many elderly provide large amounts of support to their families and to their communities and in particular, "down the generational ladder." There is also a great deal of diversity with respect to the economic standing and resources of older adults (Chappell et al., 2003).

Some critics also argue that, in part, many of these images have been "oversold" or overstated because they sell services and products like newspapers or because they are politically motivated (e.g., see Cheal, 2002; Gee and Gutman, 2000). In this regard, it is asserted that apocalyptic demography, which forecasts a number of dismal scenarios based on rapid population aging, is used by policy makers to justify or rationalize a retreat from the welfare state. This is because escalating health care and pension costs are blamed on population aging and are deemed "just too expensive" for the state to sustain. As a result, this ideology justifies family care and individual—rather than social— responsibility for the care of seniors. Indeed, many of these premises are speculative and gloss over the systemic challenges that families face, such as poverty, sexism, racism, or a lack of family support.

Further, Rosenthal (2000) reminds us that there is much more to aging family life than caregiving and dependency, and that we must adopt a more balanced view by considering both positive and negative aspects of aging-related social processes. It is also critical that we carefully evaluate what changes in family structure over time actually mean to families and family life. Indeed, there are a number of reasons why the study of aging processes and the social world of aging families is important (see Box 11.1). Cognizant of these issues, this chapter will explore a number of facets relevant to aging families and the elderly.

Defining Aging Families and the Elderly

Although, technically, we all live in aging families, it is important to define what we mean by aging families and the elderly. In keeping with our life course perspective, aging families and the elderly experience particular age-related changes or developmental transitions relevant to certain phases of the life course. These relatively unique transitional events and experiences are important to consider because they can affect family functioning, well-being, and resource and social support availability. For example, taking care of an elderly parent can bring many joys and rewards, but it can also produce economic or

---

Box 11.1
Why Study Aging and Older Adults?

- To challenge, refute, and eliminate myths about aging and older people
- To question popular, taken-for-granted assumptions about aging
- To know thyself, and others, by examining personal journeys across the life course
- To assist and support older family members as they move through the later stages of life
- To prepare for a job or career (as a practitioner, policy-maker, or researcher) where the mandate is to address aging issues to serve an older population
- To understand inter-generational relations and the status of older adults in a multicultural society
- To evaluate policies and practices for an aging population, and to identify gaps where the needs of older adults are not being met
- To enhance the quality and quantity of interaction with older people in your personal and professional life

Source: McPherson, B. 2004. *Aging As a Social Process: Canadian Perspectives.* Toronto: Oxford University Press (p. 5).

social-psychological hardship for those with limited means or little support. Moreover, social hierarchies within aging families create differential experiences both within and between families. Clearly, aging families and older people's lives and relationships are affected by inequities (e.g., gendered and social class) that generate different views and experiences of social reality and day-to-day life (Walker et al., 2001).

For the purpose of this chapter, aging families are conceptualized as mid- to later-life families who confront a number of shared transitions, despite diversity in the timing, prevalence, and nature of these events. These include such events as child launching (covered in the previous chapter), retirement, becoming grandparents, taking care of elderly parents, and the death of a family member. It is also interesting to note that with changing times and longer life expectancies, the entire life cycle has since shifted upwards (e.g., the age at retirement and grandparenthood), which has increased the age of "on time" transitions (Ambert, 2006).

With respect to defining elderly family members, gerontologists (professionals who study aging from a multidisciplinary perspective) usually regard an individual over the age of 65 as "elderly." Historically, this has been the age at which people become eligible for pension and income-security benefits and has long been associated with retirement from the paid labour force. The problem with this somewhat arbitrary definition is that it homogenizes the aged, implying that all people over this age are the same. Moreover, some researchers note that inequalities in younger life may become more pronounced in the elderly years. This is due to a chain reaction of cumulative advantage or disadvantage over the life course, which can result in increasing inequality over time (O'Rand, 1996).

Families of the Past: Golden Age or Rose-Coloured Glasses?

Many myths and stereotypes abound with respect to aging families of the past. It is commonly thought that the family life of older people was "better" in the past, which is known as the Golden Age Myth. This myth presents images of a time in which "Grandma and Grandpa's" house was a multigenerational hub comprised of a large, happy, and harmonious family of children and grandchildren, a stereotype that often serves as a standard with which to gauge today's families. Obviously, contemporary images do not measure up, since families now purportedly abandon elderly members in the embrace of materialistic consumption and individualistic pursuits (Gee, 2002: 282).

Yet contrary to popular belief, Canadian families of the past did not usually reside in three-generational households, nor were relationships necessarily better. Most fami-lies throughout the Western world, including the United States, Canada, and Europe, were nuclear in structure. High mortality rates and lower life expectancies also made the probability of multiple generations living together a rarity (Connidis, 2010). As a result, grandparents often did not get to see their grandchildren grow up, and other intimate ties were of a relatively short duration compared to today.

Furthermore, the idea that the elderly had more status and respect in previous times is controversial, given a lack of data and relatively low life expectancies. However, North

American culture is often viewed as having less reverence for the elderly relative to past cultures and other societies, such as Japan (see Box 11.2). And although this idea does receive some empirical support, it is observed that attitudes are changing among younger Japanese youth as they become more Westernized (ICGI, 2006).

The Longevity Revolution and Other Socio-demographic Patterns

As you may recall from Chapter 1, three major factors contribute to the longevity revolution phenomenon: increased life expectancy or decreased mortality, immigration patterns (which lower the relative age of the population), and declining fertility (including smaller family sizes). As a result, the population of Canada will progressively contain larger proportions of people in older age groups. This process is projected to have a significant impact on society and family life over the next 40 years.

The United Nations defines an aged population as one in which more than 7 percent of the population is over the age of 65. According to Statistics Canada (2010), an estimated 4.8 million (14.1 percent) Canadians were 65 years of age or older in 2010, a number that is expected to double in the next 25 years to reach 10.4 million seniors by 2036. It is also interesting to note that those 80 and over constitute the fastest-growing segment of the elderly and that the number of centenarians is also rising (McPherson, 2008). As shown in Figure 11.1, the age group to increase at the fastest pace was that aged 80 and over.

Box 11.2
Japanese Attitudes toward Older Adults

- Japanese law requires the Japanese National Railways to reserve seats for the aged and the handicapped. The seats are silver-gray color and are called the "Silver Seats."
- Older adults in Japan usually do not try to hide their age. In Japan, it is proper etiquette to ask older persons their ages and to extend congratulations to them for their old age.
- Most Japanese over 70 receive all of their medical care free, including physician-prescribed medicines. All older Japanese receive free yearly medical examinations.
- Traditionally, the first son's wife (the daughter-in-law) assumes most of the responsibility for taking care of older parents.
- In 1963, the Japanese made "Respect for Elders Day" a national holiday. Octogenarians (80 years old) and centenarians (100 years old) are awarded medals for reaching old age.

Source: ICGI, 2006, retrieved July 4, 2006 from www.ithaca.edu/aging/schools.

From 2001 to 2006, their numbers soared 25 percent to 1.2 million (Statistics Canada, 2008). Moreover, there were 4,635 Canadians over the age of 100 or centenarians, an increase of 22 percent since 2001 and 50 percent since 1996. And, not surprisingly, five of every six persons over 100 years of age were women since women generally outlive men (Statistics Canada, 2008).

It is also noteworthy that the population of children aged 14 and under has declined by 2.5 percent from 2001, totalling 5.6 million in 2006. Population projections indicate that those aged 65 and over will outnumber children 14 and under by the year 2016. Overall, the growth of Canada's older population will start accelerating in 2011 when the front edge of the baby boomers reach 65 years of age. Currently, the baby boom generation comprises 30 percent of the population in Canada (McPherson and Wister, 2008).

Life expectancy is the average number of years a person is expected to live and this has increased substantially over the last century. In the early 1880s, average life expectancy was only about 40 years, and this increased to about 50–55 by the late 1800s. Put another way, in 1900 a 20-year-old had only a 52 percent probability of surviving to age 65 (McPherson and Wister, 2008). Based on averaging 2006 to 2008 data, Canadian women can expect to reach age 83, while men can anticipate to live to be 79 (see Table 11.1). However, life expectancy varies by geographic region, gender, ethnicity, race, education, and

Figure 11.1
Elderly Aged 80+ Fastest Growth Rates, Canada, 1991, 2001, and 2011

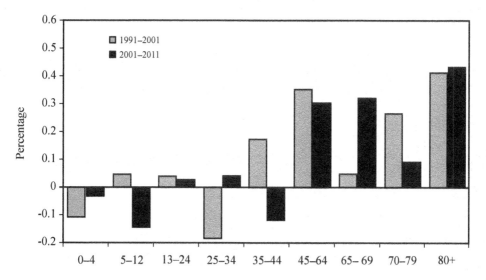

Source: Statistics Canada, *2001 Census: Age and Sex Profile: Canada* (from chart: "Growth Rates, Selected Age Segments, Canada, 1991, 2001, and 2011, under Population Gain Fastest among the Oldest"); retrieved August 10, 2006 from www12.statcan.ca/english/census01/Products/Analytic/companion/age/canada.cfm.

lifestyle (such as diet, exercise, smoking, and drinking). For example, among Aboriginal peoples, life expectancy is, on average, several years lower for both men and women.

Other important socio-demographic patterns are important to consider. As Gee (2002: 287) notes, "who lives (or does not) with whom is an important dimension of family life—even though we must remember that families and households are not necessarily the same thing." Statistics Canada (2008) reports that 53 percent of people aged 65 and older live with a spouse or partner, including same-sex partners. The majority of these marriages are first-time, with less than 5 percent involving a remarriage (Novak and Campbell, 2006). And although common-law unions were previously uncommon for older-aged couples compared to younger age groups, this trend appears to be reversing. Although the highest growth rates for persons in common-law couples between 2001 to 2006 were observed for age groups between 40 and 65 years of age, there was a 54.9 percent growth rate for those aged 65 and over. Conversely, the age group 15 to 19 years had the lowest growth rate at 0.4 percent (Statistics Canada, 2012).

Connidis (2010) suggests that the trend toward cohabitation in later life usually follows rather than leads to marriage, unlike the pattern observed among younger cohabitors. This pattern may also be reflective of an adaptive, contemporary alternative to marriage rather than as an indicator of a declining commitment to intimate relationships. For example, cohabitation is shown to offer a more egalitarian relationship than marriage and better protects the interest of adult children (for example, financial interests related

Table 11.1
Life Expectancy at Birth, by Sex and Province, 2006–2008

	Males	Females
Canada	79	83
Newfoundland and Labrador	76	81
Prince Edward Island	78	83
Nova Scotia	77	82
New Brunswick	78	83
Quebec	79	83
Ontario	79	83
Manitoba	77	82
Saskatchewan	77	82
Alberta	78	83
British Columbia	79	84

Source: Statistics Canada (2011). CANSIM, Table 102-0512 and Catalogue no. 84-537-XIE, retrieved December 30, 2011 from www40.statcan.gc.ca/101/cst01/health 26-eng.htm.

to inheritance). Later life cohabitation can also provide a financial cushion for those with less economic security, particularly women, through the sharing of expenses. It also appears to have a positive impact on well-being since it is also an attractive alternative to being single or to facing a second or third marriage.

Yet living alone is particularly common for older women—37 percent aged 65+ years live in private households alone, as do approximately one-half of women aged 75 years and older. This usually follows divorce or widowhood, although it should be noted that a small proportion (about 6 percent) of older people have never been married (Statistics Canada, 2008). Overall, we have witnessed a dramatic rise in one-person households, with about one-third being formed by those aged 65 and older (McPherson and Wister, 2008).

Another notable trend in living arrangements is the increase in multigenerational households, defined as three or more generations living under one roof. It is estimated that approximately 13 percent of elderly live in this family structure. These households have risen dramatically over the last several decades due to increased immigration from societies in which extended living and filial piety (respect, obligation, and reverence for aged parents) have been part of a cultural tradition. Cultural, economic, and other factors (e.g., the need for co-residence due to language barriers) are found to fuel this trend, which has a number of important implications for facilitating exchanges of support across the generations. For example, grandparents often play an important role in the socialization of grandchildren and help out with domestic tasks, and the middle generation can provide daily care for elderly parents requiring assistance (Gee and Mitchell, 2002).

The Ties that Bind: Patterns of Support across the Generations

The majority of support (over 80 percent) provided to older adults comes from non-paid or informal sources such as families and friends (Connidis, 2010). Indeed, many older people report that they receive informal "family" support from community ties in places ranging from RV (recreational vehicle) networks to institutionalized settings such as retirement homes (see Box 11.3). Older people benefit from this assistance in the form of emotional support, companionship, help with domestic activities, and a range of other help. However, older adults are not passive recipients of support since reciprocal support is often provided. For example, older adults often provide financial or emotional support for other family members and for friends during illness or other crises (Novak and Campbell, 2006). In this way, families tend to be engaged in exchange relations involving global reciprocity. That, is exchanges are balanced over time, rather than at one specific point in the life course (Norris and Tindale, 1994).

Types, Sources, and Exchanges of Support

Assistance being given or received usually falls into five categories of instrumental help: home maintenance, transportation, household help, personal care, and financial support. This represents a wide range of activities that can entail relatively low duration or intensity (e.g., driving an elderly parent to the shopping mall) to relatively high duration or

Box 11.3
Metaphors of Community: They're My Family Now

"Home is Where I Park It"

—Bumper sticker on a recreational vehicle

…RVers frequently use the metaphor of family to describe their feeling of community. To describe the family feeling they use words such as "friendship," "love," "trust," and "caring," and recount times when other RVers helped and supported them in a crisis. Some, like Polly Neuhaus, use sibling terms to describe their relationship with other RVers. A fellow Skip [or SKP which is an acronym for the value of Sharing, Karing People] helped her when she was in hospital. She says of her friend, "I could not have received better or more loving care from my family, and take her as my 'chosen' sister." Judy Parrack, who was widowed in 1988 describes a similar experience. Her letter is an eloquent testament to the community feeling among Escapees [an RV club]: "Family was with me for a week after Ernie died, but it is the continuing support of my SKP [Co-op] Family who write and drop by to visit that keeps me going. I don't think I'd have made it without SKPs! You'll never know how grateful I am."

The founders of Escapees consciously used the metaphor of family to describe and shape the relationships they hoped to foster among members of the club:

> Our main goal has always been to unite SKPs into an RV "family" that cares about each other. Chapters, Co-ops, and BOF groups provide a close family feeling in the same way that it works with any large family. The family unit consisting of parents and children is closer than the extended family that includes aunts, uncles, and cousins. Yet when the small units come together, they are all parts of the larger family unit.

RVers also create community by sharing activities—work as well as play. They play games of all kinds, from bridge, to bingo, to washer toss. People gather to learn line-dancing and square dancing. They meet to share knowledge with one another: how to use computers, how to do crafts. They volunteer to build and maintain their parks, organize holiday feasts, and clean park trails and buildings.

The most common food-sharing ritual among RVers is the pot-luck dinner. Pot-luck dinners are a regular event at RV resort parks, at many state parks during the winter, in boondocking areas, and at RV parks of all sorts at Thanksgiving and Christmas. RVers who are away from their families during the holidays may pool their funds to buy a turkey and share a holiday meal. Some RVers travel year after year to the same park where they meet friends to share Christmas or Thanksgiving dinner. Finally, any important celebration—such as a wedding—includes a pot-luck dinner.

Source: Counts, D.A., and D.R. Counts. 2001. *Over the Next Hill: An Ethnography of RVing Seniors in North America.* Toronto: University of Toronto Press (pp. 228–234).

intensity (e.g., providing daily personal care such as help with bathing). Support may also be affective or emotional, such as companionship or giving advice.

The hierarchical-compensatory model (Cantor, 1979) assumes that older people have a hierarchy of favoured relationships from which all forms of support are sought. Spouses and children typically top the list, but if these are not available, substitutes can be found, such as other family relatives or friends. However, Connidis (2010) argues that this model does not offer a dynamic view of social support with its fixed notions of support networks, which are subject to change over time. In fact, the average middle-aged caregiver is 54 years old and is caring for a parent or parent-in-law with a long-term disability or physical limitation. In contrast, the typical older caregiver is 73 years old and is looking after a spouse, close friend, or neighbour. Also, women devote more time to personal and emotional caregiving tasks than men, regardless of age (Stobert and Cranswick, 2004). Siblings also represent an important source of support for older adults, and assistance is related to factors such as gender, marital status, age, proximity, relationship history, and availability of other family members (Connidis, 2010). For example, siblings, especially if widowed or childless, may be the only source of support for each other in the later years (McPherson and Wister, 2008).

Life course trajectories are relevant when considering the capacity of families to provide informal social support for older people. Given falling fertility rates, one concern that is commonly voiced is whether there will be a shortage of family members (i.e., adult children) to provide care for these seniors. However, many counter this view by noting that one critical distinction in provisions of support from adult children is whether a parent has no children versus one or more (Rosenthal, 2000). And since most women who entered old age at the beginning of the 21st century were less likely to be childless than women in preceding cohorts, researchers argue that this is a fallacious contention. Furthermore, three-quarters of those over the age of 80 also have at least one living sibling, and siblings (as well as other family members or friends) also constitute a potential source of support (Connidis, 2010).

Moreover, it is important to consider the positive effects of population aging on family life. For example, in Chapter 1 we considered the "family decline" hypothesis, which purports that many families are "at risk" in contemporary times due to high rates of divorce and remarriage. However, as Bengtson (2001) argues, a more optimistic scenario emphasizes expansion of the family as well as increasing availability of extended kin such as grandparents, great-grandparents, uncles, and aunts. Also due to increased generational overlap, many grandparents can experience longer relationships with their grandchildren.

In summary, the provision of assistance between parents and children is affected by a number of factors such as age, gender, availability, and life course stage. Parents typically receive the most help when they are at advanced ages, reflecting the changing needs of the generations over time. And parents tend to give more help to children than they receive from them until very old age (Gee, 2002). Moreover, Connidis (2001) asserts that a useful way to understand social support within families is to combine the influences of social structure, culture, family history, as well as individual preferences. For example, in certain cultures, daughters-in-law are traditionally expected to care for their husband's aging parents such that these women may have little option but to fulfill this obligation. Moreover, studies show that many elderly creatively develop strong and diverse social networks with "fictive kin," such as friends, neighbours, and other voluntary associations (e.g., see Novak and Campbell, 2006).

Selected Issues Facing Today's Aging Families

In this section we will briefly highlight a number of additional topics that are particularly salient for aging families and the elderly. These include: (1) increased cultural diversity; (2) caregiving; (3) dating, cohabitation, remarriage, and sexuality; (4) the transition to retirement; (5) grandparenthood; and (6) institutionalization and end-of-life issues. Other important issues, such as poverty, elder abuse and neglect, and Alzheimer's disease, are covered in more detail in other chapters.

Increased Cultural Diversity

Canada's elderly population is more ethnically diverse than is the Canadian population as a whole. While 17 percent of the total Canadian population is foreign-born, 27 percent of residents aged 65 and over were born outside Canada (Chappell et al., 2003). Continuing high rates of immigration contribute to the increased cultural diversity of the population. And since ethnic groups may exhibit distinctive norms, values, and preferences, it is important to consider them in relation to such aspects as filial obligation and patterns of support (e.g., see Kobayashi, 2000; Kobayashi and Funk, 2010). Certain cultural groups such as Italians and Asians, for instance, have strong beliefs about not "abandoning" relatives to nursing homes (Maurier and Northcott, 2000).

Furthermore, as Canada's aged population becomes more ethnically diverse, we need to revisit many of our assumptions about "ethnic" family life and family ties. For instance, in the case of elderly widowed women, many have assumed that daughters are a strong and supportive tie. However, "it is rather ethnocentric for [North] Americans to assume that the mother-daughter tie is inevitably the closest one, since that is not the case for many societies" (Lopata, 1995: 121–122). Throughout much of Asia and the Middle East, for example, it is the son rather than the daughter who has the closest relationship with an elderly mother (Martin-Matthews, 2005).

Providing Care

As previously noted, most older adults are in relatively good health and therefore do not require intensive caregiving from family and friends. That being stated, unique rewards and challenges can occur when it comes to caring for seniors with long-term health problems, disabilities, or physical limitations. In 2007, there were about 2.7 million Canadians who provided unpaid care for people aged 65 and over with some type of long-term health care problem. Based on analyses of the 2002 and 2007 General Social Surveys, the proportion of persons aged 45 or over who are caregivers has increased from 19.5 to 28.9 percent. Gendered patterns are also highlighted, with about 56.5 percent women caregivers compared to 43.5 percent men caregivers (Fast et al., 2010). It has also been estimated that family/friend caregivers provide 70–80 percent of care to persons with a chronic health problem or disability at an estimated value of $25–26 billion annually (Fast et al., 2010).

Many of these caregivers are aged 45–64 and are members of the so-called sandwich generation, since they are wedged between the responsibilities of raising children and caring for seniors. Approximately 75 percent of these individuals also engaged in paid work. The sandwiched workers found that in caring for a senior, 15 percent had to reduce their paid work hours to provide caregiving. Many also felt burdened in terms of their health and social life (Fast et al., 2010).

Another recent study by Statistics Canada shows that many other people, such as friends, neighbours, and other relatives also provide care to seniors, as highlighted in Figure 11.2. Data shown in Figure 11.3 further reveal that physical and emotional health can be compromised by these care responsibilities. In particular, a significant proportion of caregivers report high levels of role stress (50 percent of women and 25 percent of men), negative changes in their sleep patterns (18 percent of women and 10 percent of men), and negative changes in their health status (20 percent of women and 7 percent of men).

Figure 11.2
Caregivers Most Often Provide Care for a Family Member, but Friends Provide Care as Well

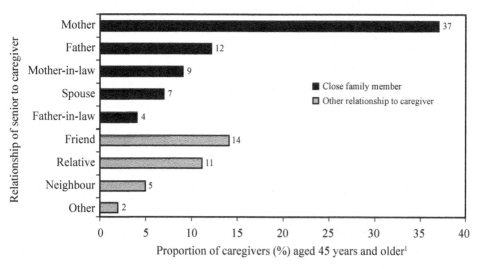

1. Due to rounding, totals might not add up to 100.
Note: Close family members (mother, father, mother-in-law, spouse, father-in-law) made up 69% of those seniors who received care from caregivers 45 years and older.

Source: Cranswick, K. And D. Dosman. 2008. "Eldercare: What We Know Today."*Canadian Social Trends*, Statistics Canada, Catalogue no. 11-008, based on General Social Survey, 2007 data; Chart 1, p. 50, retrieved August 15, 2011 from /www.statcan.gc.ca/pub/11-008-x/2008002/article/10689-eng.htm.

Figure 11.3
Health Consequences of Family Caregiving for the Elderly

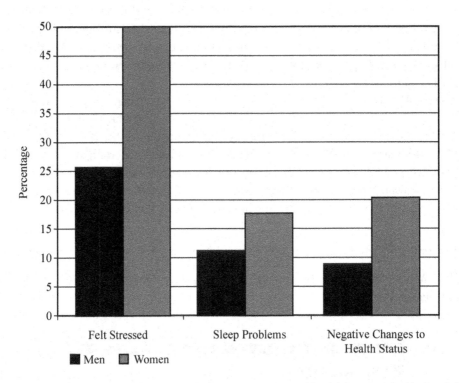

Source: Statistics Canada, General Social Survey on Aging and Social Support, cited in D. McCloskey, "Caregiving and Canadian Families," *Transition Magazine* 35 (Summer 2005): 1–16.

The most common type of help wanted among both sandwiched care providers and those providing only elder care was respite care, or occasional relief or sharing of responsibilities (see caregiver's wish list in Table 11.2). Other types of help, such as information to improve their skills or about the nature of long-term illnesses, more flexible work arrangements, and financial compensation, were also suggested by a substantial portion of caregivers.

Seniors living in rural areas can also experience greater challenges in receiving care relative to their urban counterparts (Keefe et al., 2004). For example, their family members may live in a different town or city. Rural areas also often lack adequate transportation services and many of the health-related services and organizations found in more urbanized areas. Since many rural and remote communities have a shrinking population base, it is challenging to develop a sufficient and efficient health care system for them. While more than 20 percent of older Canadians reside in rural areas, many public policies overlook this sector in the allocation of health care resources (Keating, 2008; Keating et al., 2011). The situation has deteriorated in recent years with fragmentation of services, the closing of small rural hospitals, restructuring and regionalization of health

Table 11.2
Caregiver's Wish List

	Employed	
	Sandwiched	**Elder Care Only**
	%	
Respite care	52	46*
Flexible work or study arrangements	46	36*
Information on long-term disabilities	43	39
Information on caregiving	42	37
Financial compensation or tax breaks	36	35
Counselling	28	24
Other	12	10

*Indicates statistically significant difference from sandwiched group (those who provide elder care to someone over 65 and had single children younger than 25 living at home; sandwiched workers had a paid job or business as their main activity in the past 12 months).

Source: C. Williams. 2005 (summer). "The Sandwich Generation," *Canadian Social Trends* (Ottawa: Statistics Canada), Catalogue no. 11-008, p. 20.

services, and the continuing difficulty that rural communities encounter in attracting and retaining physicians and other health care and social service workers.

Dating, Cohabitation, Remarriage, and Sexuality
McPherson and Wister (2008) observe that a majority of older men have partners, whereas the majority of older women do not (see Table 11.3). This difference is partly due to the fact that women tend to outlive their spouses and fewer eligible men are available, but also because of societal and individual-level attitudes. For example, many older women report that although they are still attracted to men, they do not want to marry. Many report that they enjoy the freedom of being single after divorce or widowhood. As one older woman stated in a study on this topic, "For the first time in my life, I have no responsibilities except for myself.... In other words, I'm just learning to fly a little bit. And I love it. Selfish, huh?" (cited in Talbott, 1998). Men, on the other hand, are seven times more likely to remarry than women (Connidis, 2010).

Generally, the decision to date, cohabit, or remarry in later life is a complex decision that is influenced by economic, social, legal, religious, and demographic factors (McPherson and Wister, 2008). Other family members can also create barriers through disapproval or by being unsupportive of a particular relationship. Nonetheless, many older adults are using introduction or dating agencies, placing personal ads in local newspapers or in magazines for retired people, or using Internet dating sites (i.e., "Silver Singles") to meet potential partners (McPherson and Wister, 2008). Divorce rates among older adults, although historically quite low, are also rising and, combined with longer life expectancy, will probably create more demand for these kinds of services.

It is also important to recognize the link between sexuality and ageism, which can also act as a barrier to the formation of intimate relations. In their book entitled *Sex May Be Wasted on the Young*, Stones and Stones (1996) argue that ageist views of sexuality are still prevalent in today's society. They note that young people in their teens and twenties often think of their grandparents as "way past it." Indeed, "the idea of their own relatives making love with passion evoked reactions from giggles at the improbable to horror at the unimaginable" (p. x). Older people in institutional settings may also face unique challenges when they try to express their sexuality. For example, attitudes of staff and facility policies (e.g., no locks on doors) can limit sexual activity, and even married couples who share a room may feel inhibited (Connidis, 2010).Yet, studies show that, provided both partners are in good health, many desire and can enjoy active sex lives well into their sunset years. Further, drugs (such as Viagra) now exist to restore or enhance sexual performance in older adults and are sometimes used to overcome impotence (Jacoby, 1999).

Turning to gay/lesbian seniors, unique challenges may occur if these older adults are estranged from or rejected by family members. However, as Laird (1996) (who is a mother, grandmother, and lesbian) claims, many gays and lesbians have good, although complicated, family relationships. They also may create a surrogate family comprising a network of gay, lesbian, and heterosexual friends. Yet, gay and lesbian seniors (especially gay men because of AIDS) can face problems in accessing medical care, home care, and community services. Partners may also have limited legal rights and may be denied access to employer drug and health benefit plans. Administrators of rental housing or long-term care facilities may reject their applications, and there are very few retirement or nursing facilities available to serve this community (McPherson and Wister, 2008).

The Transition to Retirement

Szinovacz (2006) asserts that retirement processes and experiences are usually examined from an "individualistic" perspective. In other words, they are viewed almost exclusively in relation to individual characteristics such as health, work history, or social security and pension coverage. He argues that this perspective glosses over the intricate linkages between family and retirement experiences and their relationship to policies. It also underplays the significance of life course transitions and how they are contextually embedded in the planning of, and adjustment to, this process. As such, retirement transitions are often related to past work experiences, yet family contexts (e.g., rules regarding benefits of spouses) also play a significant role.

Figure 11.4 summarizes his model of these family-retirement linkages, which is grounded in life course theoretical concepts of linked lives, interdependence, timing and sequencing of transitions, and contextual embeddedness. Family contexts consist of marital and family characteristics that precede the retirement transition and can impinge on decisions and adaptation processes. They include family-related statuses, spouse characteristics, activities, the quality of the relationship, and norms/attitudes. Statuses are the family positions held by workers, such as marital and grandparent status. The influence of these contexts may be direct (e.g., wives tend to retire at the time of husbands) or indirect (e.g., if sibling cares for elderly parent, worker can remain in workforce). The impact of family statuses will be further conditioned by the type of activities involved in each role, the quality of each relationship and pertinent attitudes and norms. For example, the "push" effect of husbands' retirement on wives' retirement may depend on the couple's

Figure 11.4
Linkages between Family and Retirement Experiences

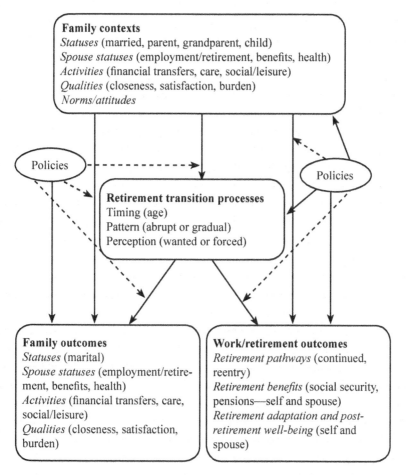

Source: Statistics Canada (2008), *New Frontiers of Research on Retirement*, Catalogue no. 75-511-XWE, Figure 11.1. Retrieved August 12, 2011 from http://www.statcan.gc.ca/pub/75-511-x/2006001/figures/5203436-eng.htm.

gender role attitudes. Notably, if spouses follow traditional roles that stress the husband's role as main family provider, the continued employment of the wife after the husband's retirement might be problematic.

Szinovacz (2006) also observes that increases in the labour force participation of women in general, and middle-aged women in particular, suggests that retirement is becoming a "couple phenomenon." Studies indicate, for example, that retired husbands' attitudes toward their wives' continued employment proved to be one of the most potent predictors of wives' retirement. Other reasons include spouses' preference for joint leisure activities, similarities in spouses' background (age, education) or shared economic restrictions. Yet, couples are not always able to implement these preferred timing patterns, since their decisions may also depend on benefit eligibility and pensions of both spouses. Another factor is a spouse's health or disability; for example, one spouse may have to retire to care for the other spouse.

Overall, it is expected that the transition to retirement will continue to transform as people live longer, gender roles transform, and economic conditions and the labour force continue to change. The abolishment of mandatory retirement at age 65 (with the exception of New Brunswick) means that many people can choose to retire or not, based on their own need, lifestyle preferences, circumstances and priorities. Yet, it is also expected that the number of retirement-aged Canadians in the workforce will continue to increase over the next 10 years, a trend that has again sparked "apocalyptic" fears of increased pressure on public pensions and raises issues of intergenerational inequity (Hill, 2010).

The financial meltdown of the financial markets in 2008 and the subsequent global recession also exposed a number of weaknesses in pension plans, such as underfunding of corporate pension plans and the need to restructure CPP/QPP (McDonald and Donahue, 2011). While the proportion of workers in Registered or Employment Programs provided by companies or the public sector has diminished, and there has been a shift to defined contribution over defined benefit plans, the proportion of workers with private pension plans (e.g., RRSPs) has risen. A significant implication of these patterns is that more responsibility for economic security in retirement will fall on the shoulders of individuals and their families during a period of increasing economic instability.

The Modernization of Grandparenthood and Skipped-Generation Households

The vast majority of Canadian women (80 percent) and men (74 percent) over 65 years of age are grandparents. At birth, approximately 66 percent of children have four living grandparents (including step-grandparents) and by 30 years of age, three-quarters have at least one grandparent (Connidis, 2010). Because of socio-demographic change, it is also not surprising that grandparenthood—as a distinct and nearly universal stage of family life—is largely a post–World War Two phenomenon. According to Cherlin and Furstenberg (1992), we have witnessed the modernization of grandparenthood. This has occurred because of several factors: declines in mortality, falling birth rates, technological advances in travel and long-distance communication (e.g., e-mail, webcams), retirement and increased affluence (e.g., pensions), and more leisure time. In other words, grandparents are living long enough to enjoy a lengthy life as grandpar-

Figure 11.5
Technology and Aging Families

*"Can you believe we got married, raised a family and retired, all
without the help of a hand-held computer?"*

Source: CartoonStock.com

ents, they can keep in touch more easily with grandchildren, they have more time to devote to them, and they have more money to spend on them. They are also less likely to still be raising their own children.

To further illustrate this concept, many families did not own cars before World War Two, and long trips could take quite some time. As one grandchild recounts (as cited by Cherlin and Furstenberg, 1992: 3):

> Well, I didn't see my grandmother that often. They just lived one hundred miles from us, but back then one hundred miles was like four hundred now, it's the truth. It just seemed like clear across the country. It'd take us five hours to get there, it's the truth. It was an all-day trip.

Grandparents today generally play an active role in the lives of their grandchildren, although there is diversity with respect to grandparenting styles. For example, grandmothers tend to be more involved in matters related to family relationships and caregiving, while grandfathers tend to be more involved in instrumental or practical matters, such as giving advice. However, in keeping with our theme of heterogeneity in family life and in gendered processes, it should be recognized that grandfathers are increasingly being recognized for their ability to adopt caring, supportive, and mentoring roles that appear to become more pronounced in later life. Indeed, Mann (2007) argues that one of the pitfalls of the previously dominant feminist perspective in this area of study is that it underestimated or ignored the experiences, contributions, and capacities of older men to provide emotional care to family members.

Some grandparents can also play a particularly active role as family "watchdogs," arbitrators, or historians, or in practising family traditions. These grandparents often look out for the well-being of younger relatives, help them when they can, and try to mediate or create linkages between family members and across the generations. As such, some grandparents play an important role in passing down important family memories through the retelling of family stories as well as by reproducing long-standing family traditions. For example, in a recent qualitative study by Kemp based on life-history interviews (2004: 512), one grandfather, age 88, states, "I think story telling is perhaps one of the main roles ... true stories too that could give you a sense of history that a lot of families lose." Conversely, some grandparents are more detached, and tend to see or contact their grandchildren less often. These grandparents take a more "hands-off" approach, which might be because of age, health status, distance, or because their children obstruct visits (Novak and Campbell, 2006).

Another important feature of contemporary life is the formation of family units whereby a middle generation is absent, known as skip-generation households. Skip-generation households (estimated to be at about 5 percent) are increasing in Canada because of more drug abuse by one or both parents, more divorces, and more reporting of child abuse and neglect (Milan and Peters, 2003).

Institutionalization and End-of-Life Issues
Contrary to popular belief, only a minority of elderly live their last years in nursing homes or other institutionalized settings. According to the 2006 Census, 4 percent of men and 8 percent of women over 65 lived in an institution. Declines in health are associated with moves to institutions. For example, many elderly with Alzheimer's disease ultimately require 24-hour care, such that families have little option but to move an older person into a residential-care facility. This relocation is necessary for their care and safety, and for the relief of family caregivers who cannot manage the behavioural problems, such as agitation, aggressiveness, and wandering.

Further, even though older people usually want to die in their own home, the vast majority end their life journey in a hospital or long-term care facility. As a result, new models and practices for end-of-life care are being offered. Some of these proposals include palliative care in other primary health-care facilities and support systems or groups for family and paid caregivers (see Box 11.4). Many of these proposals also try to account for cultural and religious diversity associated with death and dying among Canadians (McPherson and Wister, 2008).

While there is considerable diversity with respect to institutionalized care for the elderly, profit motives can undermine the delivery of care. In *Making Gray Gold*, Diamond (1995) uses personal narratives to describe how the work of nurses and other

Table 11.3
The Living Arrangements of Older Canadians (in Percentages)

	With Spouse or Partner*	With Children	With Relatives/ Non- relatives	Alone		Institution	
	65+	65+	65+	65+	85+	65+	85+
Women	41	13	9	37	59	8	28
Men	65	13	5	17	29	4	18

*Includes same-sex partners

Sources: Adapted from Statistics Canada Persons in Private Households Showing Living Arrangement, Age Groups and Sex, for Canada, 2006 Census 20% Data, 97-553-xcb2006007, 2008; and Statistics Canada Institutional Residents, for Canada, 2006 Census 100% Data, Custom Table, 2008.

Box 11.4
A New Era in Canadian Palliative and End-of-Life Research

The term palliative care refers not only to the care and management of patients approaching the end of life but also addresses the reduction of suffering throughout the course of illness and, for family, into bereavement. Palliative and end-of-life care, although traditionally associated with cancer care, intersects with a number of other clinical disciplines....As our aging population continues to grow and modern medicine provides the means to prolong the life of individuals with a variety of life-limiting diseases and conditions, society struggles with the ethical and legal questions around "appropriate" use of health care resources. Many of the people who could benefit from palliative and end-of-life care do not receive it. All too often it is left to patients, their families, and a loosely knit community of volunteer organizations to sort through the myriad of physical, psychological, spiritual, and ethical choice...The key to change lies in rigorous, scientific research that will provide the evidence for informed decision-making by clinical practitioners and policy makers.

Source: Excerpt retrieved October 31, 2005 from *The Canadian Institutes of Health Research,* www.cihr-irsc.gc.ca.

---

caregivers in a nursing home is set powerfully in the context of wider political, economic, and cultural forces that shape and constrain the quality of care for the elderly. Overall, this study of what it's like to work in and live in a nursing home shows the price that business policies extract from the elderly and their families as well as those whose work it is to care for them.

Finally, the ethical issue of euthanasia, which is sometimes referred to as "mercy killing," is likely to become more hotly debated as our population ages. "Euthanasia" is a term that comes from the Greek word for "good death" and means helping someone end his or her life. A distinction is often made between passive euthanasia (which means withholding or ceasing treatment for someone, such as turning off a life-support system), or active euthanasia (which means intervening actively to end a person's life, such as by administering a lethal dosage of sedatives). Currently, euthanasia is illegal in Canada, although the law in Canada today does not require doctors to take heroic measures to keep a terminally ill patient alive (Novak and Campbell, 2006). And given that family members and physicians sometimes differ in their judgment of the person's will to live and of the person's end-of-life preferences, increasing numbers of individuals are drafting living wills. This advance directive allows a person to think about his or her preference while in a sound state of mind (Lawton, 2001).

Summary

This chapter explores a broad range of issues relevant to family ties in the context of social change and rapid population aging. Many stereotypical assumptions about aging families and the elderly are critically evaluated in conjunction with an overview of structural socio-demographic change and its implication for patterns of support across the generations. Overall, the tendency to view aging families of the past with "rose-coloured glasses" is problematic. Instead, a life course perspective allows us to appreciate that not only has family life always been diverse, but aging families have always faced unique challenges relative to their socio-historical and geographical location (Gee, 2002).

This chapter also considers both the challenges and opportunities created by the longevity revolution. For example, for the first time in history, many grandparents can now watch their grandchildren grow up. However, increased life expectancy also means that many elderly—particularly women—are living their final years with chronic health problems. This is particularly worrisome given inequality in later life and the decline of our welfare state. In short, discourse about the "alleged fiscal crisis" facing the Canadian government affects our most economically and socially vulnerable seniors, all in the name of "deficit reduction" (McDonald, 2000). The phenomenon of population aging also raises ethical issues with respect to end-of-life issues. Finally, it is also recognized that we need to consider family issues beyond caregiving, including such topics as reciprocity in exchanges of support across the generations, friendship, sexuality, and sibling relationships. Clearly, all of these topics will gain added significance in the future as they become increasingly salient to more members of the Canadian population.

Box 11.5
Insights on Death and Dying

Since 1987, Joy Ufema has written her popular column, "Insights on Death and Dying," for Nursing journal in which she focuses on the emotional well-being of everyone involved. Below find one of Joy's favourite firsthand accounts of how she helped families, patients, and co-workers through stressful times.

Someone's waiting for her
I'm a family practice physician and my wife's a surgical nurse. I've read your column and wonder what you think about a patient's participation in his own death. I don't mean someone who commits suicide, but one who wills himself to die.
—D.B., British Columbia.

Actually, doctor, I believe that all patients live or die in spite of our care. (That's rather humbling to those of us in nursing and medicine).

Many times I've seen patients choose to finish their own lives rather than go to a nursing home, endure another amputation, or continue with futile chemotherapy. We all need a reason or purpose to wake up every morning. No one can give that to another.

Last week, one of my favourite physicians shared a story with me. As an intensivist, Dr. Peters was caring for a 91-year-old woman who'd had an episode of heart failure. As she typically does with ICU patients, Dr. Peters spoke to Mrs. Dobbs about her wishes regarding heroic measures.

"Oh, don't worry about that, dear," said Mrs. Dobbs. "I signed my living will and all that business is taken care of."

Dr. Peters assured her patient that her wishes would be honoured. Then she added, "I want to tell you that you're doing better, so we really don't need to dwell on that."

"Oh, but you see, dear, I have someone waiting for me," replied Mrs. Dobbs. "Mr. Dobbs has been gone for years. I miss him and I want to see him."

Dr. Peters nodded respectfully but again reassured Mrs. Dobbs that her condition was improving.

Later that evening, Mrs. Dobbs begin singing "Amazing Grace." She asked her nurse to join in, which she did. As another physician entered her ICU cubicle to assess her, Mrs. Dobbs waved him away. "Don't come in now," she said. "I'm focusing."

A few hours later she complained of "pain all over" and the nurse administered morphine. A short time later, Mrs. Dobbs left this world. She'd already explained why: She had someone waiting for her.

—Joy Ufema, R.N., M.S.

Source: Ufema, J. 2007. *Insights on Death and Dying*. New York: Lippincott Williams and Wilkins (pp. 176–177).

Questions for Critical Reflection and Debate

1. Critically evaluate the popular viewpoint that the elderly in Canadian society have been abandoned by their families.
2. Why are older men more likely to remarry than older women? Also discuss how families can help or hinder the formation of intimate relations among older adults following divorce or widowhood.
3. To what extent does the media (e.g., films, TV commercials, print) promote positive images of sexuality and the elderly?
4. How can a cross-cultural study of aging families help us to better understand Canadian aging family life and the role of seniors in families?
5. Debate the following: Euthanasia should be made legal in Canada to help families end the suffering of elderly, frail family members.
6. Evaluate the common "apocalyptic" statement that, "As the population ages, social policy will be challenged."

Glossary

Apocalyptic demography is the tendency to equate rapid population aging with a number of negative implications for society and for the family, especially with respect to escalating health care and pension costs and associated caregiving issues.

Filial piety is rooted in the idea that the core of moral behaviour lies in several obligations that children owe to parents (e.g., respect and caregiving).

Global reciprocity refers to the tendency of families to balance exchanges of support over the course of their lives rather than at one particular point in time.

Golden age myth is the tendency to assume that, historically, elderly people tended to reside in multigenerational households with strong ties across the generations, and that they enjoyed more status and respect than they do today.

Hierarchical compensatory model suggests that people choose their supports initially from their inner family circle and then outward to receive assistance from less intimate sources as they need more help.

Modernization of grandparenthood is the phrase used to describe the phenomenon of contemporary grandparenthood due to increased longevity, technology, affluence, and leisure time.

Palliative care is a program of active compassionate care primarily directed toward improving the quality of life for the dying.

Skip-generation households are those households in which grandparents live with at least one grandchild without the presence of the middle (parent) generation.

Further Reading

Chappell, N., L. McDonald, and M. Stones. 2008. *Aging in Contemporary Canada*, 2nd ed. Toronto: Pearson Prentice-Hall. This textbook provides a good overview of many issues relevant to seniors in Canada, with substantial focus on issues pertaining to family life.

Connidis, I.A. 2010. *Family Ties and Aging*, 2nd ed. Thousand Oaks: Sage. This book provides a comprehensive overview of research and issues on aging families in North America. Particular attention is paid to diverse family relationships and how they are structured by gender, ethnicity, socio-economic status, and sexual orientation.

Izuhara, M. 2010. *Ageing and Intergenerational Relations: Family Reciprocity from a Global Perspective*. Bristol: Policy Press. Examines new patterns of family relations both conceptually and empirically from a global perspective. Covers Europe, East Asia, Sub-Saharan Africa, Thailand, and the United States.

Novak, M., and L. Campbell. 2010. *Aging and Society: A Canadian Perspective*, 6th ed. Toronto: Thomson Nelson. Presents a positive look at issues relating to aging within the context of Canada's history, family, and social life.

Settersten, R.A., Jr. and J.A. (Eds.). 2011. *Handbook of Sociology of Aging*. New York: Dordrecht. This handbook presents a new framework for understanding the sociology of aging from three core perspectives: social phenomena, the life course, and social policy. Also makes many linkages to individuals, families, communities, and societies and explores issues of inequality, intergenerational relations, and health.

Wister, A.V., and B. McPherson. In press. *Aging as a Social Process*, 6th ed. Toronto: Oxford University Press. The most comprehensive and up-to-date overview of topics relevant to aging Canadians. Topics include many issues relevant to aging families, such as life course issues, social networks and participation, the health contexts of aging, social inequality, and social change, and work, retirement, and economic security.

Related Web Sites

Canadian Association of Gerontology offers information on the organization in addition to sources about publications and research from a multidisciplinary perspective, http://www.cagacg.ca/.

Canadian Association of Retired Persons (CARP) is a national, non-partisan, non-profit organization committed to a "New Vision of Aging for Canada" promoting social change that will bring financial security, equitable access to health care, and freedom from discrimination, http://www.carp.ca/.

CANGRADS is a Canadian not-for-profit organization that provides support for grandparents and others who are raising grandchildren or other kin, www.cangrands.com.

Division of Aging and Seniors at Health Canada provides federal leadership in many areas pertaining to aging and seniors in order to optimize healthy aging. Its many publications (e.g., Caring for Seniors) are a good source of information for and about seniors, http://www.hc-sc.gc.ca/hl-vs/seniors-aines/index-eng.php.

Gerontological Society of America is a large non-profit professional organization that provides researchers, educators, practitioners, and policy makers the opportunity to share information on aging to improve the quality of life for seniors and their families, http://www.geron.org.

References

Ambert, A.M. 2006. *Changing Families: Relationships in Context*. Toronto: Pearson.

Bengtson, V.L. 2001. "Beyond the Nuclear Family: The Increasing Importance of Multi-generational Relationships in American Society." *Journal of Marriage and the Family* 63: 1–16.

Blakeborough, D. 2008. "'Old People are Useless': Representations of Aging on the Simpsons." *Canadian Journal on Aging* 27: 57–67.

Canadian Press. 2007. "Solo-dwellers on the Rise as Young, Independent Singles Delay Marriage." Retrieved September 13, 2007, from canadianpress.google.com/article.

Cantor, M.H. 1979. "Neighbours and Friends: An Overlooked Resource in the Informal Support System." *Research on Aging* 1: 434–463.

Chappell, N., E.M. Gee, L. McDonald, and M. Stones (eds.). 2003. *Aging in Contemporary Canada*. Toronto: Prentice-Hall.

Cheal, D. 2002. *Aging and Demographic Change in Canadian Context*. Toronto: University of Toronto Press.

Cherlin, A.J., and F.F. Furstenberg, Jr. 1992. "The Modernization of Grandparenthood." In A.S. Skolnick and J.H. Skolnick (eds.), *Family in Transition*, 7th ed. (pp. 105–111). New York: HarperCollins.

Connidis, I.A. 2010. *Family Ties and Aging*, 2nd ed. Thousand Oaks: Sage.

Diamond, T. 1995. *Making Gray Gold: Narratives of Nursing Home Care*. Chicago: University of Chicago Press.

Fast, J. et al. 2010. "Gender Differences in Family/Friend Caregiving in Canada." *Research on Aging Policies and Practices*. December Issue: 1–4. Edmonton: University of Alberta.

Gee, E.M. 2002. "Families and Aging." In Neena Chappell, E. Gee, L. McDonald, and M. Stones (eds.), *Aging in Contemporary Canada* (pp. 278–308). Toronto: Prentice-Hall.

Gee, E.M., and G.M. Gutman. 2000. *The Overselling of Population Aging: Apocalyptic Demography, Intergenerational Challenges, and Social Policy*. Toronto: Oxford University Press.

Gee, E.M., and B.A. Mitchell. 2002. "One Roof: Exploring Multi-generational Households in Canada." In M. Lynn (ed.), *Voices: Essays on Canadian Families* (pp. 291–311). Toronto: Thomson Nelson.

Hill, J. 2010. "In-Depth, Aging Population: Mandatory Retirement Fades in Canada," *CBC News*, Monday, October, 18, retrieved August 15, 2011 from www.cbc.ca/news/canda/story/2009/08/20/mandatory-retirement.

ICGI (Ithaca College Gerontology Institute). 2006. *A Comparison of Japan and the United States on Issues of Aging.* Retrieved July 4, 2006, from www.ithca.ed/aging/schools.

Jacoby, S. 1999. "Great Sex: What's Age Got to Do with It?" *Modern Maturity* (October): 41ff.

Keating, N. (Ed.). 2008. *Rural Ageing: A Good Place to Grow Old?* London, UK: Policy Press.

Keating, N. et al. 2011. "Aging in Rural Canada." *Canadian Journal on Aging* 30: 323–338.

Keefe, J., P. Fancey, N. Keating, J. Frederick, J. Eales, and B. Dobbs. 2004. *Caring Contexts of Rural Seniors—Phase I Technical Report.* Veteran Affairs Canada. Edmonton: University of Alberta.

Kemp, C. 2004. "'Grand' Expectations: The Experiences of Grandparents and Adult Grandchildren." *Canadian Journal of Sociology* 29: 499–525.

Kobayashi, K.M. 2000."The Nature of Support from Adult Children to Older Parents in Japanese Canadian Families." *Journal of Cross-cultural Gerontology* 15: 185–205.

Kobayashi, K.M., and L. Funk. 2010. "Of the Family Tree: Congruence on Filial Obligation and its Implications for Social Support among Older Parents and Adult Children in Japanese Canadian Families." *Canadian Journal on Aging* 29(1): 85–96.

Laird, J. 1996. "Invisible Ties: Lesbians and Their Families of Origin." In J. Laird and R. Green (eds.), *Lesbians and Gays in Couples and Families: A Handbook for Therapists* (pp. 89–122). San Francisco: Jossey-Bass.

Lawton, M.P. 2001. "Quality of Life and End-of-Life." In J.E. Birren and K.W. Schaie (eds.), *Handbook of the Psychology of Aging*, 5th ed. San Diego: Academic Press.

Lopata, H.Z. 1995. "Feminist Perspectives on Social Gerontology." In R. Bleiszner and V.H. Bedford (eds.), *Handbook of Aging and the Family*. Westport: Greenwood Press.

Mann, R. 2007. "Out of the Shadows? Grandfatherhood, Age, and Masculinities." *Journal of Aging Studies* 21: 281–291.

Martin-Matthews, A. 2005. "Aging and Families: Ties over Time and Generation." In N. Mandell and A. Duffy (eds.), *Canadian Families: Diversity, Conflict, and Change* (pp. 311–345). Toronto: Thomson Nelson.

Maurier, W.L., and H.C. Northcott. 2000. *Aging in Ontario: Diversity in the New Millennium.* Calgary: Detselig Enterprises.

McDonald, L. 2000. "Alarmist Economics and Women's Pensions: A Case of 'Semanticide.'" In E.M. Gee and G.M. Gutman (eds.), *The Overselling of Population Aging: Apocalyptic Demography, Intergenerational Challenges, and Social Policy* (pp. 114–128). Toronto: Oxford University Press.

McDonald, L., and P. Donahue. 2011. "Retirement lost?" *Canadian Journal on Aging* 30: 401–422.

McPherson, B., and A.V. Wister. 2008. *Aging as a Social Process,* 5th ed. Toronto: Oxford University Press.

Milan, A., and A. Peters. 2003. "Across the Generations: Grandparents and Their Grand-children." *Canadian Social Trends* 71(Summer): 2–6.

Norris, J.E., and J.A. Tindale. 1994. *Among Generations: The Cycle of Adult Relationships.* Toronto: W.H. Freeman and Company.

Novak, M., and L. Campbell. 2006. *Aging and Society: A Canadian Perspective*, 5th ed. Toronto: Thomson Nelson.

O'Rand, A.M. 1996. "The Precious and the Precocious: Understanding Cumulative Advantage and Cumulative Disadvantage over the Life Course." *The Gerontologist* 36: 230–238.

Rosenthal, C. 2000. "Aging Families: Have Current Challenges Been 'Oversold'?" In E.M. Gee and G.M. Gutman (eds.), *The Overselling of Population Aging: Apocalyptic Demography, Intergenerational Challenges, and Social Policy* (pp. 45–65). Toronto: Oxford University Press.

Statistics Canada. 2000. "Family over the Life Course." Catalogue no. 91-543. Ottawa: Minister of Industry.

Statistics Canada. 2001. *2001 Census: Age and Sex Profile: Canada.* Retrieved August 10, 2006, from www12.statcan.ca/English/census01/Products/Analystic/companion.

Statistics Canada. 2003. *Population by Sex and Age Group.* Retrieved June 17, 2005, from http://www.statcan.ca/english/Pgdb/demo31d.htm.

Statistics Canada. 2008. *Age and Sex, 2006 Counts for both Sexes, for Canada, Provinces, and Territories, 100 percent Data.* Retrieved February 14, 2008 from http://www12.statcan.ca/english/census06/data/highlights/agesex/pages.

Statistics Canada. 2010. *Population Projections for Canada, Provinces and Territories (2009–2036)*, Statistics Canada catalogue number 91-520 XIE, table 052-0005.

Stobert, S., and K. Cranswick. 2004. "Looking after Seniors: Who Does What for Whom?" *Canadian Social Trends* (Autumn): 2–6.

Stones, L., and M. Stones. 1996. *Sex May Be Wasted on the Young.* North York: Captus.

Swartzwelder, J. (Writer) & J. Reardon (Director). 1994, January 6. "Homer the vigilante." In J.L. Brooks, M. Groening, and S. Simon (Executive Producers), *The Simpsons.* New York: Twentieth Century Fox.

Szinovacz, M.E. 2006. "Families and Retirement." In L. Stone (editor in chief), *New Frontiers of Research on Retirement*, Statistics Canada catalogue number 75-511-XWE pp. 165–187. Ottawa: Minister of Industry.

Talbott, M.M. 1998. "Older Widows' Attitudes towards Men and Remarriage." *Journal of Aging Studies* 12: 429–440.

Walker, A.J., M. Manoogian-O'Dell, L.A. McGraw, and D.L.G. White. 2001. *Families in Later Life: Connections and Transitions.* Thousand Oaks: Pine Forge Press.

Zimmerman, L. 2000. "Foreword." In E.M. Gee and G.M. Gutman (eds.), *The Overselling of Population Aging: Apocalyptic Demography, Intergenerational Challenges, and Social Policy* (p. ix). Toronto: Oxford University Press.

Part III

Families on the Fault Line and Social Policy Issues

While life for many Canadians is relatively comfortable and trouble free, a significant number of families face considerable hardship and challenge. Some of these problems may be relatively short term with relatively modest consequences, such as temporary unemployment or a brief illness. Or, these challenges can be chronic or long term (e.g., having a child with special needs) or occur at certain points in the life course (e.g., Alzheimer's disease in old age). Although previous parts of this text have also highlighted some critical issues facing families, in this section, we focus on a number of particularly problematic areas for families, with continued emphasis on how many of life's challenges are socially structured over the life course. In other words, social problems and what we often view as "private troubles" are often related to access to key social and economic resources. They therefore vary according to such aspects as gender, ethnicity, social class, and geographical locale. We will also consider how these challenges affect, and are affected by, family relationships and shape family interactions.

In Chapter 12, for instance, we will learn that many serious health problems are more likely to occur among individuals who live in poverty than those who are wealthier. Health problems can also impact the entire family system, such as when a family member has physical or mental health issues. And poverty and financial hardship (which will be covered in Chapter 13) are more likely to occur within certain social groups, such as among women, recent immigrants, the disabled, and Aboriginal populations. Similarly, certain social groups are more likely to experience violence, stress, and abuse (the focus of Chapter 14) because they are more vulnerable and dependent. They may also not have access to important community resources and programs. As such, social policy can play an important role in the distribution of societal resources and can play a pivotal role in the overall general health and well-being of Canadian families. Thus, in Chapter 15, we will examine some key social and family policy issues as well as some salient policy concerns for the present and future. These "critical" issues will be reviewed in light of many of the key family-related life course patterns uncovered throughout this book.

Chapter 12

In Sickness and in Health

Families Facing Health Challenges and the Creation of Healthy Lifestyles

Learning Objectives

In this chapter you will learn that ...
- experiences of health and well-being in families are embedded in socio-cultural, economic, and political contexts
- definitions of health and "ableness" are multifaceted and there are multiple social determinants of health
- health challenges can significantly affect family roles and relationships, presenting unique challenges, particularly for low-income families and those without social support
- health policies and promotion strategies need to target families and social conditions early in life
- healthy public policy can improve population health and reduce structural barriers for those experiencing problems and thereby reduce social and economic costs in the future

Introduction

Our health and well-being is shaped by many factors and social contexts, such as where we live, our income and education level, the quality of our home environment, genetics, and our relationships with our friends and family. Fortunately, most Canadians report being in good to excellent health, which is defined by the World Health Organization as "a state of complete physical, mental, and social well-being and not merely the absence of disease or infirmity." The widespread use of this over-arching definition reflects how our perception of health has shifted beyond the traditional Western biomedical model that was prevalent in our society for most of the last century. This definition also suggests that health encompasses more than the absence of illness and disease—it is multidimensional, multidetermined, and also incorporates a subjective component (Canadian Health Network, 2005).

Although Canadians are among the healthiest in the world, "good health" is not enjoyed equally by everyone, according to a federal-provincial study, *Toward a Healthy Future* (Anisef and Kilbride, 2003). Indeed, not all social groups and individuals are healthy. Families living in poverty, for example, are particularly vulnerable to health problems, and this raises a number of implications for families, society, and the Canadian health care system. In this chapter we will review key social determinants of health. Selected health and well-being issues and how they affect family relationships will also be examined, with a focus on families and disabilities, special needs children, HIV/AIDS, mental health, caregiving for the elderly, and the death of a family member. Finally, we will consider health promotion initiatives and state supports in the context of healthy public policy and community programs.

The Social Determinants of Health: Why Are Some Families Healthier Than Others?

As previously noted, our health and well-being are influenced by factors that extend beyond genetic endowment or biological realms. This has led Health Canada and researchers to the social determinants of health framework, which refers to "the economic and social conditions that influence the health of individuals, communities, and jurisdictions as a whole" (Raphael, 2004: 1). While definitions differ across studies, 11 social determinants of health have been identified, as shown in Box 12.1. These include early life, education, employment and working conditions, food security, health care services, Aboriginal status, housing, income and its distribution, social safety net, social exclusion, and unemployment/employment security, all of which interact with gender.

A social determinant of health framework highlights how structured inequality produces inequality of health conditions, and how health is profoundly influenced by governments' social policy decisions. For example, we see in Figure 12.1 that Canadians are more likely to report having unmet health care needs when they are living in poverty. Poor Canadians are also less likely to report having unmet health care needs than poor Americans, with cost being the primary barrier cited in the United States (regardless of health insurance status). Indeed, social epidemiology, which is the study of the socio-cultural, economic, and political forces that shape patterns of

---

Box 12.1
What Are the Social Determinants of Health?

The 11 social determinants of health (identified by the organizers of a 2001 York University conference on this theme) are:
- Aboriginal status
- Early life
- Education
- Employment and working conditions
- Food security
- Health care services
- Housing
- Income and its distribution
- Social safety net
- Social exclusion
- Unemployment and employment security

Source: Raphael, D. 2003. "Introduction to the social determinants of health," in D. Raphael (ed.), *Social Determinants of Health: Canadian Perspectives.* Toronto: Canadian Scholars' Press (p. 6).

disease and death in human populations, differentiates health status of the population by inequities such as socio-economic status. The health gap between the rich
and poor continues to exist, and upper-income Canadians live longer, are healthier,
and lead more disability-free lives on average than do poor Canadians. Poor material and social conditions, such as inadequate housing and poor nutrition contribute
to high mortality in the low-income population. For example, Figure 12.2 highlights
how housing affects other health determinants. Studies also show that children in the
poorest neighbourhoods have twice the infant mortality rate of children in the richest
neighbourhoods (e.g., see Bolaria and Dickinson, 2002).

Figure 12.1
**Individuals Reporting an Unmet Health Care Need by Household Income
Quintile, Canada and the United States, 2002–2003, in Percentages***

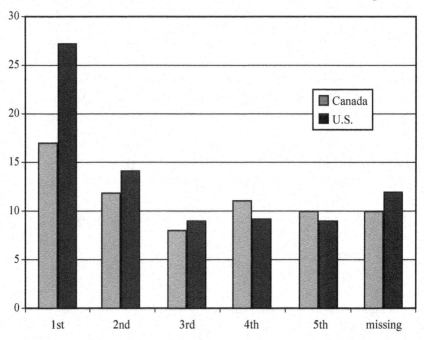

Notes: First quintile (poorest); fifth quintile (richest, but interpret with caution due to high sampling
variability); *age-adjusted percents calculated using the projected 2000 U.S. standard population. Data
include household population aged 18 and older and missing data (e.g., "I don't know" are excluded).
There are statistically significant differences between Canada and the U.S. (p.<0.05).

Sources: Statistics Canada, "Canadian Community Health Survey," *The Daily* (June 15, 2004), p.
8 (taken from table); Statistics Canada, "Joint Canada/United States Survey of Health, 2002/03,"
The Daily (June 2, 2004), retrieved August 12, 2006 from www.statcan.ca/Daily/English/040602/
d040602a.thm.

Figure 12.2
How Housing Affects Other Health Determinants

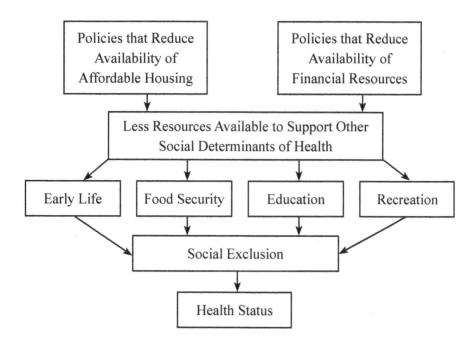

Source: T. Bryant, "Housing and Health," in D. Raphael (ed.), *Social Determinants of Health: Canadian Perspectives* (Toronto: Canadian Scholars' Press Inc., 2004), p. 223.

Research also documents that those with higher socio-economic status, particularly education level, have access to resources that are conducive to better health habits and lifestyles than those with lower socio-economic status. For instance, those with higher education tend to engage in healthy behaviours such as exercising, avoiding smoking and obesity, moderate drinking, and they are more likely to seek preventative health check-ups (Mirowsky and Ross, 1998). They also tend to have a greater sense of control and autonomy in their work lives, which increases general health and well-being (Mirowsky, Ross, and Reynolds, 2000).

The life course perspective, synthesized with the concept of "social capital" (covered in Chapter 3), is particularly useful when considering the social determinants of health. As stated by Raphael (2004: 16):

Adopting a life course perspective directs attention to how social determinants of health operate at every level of development ... to both immediately influence health as well as provide the basis for health or illness during following stages of the life course.

For example, "human capital" (i.e., education in the form of skills and knowledge), combined with strong social support from family, friends, and our communities (forms of social capital) earlier in life, can help buffer the effects of stress, and this can positively affect one's health later in life. An example of this is illustrated in Box 12.2, which summarizes key findings of "The Nun Study." This research uncovers links among supportive networks of relations, stress, education, and a positive attitude and how these factors contribute to health outcomes in later life. This research also illuminates how social support is not the sole domain of blood or formal kinship ties in families, since it can be found in other kinds of close relationships.

Box 12.2
Nuns' Story of Aging Study Links Sharp Minds to a Positive Mindset

....In *Aging with Grace: What the Nun Study Teaches Us About Leading Longer, Healthier, and More Meaningful Lives* (New York: Bantam), Snowdon (2002) yields some startling, often encouraging discoveries...not the least of which is that an educated mind, healthy habits and, maybe most important, a sense of joy in living can lead to a long, vibrant and productive life, and may even block the effects of Alzheimer's disease. "Those who are hopeful, happy, optimistic in attitudes live much longer," Snowdon says. "That happy state is probably also a healthy state." The nuns involved in the study range in age from 75 to 106, and they are members of the School Sisters of Notre Dame congregation...Because the sisters share similar lifestyles and can be followed for so many years, "it's as close as you can get to a laboratory-pure environment, a unique model of aging in a population," Snowdon says...."You don't have to join a convent to learn from these sisters...Buckle your seat belt, watch your blood pressure, eat a prudent diet, and be good at what humans are good at—language and social intercourse."... The nuns in the study aren't representative of American society. They're better educated...and their overall health reflects a life without tobacco, alcohol, or excesses of any kind... "They're very mellow," Snowdon says. He attributes that to a life of prayer and community..."Part of it is the social support they have, and I think the spiritual part is the way they get through some of the ups and downs of life." The sisters remain interested in each other and in life around them. "They're always looking forward," he says.

Source: Excerpt from USA TODAY.com, USA Today Information Network, Anita Manning, May 14, 2001, retrieved October 29, 2001 from http://pqasb.pqarchiver.com/USAToday.

Selected Health Challenges and Implications for Family Relationships

Families and Disabilities and Special Needs Children

As recognized by Statistics Canada (2012), disability is a fluid concept in that conceptions of disability have changed dramatically over time. Before the 20th century, many definitions involved religious and supernatural explanations, ranging from karma (a destiny or fate based on one's previous actions) to "God's Will." According to Statistics Canada (2007), in 2006 approximately 4.4 million Canadians—or 14.3 percent of the population (one in seven)—reported that they had one or more disabilities. This is defined as having difficulty in performing certain kinds of "normal" daily activities such as hearing, seeing, walking or climbing stairs or in having certain conditions that limit participation in these activities.

Owen (2010) further emphasizes how self-identification is critical to a disability perspective. This is because it shifts the power of naming disability away from those in authority and more toward the subjective identities of those imposed with disability labels. Against this backdrop, it is easy to understand how definitions of "disability" and the usage of this terminology have been hotly debated by disability activists and in the literature. In this regard, Owen (2010) rightfully acknowledges how defining words is a political act, as feminists and critical race theorists have struggled to emphasize. Disability connotes a lack of ability, carrying the label of inferiority and dependency. Similarly, there are differing perspectives on disability, as suggested by the Office for Disability Issues (2001: 42):

> The biomedical perspective sees disability as a disease, disorder, medical condition or biological "abnormality" within the individual. The functional perspective understands disability as a restriction in ability to perform certain standard tasks in a way that is considered "normal." The social/environmental perspective presents disability as the result of barriers in the social environment that prevents persons with disabilities from participating fully in community, work, and learning. Finally, the human rights perspective focuses on respect for human dignity and on protection against discrimination and exclusionary practices in the private and public spheres.

Overall, the emphasis in defining disability has moved away from a medial model of (ab)normality to a focus on social structure. As observed by Owen (2010) this shift has been a significant move in the rethinking of disability and the beginning of political action. Previously, disability was centred on individual impairments and people with disabilities were "othered" because of their difference from the ableist norm. Alternatively, from a social model of disability lens, it is the external obstacles that limit "ableness" rather than individual characteristics per se. For example, the lack of a ramp in a public place is the problem, not the condition that someone uses a wheelchair.

Cognizant of these important issues, a significant number of Canadian families are confronted with the associated health and economic challenges that result from disability. These challenges can be chronic or temporary, and they can occur at any point in the family life course and at any age, although generally, the prevalence of disability tends to increase with age. Yet a common theme echoed across many different kinds of family circumstances—for example, from having a child with cerebral palsy to being a parent with a learning disability to having a grandparent with Parkinson's disease—is how a lack of support and the obstacles that prevent a full life are the problem rather than the disabilities themselves.

By way of example, Owen (2010) finds that many parents of children with disabilities experience significant frustration, largely rooted in a lack of support rather than dealing with their child's disability. In some cases, children may be placed in residential or foster care because of this lack of support, and family breakdown, poverty, and unemployment can result. There are also reciprocal effects between disability and poverty, as well as ripple effects for the health and well-being of all family members. For instance, low-income parents with a disabled child may have less access to good housing and certain health or educational services, which in turn can lead to further family health problems. Also, disabled individuals of working age may not be able to find employment, which can exacerbate their health and functioning due to a lack of resources.

Although not all special needs children are necessarily considered disabled, it is estimated that between 5 percent and 20 percent of children have special needs because of their physical or intellectual disabilities, behavioural problems, or giftedness (Child and Family Canada, 2005). These children and their families can face unique challenges.

Figure 12.3

Impact of Child's Condition on Parental Employment for Parents of Children with Disabilities Aged 0 to 14, Canada, 2006

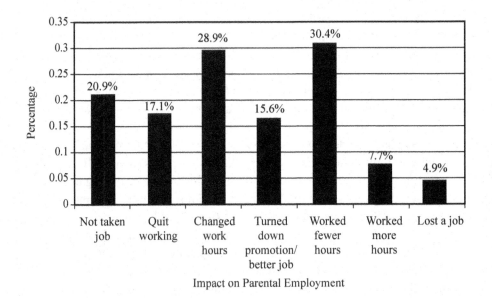

Source: Participation and Activity Limitation Survey. Ottawa: Statistics Canada, 2006.

For example, parents with autistic children may require specialized child care and educational programs. And while many parents of these children report that the experience has enriched their lives, parents can also face frustration and stress in trying to raise a special needs child, particularly when they lack support. There is also growing concern that special needs often go unaddressed in schools and communities (Child and Family Canada, 2005), which can create additional problems for families and society. In fact, it is estimated that only 3 percent of school-aged children with learning disabilities receive special needs services within their schools.

Of notable concern are children born with fetal alcohol syndrome (FAS), which is caused when mothers abuse alcohol during pregnancy. It can cut across all socio-economic groups, but it has been observed to be particularly prevalent in select Aboriginal communities in Canada (Canadian Paediatric Society, 2002). FAS is deemed one of the leading causes of learning and behavioural difficulties, and this can put youth at increased risk of developing a number of other problems. For example, research shows that 30–70 percent of young offenders and inmates have experienced learning problems (Boland et al., 1998). Moreover, almost 50 percent of adolescents who had committed suicide had previously been diagnosed with learning disabilities (Child and Family Canada, 2005).

Another type of special needs children are those with attention deficit hyperactive disorder (ADHD). This neurologically based developmental disorder (also viewed as a mental health disorder) is accompanied by symptoms of hyperactivity, impulsivity, and distractibility. These symptoms begin in infancy and sometimes continue into adulthood and affect academic progress, social skills development, and, later on, job performance. The impact is felt at home, at school, on the job, and within the community (ADHD Canada, 2007). While caring for these children presents a number of challenges, low-income mothers are found to face unique demands relative to more privileged mothers due to deep-rooted inequalities.

Overall, low-income mothers have fewer personal resources and are confronted with dwindling government support services for poor disabled children or children with special needs. Based on qualitative interview data, Litt (2004: 640) shows how these mothers are caught within "inflexible and punitive environments" and how "notions of disability disregard the lived experiences of the care needs of these children." In particular, these women must experience and negotiate a system that expects them to both financially support their children while also providing care to their children. As a result, these mothers face unrealistic work demands and inadequate public supports. Unfortunately, this undermines their employment and education options as well as their long-term prospects for financial stability. Visible minority women face additional burdens, since limited access to health care continues to be a problem in these communities.

HIV/AIDS

Globally, more than 40 million women, men, and children are infected with HIV/AIDS (human immunodeficiency virus/acquired immune deficiency syndrome). While 99 percent of infected individuals live in developing countries (Galambos, 2004), a significant number of Canadian families have been ravaged by HIV/AIDS. The first Canadian AIDS case was reported in 1982 (Health Canada, 2002). Since the AIDS epidemic began in the 1980s, 17,000 people in Canada have been diagnosed with AIDS, and 48,014 HIV cases have been reported to the Centre for Infectious Disease Prevention and Control in Canada. HIV cases are those diagnosed with the virus but have not yet developed full-blown AIDS (Canadian Health Network, 2005). Since 1995, the number of positive HIV tests reported annually has begun to decline, although 15 percent of new HIV and AIDS infections occur in Aboriginal people, which represents 9.2 percent of all AIDS cases (Health Canada, 2012).

HIV can be contracted through a variety of ways, such as unprotected heterosexual or homosexual intercourse; sharing of needles or syringes for drug injection; contaminated blood transfusions or blood products; or transmission from mother to baby during pregnancy, delivery, or breastfeeding. Groups at high risk for HIV/AIDS include men having sex with men, injection drug users, and women. The exposure category of men having sex with men represents the majority of AIDS cases (73.3 percent), even though the number of newly reported cases (incidence rates) has declined over the past decade. Aboriginal peoples are at especially high risk due to earlier experiences with sexual abuse, poverty, exploitation and sex trade participation, injection drug use, and poor mental health. And in contrast to the non-Aboriginal population, females make up a comparatively larger proportion of Aboriginal HIV/AIDS cases (Health Canada, 2012; Hoffman-Goetz and Friedman, 2005). As a result (and as shown in Table 12.1), the HIV epidemic among Aboriginal peoples shows no sign of slowing down, and they tend to be infected at a younger age than non-Aboriginal peoples. It is also interesting to note that older adults aged 50 and older have relatively high prevalence rates. In part, this may be due to earlier high-risk behaviours, but also because ageist attitudes perpetuate the view that older adults do not need "safe sex" prevention initiatives.

The effects of HIV/AIDS on families are enormous. Individuals diagnosed with the disease may be reluctant to disclose their health status to their parents and families because of shame and stigma. Unfortunately, they may be denying themselves an important source of support (Shehan et al., 2005). And for those who do tell their families and friends of their HIV or AIDS status, disclosure can also lead to stigmatization, discrimination, and disruption of personal relationships. Indeed, HIV/AIDS is frequently linked with behaviours that are often considered deviant, such as homosexual sex and injected drug use. Thus, some families may view the illness as "fitting punishment" for those who engage in shameful or illegal activities, and this can affect the kinds of support given to those who carry the disease (Shehan et al., 2005).

Although some individuals afflicted with HIV/AIDS may need to rely more heavily on outside social supports, most family members do help out with varying degrees of assistance. In some cases, parents of HIV/AIDS victims take over primary responsibility for the care of their grandchildren. HIV-infected parents, for example, may be unable to care for their children because of substance use, deteriorating health, or death. And while many grandparents experience some positive rewards as a result of their new roles, primary caregivers often must face a new set of challenges. For instance, they may incur considerable economic and social costs. Some of the children may also be HIV-infected with special health needs (Linsk and Mason, 2004).

Table 12.1
Comparison of Age at Time of Diagnosis of Reported AIDS Cases and at
Time of Test for Positive HIV Tests by Indigenous Status*

	Indigenous	Non-Indigenous
AIDS	**n = 52**	**n = 16,464**
<20 years	1.9%	1.5%
20–29 years	21.0	14.9
30–39	47.9	44.0
40–49	22.3	28.0
50+ years	6.9	11.6
HIV	**n = 879**	**n = 2,879**
<20 years	4.1%	1.6%
20–29 years	27.3	19.9
30–39 years	40.2	39.5
40–49 years	22.6	26.1
50+ years	5.8	13.0

*Indigenous ethnicity refers to Aboriginal (Inuit, Métis, Native Indian, and Aboriginal unspecified). Also, these data include reported AIDS cases up to December 31, 2003, and positive HIV tests from 1998 to December 31, 2006, from provinces/territories that report ethnicity.

Source: Public Health Agency of Canada, "HIV/AIDS epi Notes: Understanding the HIV/AIDS Epidemic among Aboriginal Peoples in Canada: The Community at a Glance" (Ottawa: Centre for Infectious Disease Prevention and Control, 2004); retrieved August 11, 2006, from http://www.phac-aspc.gc.ca/publicat/epiu-aepi/epi-note/index.html.

Mental Health Issues

Mental illness refers to a broad classification for many disorders such as anxiety, depression, bipolar disease, schizophrenia, and eating disorders, and it accounts for a large percentage of hospital stays every year (CMHA, 2006). It is also relatively common— statistics indicate that one in every five Canadians will have a mental health problem at some point in their lives. However, there is considerable variation in duration and intensity, as well as in actual and perceived root causes. For example, in Table 12.2, it is shown that while many Canadians believe that the primary cause of stress, anxiety, or major depression (apart from work) stems from money problems, others believe that it can be the result of other family or health problems, or "daily life in general."

Families can be devastated and torn apart by mental illness. Fear, frustration, embarrassment, ambivalence, and social stigma can create significant emotional repercussions

Table 12.2
Perceived Causes of Stress, Anxiety, or Major Depression, Apart from Work

"In your opinion, what are the primary causes of stress, anxiety, or major depression in your personal and family life, apart from work?"

Cause	Percentage Reporting
Money problems	44
Illness of someone close to you	13
Conflicts or disputes with children	11
Conflicts or disputes with spouse	10
Family matters/family problems	10
Staying healthy/personal health problems	9
Interpersonal relations/interactions with people	7
Death of someone close to you	6
Everything/life in general/daily life/the future	6
Parenting/concern for children/meet children's needs	5
Don't know/didn't answer	6

Notes: Based on a 2006 telephone survey of 1,501 randomly selected Canadian adults, conducted by SOM about health and financial security.

Source: "Desjardins Financial Security Survey on Health and the Desjardins National Financial Security Index," report posted by the Canadian Mental Health Association, 2006, p. 25, retrieved August 11, 2006, from www.cmha.ca (research reports: 2006 Survey on Canadian Attitudes towards Physical and Mental Health at Work and at Play).

for families. Jones (2004) documents that those families who have a family member who suffers from serious mental illness often experience complex loss. This loss is complicated by the continuing presence of the person who is felt to have been "lost," feelings of anger, and subsequent guilt, and feelings of shame. Some families may be hesitant to seek professional help. And even if professional help is solicited, there may be problems with denial and the patient's adherence to medication and therapy. And from a legal standpoint, there may be barriers to forcing a mentally ill individual to comply with doctor's recommendations. To illustrate, family members suffering from severe psychosis or delusional behaviour may believe that others are "the enemy," that the medication is part of a conspiracy to poison them, and that they are not the ones who "really need the help." And although far from the norm, mental illness can result in dangerous or deadly consequences, such as violent behaviour, suicide, or the death of innocent family members. A well-publicized example is the case of Andrea Yates, a mother who suffered from severe postpartum depression and psychosis and drowned her five children in the bathtub (see Box 12.3).

Finally, while mental illness can strike any family, poverty can contribute to mental health problems (i.e., stress), although the majority of poor people are not mentally ill. This makes it very difficult for individuals and families to rise above the poverty line. Recent studies on homelessness, for example, show that a large proportion of homeless people suffer from mental illness and a lack of family support (e.g., CMHA, 2006). Alcohol and drug abuse are also often used by the homeless in an attempt to self-medicate, which can lead to other health and social risks. These circumstances make it very difficult to achieve social connectedness and stability, including steady employment. Unfortunately, this perpetuates a vicious cycle of poverty, vulnerability, and other related problems.

Caregiving for the Elderly and Those with Alzheimer's Disease

Although most seniors are relatively healthy and generational support tends to be reciprocal, as discussed in the last chapter, a significant proportion of families provide informal support to a physically disabled or cognitively impaired older person. This assistance may be emotional or instrumental, such as help with personal care, rides to the doctor or shopping centres, and help with daily activities. Spouses, adult children, siblings, and friends are the most common sources of support. Married people, in particular, have a built-in caregiving system. This may keep many old people with serious functional dis-

---

Box 12.3
Andrea Yates

Andrea Pia Yates (born July 2, 1964) is a woman from Houston, Texas, U.S.A. who is currently serving a life sentence for methodically drowning her five children (ages six months to seven years) in a bathtub on June 20, 2001. She was suffering from a severe case of psychotic depression, recurring, after having her last baby. She immediately called 9-1-1 after the murders and was arrested shortly thereafter.

....Some believe or believed that her husband, Russell "Rusty" Yates, an employee of the Johnson Space Center, was responsible for creating the conditions that culminated in the tragedy. Andrea's psychiatrist, Dr. Eileen Starbranch, testified that she urged the couple not to get pregnant again to avert future psychotic depression, but the procreative plan taught by the Yates' preacher, Michael Peter Woroniecki, a doctrine to which Rusty Yates subscribed, insisted she should continue to have "as many children as nature allows."

Andrea Yates told her jail psychiatrist, "It was the seventh deadly sin. My children weren't righteous. They stumbled because I was evil. The way I was raising them they could never be saved. They were doomed to perish in the fires of hell."

Source: Retrieved October 31, 2005 from http://en.wikipedia.org/wiki/Andrea_Yates.

abilities out of institutions. Indeed, married people have half the institutionalization rate of unmarried older people (Novak and Campbell, 2010).

Caregiving can bring many joys and rewards, such as an opportunity to reciprocate previous care. However, it can also lead to feelings of caregiver burden. This refers to problems and stress due to caregiving, such as depression, psychological distress, and negative feelings about caregiving. Some studies also show that spouses of those receiving care suffer a greater burden from caregiving than do adult children. This strain may be particularly acute as caregivers watch their partners decline, both mentally and physically. They may also be experiencing health problems of their own, which adds to the burden. Older caregivers may also have fewer financial and social resources than middle-aged caregivers (Novak and Campbell, 2010). However, this should not downplay the considerable toll that can be placed on a minority of families in the "sandwich generation," particularly those with few social and economic supports.

Dementia is a particularly challenging health problem for families. This syndrome consists of a number of symptoms that includes loss of memory, judgment, and reasoning, and changes in mood, behaviour, and communication abilities. For example, an elderly family member could have an inability to start a conversation, have difficulty in planning and making decisions, become unusually aggressive, or engage in dangerous, inappropriate, or repetitive behaviours, such as wandering (Wister and McPherson, in press). Alzheimer's disease (AD) is the most common form of dementia and accounts for 64 percent of all dementias in Canada. An estimated 480,600 (1.5 percent of the Canadian population) in 2008 have AD or a related dementia, and women account for over two-thirds of all cases. Some projections indicate that this number might reach 1,125,200 (2.8 percent) by 2038, with the economic cost of caregiving rising from approximately $15 billion in 2008 to $153 billion in 2038 (Alzheimer Society of Canada, 2010). Unfortunately, there is no known cause or cure for AD, and its prevalence is expected to grow rapidly as our population ages (News-Medical.net, 2005).

From a symbolic interactionist perspective, MacRae (2002) studied how family members help a parent or spouse cope with the loss of self that the disease causes. She found that family members use a number of strategies to help their relative preserve some of his or her former identity. One technique entails concealing the diagnosis from others to avoid the label of dementia. Another strategy involves interpreting inappropriate behaviour as caused by the disease and not by the "real person." A third strategy is to assist the relative with dressing and grooming so he or she will present an unchanged image of self to others.

Death of a Family Member

At some point, all families must confront death and dying and a process of bereavement. These experiences are shaped by cultural contexts and religious beliefs, support systems, family relationship history, as well as the circumstances surrounding the death. Life course researchers find that unexpected deaths occurring "off time" or "too early" may be particularly difficult to cope with, such as the death of a child. A recent study by Song et. al (2010) examined the long-term effects of a child's death on the bereaved parents' health-related quality of life (HRQoL). Bereaved parents were found to have significantly worse HRQoL than comparison group parents. While gender differences, age of the child, or the amount of time since the child's death did not significantly predict health outcomes, bereaved parents whose child died in violent circumstances had particularly low levels of HRQoL. The authors suggest that this finding provides evidence that having an opportunity to say goodbye before the death of a loved one is related to better adaptation after bereavement and possibly to better outcomes in later life. In addition, the researchers find that marital closeness plays a critical role as a source of social support for spouses and is also a significant predictor for better health for bereaved couples.

Generally, death typically takes place in old age and in hospitals, even though most people want to die at home surrounded by their loved ones. Palliative care can also be very helpful to family members, which was introduced in Chapter 11. It refers not only to the care and management of patients approaching the end of life but also addresses the reduction of suffering throughout the course of illness and, for family, into bereavement. A complete program would include symptom control and spiritual support, as well as bereavement support and education (Novak and Campbell, 2010). Palliative care and other approaches to the treatment of dying family members raise many moral and ethical questions. For example, how much information should family members give a dying person about his or her condition?

Lifestyles, Families, and Communities: A Political Economy Perspective

The study of lifestyles, health, and the interplay among families, communities, and social-structural conditions has received considerable attention in the literature. The term "lifestyle" denotes certain behaviours such as poor diet, smoking, drinking, inactivity, and drug abuse that are often considered sources of illness and disease, such as FAS, cancer, and obesity. And although it is individuals who engage in these behaviours, lifestyle choices are not made in a vacuum. Lifestyles are structured by one's social situation, and are constrained by one's life chances. These life chances are influenced by factors such as family background, socio-economic status, age, gender, race, ethnicity, and geographical locale. They are also shaped by government policies and community programs that can facilitate or hinder the formation of certain behaviours.

Let us consider the health issue of addictive behaviours, such as the cigarette smoking behaviour of Canadians (see Figure 12.4). Tobacco use is the single most preventable cause of morbidity and mortality in most developed nations. It also kills more people in this country than HIV/AIDS, car accidents, murder, suicide, and illicit drug use combined (BC Ministry of Health Services, 2004). Yet, despite a significant decline in smoking over the past several decades, there are striking regional variations in daily smoking behaviour for those aged 18+, as shown in Figure 12.4. The lowest rates of smoking are reported in British Columbia (13.3 percent) while in the territories, the rates are all above 30 percent (e.g., Nunavut, 50.3 percent).

Figure 12.4
Self-Reported Daily Tobacco Smoking among Individuals Aged 18 Years and Older, by Province and Territory, Canada, 2009–2010*

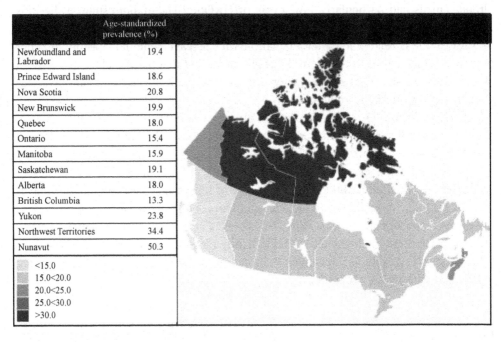

	Age-standardized prevalence (%)
Newfoundland and Labrador	19.4
Prince Edward Island	18.6
Nova Scotia	20.8
New Brunswick	19.9
Quebec	18.0
Ontario	15.4
Manitoba	15.9
Saskatchewan	19.1
Alberta	18.0
British Columbia	13.3
Yukon	23.8
Northwest Territories	34.4
Nunavut	50.3

<15.0
15.0<20.0
20.0<25.0
25.0<30.0
>30.0

*Age-standardized to the 1991 Canadian population.

Source: Public Health Agency of Canada (2011); using 2009–2010 data from the Canadian Community Health Survey (Statistics Canada).

Why do such disparities in smoking behaviours exist? Part of the explanation lies in the social conditions that can encourage/discourage this kind of addictive behaviour. British Columbia is a leader in tobacco control nationally and internationally and has introduced some of the most progressive anti-smoking programs in the country. Strongly supported by the provincial government, these programs have placed a strong emphasis on youth issues, with many school and community resources dedicated to ensuring that youth never start smoking. B.C. has also initiated programs to increase awareness of tobacco issues and to support smokers who have wanted to quit (BC Ministry of Health Services, 2004).

Alexander (2008) offers another provocative perspective on addictions more generally, focusing on a broad range of unhealthy and destructive behaviours that range from smoking and alcohol to porn, compulsive shopping, and dysfunctional social relationships. His central thesis is that addiction is particularly endemic in a Western free-market society. Drug abuse, for instance, is found to be particularly high among certain socially dislocated groups, such as Aboriginal people. This is because free markets inevitably dislocate people from traditional sources of psychological, social, and spiritual support and meaning. In this way, a lack of social integration in this broad sense is the precursor of addiction. Overall, his social theory on addiction provides added weight to the argument that individualizing unhealthy conditions or behaviours can be problematic. Hence, he argues that recognition of the social determinants of health and social-environmental and political responses to health problems are critical, a topic that we will examine in further detail in the next section.

Health Promotion and Healthy Public Policy: Should We Target Individuals, Families, or Social Conditions?

A central goal of health policy is to improve the health status of our population. How society should achieve this objective, however, is subject to a great deal of controversy. We all tend to agree that Canadians are very fortunate to have universal health coverage and that the health care system is one of the better ones in the world. It is also recognized that the health care system needs reform, but there is no consensus as to what those changes should be. For example, some analysts argue that we need to move away from a medically dominated, hospital-based health care system and toward more community care, community programs, and prevention/health promotion approaches. Others propose that we require improved medical care and hospital services, including more hospital beds (e.g., see Bolaria and Dickinson, 2002).

Despite this controversy, there are a number of issues highlighted in this chapter that are worthy of further consideration. The first is that health-promotion policies need to target not only individuals and their families but also the underlying conditions that contribute to, or further exacerbate, health inequities and health problems. For example, it may be difficult for an individual to quit smoking if other family members smoke and if they live, work, or socialize in "smoker-friendly" environments. There is also growing concern over the advertising of "junk food" and the fast-food industry, given that fast-food diets are generally low in nutrition and high in fat (Wister, 2005). This type of diet contributes to many health conditions such as obesity, which is related to diabetes and other health problems. Indeed, obesity rates have skyrocketed over the past two decades (especially among lower-income individuals and children) in tandem with the proliferation of fast-food chains in shopping malls, schools, and even hospitals. This observation calls into question theories that obesity is usually the direct result of genetics since it is highly improbable that our genes have changed much during this short time frame (Wister, 2005).

In Schlosser's well-known book (later made into a movie), *Fast Food Nation* (2002), we learn how the fast-food industry has been driven by fundamental changes in American society and has dramatically altered the diets of families (see Box 12.4). This searing portrayal of this industry also shows an almost complete lack of government regulation that manipulates and exploits workers at every point of the production process. Overall, this history of the development of the fast-food industry—similar to the tobacco industry—reveals the power and greed of corporate capitalists and governments. In short, by illuminating the role of corporate giants in fostering unhealthy lifestyle choices and a variety of health problems, we are exposed to "what really lurks between those sesame-seed buns" (Schlosser, 2002: 10).

However, in times of economic constraint, individual-level approaches for solving health problems tend to receive the most support from the government, although the government is beginning to play a role in regulating the quality of food sold by fast-food chains (e.g., through the reduction of trans fats). However, generally, it is argued that the government adopts a victim-blaming epidemiology. From this ideological stance, individuals are to blame for their own problems and it is up to them to adopt a healthier lifestyle (Doyal and Pennell, 1979). Similar to the Victorian notion of "the undeserving poor" (also discussed in Chapter 13), this idea applies an equally inappropriate notion of "the undeserving sick," which has strong implications for health care policy (Bolaria and Bolaria, 2002).

Yet, as we have seen throughout this chapter, strategies aimed solely at individuals mask the social production of inequality and social variability in health. A focus on factory workers' individual lifestyles, for instance, diverts attention from unhealthy and unsafe work environments and a lack of family-friendly policies. The end result is that health policies are not comprehensive or holistic, since they do not treat individuals' illnesses in the context of their everyday lives. They also do not address the systematic root cause of their behaviour (e.g., not having enough money to buy a high-quality family dinner in a restaurant) or illness (e.g., poverty and a lack of resources, exploitation). And since earlier health problems contribute to later ones, these strategies do not invest in long-term solutions.

Moreover, there is concern over the growing power of the pharmaceutical industry and adjacent "growth industries" (e.g., psychiatry) in our capitalist economy to "manufacture" and treat health problems once they occur. This is because their primary motivation is making drugs or selling treatments for profit. Consequently, many people are highly critical of these industries and how they treat purported "disorders." For example, Angell (2011) in her *New York Review of Books* article titled, "The Illusions of Psychiatry," critically examines the American Psychiatric Association's Diagnostic and Statistical Manual of Mental Disorders (DSM), often referred to as the bible of psychiatry and its enormous influence within American society. She also discusses a recent book that provides a disillusioned insider's view of the psychiatric profession and the widespread use of psychoactive drugs in children, which she views as "the baleful influence of the pharmaceutical industry on the practice of psychiatry" (p. 2).

In Angell's (2011) review article, she further notes that the 1980 publication of the DSM contained 265 diagnoses (up from 182 in the previous edition). The most recent version (the DSM-IV-TR, revised in 2000) contains 365 diagnoses and a forthcoming edition is expected to be even larger and more expensive. She also documents how it

Box 12.4
Fast Food Nation: The Dark Side of the All-American Meal

The extraordinary growth of the fast food industry has been driven by fundamental changes in American society. Adjusted for inflation, the hourly wage of the average U.S. worker peaked in 1973 and then steadily declined for the next twenty-five years. During that period, women entered the workplace in record numbers, often motivated less by a feminist perspective than by a need to pay the bills. In 1975, about one-third of American mothers with young children worked outside the home; today almost two-thirds of such mothers are employed. As the sociologists Cameron Lynne Macdonald and Carmen Sirianni have noted, the entry of so many women into the workforce has greatly increased demand for the types of services that housewives traditionally perform: cooking, cleaning, and child care. A generation ago, three-quarters of the money used to buy food in the United States was spent to prepare meals at home. Today about half of the money used to buy food is spent at restaurants—mainly at fast food restaurants.

The McDonald's Corporation has become a powerful symbol of America's service economy, which is now responsible for 90 percent of the country's new jobs. In 1968, McDonald's operated about one thousand restaurants. Today it has about thirty thousand restaurants worldwide and opens almost two thousand new ones each year. An estimated one out of every eight workers in the United States has at some point been employed by McDonald's. The company annually hires about one million people, more than any other American organization, public or private. McDonald's is the nation's largest purchaser of beef, pork, and potatoes—and the second largest purchaser of chicken. The McDonald Corporation is the largest owner of retail property in the world. Indeed, the company earns the majority of its profits not from selling food but from collecting rent. McDonald's spends more money on advertising and marketing than any other brand. McDonald's operates more playgrounds than any other private entity in the United States. It is responsible for the nation's bestselling line of children's clothing (McKids) and is one of the largest distributors of toys. A survey of American schoolchildren found that 96 percent could identify Ronald McDonald. The only fictional character with a higher degree of recognition was Santa Claus. The impact of McDonald's on the way we live today is hard to overstate.

Source: Schlosser, E. 2002. *Fast Food Nation: The Dark Side of the All-American Meal.* New York: Perennial (pp. 4–5).

came into nearly universal use, not only by psychiatrists, but by insurance companies, hospitals, courts, prisons, schools, researchers, government agencies, and the rest of the medical professions. As psychiatry became a drug-intensive specialty, the pharmaceutical industry was eager to forge bonds with the psychiatric profession. As a result, drug companies began to lavish attention and gifts on psychiatrists, and even began to subsidize meetings of the American Psychological Association and other related conferences. In addition, drug companies began to heavily support many related patient advocacy groups and educational organizations. Yet, according to many outspoken critics of these practices, the use of these drugs is often ineffective, inappropriate, and often has dangerous side effects.

Angell (2011) also argues that "there seem to be fashions in childhood psychiatric diagnoses, with one disorder giving way to the next" providing the example of ADHD and how juvenile bipolar disorder quickly came to replace it to become one of the fastest-growing diagnoses. Arguing that one "would be hard pressed to find a two-year-old who is not sometimes irritable, a boy in fifth grade who is not sometimes inattentive, or a girl in middle school who is not anxious," she observes that whether such children are labelled as having a mental disorder and treated with prescription drugs depends a lot on who they are and the pressures their parents face.

Notably, as low-income (American) families experience growing economic hardship, many are finding that applying for Supplemental Security Income (SSI) payments on the basis of mental disability is one strategy to survive. Hospitals and state welfare agencies also have incentives to encourage uninsured families to apply for SSI payments, since hospitals will get paid and states will save money. Citing a Rutgers University study that showed that children from low-income families are four times as likely as privately insured children to receive antipsychotic medicines, Angell concludes that "we need to rethink the care of troubled children. Here the problem is often troubled families in troubled circumstances....Our reliance on psychiatric drugs, seemingly for all of life's discontent, tends to close off other options. In view of the risks and questionable long-term effectiveness of drugs, we need to do better. Above all, we should remember the time-honoured medical dictum: first, do not harm (*primum non nocere*)" (p. 10).

Summary

In this chapter, health and well-being are recognized as more than the absence of disease and illness. An overarching theme of this chapter is that experiences of health and well-being need to be understood within the context of social, cultural, economic, and political environments. For example, government policies and the enormous power of corporations (e.g., tobacco, fast food) shape the ability of families to adopt healthy lifestyles. Several key social determinants of health are also identified (such as education and income), since these factors play an influential role in the health status of Canadians. However, it is recognized that complex processes underlie structural conditions, such as access to health care and the availability of personal and public supports. Selected serious health problems and their implications for family relationships are also highlighted. These conditions illustrate how health status and behaviour reciprocally shape family experiences that are embedded within unique ecological or community contexts.

Another central theme of this chapter is that we need to create and implement health promotion (a term that refers to the process of improving knowledge and the capacity to improve health) strategies and health policies that target macro-level conditions and families rather than place the responsibility on individuals. For instance, it is noted that low-income families are vulnerable to special risks and conflicts with health-related caregiving demands. In short, they can face "triple jeopardy," with no paid sick leave, no paid vacation leave, and no scheduling flexibility (Heymann, 2000). This creates conditions that place unique strains on caregivers and makes it very difficult to maintain paid employment and achieve financial stability. Also, in an increasingly ethnically diverse society, we require a culturally sensitive health care system that addresses the unique needs of Canadian families in addition to the significant health challenges faced by various cultural groups, in particular, Aboriginal families. For example, some recent immigrant groups and refugees have language difficulties, financial barriers, and cultural meanings of health and illness that can affect their access and utilization of health care programs (e.g., see Waxler-Morrison et al., 2005).

Finally, given the link between poor health in early life and poor health in later life, it is critical to adopt a life course lens in the development of health policies. In particular, policies and programs need to invest in preventing and reducing inequities early in life rather than "band-aid solutions," a theme that will be revisited in Chapter 15. These kinds of efforts will collectively improve our family and collective health and well-being and save health dollars in the future.

Questions for Critical Reflection and Debate

1. Discuss the limitations of the persistence of a biomedical clinical framework in the understanding of health and illness and disability.
2. Szasz (1972) argues that mental illness is a myth and that the problems being diagnosed and treated as medical problems by psychiatry are really "psychosocial problems with living." Do you agree or disagree with this viewpoint?
3. To what extent is the media responsible for the health and well-being of young adult men and women? To what extent can our families mitigate these influences, if any?
4. What are some key ideological and health policy implications of a focus on individual lifestyles and self-imposed risky behaviours such as smoking, unprotected sex, and heavy drinking?
5. Identify some vulnerable populations and their respective challenges in accessing health services and programs.
6. Adopting a life course perspective, highlight how poor health in the womb, infancy, and during childhood shapes one's life chances and health status in old age.

Glossary

Caregiver burden refers to problems and stress due to caregiving, such as depression, and psychological distress.

Health is a state of complete physical, mental, and social well-being and not merely the absence of disease and illness.

Health promotion is the process of increasing the knowledge and capacity to improve health among individuals, groups, and communities.

Lifestyle or styles of life is used to denote certain individual behaviours such as smoking and drinking that are structured by one's social situation.

Social determinants of health are the socio-economic, political, cultural, and environmental forces and factors that influence our health status.

Social epidemiology is the empirical study of the socio-cultural, economic, and political forces that shape patterns of disease and death in human populations.

Social model of disability emphasizes the external obstacles that limit "ableness" rather than individual characteristics per se.

Victim-blaming epidemiology is the tendency to shift the responsibility for illness and disease back onto the individual rather than on social conditions.

Further Reading

Alexander, B.K. 2008. *The Globalization of Addiction: A Study in Poverty of the Spirit.* Toronto: Oxford University Press. Presents an intriguing social theory on the nature of addictions (ranging from drugs and alcohol to relationship problems, internet porn, and compulsive shopping) from a global perspective by considering the role of social dislocation in a free-market society.

Barnes, C. 2010. *Exploring Disability: A Sociological Introduction.* Cambridge, UK: Polity Press. A comprehensive overview of the literature on disability including coverage of a broad array of areas, including the family and children, culture, and social policy.

Grochowski, J.R. 2010. *Families and Health.* Boston: Allyn & Bacon. This interdisciplinary text examines five different components of family health—biology, behaviour, social-cultural circumstances, the environment, and health care—and the ways they affect the abilities of family members to perform well in their homes, workplaces, and communities.

Patton, C. 1990. *Inventing Aids.* New York: Routledge. Offers a disturbing critique of the commitments of scientific knowledge as they relate to the AIDS epidemic, often conflicting with the human needs of HIV/AIDS patients and their families.

Waxler-Morrison, N., J.M. Anderson, E. Richardson, and N.A. Chambers (Eds.). 2005. *Cross-cultural Caring: A Handbook for Health Professionals.* Vancouver: UBC Press. This informative and practical manual looks at Vietnamese, Cambodian, Laotian, Chinese, Japanese, Iranian, South Asian, and Central American immigrant group health issues in relation to their "cultures of medicine," income, work, and family life.

Weitz, R. 2010. *The Sociology of Health, Illness, and Health Care: A Critical Approach.* Belmont: Wadsworth Pub. Presents a comprehensive overview of contemporary sociological topics and challenges readers to question their previously held beliefs about health, illness, and health care.

Related Web Sites

Canadian Institute of Child Health is dedicated to promoting and protecting the health, well-being, and rights of all children and youth through monitoring, education, and advocacy, www.cich.ca.

Canadian Mental Health Association was founded in 1918, and is one of the oldest voluntary organizations in Canada. It provides research and information, services, workshops, seminars, pamphlets, newsletters, and resource centres, www.cmha.ca. Facebook: Canadian Mental Health

Canadian Public Health Association is a national, independent association representing public health in Canada with links to the international public health community. Its members believe in universal and equitable access to basic conditions, www.cpha.ca.

DisAbled Women's Network (DAWN) Canada is a national feminist organization controlled by and comprised of women who self-identify as women with disabilities and provides personal profiles, a chat room, and related links, www.dawncanada.net.

Health Canada is the federal government department that encourages the health of Canadians through promotion and prevention activities. It also produces publications such as *Schizophrenia: A Handbook for Families,* in co-operation with the Schizophrenia Society of Canada, www.hc-sc.gc.ca.

World Health Organization is the United Nations's specialized agency for health and provides numerous publications and resources on health topics from around the globe, www.who.int/en/.

References

ADHD. 2007. "A Canadian Resource for ADD/ADHD for Parents, Patients, and Professionals." Retrieved February 5, 2007, from www.adhdcanada.com.

Alexander, B.K. 2008. *The Globalization of Addiction: A Study in Poverty of the Spirit.* Toronto: Oxford University Press.

Alzheimer Society of Canada. 2010. *Rising Tide: The Impact of Dementia on Canadian Society.* Toronto: Alzheimer Society of Canada.

Angell, M. 2011 (July 14). "The Illusions of Psychiatry." *The New York Review of Books,* retrieved January 16, 2011 from www.nybooks.com/articles/archives/2011/jul/14/illusions-of-psychiatry.

Anisef, P., and K.M. Kilbride (Eds.). 2003. *Managing Two Worlds: The Experiences and Concerns of Immigrant Youth in Ontario.* Toronto: Canadian Scholars' Press Inc.

310   Families on the Fault Line and Social Policy Issues

BC Ministry of Health Services. 2004. *BC's Tobacco Control Strategy: Targeting Our Efforts.* Retrieved December 28, 2006, from www.gov.bc.ca.

Ben-Zur, H. 2001. "Your Coping Strategy and My Distress: Inter-spouse Perceptions of Coping and Adjustment among Breast Cancer Patients and Their Spouses." *Family, Systems, and Health* 19: 83–94.

Boland, F.J., et al. 1998. *Fetal Alcohol Syndrome: Implications for the Corrections Service.* Ottawa: Correctional Service Canada.

Bolaria, B.S., and R. Bolaria. 2002. "Personal and Structural Determinants of Health and Illness: Lifestyle and Life Chances." In B.S. Bolaria and H.D. Dickinson (eds.), *Health and Illness and Health Care in Canada,* 3rd ed. (pp. 445–459). Toronto: Nelson-Thomson Learning.

Bolaria, B.S., and H.D. Dickinson (Eds.). 2002. *Health, Illness, and Health Care in Canada,* 3rd ed. Toronto: Nelson Thomson.

Canadian Health Network. 2005. "What Are HIV and AIDS?" Retrieved October 25, 2005, from www.canadian-health-network.ca/servlet.

Canadian Paediatric Society (Indian and Inuit Health Committee). 2002. "Fetal Alcohol Syndrome." *Paediatrics and Child Health* 7: 161–174.

Child and Family Canada. 2005. *Fact Sheet #18—Children with Special Needs.* Retrieved October 20, 2005, from www.cfc-efc.ca/docs/vocfc/00018_en.htm.

CMHA (Canadian Mental Health Association). 2006. "Understanding Mental Illness." Retrieved February 4, 2006, from www.cmha.ca.

Doyal, L., and I. Pennell. 1979. *The Political Economy of Health.* London: Pluto Press.

Galambos, C.M. 2004. "The Changing Face of AIDS." *Health and Social Work* 29: 83–85.

Health Canada. 2012. "Diseases and Health Conditions: First Nations, Inuit and Aboriginal Health." Retrieved February 1, 2012, from http://www.hc-sc.gc.ca/fniah-spnia/diseases-maladies/index-eng.php.

Health Canada, 2002. "The HIV/AIDS Files." Retrieved November 2, 2005, from www.hc.sc.gc.ca/english/feature/aids/transmission.html.

Heymann, J. 2000. *The Widening Gap: Why America's Working Families Are in Jeopardy and What Can Be Done about It.* New York: Basic Books.

Hoffman-Goetz, L., and D.B. Friedman. 2005. "HIV/AIDS Risk Factors as Portrayed in Mass Media Targeting First Nations, Metis, and Inuit Peoples of Canada." *Journal of Health Communication* 10: 145–162.

Jones, D.W. 2004. "Families and Serious Mental Illness: Working with Loss and Ambivalence." *British Journal of Social Work* 34: 961–979.

Linsk, N., and S. Mason. 2004. "Stresses on Grandparents and Other Relatives Caring for Children Affected by HIV/AIDS." *Health and Social Work* 29: 127–136.

Litt, J. 2004. "Women's Carework in Low-Income Households: The Special Case of Children with Attention Deficit Hyperactivity Disorder." *Gender and Society* 18: 625–644.

MacRae, H. 2002. "The Identity Maintenance Work of Family Members of Persons with Alzheimer's Disease." *Canadian Journal on Aging* 21: 405–415.

McCloskey, D. 2005. "Caregiving and Canadian Families." *Transition Magazine* 35 (Summer): 1–16.

Mirowsky, J., and C.E. Ross. 1998. "Education, Personal Control, Lifestyle, and Health: A Human Capital Hypothesis." *Research on Aging* 20: 415–449.

Mirowsky, J., C.E. Ross, and J. Reynolds. 2000. "Links between Social Status and Health Status." In C.E. Bird, P. Conrad, and A.M. Fremon (eds.), *Handbook of Medical Sociology*, 5th ed. (pp. 47–67). Upper Saddle River: Prentice-Hall.

News-Medical.Net. 2005."Alzheimer Society of Canada New Alzheimer Fact Sheet." Published Thursday, April 22, 2004, at www.news-medical.net.

Novak, M., and L. Campbell. 2010. *Aging and Society: A Canadian Perspective*, 6th ed. Toronto: Nelson.

Owen, M. 2010. "Lack of Support: Canadian Families and Disabilities." In D. Cheal, *Canadian Families Today: New Perspectives*, 2nd ed. (pp. 200–217). Toronto: Oxford University Press.

Raphael, D. (Ed.). 2004. *Social Determinants of Health: Canadian Perspectives.* Toronto: Canadian Scholars' Press Inc.

Schlosser, E. 2002. *Fast Food Nation: The Dark Side of the All-American Meal.* New York: Perennial.

Shehan, C.L., C.R. Uphold, P. Bradshaw, J. Bender, N. Arce, and B. Bender. 2005. "To Tell or Not to Tell: Men's Disclosure of Their HIV-Positive Status to Their Mothers." *Family Relations* 54: 184–196.

Song, J., F.J. Floyd, M. Seltzer, J.S. Greenberg, and J. Hong. 2010. "Long-term Effects of Child Death on Parents' Health-Related Quality of Life: A Dyadic Analysis." *Family Relations* 59: 269–282.

Statistics Canada. 2004. "Canadian Community Health Survey, 2003." *The Daily* (June 15).

Statistics Canada. 2005. "Canadian Community Health Survey: Obesity among Children and Adults." *The Daily* (July 6).

Szasz, T.S. 1972. *The Myth of Mental Illness: Foundations of a Theory of Personal Conduct.* Frogmore: Paladin.

Waxler-Morrison, N., J.M. Anderson, E. Richardson, and N.A. Chambers (Eds.). 2005. *Cross-cultural Caring: A Handbook for Health Professionals.* Vancouver: UBC Press.

Wister, A.V. 2005. *Baby Boomer Health Dynamics: How Are We Aging?* Toronto: University of Toronto Press.

Wister, A.V., and B. McPherson. In press. *Aging as a Social Process: Canadian Perspectives,* 6th ed. Toronto: Oxford University Press.

Chapter 13

Trying to Make Ends Meet

Family Poverty, Living on the Margins, and Financial Struggle

Learning Objectives

In this chapter, you will learn that ...
- Canada is a deeply stratified society, with some families and children experiencing extensive poverty
- definitions and meanings of poverty vary across time and place
- it is common for the general public and media to blame the victim for his or her condition
- many families, such as the working poor, experience great economic hardship despite living near or above the poverty line
- certain social groups (e.g., women, disabled, Aboriginal) are more vulnerable to poverty than others
- an increasing proportion of families, including middle-class families, is being "squeezed" financially
- studies establish a link between economic hardship and a number of negative outcomes that reverberate over the life course and among generations

Introduction

Many of us associate poverty with malnourished children with sunken eyes and bloated bellies who live in drought-ridden regions of the world. In our own country, we might picture poverty as homeless people who sleep in back alleys, push shopping carts with all their belongings, and hold out cups to strangers on city streets for money. And while this latter image certainly portrays poverty in Canada, it is not typical of the "average" poor Canadian. Indeed, poverty in Canada is not necessarily a matter of starving to death or begging on a street corner but rather of begging for food at shelters and food banks. It is also a matter of barely being able to make ends meet and in struggling to pay for life's basic necessities, such as shelter, transportation, clothing, and food. Moreover, poverty is not just a lack of riches, but rather an unequal distribution of riches.

A recent report card that summarizes how Canada is doing in addressing child and family poverty shows a relatively dismal assessment. Based on 2009 Low Income Cut-Off after-tax calculations, nearly 1 in 10 persons, including 1 in 10 children, still live in poverty. And, in 2010, the highest rate of food bank use (867,948 individuals) since 1997 was reported (Campaign 2000, 2010). And from an international perspective, Canada does not lag far behind many other industrialized countries such as the United States. This fact may be surprising to many of us, since we often assume significantly higher rates of poverty south or farther outside of our borders. The sad reality is that poverty and economic hardship are a significant social problem for many Canadian families, with consequences that create struggle and hardship in everyday life as well as over the life course.

Measuring Poverty

There are two basic approaches to defining and measuring poverty in Canada—absolute and relative (see Table 13.1 for definitions and examples of different measures). "Absolute poverty" is based on the idea that an absolute measure can be determined by examining an essential "basket" of goods and services deemed necessary for survival. In other words, what bare necessities are sufficient to keep the human body alive? A basic "basket," then, would have such items or components as food provided by a food bank, shelter provided by a community hostel, second-hand clothing from a thrift shop, and access to basic remedial care. The poverty line implied by such a budget would obviously be very low, such that an annual income of $2,000 would probably cover it (Child and Family Canada, 2006).

Table 13.1
Examples of Absolute and Relative Poverty and Low-Income Cut-off Concepts and Definitions: What Are We Measuring?

Absolute Poverty	Who Uses?	Applicability
$1 U.S. per day (minimum survival budget)	World Bank	Only useful for some developing countries
Meeting basic needs	Fraser Institute	Advanced industrialized allowance societies; no allowance for recreation and culture
Relative Poverty	**Who Uses?**	**Applicability**
Exclusion from mainstream resources, opportunities, and sources of well-being	Canadian Council on Social Development	Advanced industrialized societies
Exclusion from the standards of living broadly available to others in same society	Organization for Economic Co-operation and Development (OECD)	Advanced industrialized societies
Low-Income Cut-off	**Who Uses?**	**Applicability**
Higher percentage of income than average spent on necessities of life (food, shelter, and clothing)	Statistics Canada	Canada; considers family and community size; considers changes in household spending patterns

Source: Adapted from Canadian Council on Social Development, "Defining and Re-defining Poverty: A CCSD Perspective," retrieved August 12, 2006, from www.cssd.ca/pubs/2001/povertypp.htm.

Fortunately, prevailing definitions tend to be more generous, taking into consideration such factors as social well-being, the cost of living and region size, and family size. One of the most commonly used definitions is Statistics Canada's low-income cut-off point (LICOs), a definition that is more conservative than others, such as the one offered by the Canadian Council of Social Development (which therefore calculates higher rates of poverty). Statistics Canada LICOs are updated periodically and account for community and family size (see Table 13.2 for Statistics Canada low-income cut-offs), and the poverty lines are set at a level where a family spends significantly more of its income on food, clothing, and housing than the average family. The MBM (Market Basket Measure) is a more recent approach, and includes allowances for food, household expenses, clothing, personal needs, furniture, telephone, and entertainment (National Council of Welfare, 2003).

However, as argued by Ward (2002), these cut-off points are somewhat arbitrary or artificial, since a family with an income 10 percent above the poverty line could afford only a couple of cups a coffee per day more than those at the poverty line. Other critics of this approach also argue: "Who defines what is essential to keep a family out of poverty?" pointing to the fact that what is really being measured is relative poverty (Harman, 2005; Jackson, 2000).

"Relative poverty" is what is considered poor relative to what the contemporary social standards are for "normal" and "wealthy." It can also have a subjective component. For example, most of us probably feel poor compared to Donald Trump or Paris Hilton, yet we might feel wealthy relative to people living in drought-ridden parts of Africa or on Canadian streets. However, these reference points are obviously not really fair compari-

Table 13.2
Fact Sheet: 2008 Poverty Lines

Family Size	Community Size				
	Cities of 500,000+	100,000– 499,999	30,000– 99,000	Less than 30,000	Rural Areas
1	$22,171	$19,094	$18,976	$17,364	$15,262
2	$27,601	$23,769	$23,623	$21,615	$19,000
3	$33,933	$29,222	$29,041	$26,573	$23,358
4	$41,198	$35,480	$35,261	$32,264	$28,361
5	$46,727	$40,239	$39,992	$36,594	$32,165
6	$52,699	$45,385	$45,105	$41,272	$36,278
7+	$58,673	$50,529	$50,218	$45,950	$40,390

Source: Statistics Canada's Before-Tax Low-Income Cut-offs (1992 Base) for 2008; National Council of Welfare, "Factsheet 1" (Ottawa: National Council of Welfare, 2009).

sons since we are more likely to compare ourselves with our neighbours (i.e., "keeping up with the Joneses") or to our peer groups in our community. Moreover, these standards are not permanent, and can change with economic fluctuations, technological developments, and varying definitions of the "good life" (Harman, 2005). They can also fluctuate over the course of our lives in response to expectations that we might hold at certain points in time. For example, as a university student, you might feel relatively "well off" if you live at home and have access to your parents' car, some cash in your pockets, and a small savings account to meet your basic monthly expenses. However, at the age of 40 (and married with two kids) you might feel relatively poor in the same situation, when you might expect to own your own home and car, and have more financial resources.

Moreover, factors that influence the impact of poverty on families are its duration and depth. Duration refers to how long the experience of poverty lasts, since the repercussions of poverty will probably be very different. When poverty is experienced in childhood and adulthood, chances are good that its effects will be felt into old age. This is because disadvantage that begins in childhood (e.g., lack of a good education, malnutrition, stress) accumulates over time to produce deficits in employment and health in mid- and later life. Also, when poverty is prolonged, everyday resources are eventually depleted, making it difficult to get ahead. Depth of poverty, on the other hand, relates to the amount a family or individual income is below the poverty line. As such, the deeper the depth, the more difficult it is to provide basic needs (Ward, 2002).

Finally, while there are numerous definitions of economic vulnerability, its opposite, "economic security," has been defined by the Canadian Council on Social Development (CCSD) as follows:

> Economic security refers to an assured and stable standard of living that provides individuals and families with a level of resources and benefits necessary to participate economically, politically, socially, culturally, and with dignity in their community's activities. Security goes beyond mere physical survival to encompass a level of resources that promotes social inclusion. (Jackson et al., 2002)

Why Are Some Families Poorer Than Others? Blaming the Victim and Social Reproduction of Poverty Arguments

What are the origins of poverty? Obviously, this is not a simple question to answer, since most conditions are not the result of one causal factor, yet it is common to hear one of two common explanations for this phenomenon. The first explanation, which we will call the "blame the victim" argument, focuses on personal sources and places blame squarely on the shoulders of the individual. Early sociologists such as Herbert Spencer, for example, considered poverty a marker of human genetic "fitness" (or rather "unfitness"). In other words, people are poor because they do not possess the ability, such as the IQ or the creativity, to become anything else. In a similar vein, the culture of poverty thesis (Lewis, 1969) holds that certain types of cultures restrict people from reaching their potential. It is argued that poor families tend to develop fatalistic values and attitudes, low aspirations, have political apathy, devalue education, and reject middle-class defini-tions of success. Once this culture is in place, it develops mechanisms that perpetuate it, even if structural conditions change. This creates a self-fulfilling prophecy in which failure is inevitable and poverty perpetuates poverty (Harman, 2005).

Not surprisingly, this theory is not without its controversy since critics maintain that there are many problems with the culture of poverty conceptions. Notably, it assumes that an individual's behaviours are caused by their values rather than their conditions or constraints in life. It also leads to a circular or tautological argument in relating values to behaviour such as "individuals have little interest in success because they have a culture characterized by low success." Conversely, research shows that most poor people do not want to be poor and actually value middle-class lifestyles (e.g., see Liebow, 2003). However, they are unable to attain the opportunities (e.g., "good jobs") needed to afford these kinds of lifestyles. This theory also assumes that people's culture is fixed or static and cannot change. Moreover, the idea that certain groups such as racial or ethnic groups "have" a culture is not very compelling in understanding racial or ethnic disparities in poverty. Indeed, as noted in Chapter 3, a single culture can represent very diverse fami-lies such that larger intra- (within) group differences than inter- (between) group differ-ences by cultural group may exist.

A second explanation locates the source of poverty in systematic or structural sources (Ambert, 2006). These origins deal more with social conditions that generate poverty, such as discrimination and unequal opportunities in educational and occupational realms. Major causes are also linked to macro changes in the economy (i.e., the global recession; restructuring of the labour market resulting in loss of employment) and the decline of well-paid, unionized, entry-level jobs in manufacturing, and pay inequity by gender. They are also associated with a social reproduction of poverty process, or the tendency for social stratification to reproduce itself generationally. As a result, a child born into poverty "inherits" similar social and economic conditions and opportunities as his or her parents, resulting in poverty or a relatively similar socio-economic status later in life.

Even though the general public, media, and public policy makers tend to favour personal explanations (Ambert, 2006), there appears to be more empirical support for the latter argu-ment. This is despite the fact that many people think of our society as a meritocracy, or that we all have an equal chance of success such that those at the top are those with the most merit and talent. It is assumed that because we live in a liberal democracy, everyone has the same opportunity for upward mobility if they have the corresponding talent and ambition. This line of reasoning is reflected in attitudes such as, "people on welfare are lazy bums," and receives additional support from anecdotal stories of individuals who can tell "rags to riches" stories because they have "made it rich" through their hard work.

Yet, most individuals born into poverty do not become wealthy adults, just as most peo-ple born into wealth do not become poor adults, although there may be some movement in upward (or downward) social mobility. Generally, poverty is socially structured to the extent that social classes reproduce themselves. The fact that poverty tends to be socially structured also means that certain groups are more vulnerable to poverty than others.

Trends in Poverty and Social Groups Vulnerable to Poverty

As previously stated, about 1 in 10 Canadian children live in poverty and it is well documented that some children are at a greater risk of poverty than others. For example, there are regional and subgroup variations in child poverty and the average amount required reaching the poverty line. These regional differences provide a good example of how poverty is socially structured and reflect differences in employment or economic opportunities and conditions. Additionally, subgroup variations in child poverty rates show how persistent social and economic inequality produces a stronger likelihood of experiencing poverty. In Figure 13.1, for example, we can see how immigrants, racialized groups, those with an Aboriginal identity, and those with a disability are clearly at a higher risk for poverty than others (Campaign 2000, 2010).

Furthermore, there has been little progress in narrowing the gap between rich and poor families. In fact, the distribution of income between classes has remained remarkably intransigent over the past 50 years (Harman, 2005). Recent data also reveal that the average income of the wealthiest share of families with children increased more

Figure 13.1
Child Poverty Rates (in Percentage), for Selected Social Groups in Canada: Children 0–14 Years, 2006

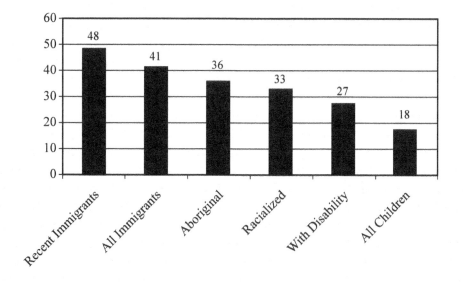

Source: Based on Canadian Census, 2006, cited in the 2010 Report Card on Child and Family Poverty (p. 5), retrieved May 31, 2011, from www.campaign2000.ca.

than twice as much (39 percent over the past 19 years) compared to family incomes for the poorest tenth of Canada's population (14 percent from 1989 to 2008). The slow growth of the average income of all families with children (20 percent over 19 years) shows why middle-income families experience economic insecurity. Furthermore, it is observed that since the early 1990s, tax changes at all levels of government have altered a somewhat progressive tax system into a less progressive one. The result of these trends show that high-income Canadians gained the most and that inequality among the classes was aggravated (Campaign 2000, 2010).

Using a feminist political economy lens, Gazo (2007) argues that the recent retrenchment of the welfare state and changes to social policy has made it increasingly difficult for many of the poorest parents to get ahead. Focusing on social assistance, it is documented that entitlement to state-based income support is increasingly contingent on employability efforts (e.g. mandatory job searches, participation in welfare-to-work programs). She states that "this entitlement relationship is implicated by simultaneous and contradictory processes embedded in neo-liberal restructuring—gendering and familization—that problematically affect parents' ability to balance their actual or potential employability expectations with family caregiving demands" (p. 32).

Consequently, it is argued that welfare reform threatens feminist gains and social justice goals. It also undermines family and financial stability, since parents are forced to adopt survival strategies (as illustrated in Box 13.1) to manage these competing demands just to "stay afloat." Hence, living on social assistance in neo-liberal times is "analogous to trying to stay afloat in a leaking life raft that keeps changing course, and at times, appears more or less buoyant" (p. 55). Thus, this research reveals growing obstacles for vulnerable families to make ends meet. It also dispels the popular idea that most of these parents are using and abusing the system for a "free ride." Not only is it very difficult for individuals to access and understand all of the complicated policy rules and regulations, but maintaining eligibility for such meagre benefits can hardly be considered a pleasant or lucrative financial experience.

The Working Poor
Many people who live in poverty have jobs and are called the working poor. According to Ross et al. (2000), the typical working poor family most likely lives in a city in Ontario, has not received much education, has many children, is fairly young, with the parents aged between 25 to 44, and likely to have only one employed wage earner. Despite this employment, parents may be earning only minimum wage, and these rates have not kept pace with inflation. In 2011, minimum wages ranged from a low of $8.75 in British Columbia to highs of $10.25 in Ontario and $11.00 in Nunavut, amounts that are deemed by many to be inadequate in covering basic living costs. Since housing is particularly expensive, families have to cut back in other ways, and one area is food. Food insecurity is the uncertainty that people can buy enough nutritious food (see Figure 13.2 for prevalence of food insecurity by household income). To fill this gap, families turn to food banks, soup kitchens, and friends or relatives for help.

Box 13.1
Staying Afloat on Social Assistance: Parents' Strategies of Balancing Employability Expectations and Caregiving Demands

Based on a qualitative study conducted by Amber Gazo (2007) at York University, the following quotes illustrate some of the experiences and coping strategies used by parents to balance policy expectations of their employability with their caregiving demands. Overall, common strategies reported by study respondents—46 parents who self-identified as being on social assistance (41 mothers—13 from common law families and 28 lone mothers; 5 lone fathers)—include "learning the system," "learning to play the system," "reliance on support systems," and "pawning." Pawning, in particular, shows the harmful and punitive effects of neo-liberal policy reforms on parents' lives.

So you know, you have to really know the legislation to be able to benefit at all. If you don't know anything about the legislation, then you're going to get your straight cheque once a month, that's it, there you go. Come back, give us your stub, you'll get another cheque next month. But if you know the legislation, you can get those extra things, which we are all entitled to. But they do not let legislation be known, publicly known (Kara, lone mother, three children).

We deal as honestly as we can. But there's other people that just can't make it...she'll go on welfare and he'll go up north and work. And there's so much of that here. Or you know, whatever. And that's just so that they can provide a good life for their kids. It's not so that they can rich. Nobody goes on welfare to get rich. You know, they go on it to get by (Doreen, common law, six children).

My mom's helped me out too you know with food and stuff like that....I have been using the food bank a lot, but she helps with uh, she'll help with food when she can and, um, just even friends you know. Like we'll help each other out you know. This month I'm having a bad month or whatever so they'll help me out. And then I'll help them out another time or whatever (Nadine, common law, two children).

I have a stereo in the pawn shop and my DVD/VCR combo. [We put them there] because we're running low on some groceries. Like on fruit and milk and stuff like that...Well I feel bad because like, you know, my kids like watching their movies and stuff like that. And plus at times it kind of gets hard to try and get them at all. I actually thought I was going to lose my VCR/DVD combo but I ended up borrowing money from my mom to pay the interest on it for another three months. Because it gets hard to pay things, you know, to keep up with bills and trying to get things out of the pawn (Janice, lone mother, two children).

Source: Gazo, A. 2007. "Staying afloat on social assistance: Parents' strategies of balancing employability expectations and caregiving demands." *Socialist Studies*, 3: 31–57.

Box 13.2
Who Is Hungry in Canada?

While anyone is at risk of food insecurity at some point in their lives, certain groups are particularly vulnerable:

Welfare Recipients
People receiving welfare assistance as their primary sources of income continue to make up the largest group of food bank users. This year, 51.6 percent of food bank clients in Canada were receiving welfare. This suggests that welfare rates in Canada do not do enough to ensure food security for low-income Canadians. According to the National Council of Welfare, welfare rates across Canada continue to fall below the poverty lines.

Working Poor
People with jobs constitute the second largest group of food bank clients, at 13.1 percent. Anecdotal evidence in the HungerCount 2005 report shows that the majority of food bank clients with jobs are employed at low wages. The expansion of the low-wage economy has generated more working poor who, even with full-time jobs, are unable to meet basic needs for themselves and their families.

Persons with Disabilities
Those receiving disability support have made up the third largest group of food bank clients in the last four years, according to successive HungerCount surveys. It is just one more example of the broader crisis of inadequate social assistance in Canada. Disability support is clearly not enough to help clients feed themselves. If current disability programs and rates do not improve we expect to see a rise in food insecurity among this demographic, since Canada has a rapidly aging society and life expectancy is increasing.

Seniors
Seniors accessing food banks cross Canada is a sad reality. HungerCount 2005 reports that seniors accounted for 7.1 percent of food bank users in a typical month of 2005. This is an increase from the previous year when 6.4 percent of food bank clients were seniors.

Children
Children continue to be over-represented among food bank recipients in Canada. This year, 40.7 percent of food bank clients were under 18. Child poverty has not improved since 1989, the year when Canada made an all-party resolution to end child poverty. Child poverty is directly tied to the level of household income. Among food bank clients, families with children make up more than 50 percent of recipients.

Lone Mothers

Lone mothers and their children are still one of Canada's most economically vulnerable groups. It is likely that many of the food bank users who are sole parents (29.5 percent), as reported in HungerCount 2005, are women; according to Statistics Canada, the majority of single-parent or lone-parent families are headed by women (85 percent of Canada's lone-parent families).

Solutions

Hunger, as a symptom of poverty, is a structural problem. Sustainable solutions to hunger and poverty require a mix of system-based policies aimed at improving the incomes and income security of poor Canadians, such as raising social assistance rates and minimum wages, improving access to employment insurance, and developing a national child care system.

Source: Canadian Association of Food Banks. 2006. Retrieved February 1 at www.cafb~acba.ca/english/EducationandResearch.html.

Shockingly, people with jobs comprise the second largest group of food bank users (see Box 13.2 for an overview of "Who Is Hungry in Canada"). Young adults also account for a sizable proportion of the working poor. Two-thirds of minimum wage workers are under the age of 25, although it should be recognized that the majority of these young people are still in school and many live at home, which is generally more economical. The good news is that many young people—especially those that complete a university degree compared to those with lower levels of education, will have a relatively lower incidence of earning a low wage as older-aged adults, as shown in Table 13.4.

Overall, some social groups are disproportionately affected by poverty and economic hardship, further revealing how social stratification has its roots in structured inequities rather than simply the result of individual failure. Moreover, although the situating is improving, among all age and social groups, women tend to be more vulnerable to poverty.

Women

It is well established that poverty tends to affect women more than men. This has led researchers to call the growth of poverty among women "the feminization of poverty," a term coined by Diana Pearce in 1978. Women at highest risk of living in poverty are single mothers—in 2000, 40.1 percent of lone-mother families were below the low-income cut-offs, making these families the group with the highest incidence of family poverty in Canada. While this percentage significantly dropped in 2009 to 21.5 percent, this rate remains three times higher than the proportion of individuals living in two-parent families (see Table 13.3). Men in single-parent families are also more

Figure 13.2
Prevalence of Food Insecurity (in Percentages), by Household Income*

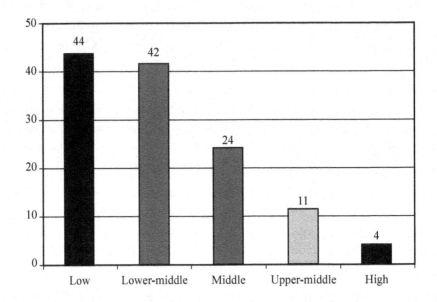

Notes: 14.7 percent of the population aged 12 or older had experienced food insecurity. Respondents aged 12 and older were asked, if, because of a lack of money, in the previous year they or someone in their household had not eaten the quality or variety of food that they had wanted; had worried about not having enough to eat; or had actually not had enough to eat. Thus, households are considered "food insecure" if they had been in at least one of these situations because of lack of money.

Source: 2000/01 Canadian Community Health Survey, cited in I. Ledrou and J. Gervais, "Food Insecurity," *Health Reports* 16, no. 3 (2005): 47.

likely than other men to experience long-term poverty (Statistics Canada, 2011). Finding affordable housing is a particularly difficult challenge for single-parent families, particularly in large urban centres.

Moreover, although the percentage of women in the paid labour market is higher than before, not only do women earn less than men, they are also more likely to be in part-time or non-standard employment that pays low or minimum wages. Women are more likely to be employed as low paid, non-unionized part-time workers in clerical, sales, and service jobs (pink-collar jobs). Men's work, conversely, has been compartmentalized into more highly paid, high-status white-collar jobs and relatively well-paid blue-collar sectors (Campaign 2000, 2006).

Table 13.3
Percentage of Persons in Low Income, 2000 and 2009*

	2000	2009
All persons	12.5	9.6
Persons under 18 years in economic families	13.8	9.5
In two-parent families	9.5	7.3
In female lone-parent families	40.1	21.5
Persons 18 to 64 years old	12.9	10.5
Persons 65 and over	7.6	5.2

*Figures based on a 1992 base after-tax income low-income cut-offs.

Source: Statistics Canada (2011). Data extracted from Table 3: Percentage of Persons in Low Income. Retrieved from www.statcan.gc/daily-quotidien/110615/t110615b3-eng.htm.

Disabled Individuals

The World Health Organization defines disability as "any restriction or lack (resulting from impairment) of ability to perform an activity in the manner or within the range considered normal for a human being." This definition suggests the essence of the experience of being in a disabled body in the sense that the world of work, family, and life in general is the privileged sphere of non-disabled people, or the "normals." It was not that long ago that those who did not conform to the category of "normal" were regarded as "freaks," not entitled to work in the public sphere, or to have love, happiness, and family in the private sphere (Goffman, 1963; Harman, 2005).

Fortunately, times have changed and opportunities for disabled individuals have broadened on many levels, yet previous and continuing discrimination have left disabled people vulnerable to poverty. Moreover, the prevalence rate of working-age people with disabilities who are living below Statistics Canada's LICO is 15 percent, compared to 6.5 percent for non-disabled Canadians. Rates also vary widely depending upon the type disability. For example, those with any cognitive or psychological disability have a poverty rate of 22.3 percent while those with a hearing disability have a poverty rate of 10.3 percent (Council of Canadians with Disabilities, 2010). Moreover, when gender, ethnic or Aboriginal status, and disability are combined, individuals can be doubly or triply disadvantaged. Finally, it should also be noted that many disabled people who are not in the workforce rely on various forms of state support, such as disability pensions, and these pensions are relatively meagre (Council of Canadians with Disabilities, 2010).

Box 13.3
Poverty and Disability: My Lived Experience

The following presentation was made on behalf of People First, an organization of people with intellectual disabilities. The speaker, Calvin Wood, was invited to speak at the "Disability Poverty/Enabling Citizenship: End Exclusion 2010" conference in Ottawa in early November, 2010. This conference was sponsored by the Council of Canadians with Disabilities and the Canadian Association for Community Living.

My name is Calvin Wood. I live in Windsor, Nova Scotia, and I am in my second term as President of People First Nova Scotia. My presentation is about poverty and disability and what it means to me. I am a person with a disability and living on social assistance. I find that after I pay my bills, like rent and phone and cable, I am left with $250 a month for food, household things like clothing, coffee, and anything else I might need or want to do. That works out to about $7 a day for everything.

The cost of food goes up and my pension cheques stay the same. Other costs go up, like cable or phone, and my disability pension stays the same. I shop for clothes at thrift shops so I don't buy anything new. I have my clothes on today from thrift shops. I like going to Tim's sometimes for lunch or for coffee, but I often don't have any money left to do that. It costs a lot to buy healthy food. I need help to pick the right food and I need more money to buy things that will keep me healthy. I would like to have more to live on.

I get $50 a month for work I do at a store in Wolfville and I get a bus pass. If I have a job making more money, I would have to deduct the wage from my pension so really, with my disability, it is hard to earn enough to make a difference in what money I have. I'm lucky, though, that I am supported by a group called SSG—the Support Services Group. I have an attendant who helps me for six hours a week and I live by myself in an apartment. I get help with washing, food shopping and other personal items. I have help from the coordinator of SSG with banking, medication, and recreation. My attendant goes with me once a month to shop. Then in between, I get the groceries I need. SSG gets $400 a month and my attendant gets $276. My rent is $550 including heat and electricity. I wish some of that money could come to me so I could do more things.

My $50 goes to the Internet. I have a laptop that my sister got me and I spend a lot of time emailing friends and being on the Internet. Some of my friends are worse off than me. Some don't get any help even though they have a disability. My friend Evelyn gets only small social assistance. My friend Donna, who is vice president of People First Nova Scotia, doesn't get help for her teeth or glasses and has to use the food bank. Another friend is not on assistance and works part-time. He can barely pay his rent and has no one to help with medications.

We are all very poor. I like being here in this nice hotel, all my expenses are paid so I'm really lucky, but I don't have any other money to go anywhere or to buy anything so I'm not really too lucky. I would like the public to be aware that living on social assistance puts the person, that is me and many of my friends and most of our People First members, in poverty. And then when we try to work, they cut back on the assistance. And how we can buy clothes for work and pay for the transportation to get there? It is like they try to keep people with intellectual disabilities poor and dependent.

I have been a member of People First for 15 years. We are trying to support each other and we come together from all over the province of Nova Scotia, and we come together from all over Canada and we discuss things that are important to us. We need jobs that will help us to be helpful in our communities and that will help us to live with some respect. We care that people with intellectual disabilities are still placed in institutions. Imagine how poor they are. No jobs, no going to Tim's with friends, no choices in what to eat. No way to get to be a member of groups like People First. No way to live like the rest us here, that is in poverty.

I'm learning that we have rights like all Canadians. What I'm not sure is if having rights will help us come out of poverty. Thank you.

Calvin would like to thank Joan Paguette for helping him to prepare this speech.

Source: Community Stories, 2010 (December). "Poverty and disability: My lived experience." Ottawa: Caledon Institute of Social Policy.

Aboriginal Families, Visible Minorities, and Recent Immigrants

As discussed previously, Aboriginal, visible minority, and immigrant families are more likely to experience poverty and economic vulnerability than other groups, and as just noted, child poverty rates are very high among these groups (Campaign 2000, 2006). Aboriginal families have faced a history of systemic discrimination at the hands of an imperialistic state. Urban Aboriginal peoples, for example, are more than twice as likely to live in poverty as non-Aboriginals (Harman, 2005). Aboriginal single parents are particularly prone to poverty, especially those with a large number of children and large households. Moreover, adult Aboriginals are more likely to face racial discrimination, be younger, have lower education levels, and are more likely to be unemployed compared to the Canadian average (McDaniel and Tepperman, 2004).

Recent immigrant families (with the majority classified as visible minority) are also highly vulnerable to living in poverty. Many find themselves among the low-wage poor compared to Canadian-born or more established immigrants (as shown in Table 13.4), or those working full-year, full-time for low wages. Moreover, some visible minority families (e.g., Arabic, Black/Caribbean, Latin American) are at a greater risk of unemployment, underemployment, and low income. Issues of education and work experience from another country (among foreign-born), language barriers, and general marginalization play a role in these patterns (Mitchell, 2005). Marginalization occurs when individuals are systematically excluded from meaningful participation in social, political, and economic activities in their communities.

Table 13.4
Incidence of Low Wage, by Highest Level of Education and Immigrant Status

		Percent in low wage					
		By highest level of education		For immigrants and the Canadian born			
		High-school or less	Non-University Post-Secondary Certificate	University degree	Canadian born	Recent immi-grants	Estab-lished immi-grants
	Total	%				%	
1993	16.1	23.4	12.4	4.5	15.2	45.7	13.6
1994	17.0	24.0	13.4	6.8	16.7	35.7	13.0
1995	15.0	20.7	12.6	6.3	14.7	36.5	11.1
1996	20.6	27.2	17.4	9.8	19.9	37.8	18.4
1997	18.0	24.8	14.9	6.4	17.4	34.0	15.9
1998	16.7	23.6	14.1	5.9	16.3	33.0	15.0
1999	14.3	20.9	10.9	4.4	13.3	33.0	13.4
2000	14.0	20.9	10.6	3.5	13.6	26.5	12.2
2001	14.0	21.5	10.3	2.9	13.5	24.0	12.4
2002	14.0	21.1	11.0	4.3	13.3	27.1	12.5
2003	14.8	22.8	12.0	4.4	14.2	25.2	13.6
2004	14.4	22.5	11.4	4.2	13.7	26.4	13.4

Source: Statistics Canada Low Wage and Low Income, Research Paper, Canada Year Book 2008, Income Research Paper Series, Catalogue no. 75F0002MIE – No. 006, Table 4, p. 9, based on the Survey of Labour and Income Dynamics.

The Senior Situation
Over time, there has been a significant decline in poverty among seniors (defined as persons aged 65 and over) as a result of improved pensions and government benefits. As shown in Table 13.3, seniors are the least vulnerable to poverty, since only 5 percent of seniors are classified as living under the LICO. Most elderly receive their income from public programs rather than paid employment. Yet, there is an overall trend toward delayed retirement for both financial and personal reasons, a topic that was covered previously in Chapter 11. If the individual was employed, Canada or Quebec Pension Plans supply an income. Old Age Security (OAS) is paid to all seniors, although it is subject to clawback at higher income levels. Those with low incomes can receive additional benefits through the Guaranteed Income Supplement (GIS).

The combination of these benefits keeps many seniors above the poverty line, although a large number are among the near-poor (Ward, 2002). Unfortunately, many of the elderly poor are women, since they are more likely to be unattached and they live longer than men. This means that they are at greater risk of using up their savings over time. Women who are separated or divorced have much lower retirement incomes than do widows or single women (who have likely invested in their career and have accrued higher retirement incomes), as most divorced women do not claim a portion of their former spouse's pension despite being entitled to it. They are also less likely to have contributed to the Canada or Quebec Pension Plan and are more dependent on the Supplement (65 percent of GIS beneficiaries are women).

Many elderly visible minority people do not qualify for pensions, making them especially vulnerable to poverty. As a result, many must rely on other family members for food and shelter, which can create strain, overcrowding, and dependency issues (Mitchell, 2005). In general, poverty is most common among seniors living alone, women over the age of 80, visible minorities, and immigrants (National Advisory Council on Aging, 2005).

Under Pressure: The Shrinking Middle Class and the Financial Squeeze

Although middle-class families are generally able to afford the basic necessities of life and enjoy a fairly decent standard of living relative to poorer families, it should not be assumed that these families never have to struggle financially to make ends meet. Middle-class families are usually defined as the 60 percent of families who are neither the poorest 20 percent, nor the richest 20 percent. These families are also diverse, for example, in 2007 this group included families with after-tax incomes as low as $37,101 or as high as $97,600. And although median family income in Canada is higher today than it was three decades ago, it is well documented that the middle class is facing considerable financial pressure, despite the fact that their work time has dramatically increased. Moreover, the overall proportion of middle-income families has been reduced, while the share of low- and high-income families has grown, trends largely attributed to rising inequalities in income distribution (Vanier Institute of the Family, 2010).

As a result, many "average" Canadian households are increasingly carrying a large debt load and are finding it difficult to get ahead. Yalnizyan (2010) reports that not only do Canadians have one of the worst debt-to-income ratios of 20 OECD nations, but that the savings rate of Canadians ($2.80 on every $100 of household income) is less than half that of the U.S. Overall, a rising number of middle-class families report financial difficulties related to paying bills and heavy debt (e.g., credit card, mortgages) due to the high costs associated with daily living, especially in urban areas with high food and housing costs. Middle-class parents are also increasingly relied upon by their older-aged children for housing assistance, rising educational costs, transportation, and other expenses (e.g., consumer goods) due to changing socio-demographic and labour market conditions, as discussed in Chapter 10.

Poverty, Negative Outcomes, and the Life Course

As presented in Box 13.4, the potentially adverse consequences of poverty and economic hardship on families are numerous and often persist over the life course. These consequences are well documented and are intensified the longer an individual is impoverished. However, poverty can strike at any time due to certain circumstances like unemployment, sickness, divorce, or addiction. Moreover, although most research focuses on negative consequences, it should not be assumed that being poor translates into a wretched existence, devoid of happiness, love, and close-knit family relations. For example, economic hardship might bring some family members closer together since there is a greater need to collectively pool resources and rely on each other for various types of support.

Box 13.4
Pathways to Poverty

There is clustering of advantage and disadvantage among Canadians. Individuals who are advantaged as children by way of income and wealth are more likely to achieve higher education levels, better paying and more secure employment. The availability of greater amounts of income and wealth also facilitate access to a variety of other commodities that shape health and quality of life (Bryant, 2004).

These include quality daycare, cultural and educational activities, leisure opportunities, and food and housing security. These material living conditions shape psychological understandings of the world and promote a sense of control over one's life, feelings of self-efficacy, and a belief that the world is understandable. Those living in poverty are likely to experience the opposite living conditions and develop little sense of control, self-efficacy, and a belief that the world is understandable.

Together, these positive or negative life experiences and the psychological concomitants of experiencing these conditions shape an individual's trajectories over time. Material and social disadvantage associated with poverty contributes to lower educational achievement and employment that provides less compensation and security, which then contribute to continuing material and social disadvantage.

Similarly, policies that reduce the availability and affordability of housing and the amount of financial resources available to people affect resources available to Canadians. This is so since these policies—low social assistance rates and minimum wages, lack of affordable housing—reduce the resources that can support other social determinants of health such as early life, food security, education, and recreation. Together these issues come together to have direct effects upon health and quality of life.

Source: Raphael, D. 2007. "Pathways to poverty," in *Poverty and Policy in Canada: Implications for Health and Quality of Life.* Toronto: Canadian Scholars' Press (Excerpt from Chapter 5, p. 21).

With this in mind, compared to other children, those exposed to poverty (especially over a long duration) or suffer severe economic loss generally have poorer physical health and more chronic health problems. They are more likely to be born with nutritional deficiencies and low birth weight, which are linked to developmental processes. In general, poor children tend to have more socio-emotional mental health and behavioural problems (e.g., depression, attention deficit disorder) than do more affluent children (Seccombe and Warner, 2004; Ward, 2002). They also have more frequent accidents because their surroundings are less safe (Ambert, 2006).

There are also strong associations between poverty and educational outcomes—poor children typically have fewer resources and opportunities for learning and educational achievement. This decreases their stock of cultural capital or knowledge of middle-class or "high culture." It is argued that access to cultural capital results in certain behaviours, lifestyle preferences, and predispositions that help children do better in school. For example, poor children may have limited vocabularies and less frequent participation in "high society" cultural activities, such as travelling or going to museums and libraries. As a result, teachers tend to give these children less attention and assistance and perceive them less favourably. In turn, poor children typically receive lower grades and are less likely to graduate from high school and to attend college or university. And since educational attainment is associated with adult socio-economic status, poor children often grow up to be poor adults. For example, those with less than a high school diploma are almost 10 times as likely to be working for minimum wage or less than those with a university degree (Statistics Canada, 2005). In this way, a lack of cultural capital, as well as social capital (which creates opportunities through social networks or "connections") contributes to the reproduction of the structure of power relationships and symbolic relationships between classes (Bellamy, 1994).

Overall, poor adults have significantly higher morbidity (sickness), in addition to lower rates of life expectancy than other adults (Seccombe and Warner, 2004). This is because income is highly correlated with health and disease, using both objective and subjective diseases, as outlined in Chapter 12. They are also more likely to work in dangerous occupations and live in unsafe or crime-ridden neighbourhoods. Housing problems are more common, which results in a higher likelihood of becoming homeless or living in crowded or substandard living conditions. In fact, homelessness is a serious problem in Canada, and the situation does not seem to be improving.

Poverty can also affect the formation and quality of intimate relations. This is because financial struggle often creates stress and strain, which can spill over into family relationships. For example, the chronic unemployment of one spouse can undermine marital stability and marital happiness. Poor families are also more likely to move than wealthier families, which can disrupt the formation of friendship and social networks in the community (Ward, 2002). This trajectory contributes to isolating people socially, and deprives families of social capital. Indeed, low-income Canadians are less likely to report that they trust other people or to participate in community activities than are other Canadians (Statistics Canada, 2004).

Box 13.5
How Paying People's Way Out of Poverty Can Help Us All

[...] When people are poor, out of work or homeless, it hurts the bottom line of all Canadians. And as the country struggles to maintain a shaky recovery amid growing global economic uncertainty, that's not a hit they can afford to take.

If Ottawa and the provinces fail to make this a priority, Tory Senator Hugh Segal predicts, "over time, we will begin to run out of the money that we need to deal with the demographic bulge because it will be consumed in the health care requirements of the poor, which will increase. It will be consumed in the costs of the illiteracy and unemployment which relate to poverty. ... And it'll be unsustainable."

It's not just Canada's problem: income inequality is sparking social unrest in the Middle East, North Africa and China. It rang alarm bells at the Organization for Economic Co-operation and Development's conference in Paris this week, where the think tank warned that if a slew of countries—from Sweden to Canada to the United Kingdom—don't take drastic action by raising taxes for the richest, they risk runaway increases in inequality.

[...] Calgary's business community crunched the numbers: It costs four times more to pay for a year's worth of emergency shelter, emergency-room medical care and law enforcement for one homeless person than it costs to fund that person's supportive housing for a year.

More recent figures have backed them up when it comes to the costs of poverty: a study earlier this year from Toronto's St. Michael's Hospital found homeless patients cost hospitals an average of $2,559 more than their housed counterparts.

By the numbers
$134,000
Estimated amount for emergency shelter, emergency hospital care, law enforcement and other social services for one homeless person in Calgary, for one year
$34,000
Estimated cost to provide supportive housing for one person in Calgary, for one year
$12,555
Average cost of hospital stay for non-homeless patient at St. Michael's Hospital in Toronto
$15,114
Average cost of hospital stay for homeless patient at St. Michael's Hospital in Toronto

At the same time, research into projects that guaranteed people a minimum annual income indicated savings in everything from social services and health care to law enforcement. The philosophy behind this is simple: people making a decent living are more likely to stay in school, out of emergency rooms and out of jail; they contribute to their economy through purchases; they are more likely to move eventually above the poverty line and pay taxes.

Source: Paperny, Anna Mehler, and T. Grant. Excerpt take from *The Globe and Mail*, 5-6 May, 2011, retrieved from www.theglobeandmail.com/news/politics/how-paying-peoples-way-out-of-poverty-can-help-us-all/article2011940.

Summary

Contrary to the perception that Canada is a relatively egalitarian society with a fair distribution of income across social groups, it is a deeply stratified, class-based nation, with some families experiencing great economic struggle. And regardless of the fact that Canada is one of the wealthiest countries in the world and has experienced continued economic growth, rising employment, and record job creation, poverty remains a rampant and serious problem. Moreover, despite a political landscape "littered with political rhetoric about children," Canada has had only modest success in reducing child poverty (National Council of Welfare, 1999). Certain social groups are also more vulnerable to poverty than others, such as women, the disabled, Aboriginals, and visible minorities. For example, at every stage of their lives, women are more vulnerable to poverty than men, and more prone to be trapped, and eventually die in a state of poverty (Harman, 2005). And for a significant number of older-aged Canadians, the prospect of a golden retirement simply does not exist (National Advisory Council on Aging, 2005).

And while it is common to "blame the victim" for their situation, it is clear that some families simply do not have access to the same types of opportunities, resources, and privileges. Indeed, there is a tendency for social classes to reproduce themselves, as is shown in the tendency for individuals from poor family backgrounds to be underrepresented in higher education and professional or managerial occupational sectors. In short, available evidence shows that it is the economy and class system that usually create these conditions rather than personality traits such as a lack of motivation, a rejection of middle-class values, or poor parental socialization.

In closing, "blaming the victim" for their poverty does little to improve the situation. Instead, it is more fruitful to examine the interaction between individuals and society and to look at the processes by which people struggle to overcome their challenges and obstacles (McDaniel and Tepperman, 2004). This idea also beckons us to dig deeper beyond mere labels of poverty to understand systematic sources of inequality and behooves us to contemplate how this social problem costs us all (also refer to Box 13.5). Hence, it prompts us to think about ways to reduce the negative experience and consequences of poverty, in order to break the vicious cycle of economic hardship.

Questions for Critical Reflection and Debate

1. Debate the following: If people work hard enough in life, they will not have to experience poverty.
2. How might poverty affect the kinds of intimate relations or unions that people form?
3. Do you think that processes of globalization and future technological advances will deepen or decrease the prevalence of poverty in Canada and in other societies?
4. Critically outline strategies at the government and community level to reduce poverty and its effects. Why have previous strategies failed?
5. Studies show that homeless children suffer high rates of developmental, mental, and behavioural problems and that many of their problems persist into adulthood. Discuss possible reasons for these outcomes.
6. Analyze the following statement: financial wealth broadens families' social and cultural capital.

Glossary

Absolute poverty is a condition of mere physical survival.
Culture of poverty refers to a fatalistic set of values, behaviours, and attitudes that is not conducive to middle-class standards of financial or material success.
Economic security refers to a standard of living that provides resources and benefits necessary for social and economic participation and social inclusion.
Feminization of poverty is the tendency for women to be poor relative to men.
Marginalization occurs when individuals are systematically excluded from meaningful participation in social, political, and economic activities in their communities.
Relative poverty is what is considered poor relative to what the contemporary social standards are for "normal" and "wealthy."
Social reproduction of poverty is the tendency for individuals born into poor families to become poor later in life.
Working poor are those individuals who experience poverty while working in the paid labour force.

Further Reading

Albanese, P. 2009. *Child Poverty in Canada*. Toronto: Oxford University Press. Provides the latest research on child poverty through an examination of trends over time, across provinces, and among various groups. She also considers theories and incorporates a global perspective.
Chappell, M. 2011. *The War on Welfare: Family, Poverty, and Politics in Modern America*. Pennsylvania, PA: University of Pennsylvania Press. Contributes to our understanding

of the effects of welfare reform on families by incorporating both conservative and liberal views, including traditional women's organizations and feminist perspectives.

Ehrenreich, B. 2008. *Nickel and Dimed: On (Not) Getting by in America*. New York: Henry Holt and Co. Provides an insightful case study of a woman who worked as a waitress, hotel maid, cleaning woman, nursing home aide, and a Wal-Mart sales clerk and her efforts to survive on minimum wage.

Hill, S.A. 2011. *Families: A Social Class Perspective*. Thousand Oaks, Calif.: Sage Publications. Examines the impact of economic systems and social class on the organization of family life and how the economy shapes the prospects families have for earning a decent living.

Kerbo, H.R. 2006. *World Poverty: Global Inequality and the Modern World System*. Boston: McGraw-Hill. Is a provocative look at development and poverty from an international perspective, and includes case studies based on Latin American, African, Asian, and the Middle Eastern nations in a global economy.

Raphael, D. 2011. *Poverty in Canada,* 2nd ed. Toronto: Canadian Scholars' Press. Presents an interdisciplinary perspective on poverty and its significance to the health and quality of life of Canadians. Particular focus is placed on the lived experience throughout the book.

Wallis, M.A., and S. Kwok (Eds.). 2011. *Daily Struggles*. Toronto: Canadian Scholars' Press. Offers a critical perspective on poverty with an emphasis on gender and race in a Canadian context. Also connects issues of human rights, political economy perspectives, and citizenship issues to other areas of social exclusion such as class, sexuality, and disability.

Related Web Sites

Campaign 2000 is a non-partisan, cross-Canada network of over 90 national, provincial, and community partner organizations committed to working together to end child and family poverty in Canada, www.campaign2000.ca. Twitter: Campaign2000

Canadian Children's Rights Council is a non-profit, non-governmental educational and advocacy organization concerned with Canadian children's human rights and responsibilities. The web site provides a virtual library, resources centre, archives, and advocacy centre for those interested in children's rights, http://www.canadiancrc.com/child_poverty_in_canada.aspx.

Food Banks Canada is a charitable organization aimed at ending hunger in Canada. The web site contains personal stories, research studies, position papers, information on advocacy and community action, as well as a link to HungerCount 2010, http://www.cafb-acba.ca/main.cfm.

National Council of Welfare is a government-funded organization that produces many reports and the most recent low-income cut-offs for different categories of people who live in poverty, http://www.ncw.gc.ca/h.4m.2@-eng.jsp.

People First of Canada is an organization and movement that is organized and directed by people who have been labelled with poverty and promotes citizenship and equality for everyone, http://www.peoplefirstofcanada.ca/index_en.php. Facebook: People First of Canada.

Raising the Roof is an advocacy-oriented organization devoted to eliminating homelessness, www.raisingtheroof.org. Facebook: Raising the Roof

References

Ambert, A.M. 2006. *Changing Families: Relationships in Context.* Toronto: Pearson Education.

Bellamy, L. 1994. "Capital, Habitus, Field, and Practice: An Introduction to the Work of Pierre Bourdieu." In L. Erwin and D. MacLennan (eds.), *Sociology of Education in Canada: Critical Perspectives on Theory, Research, and Practice* (pp. 120–136). Toronto: Copp Clark Pitman, Ltd.

Campaign 2000. 2006. *One Million Too Many: Implementing Solutions to Child Poverty in Canada, 2004 Report Card on Child Poverty in Canada.* Retrieved January 31, 2006, from www.campaign2000.ca.

Child and Family Canada. 2006. "An Introduction to Poverty in Canada." Retrieved January 30, 2006, from www.cfc~efc.ca/docs/ccsd/00000323.htm.

Council of Canadians with Disabilities. 2006. "A Call to Combat Poverty and Exclusion of Canadians with Disabilities by Investing in Disability Supports." Retrieved February 3, 2006, from www.ccdonline.ca/ccpe.htm.

Council of Canadians with Disabilities. 2010. "As a Matter of Fact: Poverty and Disability in Canada." Retrieved June 23, 2011, from www.ccdonline.ca/en/socialpolicy.

Gazo, A. 2007. "Staying Afloat on Social Assistance: Parents' Strategies of Balancing Employability Expectations and Caregiving Demands." *Socialist Studies* 3: 31–57.

Goffman, E. 1963. *Stigma: Notes on the Management of Spoiled Identity.* New York: Simon and Schuster.

Harman, L.D. 2005. "Family Poverty and Economic Struggles." In N. Mandell and A. Duffy (eds.), *Canadian Families: Diversity, Conflict, and Change*, 3rd ed. (pp. 241–275). Toronto: Thomson Nelson.

Jackson, A. 2000. "Defining and Redefining Poverty." *Perception: Canada's Social Development Magazine* 25: 3–6.

Jackson, A, S. Tsoukalas, L. Buckland, and S. Schetagne. 2002. "The Personal Security Index 2002: After September 11." Ottawa: Canadian Council on Social Development.

Lewis, O. 1966. "The Culture of Poverty." *Scientific American* 2: 19–25.

Liebow, E. 2003. *Tally's Corner: A Study of Negro Streetcorner Men.* New York: Rowman and Littlefield.

McDaniel, S.A., and L. Tepperman. 2004. *Close Relations: An Introduction to the Sociology of Families*, 2nd ed. Toronto: Pearson Education.

Mitchell, B.A. 2005. "Canada's Growing Visible Minority Population: Generational Challenges, Opportunities, and Federal Policy Considerations." In *Canada 2017: Serving Canada's Multicultural Population for the Future* (pp. 51–62), Policy Forum Discussion Papers. Gatineau: The Multiculturalism Program, Department of Canadian Heritage.

National Advisory Council on Aging. 2005. *Seniors on the Margins: Aging in Poverty in Canada*. Ottawa: Minister of Public Works and Government Services.

National Council of Welfare. 1999. *Children First: A Pre-budget Report by the National Council of Welfare*. Ottawa: National Council of Welfare.

National Council of Welfare. 2003. "Fact Sheet: Definitions of the Most Common Poverty Lines Used in Canada—June 2003." Ottawa: National Council of Welfare.

Ross, D.P., K.J. Scott, and P.J. Smith. 2000. *The Canadian Fact Book on Poverty—2000*. Ottawa: Canadian Council on Social Development.

Seccombe, K., and R.L. Warner. 2004. *Marriages and Families: Relationships in Social Context*. Toronto: Thomson Wadsworth.

Statistics Canada. 2002. "Family Income, 2000." *The Daily* (October 30).

Statistics Canada. 2004. "General Social Survey: Social Engagement." *The Daily* (July 6).

Statistics Canada. 2005. "Fact Sheet on Minimum Wage." *Perspectives on Labour and Income*. Ottawa: Minister of Industry.

Vanier Institute of the Family. 2010. *Families Count: Profiling Canada's Families IV*. Ottawa, ON: Vanier Institute of the Family.

Ward, M. 2002. *The Family Dynamic: A Canadian Perspective*, 3rd ed. Toronto: Nelson Thomson Learning.

Yalnizyan, A. 2011. "Canadian Households: Among Highest Debt to Income Ratios in the World." Ottawa: Canadian Centres for Policy Alternatives.

Chapter 14

Families in Crisis

Family Violence, Abuse, and Stress

Learning Objectives

In this chapter you will learn that ...
- there is a dark side to family life, and that certain individuals are more vulnerable to violence, abuse, and stress
- there are many definitions and various forms of violence, abuse, and stress
- this area of study is fraught with definitional and methodological challenges
- there are short- and long-term consequences of violence and abuse
- a life course, ecological perspective is important and helps us to critically evaluate explanations for violence, abuse, and stress
- there are several issues relevant to prevention and intervention

There was an old woman who lived in a shoe,
She had so many children she didn't know what to do.
She gave them some broth without any bread,
And whipped them all soundly and sent them to bed.
                    —Anonymous Mother Goose rhyme (cited in Engelbreit, 2005: 29)

Introduction

For most us of, the family represents a sacred institution that provides "a haven in a heartless world" (Lasch, 1979). As such, the family home symbolizes a cozy and safe retreat from a violent world with its legacy and repertoire of conflict, war, and terrible human atrocities, yet for many people, especially for women and children, there is a dark side to family life. In fact, our families may be one of the most violent and cruel groups to which we belong. According to one study, one-quarter of all violent crimes reported to a sample of police services involved cases of family violence (Statistics Canada, 2003). Moreover, despite fears to the contrary, it is not a stranger but a so-called loved one who is more likely to assault, rape, or murder us (DeKeseredy, 2005).

Unfortunately, many of us do not reveal these private troubles to others, and this topic has only been recently discussed in public domains. The popular daytime talk show *The Oprah Winfrey Show* was one of the first mass media forums to openly discuss familial child abuse in 1985. This landmark show included Oprah's own personal account of her childhood sexual molestation by a family member while growing up. Similarly, violence in intimate relations was kept hushed until relatively recently in scholarly realms. A review of the table of contents of *The Journal of Marriage and the Family*, the leading international journal in the field of family studies from its inception in 1939 through 1969, also shows a complete absence of the word "violence." A survey by Eichler (1983) in the 1970s further documented that violence in the family continued to be ignored by social scientists. Out of 18 textbooks on the family published or reprinted in the 1970s, only three mentioned family violence. Norms of family privacy, coupled with the sensitive nature of the issue and the assumption that it rarely happened, contributed to this "blind eye to reality" (Drakich and Guberman, 1987). Fortunately, over the last two decades studies and public awareness of this significant social problem have grown considerably.

In light of these issues, the purpose of this chapter is to examine family violence, abuse, and stress across the life course. We will begin by defining key terms and various forms of family violence, as well as providing an analysis of their consequences and explanations. Sources of family stress are also highlighted. The chapter concludes with recommendations for prevention and intervention.

What Is Family Violence and Neglect? Definitions, Forms, and Prevalence

Directly or indirectly, virtually all of us have experienced some form of family violence or neglect in our lives, but what is family violence and neglect? Defining and measuring family violence is not an easy task, since there is seldom consensus as to what constitutes a violent act. Therefore, most controversies centre on how broad (or narrow) these definitions should be. These definitions are significant since they can affect the collection of data and prevalence rates, which can have enormous social and legal implications. As a result, definitions can influence the quality and quantity of policies and social support services implemented by official agencies to deal with the issue (DeKeseredy, 2005). This can be problematic if narrow definitions are used. For example, if spousal abuse is defined by only extreme acts of violence (i.e., broken bones, murder), then government officials may be led to believe that violence against women is not a pressing social problem. As a result, they may channel fewer resources into programs and services designed to prevent and control the phenomenon (Jiwani, 2000).

Violence is defined by the World Health Organization (2005: 1) as "the intentional use of physical force or power, threatened or actual, against oneself, another person, or against a group or community that either results in or has a high likelihood of resulting in injury, death, psychological harm, maldevelopment, or deprivation." Three broad types can be identified: self-directed, interpersonal, and collective. Each is further divided to reflect more specific types of violence. Interpersonal violence (depicted in Figure 14.1) distinguishes family violence, which occurs largely between family members and intimate partners. Usually, this type of violence takes place in the home. Community violence, on the other hand, generally takes place outside the home and between individuals who are not related and who may or may not know each other.

This typology also illustrates that the nature of violence can be physical (including sexual assault), psychological, or involve deprivation or neglect. Abuse can also entail financial exploitation, as shown in Table 14.1. Additionally, recent research on poly-victimization establishes the need to theorize and study the connections between the various types of violence since they often do not occur in isolation from one another. Indeed, it is common for multiple types of abuse to co-occur in the lives of victims, a finding that helps us to better understand the effects of abuse on victims (Anderson, 2010).

Table 14.1
What Is Abuse and Neglect?

Type	Definition and Examples across the Life Course
Physical	Inflicting discomfort, pain, or injury by slapping, punching, rough handling, sexual assault, over- or undermedicating, or excessive use of physical restraint. *Example:* Father straps son with belt because son had slapped brother.
Psychological	Diminishing dignity and self-worth by name-calling, insulting, threatening, ignoring, isolating, excluding from meaningful events. *Example:* Uncle cannot accept gay niece and calls her a "freak of nature" and "stupid dyke," among other insulting names.
Financial	Misuse of money or property, stealing money or possessions, forging signatures or legal documents. *Example:* Adult grandson tricks elderly grandmother into signing cheques to cover his personal expenses and money for drugs.
Neglect	Failing to meet the needs of family members unable to meet those needs alone. Denial of food, water, medication, treatment, health aids, clothing, visitors. *Example:* Mother and father keep young child locked up in room while they work and provide inadequate diet and social interaction.

Source: Adapted from the National Advisory Council on Aging, "Hidden Harm: The Abuse of Seniors," *Expression: Bulletin of the National Advisory Council on Aging* 17, no. 1 (Ottawa: Government of Canada, 2003–2004), p. 2.

From this lens, family violence and abuse is as an umbrella term covering a range of different types of violence among different sets of family members (McDaniel and Tepperman, 2004). And from a life course perspective, certain types of violence may be inflicted on certain family members at particular stages of the family life cycle, such as during childhood (i.e., child abuse, including sibling abuse), young adulthood and adulthood, and the elderly years. This is because age interrelates with conditions related to vulnerability, dependency, and access to resources that can influence the risk of being injured. In the next section, we will focus on common kinds of violence that occur in families, using a life course organizational framework.

Child Abuse and Neglect
From a historical perspective, children have often been considered the property of their parents, especially of their fathers. As a result, children have had few rights and have

Figure 14.1
Typology of Violence

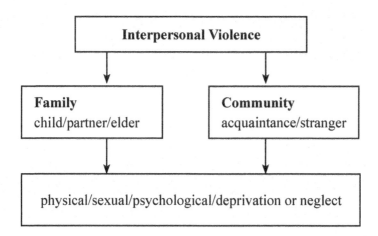

Source: Adapted from World Health Organization, *Violence Prevention Alliance*, retrieved October 11, 2005, from www.who.int/violenceprevention.

been vulnerable to abuse and neglect. Moreover, it was common for both parents and teachers in the past to have condoned physical discipline, often quoting the biblical phrase "Spare the rod and spoil the child" to justify this behaviour. Sexual abuse was also prevalent. For example, in ancient Greece it was not unusual for men to use boys for sexual pleasure (Ward, 2002). Also from a historical and global perspective, various types of child abuse, such as the trafficking, sexual exploitation, and genital mutilation of young girls has been and continues to be commonplace.

In Canada, the first Children's Aid Society was formed in Toronto in 1891. Yet, initial concern of reforms focused on child employment and substitute caregivers rather than on neglect and abuse by parents (although the latter was covered by the legislation). For many years, Canadian concerns and legislation changed little. Following popularization of the phrase "battered child syndrome" (coined by Kempe in the early 1960s), mandatory reporting laws were passed. By the late 1970s, nine of the 12 provincial and territorial jurisdictions had passed such laws and the rest had implemented monitoring programs (Wachtel, 1989; Ward, 2002).

With respect to defining child abuse, there is much controversy over its definition and manifestation. For example, while many Canadians view spanking as an aggressive act intended to harm or injure, many do not view it as abuse since it "is the norm rather than the exception" (Flynn, 1998). This is partly because it is legal, except under certain conditions (see Box 14.1). It is also interesting to note that while spanking is relatively common throughout the world, it is illegal in some countries such as Sweden.

Box 14.1
Spanking Laws in Canada

A Supreme Court of Canada ruling handed down on January 30, 2004 upholds the "spanking laws" in Canada, but for the first time, the high court has issued guidelines that spanking teenagers or children under the age of two, hitting a child in the head, or using objects such as belts or rulers are actions that go too far.

In a deeply split six-three decision, the court ruled...the so-called "spanking" defense in Canadian law does not protect or excuse "outbursts of violence against a child motivated by anger or animated by frustration." Still, parents, their stand-in caregivers, and teachers may use reasonable force if it is for "educative or corrective purposes," Chief Justice Beverley McLachlin wrote for the majority.

"The reality is," wrote McLachlin, that without such a defense, Canada's "broad assault law would criminalize force falling far short of what we think as corporal punishment, like placing an unwilling child in a chair for a five-minute 'time-out.'"

Source: CanadianLawSite.Com (2004: 3).

It is virtually impossible to know the full extent of child abuse and neglect in Canada. This is because only the most extreme cases come to the attention of the professional community, and there are no Canadian national representative sample survey data. Also, many people do not disclose incidents because of fear of reprisal, shame, and denial (DeKeseredy, 2005). Despite these limitations, most substantiated reports of child maltreatment are neglect at 34 percent (i.e., failure to meet the emotional or physical needs of a child), followed by exposure to domestic violence (34 percent), physical abuse (20 percent), emotional maltreatment (9 percent), and sexual abuse (3 percent), based on a recent government report (see Table 14.2).

While any of these types of abuse is inexcusable and unacceptable, one particularly traumatizing crime that is committed in families—falling under the category of sexual abuse—is that of incest. The Criminal Code of Canada defines incest in section 155(1): "Everyone commits incest who, knowing that another person by blood relationship is his or her parent, child, brother, sister, grandparent or grandchild, as the case may be, has sexual intercourse with that person." However, according to the organization Victims of Violence, a federally registered charitable organization devoted to providing support to victims and the general promotion of public safety, this definition does not include touching, fondling, oral sex or masturbating, which can be considered to be forms of sexual abuse. Instead, they argue that a more appropriate definition would take into account those other acts. It also does not encompass non-biological family ties, although these individuals can be charged under different criminal codes (e.g., having sex with a minor).

Table 14.2
Primary Categories of Substantiated Child Maltreatment Investigations in Canada in 2008

Primary category of maltreatment	Number of investigations	Rate per 1,000 children	%
Physical abuse	17,212	2.86	20%
Sexual abuse	2,607	0.43	3%
Neglect	28,939	4.81	34%
Emotional maltreatment	7,423	1.23	9%
Exposure to intimate partner violence	29,259	4.86	34%
Total substantiated investigations	**85,440**	**14.19**	**100%**

Based on a sample of 6,163 substantiated investigations. Percentages are column percentages.

Source: Public Health Agency of Canada (2011). *Canadian Incidence Study of Reported Child Abuse and Neglect – 2008*, Table 4-1. Retrieved August 10, 2011 from http://www.phac-aspc.gc.ca/ncfv-cnivf/pdfs/nfnts-cis-2008-fact-feuil-eng.pdf.

Victims of Violence (2011) also report that victims of incest can be any age, although most are victimized between the ages of 8 and 12. Incest is also found to be more likely to occur in families of low socio-economic status, or families in which substance abuse is a factor, although it can occur in many diverse settings and contexts. And although victims can be either male or female, statistics show that female victims outnumber male victims 10 to 1. Regarding perpetrators, they tend to be male, are usually considerably older than their victims, and 75 percent of cases are step-father/step-daughter relations.

However, researchers caution against a complete reliance on these statistics to produce a profile of victims/perpetrators since certain individuals may be more (or less) likely to report the crime to authorities, such as the police. For example, boys may be more reluctant to report the abuse than girls due to the pressures that stem from societal norms of masculine behaviour, such as "all boys want sex" and "big boys don't cry." Biological children may also be less likely to report this type of abuse (categorized as "consanguine" since it involves blood relatives) than step-children or children of "quasi relatives" (e.g., live-in parental partners or foster parents).

Furthermore, it should be recognized that children can also abuse, or, in extremely rare cases, murder their own parents. This is illustrated in the recent case of 26-year-old Gregory White, who lived with his parents in a single-storey house northwest of Barrie, Ontario. He was charged with the first-degree murder of his parents, aged 53 and 51, in addition to indecently interfering with human bodies (CBC News, 2011). Estimates suggest that 7–13 percent of children attack their parents, and most are between the ages of 10 and 24 with a peak in the late teens. Older children tend to be more violent than younger ones, and substance abuse, delinquency, and a lack of interest in school is common among these abusers. Moreover, some researchers suggest that parent abuse is an attempt to retaliate for earlier abuse by a parent, although this aggression tends to be targeted at the less powerful parent rather than the one who was the abuser. Generally, parent abusers use assault to gain power and control in the family (e.g., see Ward, 2002).

Sibling Abuse

Sibling violence can be defined as any form of intentional harm inflicted by one child in a family unit on another. Children do not have to be related by birth in order for it to take place (e.g., abuse between step-siblings). It also includes highly injurious physical, psychological, and sexual behaviour. For example, in Table 14.3 we see an overview of the different types and prevalence of physical violence between siblings. Unfortunately, researchers and parents often regard violence between siblings as a "normal" part of sibling rivalry and growing up (with the exception of sibling incest). Most parents rarely discourage their children from engaging in aggressive behaviours such as slapping, shoving, and hair pulling, and intervene only when "minor" events are seen as escalating into major conflict (DeKeseredy, 2004; Perozynski and Kramer, 1999).

Although Canadian research is limited, sibling violence is considered to be the most common form of violence in the family (DeKeseredy, 2004). Indeed, many siblings behave like those depicted on reality shows such as *Nanny 911*, or *Supernanny*, especially at younger ages, which often show siblings engaged in behaviours such as hitting and pushing. Older children tend to use language instead of physical aggression to resolve conflict. Research also shows that girls are not always "sugar and spice and everything nice." Contrary to stereotypes, girls are often as violent as boys (e.g., see Duffy and Momirov, 1997), although males with brothers tend to have the highest levels of sibling violence of all types of sibling pairs (Hoffman, Kiecolt, and Edwards, 2005).

Abuse between Partners

There are many different forms of abuse between partners, from emotional abuse to murder and this can occur in dating relationships, cohabiting and marital unions, and between same-sex couples. Most research has focused on abuse against women. Like child abuse, woman abuse is rooted in history, since women have long been viewed as possessions of men. In England, for instance, women and children were considered property of the husband and father. His obligation was to control and discipline them, and he was allowed to beat his wife as long as the stick was no thicker than his thumb (hence, the popular phrase "rule of thumb"). This law was not repealed until 1820, and from 1909–1960 the Canadian Criminal Code included the separate offence of wife battering. However, the victim had to show a greater level of harm than was required in cases of assaults by strangers. Further, it was not until 1983 that a man could be charged with raping his wife (Ward, 2002).

Table 14.3
Types of Sibling Violence Ever Experienced by Respondent in Senior Year of High School

Type of Violence Perpetrated	% of Respondents Who Had Experienced
Slapped	26.1
Pushed, shoved, grabbed	60.1
Physically restrained or pinned down	29.0
Scratched	20.9
Pulled hair or pinched	25.5
Threatened to hit or throw something	39.6
Hit with hands or objects	34.8
Punched	25.8
Kicked or bit	21.4
Thrown against a wall or pushed down	14.7
Choked or smothered with pillow	4.3
Burned	0.6
Beaten up	3.7
Threatened to use weapon	4.8
Used a weapon	1.8
Done any of the above acts	68.7

Notes: Based on a sample of 651 young adults. Mean number of types of violence perpetrated = 3.13 (range 0–15).

Source: K.K. Hoffman, K.J. Kiecolt, and J.N. Edwards, "Physical Violence between Siblings: A Theoretical and Empirical Analysis," *Journal of Family Issues* 26, no. 8 (2005): 1103–1130. (Extracted partial data from table 1, p. 115.)

With respect to family-related incidents of spousal violence (i.e., violence committed by a spouse or ex-spouse) reported to police, from 1995 to 2001 rates increased for both men and women but have remained relatively stable since that time (Statistics Canada, 2011). However, this does not mean that spousal violence was less common prior to 2001, since victims may be more willing than ever to report these experiences than in the past. The vast majority of victims (85 percent) are females. Yet, this report and research more generally shows that many assaults and other types of abuse (e.g., emotional) also occur against husbands. Thus, it may be the case that men are more reluctant than women to report this abuse to authorities for fear of shame or ridicule.

Despite the existence of abuse against males by females, it is well documented that women are more likely to suffer more serious injuries and death than men. Women are three times more likely to be killed by husbands than vice versa, although the risk of spousal homicide declines with age, with the highest incidence for females aged 15 to 24, as shown in Figure 14.2. Moreover, the type of spousal relationship differs, depending upon the gender of the victim. According to Statistics Canada (2011), while most male victims were killed by a common-law partner (66 percent), female victims were more likely to have been killed by their legally married spouse (39 percent) than by a common-law partner (33 percent). In addition, more men than women "hunt down" and kill partners who left them or were unfaithful, as well as kill their children along with their spouse. Furthermore, women who kill partners usually do this as a defensive action following years of abuse, and often because they see no other way out (Pottie Bunge and Locke, 2000).

Figure 14.2
Spousal Homicides by Sex and Age Group, Canada, 2000 to 2009

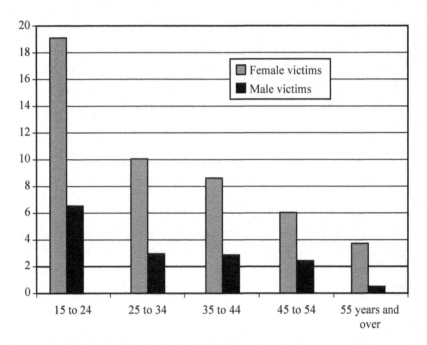

Note(s): Rates are calculated on the basis of 1,000,000 population. Populations based upon July 1st estimates from Statistics Canada, Demography Division. Includes legally married, common-law, separated, and divorced persons age 15 years or older. Excludes homicides of same-sex spouses due to the unavailability of population data on same-sex couples. Based on the Statistics Canada, Canadian Centre for Justice Statistics, Homicide Survey.

Source: Statistics Canada (2011), *Family Violence in Canada: A Statistical Profile*, retrieved August 3, 2011 from http://www.statcan.gc.ca/pub/85-224-x/2010000/ct016-eng.htm.

Finally, although spousal or woman abuse cuts across all socio-economic groups, some individuals are more vulnerable than others. For example, Papp (2010) argues that culturally driven violence against women is a growing problem in Canada's immigrant communities (see Box 14.3). Aboriginal women also report a higher prevalence rate than non-Aboriginal women, and poverty and unemployment are powerful determinants of various types of woman abuse (e.g., see DeKeseredy, 2004).

Although gender or patriarchal ideologies are not as much of an issue, same-sex partner violence is as much a matter of power and control as it is in heterosexual violence,

---

Box 14.2
Woman Abuse: Two Stories

I'm making a life for myself and my kids. I'm really scared. No matter how bad things got with the beatings and all, it was home. There were some good times, good memories. He wasn't bad to the kids. I got taking Valium then. The doctor gave me a prescription because he said I had bad nerves. I got addicted. So, it's tough. I have to deal with that too. The kids are mad at me. They don't like the apartment. They want their house, their friends, their old school back. So, it's hard sometimes to know if I'm doing the right thing. Will my kids hate me in ten years? When I think like that, I have to believe that they'll understand when I tell them the whole story. I hope that they'll learn from me that you have to have the courage to stand up for yourself. You have to have the courage to let go and make changes. I left to give my kids a better life, with more self-respect. But it's hard (Lisa, a 28-year-old woman with two children, five and six, who left her husband a year earlier).

The worst thing for me was realizing that you really are alone in this world. You feel so alone when the person you thought loved you turns on you. But you still hope that there's someone out there who will help you. Maybe there's someone out there who will really love you the way you thought your husband would. It's not till you turn to someone for help that you know how really alone you are. No one ever helped me. Oh, my minister gave me numbers for services. My neighbours took me to the hospital. They called the police. I guess they tried. But I always felt like they thought I had the plague or leprosy or something. They didn't want to catch whatever I had that made me abused. They wanted to get rid of the abuse so it wouldn't get them too. They never gave me what I needed. They pretended their pain was different from mine. Why can't people see that we all have pain and disappointment and joys and dreams? We are all a lot more the same than we are different (Kate, a woman in her late twenties who helped create a self-help group for women who are abused).

Source: DeKeseredy, W. and L. Macleod. 1997. *Woman Abuse: A Sociological Story.* Toronto: Harcourt Brace and Co. (pp. 49–50).

Box 14.3
Crimes of "Honour" in Immigrant Communities

South Asians who are determined to maintain the oppression of women and reject assimilation into the host society use religious and cultural values as a pretext to control female chastity. This effectively places the maintenance of traditional values and family honour on the woman alone. Sons are rarely punished for their lack of chastity. Because the stakes are so high, punishments for perceived rejection or disobedience of the cultural code can be severe. The "reasons" for carrying honour killings—usually offered by those perpetrating the crimes—are diverse: wearing makeup, socializing with unacceptable friends, wearing unacceptable clothes, staying out late, dating, lack of sex in the marriage, extramarital sex, gossip or challenging the authority of the dominant male in the family.

As vital as legal and human rights policies are, more invidiuals and agencies that provide services to abused women are starting to identify the magnitude of the problem by recognizing the brainwashing of children in the service of maintaining male power over females and by understanding how respect for culture and religion is being exploited to sustain this control. While legal sanctions are needed, third parties cannot establish the conditions for reform. Leaders of the South Asian immigrant communities must take responsibility for breaking the silence, to borrow a much-used locution from campaigns against Western paradigms of domestic violence. They must challenge the deep-rooted cultural thinking and traditional structures that lie at the root of women abuse in South Asian homes.

Community mobilization and outreach programs are an important part of generating dialogue within this community and of developing partnerships and networks. While there are legal options for supporting women and providing safety for them, it is imperative that we generate an open dialogue that is not threatening within the community in order to guarantee the security of all immigrant women and to ensure their right to live without fear of violence from those who, according to Canadian values, should be their most trustworthy companions and protectors.

Source: Aruna, Papp. 2010. *Culturally Driven Violence against Women: A Growing Problem in Canada's Immigrant Communities.* Winnipeg, MB: Canada Frontier Centre for Public Policy (p. 16).

and although we lack reliable data, the rate of violence between the two groups appears to be similar; albeit claims are usually based on findings from separate studies rather than theoretically informed comparative studies (Anderson, 2010). As cited in Anderson (2010: 733), research on LGBT families has not applied a structuralist theoretical framework that recognizes sexual orientation as a location within a structure of inequality: "Rarely do researchers consider the real institutional differences, that affect, for example, homosexual and heterosexual couples differently; nor do they question the strategy of directly comparing gay and straight couples without regard for their distinct circumstances." Notably, an additional level of intimidation can exist between same-sex partners if one threatens to expose the sexual orientation of a partner who has not informed family members or co-workers (e.g., see Leventhal and Lundy, 1999). Gay and lesbian victims of violence and abuse may also be less likely to report the abuse to authorities than heterosexual victims because of fear of shame or ridicule (Ambert, 2006).

Seniors

Seniors are vulnerable to the same types of abuse as family members at younger ages. In fact, some researchers believe that due to the aging process, some seniors are more vulnerable to being victims than younger family members. As we age, the likelihood of disability rises, and this may include mobility, hearing, vision, and speech, as well as cognitive disabilities such as Alzheimer's disease. According to some studies, people with disabilities are 50 percent more likely to be victims of violence or abuse (Roeher Institute, 1995). In short, some seniors are more at risk than others. As portrayed in Table 14.4, this includes not only those with disabilities who are dependent, but older seniors, women, those who are socially isolated and with reduced cognitive capacity, and seniors cared for by people with an alcohol or drug problem (NACA, 2003–2004).

It is estimated that 4–10 percent of seniors experience some form of abuse in later life, although it is difficult to arrive at accurate statistics given that many seniors do not want to report abuse to the authorities due to embarrassment, shame, or fear of ridicule or further abuse. Many elderly victims may even be unaware that they are being abused. Common types of abuse include financial abuse (e.g., misuse of the senior's money or property; forgery), physical, psychological, and neglect. Neglect occurs when a caregiver fails to meet the needs of an older adult who is unable to meet his or her needs alone, such as the denial of food or visitors (Spencer, 2005). In addition, older people may be

---

Table 14.4
Summary of Risk Factors for Elder Abuse

Some seniors are more at risk than others.
- Older seniors
- Women
- Socially isolated
- Seniors with reduced cognitive capacity
- Seniors with disabilities who are dependent
- Seniors cared for by people with an alcohol or drug problem

Source: National Advisory Council on Aging, "Hidden Harm: The Abuse of Seniors," *Expression: Bulletin of the National Advisory Council on Aging* 17, no. 1 (Ottawa: Government of Canada, 2003–2004), p. 3.

vulnerable to medication abuse, such as the purposeful overdosing of drugs, leaving the older person almost comatose, or a reluctance/refusal to give medications when needed.

There may also be culturally specific forms of elder abuse that can take place but that often remain hidden. Recent immigrant seniors may be isolated and completely dependent upon their families. They also commonly have language and other issues (e.g., transportation, financial) that make them particularly vulnerable to abuse and seeking outside help. Families can also hold certain cultural values on aging and care of the elderly, which can affect the experience of, and risk for, abuse. Tam and Neysmith (2006), for instance, based on a qualitative study of home care workers, found that disrespect is the key form of elder abuse that takes place in the Chinese community. The concept of disrespect can be described in many ways but was often described by the study participants as abusive, unnecessary scolding and nagging. It also included various acts of rudeness (e.g., bossy and controlling behaviour), deprivation (e.g., no Chinese television and radio), and space/mobility restrictions (e.g., forcing elders to stay in their room). These researchers further note that this type of emotional violence remains invisible under categories of elder abuse derived from a Western cultural perspective, such that a social exclusion framework is need to understand the experiences of particular immigrant populations.

Furthermore, most abuse is perpetrated by someone the senior knows. According to NACA (2003–2004), in cases of family violence, adult children and spouses account for almost three-quarters (71 percent) of abusers. Older women are as likely to be abused by a spouse (36 percent) as by an adult child (37 percent), while men are more likely to be abused by an adult child (43 percent).

Consequences of Abuse: The Ripple Effect

As depicted in Box 14.2, victims of abuse can experience a host of negative consequences in both the short- and long-term. In particular, we are becoming increasingly aware of linkages among abuse, neglect, maltreatment, and health outcomes. A recent report places family violence among contributing or causal factors for a wide range of illnesses and diseases such as sleep and eating disorders, thyroid malfunction, and irritable bowel syndrome (e.g., see BCIF, 2005). With respect to children witnessing domestic violence, reactions can include emotional, social, cognitive, physical, and behavioural maladjustment problems (e.g., see Moss, 2004). These children also tend to exhibit lower levels of social competence and higher rates of depression, worry, and frustration. They are also more likely than other children to develop stress-related disorders and to show lower levels of empathy (Dauvergne and Johnson, 2001). Poly-victims, in particular, appear to suffer greater trauma than victims who suffered from multiple incidents of a single type of violence (Anderson, 2010).

Other studies also highlight the "ripple" effect of early abuse in life. For example, various forms of child maltreatment negatively affect the victim's development physically, intellectually, and psychosocially. Child victims of neglect and/or abuse are also 1.75 times more likely to experience post-traumatic stress disorder as adults compared to individuals who did not experience neglect and/or abuse (Widom, 1999). Moreover, victims are more likely to experience anxiety and depression, eating disorders, attachment difficulties, and low self-esteem (Kolko, 1996). A recent Canadian study also showed that a history of child abuse and maltreatment was one of the leading predictors of psychological problems in adulthood (Mian, Bala, and MacMillan, 2001).

Abuse in childhood is also shown to be related to the risk of later victimization. For example, Laporte et al. (2011) find that female adolescents who had been victimized by either of their parents were at a greater risk for revictimization within their dating relationships. High-risk adolescent males who reported childhood victimization were at a significantly higher risk of being aggressive toward their girlfriends, especially if they were harshly disciplined by their fathers. Also, using a longitudinal study of college women, Smith et al. (2003) found that the risk of physical and sexual assault victimization in college was greater among respondents who reported experiencing both childhood abuse and physical abuse victimization in adolescence.

Additionally, children raised in violent or conflict-ridden homes are also more likely to run away or leave home at early ages to escape an unhappy home environment (Mitchell, Wister, and Burch, 1989). This places them at risk for dropping out of high school, homelessness, and a number of social problems, such as prostitution, drug addiction, and engaging in criminal activities. Thus, there is also a broader harm or cost to society as a whole. Not only are abuse/neglect victims more likely to engage in illegal and delinquent behaviours as teenagers and adults, but they may also create a host of additional public costs, such as to the health care system (e.g., see Widom, 2001).

What Has Love Got to Do with It? Why Do People Abuse and Neglect Their Family Members?

There are many theories as to why people abuse their family members and they vary according to the type of abuse inflicted. For example, theories of wife abuse often focus on patriarchal structures, power, and gender inequality. On a general level, theories range from blaming the perpetrator to placing responsibility on our social structure and fall into one of three categories: (1) violence as individual pathology; (2) violence as learned behaviour; (3) violence as a by-product of environmental stressors.

Violence as Individual Pathology

Violence is often studied from both the biological and psychological disciplines, and the treatment of family violence has been the focus of medical and mental health professionals. Analyses have therefore been directed to biological and psychological anomalies that produce and characterize perpetrators of violence. The medical model, also termed the "pathological model," asserts that individuals who assault or abuse members of their family possess distinguishing personality characteristics that reflect some form of mental illness or pathology. This viewpoint fits in neatly with the general diagnostic framework of practitioners and beliefs held by the general public that abusers are "sick." For example, from a biological perspective, bad behaviour is the effect of a person's physiological makeup as a result of such causes as "bad genes" or hormonal imbalances.

In the psychological framework, defective personality structures result in individuals who are impulsive, immature, depressed, and insecure. Thus, violence and abuse occur because these individuals are incapable of love or of forming empathic attachments. However, research establishes that personality disorders occur no more often in perpetrators of violence than in the general population. Moreover, many criticize this explanation because it oversimplifies behaviour and provides an easy "excuse" for the perpetrator. It also does not consider the context in which the abusive behaviour unfolds, such as opportunity structures and stressful environments.

Violence as Learned Behaviour

Social learning theory, which was covered in Chapter 2, argues that violent or abusive behaviour is learned in interaction with others. For example, children who witness violence between their parents may learn that this is an acceptable means for achieving one's goals or for resolving problems. And since the family is a primary agent of socialization, it is assumed to be a potential cradle of violence. For example, if small children are disciplined with physical punishment, they will imitate the behaviour and internalize the belief that violence and the use of power is a legitimate form of interpersonal control and behaviour. In this way, violence breeds violence, which perpetuates a cycle of violence (Drakich and Guberman, 1987).

This intergenerational transmission of family violence or social learning theory viewpoint has been extensively studied by researchers. Generally, most studies conclude that children who experience or are exposed to family violence do not inevitably grow up to become perpetrators of violence, although there is partial support for this theory. Indeed, some studies show a carry-over effect from one generation to the next, which perpetuates a cycle of violence, neglect, and maltreatment (Zuravin et al., 1996). Therefore, several other social and cultural factors must also be taken into account.

Violence as a By-product of Environmental Stressors

From this perspective, the perpetrator is considered the primary source of violence, but has been "pushed" to it by environmental triggers or stressors such as alcohol, drugs, or stress. Stress is defined as "a state which arises from an actual or perceived imbalance between demand (e.g., challenge, threat) and capacity (e.g., resources, coping) in the family's functioning" (Huang, 1991: 289). Indeed, stress as an explanation for family violence is pervasive in the literature, and the family is seen as a receptacle for both inside and outside stresses (Drakich and Guberman, 1987). This has led researchers to the famous ABCX family crisis model devised by Hill in 1949. Simply put, A (the stressor event) interacts with B (the family's crisis-meeting resources), and C (the definition the family makes of the event), which, in turn, produces X (the crisis).

Possible environmental stressors include new members added to the family structure, death of a family member, divorce, war, and natural catastrophes, such as earthquakes or hurricanes. Recently, this model has been expanded to the Double ABCX crisis model of stress. This revised model takes into account the idea that the ability to cope depends on family circumstances when the stressor is experienced. Also, since all families experience prior strains and hardships, there can be a pile-up of stresses (the AA in the model). Family coping may be helped by obtaining new resources, such as social support (BB in the model), and is also influenced by the family's perception of the demand pile-up (the CC in the model). Generally, strong families adapt more successfully to stresses. As a result, weak families have less flexibility and fewer resources for dealing with stresses, and therefore do so less effectively (White et al., 2005).

The fact that stress exists in the family or outside of it cannot be denied. Lack of social support, unemployment, relationship and health problems, workplace and child-care challenges, and other demands can create considerable stress and anxiety. This can place individuals at risk of making poor decisions, such as the one depicted in Box 14.4, in which an elderly man accidentally kills his wife who suffers from dementia. Moreover, there is also a link between stress, violence, and alcohol/drug abuse. However, not all individuals who experience stress or abuse alcohol or drugs harm their family members. Indeed, alcohol abuse is argued to be a "disavowal technique" that releases the individual from feeling responsibility for violent behaviour. Therefore, attention must extend beyond the precipitating factors of stress to social structural conditions and institutional practices that can trigger or contribute to abuse and neglect.

An Ecological and Dialectical Perspective: Social Location and Context, Contradictions, and Institutional Practices

A critical evaluation of the previous theories suggests that it is fruitful to consider various levels of risk factors from an ecological perspective, a conceptual framework that was introduced in Chapter 2. This is based on evidence that no single factor can explain why some individuals or groups are at a higher risk of interpersonal violence, while others are more protected from it (World Health Organization, 2005). As articulated by leading proponent Bronfenbrenner (1979: 3), "the ecological model environment is conceived as a set of nested structures, each inside the other like a set of Russian dolls." This model is applied in Figure 14.3, whereby violence is conceptualized as the outcome of interaction among many factors at four levels: the individual, the relationship, the community, and the societal. These range from macro-societal structures in a patriarchal capitalist society (e.g., laws, ageism, sexism, racism) to meso/exo-level factors (e.g., social networks, community resources, work-related factors, history of relationship) to micro-level individual factors (e.g., gender, age, drug abuse, personality).

A focus on these nested structures and processes illuminate how certain social structural conditions (e.g., poverty and a lack of community supports), combined with institutional practices in a variety of realms (e.g., law, policing, and social work), contribute to individual acts of violence, abuse, or neglect. For example, Swift (1995) provides a powerful critique of how many organizational practices obscure social injustices and place the blame for neglectful mothers back onto poor mothers for failing to cope. Similarly, McKendy (1997) shows how certain ideological practices work to keep "class seen but

Box 14.4
Elderly Man Sentenced in Wife's Gagging Death
Updated: Thu, 07 April 2005.

SAINT JOHN, N.B.—An elderly man found guilty of criminal negligence in the death of his wife, who had been tied up and gagged, has received a two-year sentence to be served in the community. On Wednesday, a New Brunswick judge sentenced Kenneth Leadlay, 82, who had pleaded guilty on the charge. Police found the body of his 81-year-old wife, Alice Leadlay, last September in Rothesay, N.B. The woman, who suffered from dementia, had been tied up and gagged. As a result of her condition, she roamed the house and often screamed for hours. It was revealed during the trial that Leadlay had tied her up because he hadn't slept for days and desperately needed some sleep.

Leadlay spoke to the court briefly before his sentencing. He told the judge he had met his wife when he was 13 and she was 12. He said she was his sweetheart, his wife, and his best friend. Throughout the case, the court heard evidence that backed up that claim. Witnesses testified that they considered the Leadlays to be a happy, loving couple.

Judge Jenrik Tonning said there was no doubt that Leadlay was negligent and responsible for his wife's death. He said that it was a case of bad judgment from a man who wasn't willing to admit his wife was too big a burden for him. He acknowledged that the woman's dementia had taken a physical and emotional toll on her husband. The judge also noted the man's age, his long work record, and relationship that showed no sign of prior abuse. Tonning said the two-year sentence would be served at the home of Leadlay's son in Bedford, N.S. At least two members of Leadlay's family were unhappy with that sentence. One estranged son said he wanted an inquest into his mother's death.

Source: CBC.ca News, retrieved October 4, 2005 from www.cbc.ca/story/canada/national/2005.

unnoticed" in cases of wife abuse. In particular, these practices obscure issues of inequality and the conditions faced by poor men in a patriarchal capitalist society, which place them at a greater risk for wife abuse.

Moreover, institutional practices and responses can impinge on an individual's ability to deal with and prevent further abuse or neglect from occurring. For example, Renzetti (2005) offers a dialectical approach to intimate aggression (which dates back to such classical theorists as Karl Marx) that is congruent with a life course and ecological perspective. This dialectical approach emphasizes how social location (e.g., age, gender, class, race/ethnicity, sexuality, disability, and geography) intersects with structural and institutional contexts. It is dialectical in that it considers contradictions and tensions between these domains. Notably, perpetrators and recipients react to, understand, and act on aggression

Figure 14.3
An Ecological Perspective on Family Violence: Examples of Risk Factors at Each Level

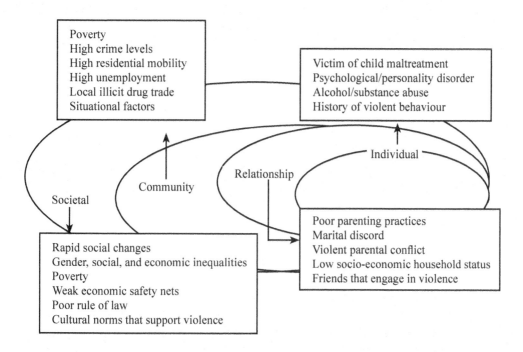

Poverty
High crime levels
High residential mobility
High unemployment
Local illicit drug trade
Situational factors

Victim of child maltreatment
Psychological/personality disorder
Alcohol/substance abuse
History of violent behaviour

Individual

Relationship

Community

Societal

Rapid social changes
Gender, social, and economic inequalities
Poverty
Weak economic safety nets
Poor rule of law
Cultural norms that support violence

Poor parenting practices
Marital discord
Violent parental conflict
Low socio-economic household status
Friends that engage in violence

Source: Adapted from World Health Organization, 2005. *Global Campaign for the Prevention of Violence*, retrieved December 2, 2007, from http://whqlibdoc.who.int/publications/2005/924159313X_eng.pdf.

within prevailing discourses of gender, intimacy, sexuality, and violence that are deeply rooted in hierarchy, patriarchy, racism, heteronormativity, and inequity. Intimate violence is also paradoxical in that it often occurs in the context of a loving or supportive relationship that is also shocking and hurtful. It may also be preceded and followed by everyday acts of care, hostility, concern, or control (Olsen, Fine, and Lloyd, 2005).

Using the scenario of women who have been abused by their partners, Renzetti (2005) notes that they often reject arrest and jailing of their violent partner because they fear negative consequences for their children. These women may rely on their partner for child care or financial support and may be unable to pay for child care in the public sector. Jailing a partner, therefore, might mean having to travel several hours a day by public transportation to a low-paying job, which further limits her ability to care for her children. As a result, certain institutional practices (which, ironically, were created to protect women and hold men accountable for their actions) can impede some women's agency in dealing with abuse as well as other aspects of their lives, particularly in the absence of alternative resources.

Overall, an ecological and dialectical perspective does not excuse the individual from violent or abusive behaviour. Rather, it provides a contextual social location explanation that anchors acts of abuse and neglect in relation to issues of vulnerability, dependency, and access to resources and ideological and institutional practices. It also provides specific implications for action-oriented solutions (e.g., eradicating poverty, changing norms) to a very serious social problem. Unfortunately, however, these solutions tend not to be implemented because this would require a significant restructuring and more equal distribution of societal resources, in addition to changing dominant societal discourse and systemic institutional practices. Nonetheless, we will briefly review some of the commonly used approaches to prevention and intervention.

Prevention and Intervention

Preventing family violence and stress from occurring is an obvious way to reduce or eradicate these problems. Three basic approaches to prevention include: (1) primary prevention; (2) secondary prevention; and (3) tertiary prevention.

Primary prevention is the attempt to keep abuse from occurring at all, and this occurs mainly through education. An example is the widespread ad campaign launched by the Canadian Federation of Students on university campuses during the 1980s. This campaign was designed to prevent date rape and dating violence against young women by educating young men that "No means no." Courses in marriage preparation, prenatal care, parental education, and caregiving for the elderly can also include discussion of abuse. They can also provide individuals with strategies and resources to prevent stress and abuse, such as the tragic scenario depicted in Box 14.4. Visits by public health nurses to new mothers, recent immigrants, and isolated elderly can also play an important role. These professionals are trained to spot early signs of stress, dependency, and abuse. As a result, they can refer stressed individuals to the appropriate educational, health, and support programs (Wachtel, 1999).

Secondary prevention programs entail working with groups deemed to be at risk for abuse. For instance, in the case of preventing child abuse, programs geared at prenatal nutrition, fetal alcohol syndrome support programs, and remedial schools (e.g., for children diagnosed with attention deficit disorder) could be helpful. Providing poor families with adequate income and housing assistance can also help to alleviate stress. With respect to elder abuse, outreach programs can reduce isolation and educational programs can teach elders how to avoid physical and financial exploitation. For example, seniors could be educated on the importance of having accurate knowledge of their finances and to be alert to unusual withdrawals from their bank accounts (NACA, 2003–2004).

The third approach, or tertiary prevention, is one of the most common approaches, and this entails treatment or some other intervention to keep abuse from recurring. For example, services for battered women help them to leave an abusive situation, such as help lines, shelters and temporary housing, counselling, and skills training. Other types include counselling and anger-management courses for perpetrators and educational programs to teach effective parenting skills to abusive parents (e.g., Wachtel, 1999; Ward, 2002). This approach is generally viewed as less costly (at least in the short term) than the first two approaches, which are more broad-based. However, it is often criticized as a "band-aid" solution, since it usually does not address systematic factors, which are often traced to deeper root issues of poverty, racism, sexism, and ageism.

Summary

In this chapter, the dark side of family life is brought to light through an exploration of what can occur behind closed doors. Tragically, violence, abuse, and stress exist in many families, and some individuals are more vulnerable to these problems, such as women, children, and seniors. Indeed, we may have more reason to fear our own family members than someone we don't know. Thus, our intense fears of "stranger danger" are not well founded (Dekeseredy, 2005). An examination of various definitional and methodological issues also shows that violence, abuse, and neglect are difficult to measure and are probably seriously underreported.

A critical analysis of general theories of violence, abuse, and stress reveal that searching for a singular cause is futile. Instead, these problems are multifactorial and can fruitfully be viewed from a life course ecological perspective that considers social location and the dialectical nature of violence, abuse, and neglect. This holistic framework incorporates a multitude of risk factors and addresses the interactions between persons, socio-cultural contexts, and institutional practices. For example, inadequate financial resources and a lack of social supports for caring for a dependent elder family member can foster caregiver resentment against the older adult or an inability to provide proper care. And when combined with cultural attitudes and values of ageism, older adults may be seen as less worthy than younger individuals. This further contributes to a climate within families that is conducive to elder abuse. Moreover, a dialectical approach reminds us that while family life has a darker and more malevolent connotation, it is also one filled with contradictions and tensions, including an odd, paradoxical mixture of aggression and tenderness (Olsen, Fine, and Lloyd, 2005). This observation suggests that family violence, abuse, and neglect are complex and multifaceted. Finally, it is critical for policy makers to make more long-term investments in addressing and eradicating a serious social problem, with its significant health and economic costs to individuals, families, and society.

Questions for Critical Reflection and Debate

1. Discuss some key methodological barriers to collecting data on the prevalence of violence and abuse within the family. What strategies might help researchers to collect more accurate data?

2. Many people believe that family life was better in "the good old days" and that violence and abuse in families is a relatively recent phenomenon. Do you agree or disagree with this assertion?
3. Why are family members often reluctant to report abuse to the authorities? Do these reasons vary by gender, age, socio-economic status, or where one lives?
4. Identify some major sources of stress in families that could trigger violence and abuse and relate these examples to the Double ABCX model.
5. Debate the following: Victims of child abuse are more likely to become abusers when they are adults compared to those who were not victimized as children.
6. What do you think the community's role should be in providing services to families and individuals under stress and at risk of inflicting violence and abuse? Should the focus be placed on prevention programs or assistance programs?

Glossary

Cradle of Violence refers to how the family environment is a potential birthplace of family violence, since it is the key agent of socialization.

Dialectical approach to intimate aggression offers theoretical integration and a focus on paradox, contradictions, and tensions in close relations that are intertwined with social, historical, and environmental contexts.

Double ABCX model of stress extends the ABCX model of stress, with its focus on pile-up events and the family's access to resources during crisis events.

Ecological perspective applied to family violence contextualizes risk factors at four nested levels: macro (societal), meso (community), exo (relationship), and micro (individual).

Family violence occurs largely between family members and intimate partners and usually takes place in the home. It can involve physical, sexual, or psychological force or power, as well as deprivation or neglect.

Intergenerational transmission of violence refers to how violence is transmitted from one generation to the next.

Primary prevention is geared toward preventing family violence and abuse in the first place and can be distinguished from intervention strategies.

Secondary prevention entails working with at-risk groups for violence and abuse.

Tertiary prevention refers to treatment or interventions to keep abuse from recurring.

Further Reading

Barnett, O., C.L. Miller-Perrin, and R.D. Perrin. 2011. *Family Violence across the Lifespan: An Introduction*, 3rd ed. Thousand Oaks: Sage. This new edition will help students achieve a deeper understanding of the methodology, etiology, prevalence, treatment, and prevention of family violence. Topics include child neglect, dating aggression, and abuse of the elderly and the disabled.

Cook, P. 2009. *Abused Men: The Hidden Side of Domestic Violence*, 2nd ed.Westport, Conn: Praeger Trade. This new edition updates one of the first books to comprehensively examine the hidden social problem of abused men and provides emotional, gripping stories.

Dekeseredy, W.S. 2011. *Violence against Women in Canada*. Toronto: University of Toronto Press. A well-documented sociological overview of the issue of violence against women. Debunks current attempts to label intimate violence as gender neutral and discusses policies to eradicate the problem.

Dorais, M. (translated by I.D. Meyer). 2009. *Don't Tell: The Sexual Abuse of Boys,* 2nd ed. Montreal, Quebec: McGill-Queen's University Press. Using first-hand accounts, the author gives male sexual abuse victims a voice and examines the effect of sexual abuse on the life of men, including their sense of self and personal relationships.

Papp, A. 2010. *Culturally Driven Violence against Women: a Growing Problem in Canada's Immigrant Communities*. Winnipeg, Man.: Frontier Centre for Public Policy. A primer on the traditions and values of selected immigrant communities; also covers issues such as "honour killing" in strong patriarchal immigrant communities and provides policy recommendations.

Peltzer, D. 2010. *A Child Called "It."* Deerfield Beach, Fl: Health Communications, Inc. The inspirational story of a child who was brutally beaten and starved by his emotionally unstable, alcoholic mother. This gripping account is told through the eyes of a child, who survives, despite extreme life-threatening odds.

Ross, L.E. (Ed.). 2010. *The War against Domestic Violence*. Boca Raton, FL: CRC Press/ Taylor and Francis. An overview of intimate partner violence among different ethnic groups (e.g., Latinos, Asian, African and Native American) and social groups (e.g., LGBT), as well as discussion on the connection between domestic violence and a number of other issues, including homelessness and substance abuse.

Related Web Sites

Canadian Health Network has a web site that contains a section on family violence and people with disabilities, www.publichealth.gc.ca.

Family Violence in Canada: A Statistical Profile 2009 is available as a free, downloadable copy of a recent Statistics Canada report, http://www.phac-aspc.gc.ca/ncfv-cnivf/ pdfs/fv-85-224-XWE-eng.pdf.

Health Canada contains a section on violence via the A to Z directory, in addition to the Child Maltreatment Division and the National Clearinghouse on Family Violence, http://www.hc~sc.gc.ca.

International Network for the Prevention of Elder Abuse is dedicated to global dissemination of information on the prevention of abuse against older people, www. inpea.net.

Woman Watch is a UN research arm and web site that tracks reproductive, health, and violence issues that affect women worldwide, www.un.org/womanwatch.

References

Ambert, A.M. 2006. *Changing Families: Relationships in Context*. Toronto: Pearson Education.

Anderson, K.L. 2010. "Conflict, Power, and Violence in Families." *Journal of Marriage and the Family* 72: 726–742.

BCIF (BC Institute against Family Violence). 2005. "The Health-Care Costs of Family Violence." *Aware Newsletter* 12, no. 1 (Summer).

Bronfenbrenner, U. 1979. *The Ecology of Human Development: Experiments by Nature and Design*. Cambridge: Harvard University Press.

CBC News. 2011. "Son Charged in Killing of Barrie-Area Couple." March 28, 2011, retrieved August 10, 2011 from cbc.ca.news/Canada/Toronto/story/2011/03/28/barrie-rem.

Dauvergne, M., and H. Johnson. 2001. "Children Witnessing Family Violence." *Juristat* 21, no. 6. Catalogue no. 85-002-XPE. Ottawa: Statistics Canada.

DeKeseredy, W. 2004. "Patterns of Family Violence." In M. Baker (ed.), *Families: Changing Trends in Canada*, 5th ed. (pp. 229–257). Toronto: McGraw-Hill Ryerson.

Drakich, J., and C. Guberman. 1987. "Violence in the Family." In K.L. Anderson et al. (eds.), *Family Matters: Sociology and Contemporary Canadian Family Patterns* (pp. 201–335). Toronto: Methuen.

Duffy, A., and J. Momirov. 1997. *Family Violence: A Canadian Introduction*. Toronto: James Lorimer.

Eichler, M. 1983. *Families in Canada Today: Recent Changes and Their Policy Consequences*. Toronto: Gage Publishing.

Engelbreit, M. 2005. *Mary Engelbreit's Mother Goose: One Hundred Best-Loved Verses*. New York: HarperCollins.

Flynn, C.P. 1998. "To Spank or Not to Spank: The Effect of Situation and Age of Child on Support for Corporal Punishment." *Journal of Family Violence* 13: 21–37.

Hoffman, K.L., K.J. Kiecolt, and J.N. Edwards. 2005. "Physical Violence between Siblings: A Theoretical and Empirical Analysis." *Journal of Family Issues* 26, no. 8: 1103–1130.

Huang, I.-C. 1991. "Family Stress and Coping." In S.J. Bahr (ed.), *Family Research: A Sixty-Year Review, 1930–1990*. Vol. 1. New York: Lexington Books, Maxwell MacMillan International.

Jiwani, J. 2000. *The 1999 General Social Survey on Spousal Violence: An Analysis*. Retrieved October 12, 2005, from www.casac.ca/survey99.htm.

Kolko, D. 1996. "Child Physical Abuse." In J. Briere et al. (eds.), *The APSAC Handbook on Child Maltreatment*. Thousand Oaks: Sage.

Laporte, L., D. Jiang, D.J. Pepler, and C. Chamberland. 2011. "The Relationship between Adolescents' Experience of Family Violence and Dating Violence." *Youth and Society* 43: 3–27.

Lasch, C. 1979. *Haven in a Heartless World: The Family Besieged*. New York: Basic Books.

Leventhal, B., and S.E. Lundy. 1999. *Same-Sex Domestic Violence: Strategies for Change.* Thousand Oaks: Sage.

McDaniel, S.A., and L. Tepperman. 2004. *Close Relations: An Introduction to the Sociology of Families*, 2nd ed. Toronto: Pearson Prentice-Hall.

McKendy, J.P. 1997. "The Class Politics of Domestic Violence." *Journal of Sociology and Social Welfare* 24: 135–155.

Mian, M., N. Bala, and H. MacMillan. 2001. "Canada." In B.M. Schwartz-Kenney, M. McCauley, and M. Epstein (eds.), *Child Abuse: A Global View.* Westport: Greenwood.

Mitchell, B.A., A.V. Wister, and T.K. Burch. 1989. "The Family Environment and Leaving the Parental Home." *Journal of Marriage and the Family* 51: 605–613.

Moss, K. 2004. "Kids Witnessing Family Violence." *Canadian Social Trends* 73: 12–16.

NACA (National Advisory Council on Aging). 2003–2004. "Hidden Harm: The Abuse of Seniors." *Expressions: Bulletin of the NACA* 17, no. 1. Ottawa: Government of Canada.

Olsen, L.N., M.A. Fine, and S.A. Lloyd. 2005. "Theorizing about Aggression between Intimates." In V.L. Bengtson, A.C. Acock, K.R. Allen, P. Dilworth-Anderson, D.M. Klein (eds.), *Sourcebook of Family Theory and Research* (pp. 315–331). Thousand Oaks: Sage.

Perozynski, L., and L. Kramer. 1999. "Parental Beliefs about Managing Sibling Conflict." *Developmental Psychology* 35: 489–499.

Pottie Bunge, V., and D. Locke (Eds.). 2000. *Family Violence in Canada: A Statistical Profile 2000.* Catalogue no. 85-224-XIE. Ottawa: Statistics Canada.

Renzetti, C.M. 2005. "The Challenges and Promise of a Dialectical Approach to Theorizing about Intimate Violence. In V.L. Bengtson, A.C. Acock, K.R. Allen, P. Dilworth-Anderson, and D.M. Klein (eds.), *Sourcebook of Family Theory and Research* (pp. 335–337). Thousand Oaks: Sage.

Roeher Institute, 1995. *Harm's Way: The Many Faces of Violence and Abuse against Persons with Disabilities.* North York: Roeher Institute.

Smith, P.H., White, J.W., and L.J. Holland. 2003. "A Longitudinal Perspective on Dating Violence among Adolescent and College-Age Women." *Journal of American Public Health Associations* 93: 1104–1109.

Spencer, C. 2005. "Abuse in Institutions." In A. Soden (ed.), *Advising the Older Client* (pp. 235–246). Markham: LexisNexis Butterworths.

Statistics Canada. 2003. "Family Violence." *The Daily* (June 23). Retrieved October 13, 2005, from www.statcan.ca/Daily/English/030623/d030623c.htm.

Statistics Canada. 2006. *Family Violence in Canada: A Statistical Profile, 2006.* Canadian Centre for Justice Studies, Catalogue no. 85-224-XIE. Ottawa: Statistics Canada.

Statistics Canada. 2011. *Family Violence in Canada: A Statistical Profile, 2011.* Canadian Centre for Justice Statistics. Retrieved August 3, 2011, from www.statcan.gc.ca/pub/85-244-x/2010000/ct016-eng.htm.

Swift, K.J. 1995. *Manufacturing "Bad" Mothers: A Critical Perspective on Child Neglect.* Toronto: University of Toronto Press.

Tam, S., and S. Neysmith. 2006. "Disrespect and Isolation: Elder Abuse in Chinese Communities." *Canadian Journal on Aging* 25: 141–151.

Victims of Violence. 2001. "Incest: Introduction, Definition, Victims, and Perpetrators." Retreived August 10, 2011 from www.victimsofviolence.on.ca/rev2/index.php.

Wachtel, A. 1989. *Discussion Paper: Child Abuse*. Ottawa: Health and Welfare Canada.

Wachtel, A. 1999. *The "State of the Art" in Child Abuse Prevention, 1977*. Ottawa: Health Canada.

Ward, M. 2002. *The Family Dynamic: A Canadian Perspective*, 3rd ed. Toronto: Nelson Thomson Learning.

White, J.M., L.E. Larson, J.W. Goltz, and B.E. Munro. 2005. *Families in Canada: Social Contexts, Continuities, and Changes,* 3rd ed. Toronto: Pearson Prentice-Hall.

Widom, C.S. 1999. "Posttraumatic Stress Disorder in Abused and Neglected Children Grown-up." *American Journal of Psychiatry* 156: 1223–1229.

Widom, C.S. 2001."Child Abuse and Neglect." In S.O. White (ed.), *Handbook of Youth and Justice* (31–48). New York: Plenum.

World Health Organization. 2005. *Violence Prevention Alliance*. Retrieved October 11, 2005, from www.who.int/violenceprevention.

Zuravin, S., C. McMillan, D. DePantilis, and C. Risley-Curtis. 1996. "The Intergenerational Cycle of Child Maltreatment: Continuity versus Discontinuity." *Journal of Interpersonal Violence* 7: 471–489.

Chapter 15

Families and the State

Family Policy in an Era of Globalization and Economic Uncertainty

Learning Objectives

In this chapter you will learn ...
- that family policy within the context of broader social policy is influenced by the processes of globalization and economic restructuring
- examples of family policy from a critical perspective will be defined and provided
- that many key policy issues face Canadian families
- the distinctions between policy advocacy, research, and evaluation
- that there are several recommendations for forward-looking family policy
- that there are salient policy challenges for future family life

Introduction

Many of us have heard our former prime minister Pierre Trudeau's highly quoted 1967 statement that "There's no place for the state in the bedrooms of the nation." And while many of us would support this general principle with respect to the sexual behaviour of consenting adults, many of us would also agree that there will always be a need for governments to support and regulate other aspects of family life. Indeed, for over a century, the state has regulated many domains of family life by enforcing government legislation and regulations (Baker, 2005).

The welfare state has been a defining feature of advanced capitalist societies, especially since the end of World War Two. It refers to government-sponsored programs designed to improve the social and economic well-being of families and individuals and is comprised of an intricate web of supports to individuals and families. This includes aspects such as income and security payments, social insurance, universal and targeted cash transfers, a wide range of social services (including housing, education, and health care), as well as several related laws and regulatory measures (Evans and Wekerle, 1997; Olsen, 2002).

As social programs became more costly (most of which were developed from the 1950s to the 1970s), governments began to question their ability to improve them or even to maintain them (Baker, 2005). During this time, we also witnessed generally slower levels of economic growth in the late 1970s through the 1990s. Spurred by factors such as globalization and world trade production, this was a period punctuated by severe worldwide recessions and rapidly escalating rates of unemployment (Olsen, 2002). As a result of these and other social, economic, and political transformations, the welfare state was dramatically restructured and reshaped. A notable outcome of this retrenchment has been massive cutbacks in state supports and a heavier reliance on family and community resources. High levels of inequality and disparities both across and within countries have also deepened. Taken together, these trends have introduced a number of new challenges for Canadian families.

Cognizant of these points, a number of family policy issues from a critical life course perspective will be examined in this chapter. First, we will define what we mean by social and family policy. This will be followed by an identification of some important policy issues relevant to the life courses of Canadian families. A brief overview of policy advocacy and research will be provided, as well as a number of forward-looking policy recommendations. Finally, salient policy issues likely to affect families in the near future will be identified, in recognition of the major trends and issues covered throughout this book.

What Is Social and Family Policy?

Broadly speaking, social policies and programs are those social arrangements aimed at the distribution of social resources and the promotion of the welfare of the individual and society, and are formed out of competing values (Gee and McDaniel, 1994). Family policy, therefore, is a subfield of social policy concerned with the problems of families in relation to society and advancement of family well-being as its goal. It can be defined as "a coherent set of principles about the state's role in family life which is implemented through legislation or a plan of action" (Baker, 1995: 5). Yet, it is important to recognize that numerous definitions have been advanced and are characterized by differences in scope, content, and target audience. For example, Kamerman and Kahn (1978: 3) conceptualize the scope of family policy as "everything that government does to and for the family."

Moreover, as summarized in Box 15.1, Baker (1995) states that family policy can be divided into three categories: (1) laws relating to family issues (e.g., marriage, adoption, divorce, child support); (2) policies to help family income (e.g., tax concessions, maternity leave); and (3) the provision of direct services (e.g., child care, home care health services, subsidized housing). Also, family policies are objectives and goals that are more or less deliberate, intended, and desirable, while programs are the practical applications that are used to achieve or fulfill the goals. Thus, the range of policies and programs affecting families is very broad—some support a nurturance or social function while others support economic ones.

It is also important to recognize that, unlike many European countries, Canada (with the exception of Quebec) has never developed explicit family policies in which the state's role is very clear (see Table 15.1). It does not have the jurisdiction to intervene in various aspects of family life. Instead, most governments have an array of policies and practices that affect families either directly or indirectly. These implicit policies establish general legislation and social programs that contain a particular ideological view of family and the role of the state in family life. Family ideologies can be found within laws, social policies, and regulations, rather than within one specific document.

Despite an absence of an explicit family policy in Canada, Eichler (1987) argues that two different models of the family have directed most family-oriented policies (see Table 15.2 for a chronology of selected family-support policies in Canada). These include: (1) the Patriarchal Model of the Family and; (2) the Individual Responsibility Model of the Family, and can be distinguished by a number of both shared and unique characteristics. In both models, the household and family are treated as identical. However, in the first model, the husband/father is viewed as responsible for the economic well-being of the family, while

Box 15.1
Families, the State, and Family Policies

The government of Canada has never developed explicit family policies, in part because it lacks the jurisdiction to intervene in many areas of family life. In addition, there is little consensus about how to create more explicit and cohesive family policies. In fact, two broad opinions are prevalent among the lobby groups pressuring government. One contends that family structure and practices reflect pressures and changes in the broader society as well as personal preferences. Therefore, governments cannot easily modify them through legislation or regulations. Nevertheless, parents make an important contribution to society by raising children, and deserve ongoing state supports to combine paid work with childcare and to raise children under difficult circumstances. The contrasting view is "the family" is deteriorating and declining as the major institution in society. The state has an obligation to fight against unhealthy influences and the intrusion and growing acceptance of alternative lifestyles. One way of doing this is to tighten welfare rules, ensure that the family remains a legal and heterosexual unit, and strictly enforce parental and spousal obligations.

In recent years, governments have tried to strengthen families but have found that new policies are difficult to create, costly to enforce, and often create unintended results. Any new initiative is fraught with controversy and opposition from various lobby groups. Interest groups from the political left and those who applaud new family forms are suspicious of the call for "a family policy" because they fear it could represent a conservative agenda opposing greater equality for women and "families of choice." Groups on the political right often argue that new programs are too expensive and reward the "undeserving" poor. Creating social policies and programs that integrate these two opposing viewpoints has been challenging, both in Canada and in other countries.

Source: Baker, M. 2005. "Families, the state, and family policies," in M. Baker, *Families: Changing Trends in Canada*, 5th ed. Toronto: McGraw-Hill Ryerson (pp. 258–276).

the wife/mother is seen as responsible for the household and personal care of family members, especially children. Women are largely viewed as dependants, and this model is premised on the notion of gender inequality, which expresses itself in a rather strict gendered division of labour. Conversely, the second model assumes that each partner is viewed as responsible for his or her own support. Also, both father and mother are seen as responsible for the household and personal care of family members, especially children.

Although Canadian social policies largely reflect the Individual Responsibility Model (especially since the late 1970s), a good example of policy based on patriarchal assumptions

Table 15.1
Defining Social and Family Policy

Term	Definition and Examples
Social Policy	Social arrangements aimed at the distribution of social resources and the promotion of the welfare of the individual and society; formed out of competing values at three levels of government (federal, provincial, and municipal); impacts all families
Family Policy	A subfield of social policy; addresses family-related conditions and problems; refers to a coherent set of generally agreed-upon (explicit or implicit) principles about the state's role in family life; implemented through legislation or a plan of action; can be divided into three categories: 1. laws relating to family issues (e.g., marriage, adoption, divorce, child support); 2. policies to help family income (e.g., tax concessions, maternity leave); 3. the provision of direct services (e.g., child welfare, home care health services, subsidized housing)

can be found in Ontario during the 1980s when the "Spouse in the House" social welfare rule was in existence. The regulation at the time was that a mother is eligible for welfare only if she does not live with a man. This is because it was assumed that the man will take over the function of breadwinner, even if in reality he is unemployed or does not contribute any income to the household. To illustrate the effects of this policy, on January 19, 1984, *The Toronto Star* reported on its first page the headline: "Mom's Welfare Fraud Blamed on 'System'" (see Box 15.2). The story presented concerned a welfare mom who allegedly defrauded welfare of more than $37,000 because she was fearful of losing her children. For 10 years, this woman had received about $270 per month to support herself and her three children.

Interestingly, her husband had been court-ordered to pay child support but had never paid any (which added up to arrears of $19,500) and warrants for his arrest were never executed. The woman had been informed that if she had no way of supporting her children, they would be turned over to the Children's Aid Society. The reason why she was accused of defrauding welfare was because she was living common-law with another man, rather than as a single woman, yet there was no evidence that this man was able or willing to support her or her children. As a result, the woman was ordered to repay the money that she received minus the amount owed by her husband over six years. However, she earned only $200 a week as a manual labourer, making it very difficult to repay the money. As she logically argued, "The system sold us out.... You took my children's rights. You didn't protect them. If they were in Children's Aid, you'd be paying $550 a month to protect them" (*The Toronto Star*, January 19, 1984: 1). It is also ironic to note

Table 15.2
Chronology of Selected Social Policies and Reforms in Canada

Social Benefit	Description and Reforms
Family Tax Benefits (1918–1993)	Tax deductions for taxpayers with dependants began with first Income Tax Act; tax credits added 1972
Mothers/Widows Pensions (1920+)	Started around 1920; date varies by province
Old Age Pension	Established in 1926 as a pension for those with low incomes; became a universal pension in 1951
Family Allowance	Paid to all mothers for each child (replaced by the Child Tax Benefit in 1993)
(Un)employment Insurance (1940)	Established as a federal social insurance program; other benefits added over time (e.g., Maternity in 1971)
Medicare (1966)	Public insurance established for hospitals and diagnostic services in 1958 and for visits to physicians in 1966
Spouses Allowance (1975)	Created as an income-tested pension for spouses aged 60–64 of old age pensioners, mainly women
Resolution to end "Child Poverty" (1989)	An all-party agreement in Parliament
Canada Child Tax Benefit (1998)	Prior Child Tax Benefit (1993–1998) merged with Working Income Supplement
Choice in Child Care Allowance (2006)	$100 per month direct payment per child under the age of six in addition to current Canada Child Tax Benefit, National Child Benefit Supplement, and Child Care Expenses Deduction (although these amounts will decrease in certain households)

Source: Derived from information presented in M. Baker, "Families, the State, and Family Policies," in M. Baker (ed.), *Families: Changing Trends in Canada*, 5th ed. (Toronto: McGraw-Hill Ryerson, 2005), table 12.1, p. 270; and updated from The Conservative Party of Canada's web site, "A new $1,200 Choice in Childcare Allowance for pre-school kids," retrieved August 14, 2006, from www.conservative.ca/EN/1091/33693.

that this rule may have produced another unintended outcome—some single mothers may have avoided the formation of live-in partnerships, unions that may have created a number of positive consequences for both the mothers and their children.

Many of these implicit policies have been developed over the years and have been influenced by the ideology of the party in power, the concerns of the day, and the pressure

Box 15.2
Mom's Welfare Fraud Blamed on "System"

The following excerpt shows an example of a controversial government welfare policy implemented during the 1980s known as the "Spouse in the House Rule."

A 37-year-old Brampton mother of four defrauded welfare of more than $37,000 because she was afraid of losing her children, a Peel County Court has been told. She was put on probation for two years and ordered to repay part of the money. But she might never have committed the crime had she received proper child support, Judge Francis McDonald said yesterday. "Our system could not pay her so she found one that would, it is as simple as that," he said. For 10 years Patricia Geall told authorities that she lived alone and was given about $270 a month to support herself and her three children although she was living with a man. Her former husband never paid her child support, which now adds up to $19,500 despite a court order. Warrants for his arrest were never executed, the court was told. "If (the husband) had been forced to pay, she might never have been pressed into the situation she has found herself in," McDonald said. Geall had been told that if she had no way of supporting her children, she could lose them to the Children's Aid Society, the court was told.

Source: Excerpted from Lynn Moore, 1984, "Mom's welfare fraud blamed on 'system,'" *The Toronto Star*, January 19, p. A1.

of powerful advocacy groups. From a historical perspective, Canada has been characterized by two fundamentally opposed value positions—conservatism and liberalism. Conservatives tend to be against family intervention in family affairs when it takes the form of income transfers to the less well-off, yet are often more in favour of it with respect to sexual matters. For example, the conservative government has generally been supportive of traditional "family values" and opposed to same-sex marriage and abortion. In contrast, the liberals tend to press for government aid for disadvantaged families but have less interest in regulating intimate relationships between consenting adults. Thus, these underlying values are especially prevalent within labour market and social welfare programs, and relate to notions of how families are defined with respect to their responsibilities, family values, and under what circumstances the state will assist or intervene in family life. As such, it may be necessary to review a wide variety of laws or to read between the lines of these laws (Baker, 1995).

Selected Policy Issues Facing Canadian Families Over the Life Course

Based upon the current trends and issues reviewed previously throughout this text, several suggestions for policy reform and community programs can be identified. This will include focus on the following five areas: (1) parenthood and child care; (2) education, income, and work; (3) partnership formation and dissolution; (4) seniors and caregiving; and (5) health care and social services. It is recognized that many of these areas intersect, but they do allow for a brief identification of key family-related policy issues relevant to the diverse and changing needs of families over the life course.

Parenthood and Child Care

Although many parents with preschool children would prefer to stay home and raise them, the reality, of course, is that most parents cannot achieve this "ideal" situation. A recent study by Statistics Canada (2005) finds that 53 percent of Canadian children between the ages of six months and five years were in some form of child care, up from 42 percent in 1995. As a result, a major policy challenge is child care. This issue is particularly salient for women, since they continue to perform most of this work while they continue to participate in the labour force in record numbers. Child care is also crucial to gender equality, since without access to affordable child care, some mothers are forced to restrict themselves to part-time work or to lower-paying jobs. Furthermore, structural and ideological barriers impede many men from taking paternity leave or time off work to care for children, which further perpetuate gender inequities. This also disadvantages men in terms of their time availability with their children.

Families need a variety of options to meet their specific child-care needs, such as corporate on-site-based daycares and after-school programs. Yet, the availability and provision of quality daycare is minimal, with the exception of Quebec, which recognizes three types of subsidized daycare services (child care and daycare centres and home care providers) and at a reasonable cost of $7 per child per day. Only those with the most resources or a wealthy few can hire nannies to provide at-home child care. Access to affordable daycare is also an enormous problem for single parents or for parents who work untraditional hours, such as night shifts, weekends, or part-time. Indeed, access to high-quality daycare should be available to all Canadians, regardless of race, ethnic background, level of competence, or ability to pay. In addition, it is often only affluent women and couples who can take advantage of many government programs, such as maternity and parental leave because of eligibility criteria. As a result, certain groups (e.g., recent immigrants) may not have access to these programs, as well as other tax credits and exceptions (Ranson, 2005).

In summary, Canada needs to have a national standard of quality and universal access to child care for those families who require or choose to use them. This means that the government should establish a consistent training and education requirement for caregivers and consistent licensing practices. Greater effort is also needed to implement and monitor programs, as well as to collect information on child-care options in a collaborative and coordinated manner across the provinces.

Education, Income, and Work Issues

Individuals from higher socio-economic families are more likely to attend post-secondary institutions and marry and have children at later ages. Similarly, they are less likely to experience poverty, drop out of school, become teenaged or young parents, and to divorce. Overall, educational qualifications are a key determinant of life chances in industrial societies and are generally a strong correlate of making a higher income. In short, higher income enables individuals to have more choices. It is also well documented that less-educated workers have been disadvantaged in the labour market during the past two decades, and that income inequality has also grown in many countries.

As revealed in Chapter 13, we should all be very concerned about the high level of poverty in Canada. The 2008 poverty rate for children in Canada was 15.1 percent, which is much higher than many other Western, industrialized countries (with the exception of the U.S., which is approximately 21.6 percent). For example, in Sweden, the rate was 7 percent; the Netherlands, 9.7 percent; France, 9.3 percent; Germany, 8.3 percent; and Britain, 12.5 percent (OECD, 2011). Therefore, aims to eradicate poverty and to improve the educational opportunities for all young people should be paramount.

It is also recognized that not all individuals are willing or able to complete high school or to attend college or university. Thus, it might be useful to devise support mechanisms or incentives to assist at-risk adolescents during secondary school. For example, it might be beneficial to have an expanded system of apprenticeship and vocational education as other options to formal college attendance. In addition, greater attention should be given to the likely impact of government policies on the economic well-being of families and children, especially those living at or near the poverty line, such as the working poor.

Moreover, there are rural/urban and regional variations in access to post-secondary institutions, as well as in the availability of good jobs. As revealed in Figure 15.1, unemployment rates are the highest in the Atlantic or eastern provinces, and generally decline as you move west; a trend that has been relatively long term. Thus, families living in economically depressed areas or regions with fewer opportunities can have different life course trajectories and require unique supports and policies. For example, in the Atlantic region, seasonal labour is common (e.g., in the fishing, mining, forestry, and produce industry). This means that these families face unique challenges in maintaining household income and in balancing work and family demands and require supports tailored to meet their unique conditions and problems. In other areas, high unemployment in single-industry, small community areas (e.g., as experienced in Nova Scotia) can force families to migrate to urban areas in search of a better life, which then further impacts the local community. For example, as families and young people leave their home communities for jobs in urban areas, schools may begin to close and local businesses can suffer, which creates a "ripple effect" impact on the lives of those wanting to remain in the smaller community.

Turning to work/family challenges, researchers often characterize this tension as the "double squeeze." This is because there is often pressure on economic resources and a simultaneous squeeze on the time and energy needed for family, work, and community commitments (Skocpol, 1997). And although many policies have emerged that provide more flexibility for employees with family responsibilities, in comparison with Europeans, many argue that North Americans have significant "policy deficits" in relation to work-family and other policy supports. For example, Sweden has vastly more generous paid maternity and parenting leave policies and paid leave to care for sick chil-

Figure 15.1
Annual Average Unemployment Rate by Province/Region, 2010, Canada (in Percentages)*

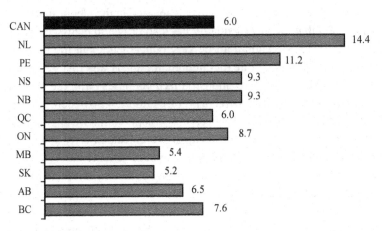

Data based on Statistics Canada Labour Force Survey Estimates (LFS), Supplementary Unemployment Rates by Region. Ottawa: Statistics Canada.

Source: Human Resources and Skills Development Canada (2011). "Work and Unemployment Rate: Regions," retrieved January 27, 2012 from http://www4.hrsdc.gc.ca/.3ndic.1t.4r@-eng.jsp?iid=16#M_4.

dren. Indeed, a major concern voiced most often by North American parents is conflict between work and family, and this may transcend class, race, ethnicity, and family structure (Moen and Jull, 1995).

A major challenge for families is trying to balance the competing demands of family and work responsibilities. As a result, many families are chronically overworked and overwhelmed in their daily lives because work becomes too much. Many studies find that about one-third of the workforce reports chronically feeling overworked. A recent study showed that 38 percent of working mothers are severely time stressed, averaging 74 hours of paid and unpaid work each week. Single mothers are particularly prone to stressful lives, since they often do not have a partner to rely on for emotional and financial support. Furthermore, women who do primarily unpaid work can be prone to isolation, and are at greater risk of physical, emotional, and or/sexual abuse (Women and the Economy, 2006).

Furthermore, other emergent economic and socio-demographic trends contribute to the need for more unpaid work within the family and also have significant consequences for families. As noted in Chapter 7, children tend to remain at home longer than in recent decades, thus prolonging the transition to the empty nest. Extended domestic responsibilities are largely borne by mothers, who continue to provide domestic labour in the form of day-to-day caring, cooking, and cleaning services for their young adult children.

Partnership Formation and Dissolution

Many Canadians still believe that legal marriage is the ideal, that children should be raised with both biological parents, and that marriage should last a lifetime. Yet, there appears to be growing consensus that we also need policy reform and community programs to support healthy families and intimate relationships more generally, with a focus that extends beyond legal, heterosexual marital relationships. This can strengthen the intimate ties of young adults and their families, as well as prevent young adults from other risky behaviours such as leaving home to marry or cohabit at an early age and teenage parenthood. Also, although some partnerships and marriages cannot be salvaged, some people argue that future generations would be well served if some of the separating or divorcing parents remained together. This is particularly germane to those relationships that could be saved with proper social and economic supports.

Overall, community resources are needed to support the diverse relationships of young people. In Chapter 8, it was noted that gays/lesbians experience more resistance to partnership choices and their decision to cohabit or marry. Generally, gay and lesbian young adults receive more support from non-family members than their families of origin. This suggests that this group of individuals and their families require community supports of a specific nature (e.g., education and support to overcome homophobic ideologies). Also, with high rates of immigration to Canada from traditional home countries, we need to provide culturally sensitive community programs and services to deal with the unique issues that these families face (e.g., discrimination, language barriers, intergenerational conflict) as they try to assimilate into a new country. For example, in some traditional ethnic groups, same-sex unions, unmarried cohabitation, and single-parenthood are socially frowned upon.

Seniors, Caregiving, and Dependency Issues

As previously mentioned, the age structure of Canada is aging, and it is expected that approximately 25 percent of the population will be over age 65 by the year 2031. As such, policy in a number of realms (e.g., health care, pension, housing) will need to be revised in order to meet the needs of this highly heterogeneous group. And as Canada's aged population becomes more ethnically diverse, we may need to devise new policies and programs. Elderly members of ethno-cultural communities are shown to have language barriers, religious and cultural differences, and economic dependency, which can reduce their access to community-based health and social services. Elderly ethnic minority women, in particular, are found to have high rates of poverty and are often not eligible for pensions such that they may face "triple jeopardy" (Brotman, 1998).

Moreover, it is important to reiterate that most elderly receive support from informal caregivers (family and friends), such that population aging will have important implications for Canadian families. And while many have argued that the purported "caregiving crunch" has been more myth than reality, many assert that sandwich-generation challenges will increase in the future, and that family caregivers need more state and community support. This can help to alleviate caregiver burden and dependency among the elderly. Moreover, the National Advisory Committee on Aging finds that caregiving can generate numerous financial, psychological, health, and social costs. As a result, they offer a number of recommendations for policy/program reform such as a federal program of home care and increasing tax credits for caregivers who incur financial loss. At the community level, programs to alleviate caregiver burden, respite care, and to provide recreation and transportation will need attention.

Health Care and Social Services

The Canadian welfare state has developed a wide range of health and social services to promote health and well-being. These services range from preventative, community-based programs to primary health care, to acute care in the case of accident or illness. Social services encompass such areas as child protection, social work interventions, settlement services for refugees and immigrants, and residential services for those unable to live independently. Yet, although Canadians enjoy relatively good health and universal coverage for most health and social services, financial and other barriers exist for many individuals. Many services are only partially insured (or not at all), including dental care, eyeglasses, prescriptions drugs, and fees arising from ambulance and ancillary services.

Geographical isolation also makes it difficult for families to access appropriate services. This is particularly problematic for Aboriginal families who live in remote areas. Moreover, the priorities set by Aboriginal peoples are often at variance from those developed by the government. In part, this is because Aboriginal peoples define health in terms of balance, holism, harmony, and spirituality rather than in terms of Western concepts of physical dysfunction and disease within the individual. Fortunately, in recent years many Aboriginal communities have assumed the administration and management of health care in their own communities. And with more land claims settlements, self-determination, and political autonomy for these families, it is hoped that their health situation (e.g., high mortality and chronic conditions), in addition to other challenges (e.g., the high number of children in the social welfare system), will continue to improve (Shah, 2005).

Furthermore, alternatives to conventional drug therapy are required given the growing strength of the pharmaceutical industry and concerns that we are headed toward an over-medicalized society, a topic that we discussed in Chapter 12. These issues may also be gendered in that women are more likely than men to be prescribed central nervous system depressants as well as sleeping pills and for longer periods of time. They are also more likely to be prescribed these pills for non-medical reasons such as to help them cope with work or family stress, grief, or for natural life events such as childbirth and menopause as well as for chronic illness and pain. Yet, no comprehensive policy or intervention strategy exists to address this serious health issue (Currie, 2003).

And with continuing retrenchment of the welfare state, many programs and services have also been reduced or cut, such as women's crisis centres and other social services. This means that important services are simply no longer available. Governments also often change the eligibility criteria with respect to who is "deserving" of such assistance in order to generate cost savings. For example, Box 15.3 provides an example on recent changes to health care benefits for autistic children in British Columbia. Moreover, many researchers and delivery providers recognize the need to enhance the cultural competence and gender-

Box 15.3
The Supreme Court of Canada Decides that Autistic Children Do Not Have a Right to Health Services

This excerpt was found in a November 9, 2004 media release from the Women's Legal Education and Action Fund.

Toronto – LEAF (Women's Legal Education and Action Fund) and its intervention partner DAWN (DisAbled Women's Network) Canada say that this morning's decision from the Supreme Court in *Auton v. British Columbia* is devastating for all disadvantaged persons. At issue is whether the B.C. Government's refusal to fund health services to ameliorate the effects of autism violates the equality rights of autistic children, rights guaranteed in the Canadian Charter of Rights and Freedoms. The Court found that the failure to provide autism-related health services does not constitute a breach of the Charter's s.15 guarantee.

The Court's decision has turned back the clock by decades on equality rights progress in Canada by its ruling in *Auton*. The court has applied a narrow and formalistic interpretation…The critical flaw with the Court's reasoning lies in its narrow conception of health services—it endorsed a conception of health services that is focused on the able-bodied norm, and accepts that norm instead of challenging it as exclusive and discriminatory. It takes the current health services framework as natural, and the implication is that anything outside of it is "extra" or "abnormal."… As a result…disabled persons are to be treated as second-class citizens because the Court did not acknowledge that the health system privileges the able-bodied. Autistic children in particular will remain at risk of isolation and institutionalization. The negative effects will be compounded for girls with autism. For example, women with autism who are institutionalized are likely to experience one of the most serious forms of gendered disability discrimination—the physical and sexual abuse that is prevalent in institutions.

Counsel for LEAF and DAWN are Dianne Pothier and Fiona Sampson.

Source: Excerpt taken from the Women's Legal Education and Action Fund web site of media releases, http://www.leaf.ca/events-media.html, retrieved June 7, 2005.

sensitivity of health care service provisions. For example, some immigrants seeking care experience outright racism and may have to experience a waiting period before they are eligible for provincial health insurance (Oxman-Martinez and Hanley, 2005).

Overall, Rioux (2006) argues that we need a human rights–based approach to health and social well-being given that this is influenced by a variety of social, economic, and environmental factors, and not just access to health care. This rights-based approach means using human rights as a framework for health development. In this way, basic principles of human rights become integral to the design, implementation, and evaluation of policies and programs. This approach can also be used to assess the human rights implications of policy, programs, and legislation. In this way, social policy can enhance rather than diminish the well-being of families. As illustrated in Figure 15.2, these fundamental human rights include political and civil rights (such as the right to life), freedom of opinion, a fair trial, and protection from torture and violence. They also include economic, social, and cultural rights, such as the right to work, social protection, an adequate standard of living, the highest possible standards of physical and mental health, education, and enjoyment of the benefits of cultural freedom and scientific progress (Rioux, 2006).

Policy Advocacy, Research, and Evaluation

Policy development and implementation is a political, complicated, and multi-faceted process, as depicted in Figure 15.3. With regard to the general policy research process (which can take place in a variety of government and non-government settings), it typi-

Figure 15.2
Linkages between Health and Human Rights

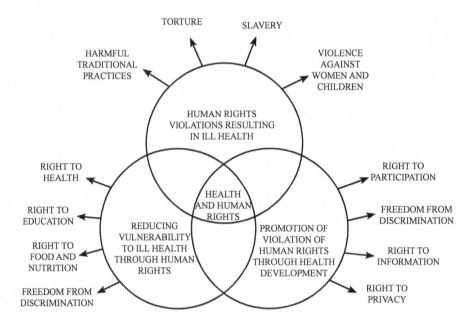

Source: World Health Organization, *Health and Human Rights*, Health and Human Rights Publication Series, no. 1 (Geneva: World Health Organization, 2002), p. 8.

Figure 15.3
The Policy Process

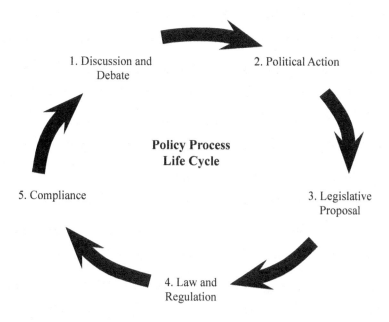

1. Discussion and
Debate

2. Political Action

Policy Process
Life Cycle

5. Compliance

3. Legislative
Proposal

4. Law and
Regulation

Source: Petersen, R.J. 2009. "The Policy Process Lifecycle," *EDUCAUSE Review*, vol. 44, no. 2 (March/
April): 74–75. Retrieved January 28, 2012 from http://www.educause.edu/EDUCAUSE+Review/
EDUCAUSEReviewMagazineVolume44/ThePolicyProcessLifeCycle/16380.

cally begins with a general statement that some kind of social action may be desirable.
Individuals can play important roles in affecting family-related policy as advocates,
community organizers, and researchers. For instance, researchers can seek to examine
whether or not recommendations need to be made with respect to changing laws, the
development of programs, or action taken to fulfill specific needs.

Generally, the advocate endorses and actively works for a course of action that improves
community and family life and the well-being of its members. This kind of advocacy
typically requires some type of leadership and group mobilization, for example, at the
local or community level. Community organizing can be defined as "a search for social
power and an effort to combat perceived helplessness through learning that what appears
personal is often political" and creates a capacity for democracy and for sustained social
change (Shragge, 2003: 41).

An example of a community-directed organization is DERA (Downtown Eastside Residents Association) in Vancouver, British Columbia. DERA was formed in 1973 by local
residents as a reaction against the general attitude of indifference and neglect that many
felt toward this area, which was then known as "Skid Row." Located in the poorest urban

neighbourhood in the nation, DERA has fought for 31 years to focus the attention of government, industry, and the public on the key components of poverty and homelessness that prevent the formation of healthy families and individuals. And while their confrontational political style has been criticized, it has empowered residents to take control over their lives by fighting for their rights. It is therefore not surprising to learn that advocacy can be a daunting task, since it requires many skills, perseverance, and pragmatism.

As researchers, there are also a variety of ways to propose and establish family policy, as illustrated in Box 15.4. These proposed policy changes (entitled, "A New Deal for Families") are recommended by researchers at the University of British Columbia and focus on families raising young children. Policy change is urged in the areas of parental benefits, child care services, and work-family balance, issues that we have previously identified as in need of critical evaluation and reform. Think tanks such as the Vanier Institute of the Family in Ottawa (established in 1965) are also actively involved in both family research and policy advocacy. Members of these types of institutes and foundations typically publish books, special reports and position papers, and press releases and convey this information to elected policy officials, policy makers, educators, researchers, and the general public.

Another type of policy research conducted is aimed at policy evaluation. As previously noted, many policies, although created with good intentions, can actually be harmful to individuals or families. Basically, policy evaluation is done at a programmatic level to determine the extent to which social programs have achieved or are achieving their stated goals. It can also evaluate what the actual impact is on families. For instance, what is the impact of a program such as Head Start on mothers as well as children? What is the consequence of not allowing dependent co-resident young adults to be eligible for welfare benefits? It is also interesting to note that evaluation research may demonstrate that intended goals are being met, while the impact analysis may show that the goals are counterproductive, producing unintended family policy consequences for families.

A recent example of a government policy that has come under fire for creating consequences that may not be good for many families is the new Choice in Child Care Allowance, introduced by the Harper government in 2006. Parents are given this allowance to spend as "they choose," such as on formal child care, a babysitter, or helping one parent stay at home. According to critics, this new allowance of $100 a month in direct payments to parents per child under the age of six provides the least benefit to the working poor and modest-income families who need help the most. As shown in Figure 15.4, this allowance pays more to most one-earner families than to two-earner and one-parent families, and more to higher-income families than to modest-income families earning $30,000. This is because the true value of this allowance is not the same as the face value that families receive. Because this allowance will be counted as taxable income in the hands of lower-income parents, these families will pay more federal and provincial/territorial income taxes, while receiving fewer benefits than the previous federal Canada Child Tax Benefit and other credits.

As a result, it is argued that one-earner families with a parent who stays home will do better than lone-parent and two-earner families (Child Care Advocacy Association of Canada, 2006). Other critics charge that this program comes at another high price since

Box 15.4
A New Deal for Families

There is a silent generational crisis occurring in homes across Canada. The generation raising young children today struggles with less time, stagnant household incomes, and skyrocketing housing costs compared to the 1970s. The failure to invest in the generation raising young children is not consistent with Canada's proud tradition of building and adapting.

Canada has become a country in which it is far harder to raise a young family. The country's economy has doubled in size since the mid-1970s, yet the reality for parents with preschool children is a decline in the standard of living. Compared to the previous generation, the average household income for young Canadian couples has flat-lined (after adjusting for inflation) even though the share of young women contributing to household incomes today is up 53 percent. Meanwhile, housing prices increased 76 percent across the country since the mid-1970s.

The generation raising young children today is squeezed for time at home, squeezed for income because of the high cost of housing, and squeezed for services like child care that would help them balance earning a living with raising a family.

A practical solution is proposed: A New Deal for Families with Young Children
The New Deal will provide a Time Dividend to families, to ensure that the generation raising young children accesses 2.8% of the economic prosperity produced today compared to the mid-1970s. The Time Dividend will...put the family back into Canadian values, while acknowledging the diversity of households, and recognizing the very different circumstances facing parents compared to the Baby Boomers; ....provide choices for women and men to contribute at home and on the job, while enabling personal responsibility for moms and dads alike as they have enough time to raise their kids, and enough time to earn a living.

The New Deal is centred on three core policy changes:
New mom and new dad benefits: WHY? To transform the uneven access to parental leave into a benefit system that ensures all parents, including the self-employed, have the time and resources to be home with their newborns. **HOW?** Extend parental leave from 12 months to 18 months, generally reserving the extra six months for dads (with exceptions for lone parents and same-sex couples). Introduce a healthy child check-in and parenting support program during a child's first 18 months to monitor for early development delays and to answer parents' questions regarding children's feeding, sleeping, crying, etc. **DETAILS:** Benefits would be available to ALL single- and dual-earner households regardless of parents' attachment to the labour market (including the self-employed). Moms and dads who currently do not qualify for leave would see their after-tax income increase by at least $11,000 in the 12 months following the birth of their child. Leave would be made affordable by insuring 80 percent of parents' income up to $60,000 a year. This increase will

double the existing maximum benefit. The minimum benefit will be $440 weekly, enough to eradicate child and family poverty for this age group.

$10/day child care services: WHY? To remedy the current system of unregulated, unaffordable child care services, thus ensuring that parents can spend enough time in employment to manage the rising cost of housing and stalled household incomes. **HOW?** Reduce child care service fees to no more than $10/day (full-time) and $7/day (part-time), making it free for families earning less than $40,000/year. Ensure quality services by providing funding for ample caregivers on site so that children spend their time in developmentally stimulating activities and play, including children with extra support needs. Caregivers will have appropriate training in child development and will be paid pay equity wages. **DETAILS:** Universal, affordable child care services would support healthy child development by supplementing, but never replacing, the care that families provide directly. Families could choose to use the services regardless of parental employment. Families could also choose to access parenting support even if they do not use child care services. Programs will reflect the diverse cultures in local communities. Where numbers permit, families could choose programs that feature a language other than English or French in recognition that Canadian families speak many languages at home. For Indigenous citizens, funding is allocated to enrich services that prioritize exposure to the languages and cultures of First Nations, Métis, and Inuit as part of Canada's commitments to Truth and Reconciliation.

Flex-time for employees and employers: WHY? To remedy workplace standards that ignore the family by ensuring all employees can choose to combine work and family successfully. **HOW?** Adapt overtime, Employment Insurance, and Canada Public Pension premiums paid by employers to make it less costly for businesses to use employees up to 35 hours per week, and more costly for hours thereafter. Overtime will kick in at 35 hours a week (average over a year). Overtime premiums will be paid either as cash or earned time away from home. **DETAILS:** With new incentives, employers would reduce the work week by 3–5 hours on average for the half of men and the third of women who work more than 40 hours/week. These employees would trade some after-tax wages (or future wage increases) in order to gain four more weeks of time per year. In negotiation with employers, this time could be taken in chunks, or as earned hours away from work each week through the year. Changes to the National Child Benefit Supplement will ensure any reduction in employment hours does not reduce income in low-earning families. This may be especially important for some lone parent households. Employees who currently work parent-time hours would gain opportunities for more employment. Within two-parent homes, flex-time may not change the total hours that parents work, but redistribute them more evenly between dads and moms.

Source: Kershaw, P. and L. Anderson. 2011. "Fact sheet: A new deal for families," Human Early Learning Partnership, University of British Columbia. Retrieved January 25, 2011 from earlylearning.ubc.ca.

it cuts the federal and provincial investments that are designed to increase the number of regulated child-care spaces. As a result, it will do little to attract and retain qualified child-care workers who are the most underpaid workers relative to their qualifications in Canada (Jacobs, 2006).

Moreover, policy evaluation can uncover improved methods of policy implementation, delivery, and cost reduction, which can provide a number of long-term advantages to both families and the state. For example, extensive research by Browne et al. (2001, 2011) shows that our current system of service delivery is inadequate because of a short-sighted "piecemeal" approach. These researchers assert that we need policies and programs that are comprehensive, holistic, and investment oriented. However, this is difficult to achieve because governments change, many sectors receive their funding separately, and there is little coordination of services across ministries and portfolios. This approach also often fails to identify the root cause of the problem, which is often the source of a chain reaction of other problems across the life course. It may also be difficult for one trained professional to ascertain links among the person's condition (e.g., chronic depression), the context in which the person

Figure 15.4
True Value of Harper Child Care Allowance, Families with Two Children (One under Six), Ontario, 2006, by Net Family Income

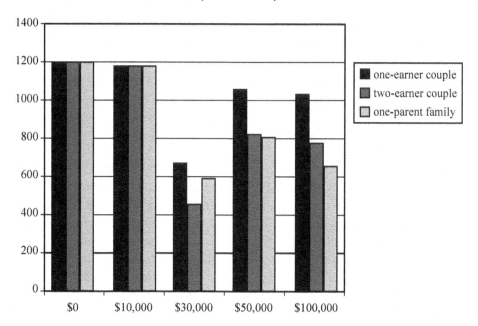

Source: Based on Table 2, cited in Child Care Advocacy Association of Canada, "The Harper Child Care Plan: Buyer Beware," retrieved August 13, 2006, from www.childcareadvocacy.ca.

lives (e.g., poverty), and the set of circumstances that led to the problem (e.g., a lifetime of little family support or "social capital," abuse and neglect, low education, and so forth).

Instead, a more effective and proactive approach is to provide individuals (particularly vulnerable individuals) with coordinated service packages. For example, in one pilot project, single parents living on social assistance were provided with a tailored package of services, such as help with child care, access to recreational facilities, job training, mental health counselling, and visits by public health nurses. At the end of the study, these parents (and the children) experienced a multitude of benefits. The single mothers were more likely to leave welfare and had improved mental health. Also, there was a savings of $300,000 in social assistance within the first year for every 100 mothers (Browne et al., 2001).

Summary

Although it is difficult to forecast how families will look in the future, it is certain that the one institution in which the majority of people live their lives will not remain unchanged. And while it is impossible to predict the kinds of environmental, economic, and social challenges that families will face, policies and programs will need to be continually revised or developed in response to the changing life course needs and conditions of Canadian families. This is because socio-demographic and technological changes affect patterns of support within families, family structure, and lifestyles in profound ways. Notable family-related trends likely to persist (or rise) in the near future include: delays in family formation, low fertility, non-marital cohabitation, same-sex and mixed-race unions, "commuter" unions/marriages (e.g., couples living apart for job-related reasons), divorce and remarriage, labour force participation of women, population aging, continuing high rates of immigration, and geographical dispersion and mobility. It is also expected that new technologies (e.g., medical, reproductive, electronic/digital) will continue to dramatically transform family patterns, including relationships and means of communication.

Therefore, issues germane to child care, intimate ties, household living arrangements, work-family balance, elder care, and population health more generally are expected to become even more salient. And with more economic opportunities for women and continued secularization, it is expected that relationship dissolution rates will continue to be relatively high, particularly as non-marital cohabitation (heterosexual and homosexual) will continue to grow in popularity. Overall, these transformations in family life will necessitate associated changes in family policies and programs, such as availability and access to programs and services and legal issues relevant to common-law relationships and child custody.

Finally, given the trend toward neo-liberalism and growing social inequality, many critics of current social policy assert that we need to develop a new model of the family that emphasizes social responsibility and promotes full citizenship (e.g., see Eichler, 1987; McDaniel, 2002) rather than economic gain and competition. In this way, personal troubles can be treated as public issues, since most events and circumstances have elements of both (Mills, 1959). For example, policies based on this model could facilitate greater involvement of fathers in child care as well as constructive solutions to workplace-family dilemmas. More importantly, implementing such policies that start from the notion that care for people is a social responsibility rather than a private one can help to create a more humane and healthier society. In short, these social policies can help to build a better Canadian society in which diverse families of all shapes, sizes, and ages can thrive and flourish.

Questions for Critical Reflection and Debate

1. Should Canadian family policy be value-free? Also, can or should family research be separated from family advocacy?
2. Debate the following: The state should not interfere with family life. Consider family issues such as adoption, marriage, reproductive technology, sexual relations, and dependency between family members.
3. Provide an argument for and against the following statement: Family policy should be established at the federal as opposed to the provincial level. Is a national family policy feasible?
4. Should policies be age-based? Consider how policies target particular age groups and identify their key limitations and advantages.
5. Do you think that it is more effective to develop policies and programs that target individuals or interpersonal relations (micro level) or at a systems level (macro level)? Also consider issues of prevention and intervention (e.g., to such areas as poverty, alcoholism and substance abuse, and family violence).
6. What predictions would you make with respect to family life and changes in family policy by 2050? Consider some of the following areas: daycare, parental roles, same-sex unions, changing parent-child relationships, and the aging of the population.

Glossary

Family ideologies incorporate a set of family-related values and beliefs that reflect the interests and beliefs of a social group or society and forms the basis of political action.
Family policy can be defined as a coherent set of principles about the state's role in family life, which is implemented through legislation or a plan of action.
Globalization refers to the world scale of economic and other market activity facilitated by the expansion of telecommunications technology.
Neo-liberalism supports the restructuring of welfare societies to better meet the demands of a global market economy. This political rationality stresses competition and personal responsibility.

Unintended family policy consequences refers to the negative consequences on family life as a result of well-intended government policy.

Welfare state refers to a wide range of government-sponsored programs and legislations designed to improve the social and economic well-being of families and individuals, particularly in times of need.

Further Reading

Baker, M. 2010. *Choices and Constraints in Family Life*, 2nd ed. Toronto: Oxford University Press. Focuses on Canada within a global context and contextualizes family life within broader structural concerns such as the economy and government policy.

Béland, D. 2010. *What Is Social Policy? Understanding the Welfare State*. Cambridge: Polity Press. Provides a concise sociological and political introduction to social policy. Helps readers to grasp the nature of social programs and the political struggles surrounding them.

Blake, R. 2008. *From Rights to Needs: A History of Family Allowances in Canada, 1929–92*. Vancouver: University of British Columbia Press. Focuses on how policies are made by examining the history of family allowances in Canada from their debut in the House of Commons in 1992 to their demise under the Mulroney government in 1992.

Bradshaw, J. and A. 2008. *Social Policy, Employment and Family Change in Comparative Perspective*. Cheltenham: Edward Elgar. A cross-national study of family change, parental employment, and social policy in the five Nordic countries, the Netherlands, Germany, and the United Kingdom.

Eichler, M. 1997. *Family Shifts: Families, Policies, and Gender Equality*. Toronto: Oxford University Press. A classic work outlining various ideological models of the family and how they have affected policy development and implementation.

Jenson, J.M., and M. Fraser (Eds.). 2010. *Social Policy for Children and Families: A Risk and Resilience Perspective*. Thousand Oaks, Calif: Sage Publications. Offers a public health framework based on ecological theory and principles of risk and resilience. Contributing authors apply this model to the domains of child welfare, education, mental health, developmental disabilities, substance use, juvenile justice, and poverty.

Lin Chang, M. 2010. *Shortchanged: Why Women Have Less Wealth and What Can Be Done About It*. Oxford, New York: Oxford University Press. Using national data and in-depth interviews, this book addresses the gender-wealth gap and its relationship to policies on equal pay, caregiving, and family-friendly workplaces.

Related Web Sites

Caledon Institute of Social Policy is a centre-left think tank based in Ottawa and offers many discussion papers on social policy issues affecting families, http://www.caledoninst.org/.

Campaign 2000 was founded in 1989 to monitor child poverty in Canada, and produces an annual report card, www.campaign2000.ca.

Canadian Policy Research Network aims to create knowledge and lead public debate on social and economic issues, www.cprn.org.

Childcare Resource and Research Unit, University of Toronto, publishes Canadian and cross-national research on child-care policy issues, www.childcarecanada.org.

Institute for Research on Public Policy was founded in 1971 and seeks to improve public policy decisions, www.irpp.org.

Vanier Institute of the Family is a family-oriented think tank national organization (established in 1965) dedicated to promoting the well-being of Canadian families through advocacy, research, and policy, www.vifamily.ca. Facebook: The Vanier Institute of the Family / L'Institut Vanier de la famille, Twitter: VanierInstitute

References

Baker, M. 1995. *Canadian Family Policies: Cross-national Comparisons*. Toronto: University of Toronto Press.

Baker, M. (Ed.). 2005. *Families in Canadian Society*, 5th ed. Toronto: McGraw-Hill Ryerson.

Brotman, S. 1998. "The Incidence of Poverty among Seniors in Canada: Exploring the Impact of Gender, Ethnicity, and Race." *Canadian Journal on Aging* 17: 166–185.

Browne, G. 2011. "More Effective/Less Expensive Health Services also Address the Social Determinants of Health." *OASW Magazine*, Vol. 37, No. 1 (March).

Browne, G., J. Roberts, C. Byrne, A. Gafni, R. Weir, and B. Majumdar. 2001. "The Costs and Effects of Addressing the Needs of Vulnerable Populations: Results of 10 Years of Research." *Canadian Journal of Nursing Research* 33: 65–76.

Child Care Advocacy Association of Canada. 2006. "The Harper Child Care Plan: Buyer Beware." Retrieved August 13, 2006, from www.childcareadvocacy.ca.

Currie, J.C. 2003. *Manufacturing Addiction: The Over-prescription of Benzodiazepines and Sleeping Pills to Women in Canada*. British Columbia Centre of Excellence for Women's Health Policy Series, Vancouver, on-line at www.bccewh.bc.ca.

Eichler, M. 1987. "Family Change and Social Policies." In K.L. Anderson et al. (eds.), *Family Matters: Sociology and Contemporary Canadian Families* (pp. 63–85). Toronto: Methuen.

Evans, P.M., and G.R. Wekerle. 1997. "The Shifting Terrain of Women's Welfare: Theory, Discourse, and Activism." In P.M. Evans and G.R. Wekerle (eds.), *Women and the Canadian Welfare State* (pp. 1–27). Toronto: University of Toronto Press.

Friendly, M., J. Beach, and M. Turiano. 2002. *Early Childhood Education and Care in Canada 2001*. Toronto: Childcare Resources and Research Unit, University of Toronto.

Gee, E.M., and S.A. McDaniel. 1994. "Social Policy for an Aging Society." In V. Marshall and B. McPherson (eds.), *Aging: Canadian Perspectives* (pp. 219–231). Peterborough: Broadview Press.

Jacobs, J. 2006. "Editorial: Conservative Child-Care Plan Comes at High Price" (February 21). Ottawa: Canadian Centre for Policy Alternatives.

Kamerman, S.B., and A.J. Kahn. 1978. "Families and the Idea of Family Policy." In S.B. Kamerman and A.J. Kahn (eds.), *Family Policy: Government and Families in Fourteen Countries* (pp. 1–16). New York: Columbia University Press.

McDaniel, S.A. 2002. "Women's Changing Relations to the State and Citizenship: Caring and Intergenerational Relations in Globalizing Western Democracies." *Canadian Review of Sociology and Anthropology* 39: 1–26.

Mills, C.W. 1959. *The Sociological Imagination*. New York: Oxford University Press.

Moen, P., and P.M. Jull. 1995. "Informing Family Policies: The Use of Social Research." *Journal of Family and Economic Issues* 16: 79–107.

OECD. 2011. "CO2:2: Child Poverty." Paris, France: Organization for Economic Co-Operation and Development, Social Policy Division, Directorate of Employment, Labour and Social Affairs.

Olsen, G.M. 2002. *The Politics of the Welfare State: Canada, Sweden, and the United States*. Toronto: Oxford University Press.

Oxman-Martinez, J., and J. Hanley. 2005. "Health and Social Services for Canada's Multicultural Population: Challenges for Equity." In *Canada 2017: Serving Canada's Multicultural Population for the Future* (pp. 17–29). Gatineau, Quebec: The Multiculturalism Program, Department of Canadian Heritage.

Ranson, G. 2005. "Paid and Unpaid Work: How Do Families Divide Their Labour?" In M. Baker (ed.), *Families: Changing Trends in Canada*, 5th ed. (pp. 99–121). Toronto: McGraw-Hill Ryerson.

Rioux, M. 2006. "The Right to Health: Human Rights Approaches to Health." In D. Raphael, T. Bryant, and M. Rioux (eds.), *Staying Alive: Critical Perspectives on Health, Illness, and Health Care* (pp. 85–114). Toronto: Canadian Scholars' Press Inc.

Shah, C.P. 2005. "The Health of Aboriginal Peoples." In D. Raphael (ed.), *Social Determinants of Health: Canadian Perspectives* (pp. 267–282). Toronto: Canadian Scholars' Press Inc.

Shragge, E. 2003. *Activism and Social Change: Lessons for Community and Local Organizing*. Peterborough: Broadview Press.

Skocpol, T. 1997. "A Partnership with American Families." In S.B. Greenberg and T. Skocpol (eds.), *The New Majority: Toward a Popular Progressive Politics* (pp. 104–129). New Haven: Yale University Press.

Statistics Canada. 2005. "Child Care." *The Daily* (February 7).

Women and the Economy. 2006. "Women and Unpaid Work." Retrieved February 10, 2006, from www.unpac.ca/economy/unpaidwork.html.

Copyright Acknowledgements

Chapter 1
Opening photo: RonTech2000, "Healthy Eating," 14388436, from www.istockphoto.com.

Box 1.1: Dorothy Smith, "The Standard North American Family: SNAF as an Ideological Code," from *Writing the Social: Critique, Theory and Investigations*. © University of Toronto Press, 1999. Reprinted with permission of the publisher.

Box 1.2: Excerpted from "Pets: An Integral Part of the Family" and "Pet Ownership: It's Good for Your Health." © Ontario Veterinary Medical Association, 2007. Reprinted with permission of the publisher.

Box 1.4: R.M. Milardo, "Relational Landscapes," from *The Forgotten Kin: Aunts and Uncles*. © Cambridge University Press, 2009. Reprinted with permission of the publisher.

Chapter 2
Opening photo: knape, "Young family and their dog," 18699527, from www.istockphoto.com.

Box 2.4: D. Popenoe, excerpted from *Disturbing the Nest*. © Aldine de Gruyter, 1988. Reprinted with permission from the publisher.

Figure 2.1: Photo and caption appeared inside the front cover of the *Encyclopedia Canadiana: The Encyclopedia of Canada*, vol. 10. © The Grolier Society of Canada Ltd., 1958.

Figure 2.2: B.B. Ingoldsby, S.R. Smith, and J.E. Miller, *Exploring Family Theories*. © Oxford University Press, 2004. Reprinted with permission of the publisher.

Chapter 3
Opening photo: Claus Mikosch, "Hands," 10606799, from www.istockphoto.com.

Box 3.2: Bettina Bradbury, "Working Families: Age, Gender, and Daily Survival in Industrializing Montreal," from *Working Families: Age, Gender and Daily Survival in Industrializing Montreal*. © University of Toronto Press, 1993. Reprinted with permission of the publisher.

Box 3.4: "Grandmothers to Grandmothers," from http://www.stephenlewisfoundation.org/get-involved/grandmothers-campaign/about-the-campaign. © Stephen Lewis Foundation. Reprinted with permission of the publisher.

Figure 3.1: Courtesy of USAID.

Figure 3.3: Bill Proud, "Globalization," wpr0063, from www.CartoonStock.com.

Figure 3.6: "Hunger on the Rise: Number of Hungry People Tops One Billion." © International Monetary Fund, 2010.

Chapter 4

Opening photo: Isaac L. Koval, "Boy Cries," 9143575, from www.istockphoto.com.

Figure 4.1: "Last Best West," C-80108 and C009652. © Library and Archives Canada.

Figure 4.3: "The Undesirables," 1910–1911. © Canadian Museum of Civilization.

Chapter 5

Opening photo: Hulton Archive, "Mother and Daughter," 18247697, from www.istockphoto.com.

Figure 5.2: "Employment Rate for Women, by Age of Youngest Child, 1976–2009." © Human Resources and Skills Development Canada, 2011.

Figure 5.4: Daryl Cagle, "True—Men do 29% of the laundry," dca0059, from www.CartoonStock.com.

Box 5.6: Arlie Hochschild, "The Second Shift, Gender Ideology, and Feeling Rules," from *The Second Shift*. © Avon, 1989. Reprinted with permission of the publisher.

Chapter 6

Opening photo: Jason Stitt, "Smiling Couple," 1505811, from www.istockphoto.com.

Box 6.1: Jeanette Stewart, "From Russia, Maybe with Love: Mail Order Brides a Booming Business." © Postmedia News, a division of Postmedia Network Inc., 2011. Reprinted with permission of the publisher.

Box 6.4: Carolyn Abraham, "Health Canada Plans to Regulate Egg Freezing: Review May Result in Limit on Number of Clinics Licensed to Perform Service." © *Globe and Mail*, 2007. Reprinted with permission of the publisher.

Chapter 7

Opening photo: Kirill Polovnoy, "Happy Family," 12234453, from www.istockphoto.com.

Box 7.1: Cameron L. Macdonald, "Manufacturing Motherhood: The Shadow Work of Nannies and Au Pairs," *Qualitative Sociology* 21. © Springer Science and Business Media, 1998. Reprinted with permission of the publisher.

Box 7.5: Diana Gustafson, excerpted from "The Social Construction of Maternal Absence," from *Unbecoming Mothers: The Social Production of Maternal Absence*. © Taylor and Francis Group, 2005. Reprinted with permission of the publisher.

Figure 7.1: Sarah Connor and Satya Brink, "The Impacts of Non-Parental Care on Child Development." © Human Resources and Social Development, 2008.

Figure 7.2: Victoria J. Rideout, Ulla G. Foehr, and Donald F. Roberts, "Generation M²: Media in the Lives of 8- to 18-Year Olds." © Kaiser Family Foundation, 2010. Reprinted with permission of the publisher.

Figure 10.2: Aaron Bacall, "I'm here to update your census form," aban689, from www. CartoonStock.com.

Chapter 11

Opening photo: Nina Shannon, "Reading," 4951135, from www.istockphoto.com.

Box 11.3: D.A. Counts and D.R. Counts, excerpted from *Over the Next Hill: An Ethnography of RVing Seniors in North America.* © University of Toronto Press, 2001. Reprinted with permission of the publisher.

Box 11.5: Joy Ufema, excerpted from *Insights on Death and Dying.* © Lippincott Williams and Wilkins, 2007. Reprinted with permission of the publisher.

Figure 11.5: David Brown, "Can you believe we got married, raised a family and retired, all without the help of a hand-held computer?" dbrn168, from www.CartoonStock.com.

Chapter 12

Opening photo: Kim Gunkel, "Mom Embracing Daughter," 12305760, from www. istockphoto.com.

Box 12.4: Eric Schlosser, excerpted from *Fast Food Nation.* © Eric Schlosser and Houghton Mifflin Company, 2001. Reprinted with permission of the publisher.

Table 12.1: "HIV/AIDS epi Notes: Understanding the HIV/AIDS Epidemic among Aboriginal Peoples in Canada: The Community at a Glance." © Public Health Agency of Canada, 2004.

Table 12.2: Data compiled from "Desjardins Financial Security Survey on Health and the Desjardins National Financial Security Index," from the report "Survey on Canadian Attitudes towards Physical and Mental Health at Work and at Play," posted by the Canadian Mental Health Association, 2006.

Chapter 13

Opening photo: Chris Fertnig, "Depressed Woman," 16939736, from www.istockphoto.com.

Box 13.1: A. Gazo, "Staying Afloat on Social Assistance: Parents' Strategies of Balancing Employability Expectations and Caregiving Demands," *Socialist Studies* 3. © *Socialist Studies*, 2007.

Box 13.2: "Staying Afloat on Social Assistance: Parents' Strategies of Balancing Employability Expectations and Caregiving Demands." © Canadian Association of Food Banks, 2006. Reprinted with permission of the publisher.

Box 13.3: "Poverty and disability: My lived experience," from *Community Stories.* © Caledon Institute of Social Policy, 2010.

Box 13.5: Anna Mehler Paperny and Tavia Grant, excerpted from "How paying people's way out of poverty can help us all." © *Globe and Mail*, 2011.

Chapter 14

Opening photo: Warren Goldswain, "Domestic Abuse," 15397089, from www.istockphoto.com.

Index

Page numbers in italics refer to glossary definitions.

one-person households, 64, 265
Ontario
    divorce rates, 214; Family Statute Law
    Amendment Act, 223; family struc-
    ture in, 137; leaving home in, 237; life
    expectancy, 264; minimum wage in,
    320; same-sex partners in, 142; sexual
    orientation in, 193, 194; smoking in,
    302; unemployment in, 374
operant conditioning, 170–72, *182*
oppression
    unpaid labour as, 33; of women, 31
Oprah Winfrey Show, 340
orientation, family of, 10, 11
*The Origins of the Family, Private Property,
    and the State* (Engels), 31
the "other"
    disabled as, 293; generalized other, 174,
    181; minorities and, 81

paid labour. *see* labour; unpaid labour
palliative care, 276, 277, *280*, 301
paradigms, 28
parental home
    cluttered nest, 246; conflict in, 353;
    home-leaving and, 234–38; pathways
    out, 235–37; "returning adult syndrome",
    246–47; returning to, 238–42
parental leave, 232
parenthood
    child care and, 372; delayed, 67, 147–
    48; hegemonic, 153; ideologies of,
    176–80; intended fertility, and family
    size, 148, 151; multiple partner fertility,
    146–47; transition to, 146–53
parenting
    commodification of, 31–32, 33; co-par-
    enting, 224–25; gay, 187, 199
parenting leave, 373
parents
    abuse of by children, 345–46; empty
    nest syndrome, 242–45; helicopter, 238,
    240–41; role in socialization of chil-
    dren, 163, 174; tether parents, 240
Parsons, Talcott, 15, 29, 120
partnership formation and dissolution, 375
part-time work, 106–7, 108, 324
Pascoe, C.J., 132

paternity leave, 121, 372
pathological model of violence, 353–54
Patriarchal Model of the Family, 367–69
patriarchy
    abuse and, 353; authority of men over
    women, 62–63; gendered division of
    labour and, 59, 120–21
patrilineal descent, 64
patrilocal residence, 64
Pavlov, Ivan, 170
pawning, 321
pedophilia, 199
peer groups
    as agent of socialization, 165, 168
Penn, Mark, 132
People First, 326–27
personal values
    family sociology and, 47
"Peter Pan Syndrome", 247
pets, as family members, 8, 9
pharmaceutical industry
    alternative therapies, 376; influence on
    psychiatry, 304–6
phenomenology, 45
physical violence, 341–42
Piaget, Jean, 172–73
pioneer families, 54
Pioneer Girl (Caswell), 57–58
plural marriage, 139, 140
Polish ethnic origin, 87
political economy theory, 30, 31–32, 33, 42,
    320
    effect of industrial economy on families,
    33; poverty and, 320; power relations in,
    31–32
pollution, opposition to, 73–74
polyandry, 61–62
polygamy, 13, 62, *76*, 139, 140
polygyny, 61–62
poly-victimization, 341, 352
Popenoe, Dave, 13–14, 14
popular culture
    changes in family life, 105–8; dating
    methods in, 131–32
population aging, 73, *76*
    apocalyptic demography and, 259–60;
    demographic focus on, 259; factors con-
    tributing to, 262–65